Eleonora Duse

Eleonora Duse

A Biography

HELEN SHEEHY

Alfred A. Knopf New York 2003

THIS IS A BORZOI BOOK
PUBLISHED BY ALFRED A. KNOPF

Knopf, Borzoi Books, and the colophon are registered trademarks
of Random House, Inc.

Grateful acknowledgment is made to Susan Bassnett for permission to
reprint excerpts from *The Flame* by Susan Bassnett. Reprinted by
permission of the author.

Library of Congress Cataloging-in-Publication Data
Sheehy, Helen
Eleonora Duse / Helen Sheehy.—1st ed.
p.   cm.
ISBN 0-375-40017-6 (alk. paper)
1. Duse, Eleonora, 1858–1924.   2. Actors—Italy—Biography.   I. Title.
PN2688.D8 S48 2002
792'.028'092—dc21
[B]   2002033997

Manufactured in the United States of America
First Edition

For Tommaso—*ancora e sempre*

Contents

Illustrations

Acknowledgments

THIS BIOGRAPHY draws on previously unpublished or unknown material, including Duse's thirty-five-page handwritten memoir. Duse's granddaughter, Sister Mary Mark Bullough, who died in April 2001, shared her memories with candor. Martin Waldron allowed me to use his Duse library and collection of unpublished letters, photographs, and memorabilia. His help, both practical and spiritual, was invaluable. Paolo Valesio of Yale University told me about a packet of Duse letters to d'Annunzio. I'm grateful to Steve Jones of Yale's Beinecke Library for his assistance in copying these letters. Eleonore Thun-Hohenstein of Vienna shared copies of Alexander Wolkoff's letters to Duse. Wendy Knopf Cooper's interview with her mother, Mildred Oppenheimer Knopf, illuminated Duse's last months. Michael Morrison, John Barrymore's biographer, sent me a transcript of Barrymore's memories of meeting Duse, which Morrison had discovered after the publication of his own book. In Venice, Paolo Puppa, playwright and professor, opened his library to me and gave me the thesis of Anastasia Plazzotta, who had done important research in Russia. I'm grateful for his kindness, and for Anastasia Plazzotta's scholarship. In Berlin, Elke Neumann generously shared information about Duse's German tours. Elliot Norton, Luisa Osti Chiarelli, Eleanor Lambert, and Beppe Menegatti all shared their memories of Duse.

I am indebted to Paola Bertolone, theatre historian and Duse scholar, who introduced me to the latest Duse scholarship in Italy, uncovered new information, shared her research into thousands of Duse lettters, and inspired me with her intellectual rigor. She led me to the work of Duse scholar Gerardo Guerrieri. The archives he left and his pioneering research are crucial references. I'm grateful to Maria Casa, who provided years of dedicated detective work, as well as the use of her apartment in Rome. I'm also grateful to d'Annunzio translator and scholar Susan Bassnet, and to Duse scholar Mirella Schino. Their work provided guidance and inspiration.

The Fondazione Giorgio Cini in Venice has a vast collection of Duse letters, scripts, costumes, memorabilia, objects, and photographs. I owe much to archivist Franco Casini for his expert and patient assistance. I'm grateful to Annamaria Andreoli, president of the Il Vittoriale Foundation and author of an important biography of Gabriele d'Annunzio. Her staff at d'Annunzio's Il Vittoriale in Gardone Riviera provided excellent service, and during my stay there they also discovered several significant Duse letters to her husband and her father.

I am indebted also to the following people, institutions, and libraries who provided assistance and information: Pam Jordan, librarian at the Yale School of Drama; Kevin Pacelli, Newspaper and Microform Reading Room, Sterling Library, Yale University; the staff of the Biblioteca Teatrale del Burcardo, Rome; Dr. Martinoli, Biblioteca Nazionale, Rome; Fondazione Primoli, Rome; Anna Perugini, Istituto Centrale per il Catalogo e la Documentazione Mario Nunes Vais, Rome; Degli Innocente, Florence; Melanie Christoudia, Theatre Museum, National Museum of the Performing Arts, London; Glasgow University Library, Special Collections; Bibliotheque de l'Arsenal, Paris; Hemeroteca Municipal Library, Madrid; Mary Ellen Rogan and Robert Taylor, Billy Rose Theatre Collection at the New York Public Library; Dance Collection, New York Public Library; Al Palko, Connecticut State Library; Melissa Miller, Harry Ransom Humanities Research Center, Austin, Texas; Paul Holmer, Southern Connecticut State University Library, Annette Fern, Harvard Theatre Collection; Danielle Green, Harvard University Archives; Houghton Library, Harvard University; Gene DeGruson, Pittsburgh State University; Geraldine Duclow, Theatre Collection, Free Library of Philadelphia; Carnegie Library of Pittsburgh; Miller Memorial Library, Hamden, Connecticut; Feuchtwanger Memorial Library, University of Southern California; Museum of Television, New York; Museum of the City of New York; Museum of Modern Art, New York; Berg Collection, New York Public Library; Alice Birney, Library of Congress; and Town Hall, Asolo, Italy.

Although our interpretations, emphasis, and conclusions often differ, I have been helped enormously by the work of earlier Duse biographers, and I admire and respect them. Olga Signorelli's books about Duse are an indispensable guide and reference. Duse's subsequent biographers have depended upon Signorelli's work, and I have as well. Luigi Rasi, Edouard Schneider, E. A. Rheinhardt, Frances Winwar, Eva Le Gallienne, Giovanni Pontiero, and Cesare Molinari all provided valuable information in their biographies. William Weaver's 1984 biography of Duse is an important resource.

During the years I worked on this book, Susan Terry of Infowhizz shared her knowledge and expertise. Dan Markley and Alison Sheehy offered hospitality and loving support. I also appreciate the help of the following people around the world, who helped in large ways and small: Martha Venter, Martha Cutts, Leslie Casanova, Micaëla Veit, Kristin Ellis, Susan Lavorgna, Drew Eliot, Ellen Burstyn, Leonard Finger, Bob Tollett, Peter Kurth, Brent Venable, Brian Kellow, Mary Layne, Stephan Chodorov, Greg Leaming, Filippo Naitana, Barry Paris, Dr. Anne Strong, Doris Abramson, Linda Davis, Sister M. Nicola, Dr. "Shep" Nuland, Edward Craig, William Gass, William Koshland, Robert Steiner, Andrea Zanotto, Otto Gugler, Richard Stoddard, Mary Jane Phillips-Matz, Rita Zambon, Lion Heart Autographs, Sotheby's, Gianmario Cipani, and Andrew Saxe.

I thank my colleagues in the Amherst Biography Group who read portions of this biography and offered commentary: Sandra Katz, Elizabeth Lloyd-Kimbrel, William Kimbrel, Ann and Michael Meeropol, Stephen Oates, and Harriet Sigerman.

I am grateful to my German translator, Steven Whiting, and to my French translators, Christopher de Haan and Vivian Benesch. Nino Ribeiro translated Brazilian documents.

From the start of my work, scholar and writer William "Bill" Christian has given me encouragement and advice. I'm abidingly grateful to poet and translator Justin Vitiello, who smoothed out my rough translations. I'm profoundly appreciative of Lorca biographer Leslie Stainton, who took time from her own work to help me with mine, including researching in Spanish archives and reading and commenting on a draft of the manuscript.

I owe a debt to all my friends in the living theatre who continue to inspire me with their imaginative and fruitful work. I'm particularly grateful to Mark Lamos and Connie Congdon, whose encouragement and belief have seen me through three biographies.

My thanks to my agent Philip Spitzer for his support and expertise. I thank my editor, Victoria Wilson, who launched me on this voyage in 1996. I am grateful for her careful reading, incisive observations, and years of friendship.

I thank Tom Sheehy for his practical support and loving criticism.

Eleonora Duse

One

"WHO CALLS? I am here. What is your will?" Repeating the lines of Shakespeare's Juliet, Eleonora Giulia Amalia Duse walked through the Palio gates into Verona on a Sunday in May 1873. She was fourteen. Slender and small-waisted, she moved with easy strides, using her whole body as one accustomed to walking great distances. Her long dark hair was shot through with bronze strands highlighted by the sun. In repose, her striking features—large, heavy-lidded black eyes, high, broad cheekbones over a square jaw, a patrician nose, and generous mouth—suggested the purity of classic sculpture.

Already a stage veteran of ten years, Eleonora was the leading lady in her family's troupe, a struggling, itinerant theatre company engaged to perform *Romeo and Juliet* that afternoon in Verona's ancient arena. As she walked, Eleonora rehearsed her lines that she had copied into a notebook. "I was choked with anxiety," she recalled.

Juliet, she imagined, had walked these same streets of swirling gray stones, looked up at the same red-roofed buildings, visited the same *palazzi* of local pink limestone, *rosso di Verona*. Perhaps Juliet had crossed the Scaligero bridge by the old castle and gazed into the depths of the Adige, which wound like a ribbon through the city. The sun bathed everything in glowing light, but at each street corner Eleonora expected to see a sombre funeral procession and Juliet's iron coffin.

In the Piazza Erbe, which had served as a market for almost two thousand years, Eleonora made her way through the stands shaded by white umbrellas. She stopped by the splashing Roman fountain with its statue of a woman representing Verona. Using all of her money, she bought pale pink roses. They would serve as a prop for Juliet—an idea suggested by her parents' first meeting, a family story her father, Alessandro Duse, had recorded in his diary. One day, walking along a street, he had felt flowers and leaves rain down upon him. He had looked up and into the eyes of a dark-haired girl tending her window box. Day after day, he followed the same path until he found the courage to walk up the stairs to her balcony. Finally, he did speak to her, and they married. Eleonora's mother's name was Angelica Cappelletto, which sounded hauntingly similar to Capulet.

From the Piazza Erbe to the arena was a short ten-minute walk. Finished by the Romans in the first century A.D., the arena could hold 25,000 people, almost half the population of Verona, in unbroken stone tiers of *rosso di Verona.* Throughout the centuries, the vast stone oval had hosted gladiator fights, mock sea battles, bullfights, fairs, equestrian performances, and grand opera. Small theatre companies like the Duse-Lagunaz troupe set up their wooden stage—their two planks and a passion—at one end of the arena, roped off a section of the seats, and charged only a few pennies for the late-afternoon performances.

Entering into the sunlit arena from the shadowy, underground corridors, Eleonora looked up at the tall grasses that grew from the crumbling parapet. A breeze stirred, and she felt her energy rise. Intoxicated by the fever of her imagination, the clear light, the dark blue sky, and the scent of the rose bouquet she carried, "the words flowed with strange ease, almost spontaneously," she remembered, "and I could hear them through the constant drumming of my heartbeat."

During the performance that day, when Juliet first met Romeo at the ball, Eleonora allowed one of her roses to drop at his feet. Later, from her balcony, she plucked the petals one by one from a rose, as if she were laying bare her heart, and they floated down to him. As the tragedy neared its end, the sun began to set, turning the top stone tier a fiery red. Under a "sky white as pearl," Eleonora heard the bells of the churches of Verona and "that almost sea-sound which quieted when I appeared." Mingling love with death, she covered Romeo, who lay in the tomb, with the last of her roses, and they wilted in the heat. When she stabbed herself with Romeo's dagger and fell upon his body, "the crowd let out such a great roar that I was terrified."

Struck by the coincidence of playing a girl of her same age in Juliet's own city, and acting as Juliet herself might have acted, Eleonora believed she was the reincarnation of Shakespeare's character. Before she spoke, every word seemed "to go right through the heat of my blood. There was not a fibre in me that did not contribute to the harmony. Oh, grace, it was a state of grace!"

In this state of boundless grace, she felt an "indescribable sense of abandonment." "Someone lifted me up," she recalled. "They held the torch close to my tear-stained face; it was crackling very loudly, it smelled of resin and was red and black with flames and smoke."

"I was Juliet," she explained. "I must have looked like death itself."

IN BECOMING JULIET, Eleonora Duse found herself. The feeling that surged through her, undoing the boundaries of her personality and uniting her in communion with the audience, was terrifying, uncanny, and as ancient as Dionysus, the god of the theatre, who embodies two opposing principles, the "ecstasy of power over others and the ecstasy of self-surrender." For the rest of her life, because she became most herself when acting other selves, she would seek this state of profound grace and ecstatic abandonment. "Art, like love," she said, "is insatiable."

Guided, she said, by a secret voice, a voice she called an "echo of the pain of the world," Duse aimed for a "transformation of life." Her grandfather Luigi Duse had taken off the traditional commedia dell'arte mask to reveal his human face. Eleonora Duse freed herself from the superficial mask of stage makeup and then she stripped away another mask. She opened her soul and revealed a woman as a human being. Her singular journey revolutionized the theatre and our understanding of what it means to be human. Duse's art embodied the past, the exact present, and the future. She was the first modern actor.

Speaking in Italian in theatres around the world, Duse was understood. Audiences, critics, and especially other artists were moved and responded to her art with acclamations and an outpouring of tributes at times so extreme as to be worthy of a deity. Critics scoured their vocabularies for words to describe her acting and yet words seemed inadequate. How could they describe what they had never seen before?

In the characters she portrayed—and she acted women only—Duse expanded the very idea of Woman. With *sprezzatura*, a seemingly effortless grace, she revealed the immense gap between accepted ideas of woman and what a woman really was. Once, she was told that in Ibsen's *The Lady from the Sea,* she was acting the drama of the female spirit. "No!" she replied, "the drama of everyone." Because she believed that language, the very words themselves, were ambiguous, cloudy, and contradictory, she ransacked her scripts, digging beneath the lines of her characters not to reveal certainty, but to portray what she called the invisible side of life. Duse's humanistic art and her revolutionary approach to language anticipated the complexity, fluidity, and impermanence of the modern world. In Duse's acting, as in her personality, there was nothing *fixed,* no national boundaries, no boundaries at all—there was only a human being, alive, ever changing, and ultimately tragic.

The world of the theatre, an active, ephemeral world that moves from light into darkness, is a metaphor for life—and death—itself. Duse understood this. After seeing her work, Konstantin Stanislavsky sought to codify her art. Duse rejected theories of art and "dared not define" her own art. While Stanislavsky sought a method to reproduce the character night after night, Duse aimed for something more. She strived to create a new woman, a new human being, in performance after performance. "Through discipline," she wrote, "with incessant control, with incessant self-domination, and squandering one's own person and soul to become a consciousness . . . to conjure from the center and journey to the most secret heart of things, not the reality of life, but the dream." Like Donatello, she wanted her art to be a new language: "the outward rendered expressive of the inward; the body instinct with spirit; the soul made incarnate."

She resisted all efforts to dissect her art. When the first biography was published about her, she wouldn't read it because she believed an academic could never understand her. Urged endlessly to write her autobiography, she refused. Except for some scribbled pages of memories, she never wrote a memoir. Unsentimental about her life, she refused to turn it into publicity or mythology. Experience had taught her fame was enhanced by mystery, and privacy created more fascination than self-promotion.

At twenty-four, with two decades of acting behind her, when pushed by a persistent critic to explain her art, Duse offered a parable instead. As a child she had been given a beautiful puppet. Intrigued by the puppet's moving arms and legs and smiling mouth that opened and closed, she had destroyed it when she took it apart to see how it was made. "And it's *art* that you wish to talk about?" she chided the critic. "It would be like trying to explain love." Those "who pretend to understand art, understand nothing," she told him bluntly. Years later, she wondered, "Who is it that arrives at art without an understanding of life?"

After she had become an international celebrity, Duse was asked which country she preferred. "The crossing," she replied. When Duse was born she had no country, and the journey would always be more important to her than any nation. The image of the sea flows through her writing. She grew up near water—the Adriatic, the lagoons and canals of Chioggia and Venice, the Adige and the Po Rivers, and the smaller rivers and streams of northern Italy. She called herself a "passionate colorist," who preferred the "emerald sea of the Adriatic with its red sails" to the blue waters and white sails of the Mediterranean. One of her earliest memories was of her father dropping her over the seawall at Chioggia into the Adriatic and then diving in beside her.

She thought of herself as a child of the sea and her life as a voyage. The theatre was her ship—the shifting planks under her feet, the air she breathed, the light she moved in. She lived in this world without self-consciousness, with the bold directness and easy grace of a creature in its natural habitat.

The world outside the theatre—the solid, bourgeois, literal world of permanent homes, schools, and churches—seemed fictional and remote. Because she was an actor and a nomad, she did not and could not belong to that middle-class world. She was an outcast, with the social standing of a Gypsy. Humiliated and ashamed, she never forgot the taunts she received from other children, who shunned her and cursed her as the daughter of *commedianti*, third-rate, lowlife *actors*.

Without formal schooling, she learned to read from the scripts they performed. Economics, philosophy, psychology, and politics she absorbed from her daily life. It was a hard school. At times, she was forced to beg. Begging is performing, after all, and poverty a powerful motivation. Eleonora learned to say one thing and think something else. She learned to read faces and gestures, and to know when a harsh word masked a generous heart. Brutal necessity made her acutely aware of her audience. She learned how to use her body and her voice—to know which delicate movement of the arm, what cunning bend of the leg or quick bow of the head, what subtle phrase spoken with enticing sweetness or silent glance with wet, pleading eyes would cause the centimes to fall into her outstretched hand.

All the different coins and money confounded the tourists. The lira nuova d'Italia, equivalent to the French franc, was used in Sardinia; the Austrian lira, equal to 87 centimes of the lira nuova, was used in the Austrian-controlled Venetian territories; and the French gold napoleons were the most desirable coins of all and good anywhere. The money reflected the confusing political reality. But for Eleonora, money simply meant bread to eat and a bed for the night. Economics and politics were personal. How do I survive? Whom do I have to please? Actually, it was a state not unlike the real world of mid-nineteenth-century Italy.

GEORGE GORDON, Lord Byron, had called Italy the garden of the world. It contained the fruits of the past in art, architecture, and poetry as well as the seeds for a new beginning. After visiting Italy, Henrik Ibsen said he didn't know how he had existed before. In Rome in 1866, Ibsen wrote the icy Nordic drama *Brand*. He wrote *A Doll's House* at the seaside in Amalfi and wrote *Ghosts* in Sorrento. Henry James shared Ibsen's view. When James arrived in Rome in 1869, he told his diary, "At last, for the first time, I live."

At the same time that foreign artists basked in the sun, soaked up history, and created their art while living cheaply and well, native theatre artists coped with simple survival. Rossini's and Verdi's operas were acclaimed around the world, the tragedians Tommaso Salvini and Adelaide Ristori were applauded in Paris, London, Moscow, and New York, but the Italian theatre, overshadowed by opera, and its audiences diminished by political unrest and poverty, was neglected and forgotten. Ristori and Salvini performed mostly Shakespeare and popular French plays. Censorship had stifled Italian literature, and the most gifted writers wrote libretti instead of plays.

Italy, which had not yet become a country, was uncertain, turbulent, and filled with so many plot twists and turns that politics resembled melodrama. In the early decades of the nineteenth century, Count Metternich of Austria played the evil villain, leading the Congress of Vienna to repress the principles of democracy, liberalism, and nationalism awakening across Europe. The Industrial Revolution and the rise of the middle class were inevitable, though, and revolutions stirred across Europe and in the ten small states that made up the Italian peninsula. The revolutionary hero Giuseppe Mazzini founded a secret society called Young Italy and worked for a dream that had eluded Italians for centuries, a united Italy under one flag.

In 1848, Venice blockaded Austrian forces and declared itself a republic, the independent island of Sardinia forced the Austrians to retreat from northern Italy, the pope was expelled from Rome, and a Roman republic was proclaimed. That year Elizabeth Barrett Browning watched celebrations of Italian unity from her Casa Guidi windows in Florence. Like many foreigners drawn to Italy, she felt liberated there. In her farseeing poetry, she championed the Risorgimento, Italy's desire for freedom and unification, but she also spoke out for the future and a wider humanity reaching to the millennium. "No more Jew nor Greek then," she wrote, "taunting / Nor taunted: no more England nor France! / But one confederate brotherhood planting / One flag only, to mark the advance, / Onward and upward, of all humanity." The celebrations were short-lived. The Austrians regrouped, regained control of Lombardy and Venetia in the north, and French forces restored the pope in Rome.

The revolution of 1848 had failed, but Victor Emmanuel II, king of Sardinia, which had a liberal constitution and flew the red, green, and white flag, the symbol of a free Italy, offered asylum to political refugees. The brilliant statesman Count Camillo Cavour became prime minister of Sardinia. In 1859 Cavour provoked war with Austria and gained Lombardy. The duchies of Parma, Modena, and Tuscany joined Sardinia. Another hero, Giuseppe Garibaldi, and his red-shirted followers won the kingdoms of Naples and Sicily. Rallying around the enormously popular music of Verdi (whose name formed an acronym for Vittorio Emmanuele Re d'Italia), the unification

Luigi Duse, Eleonora's paternal grandfather,
as Giacometto, 1830s

forces declared Victor Emmanuel II as king of Italy. In Turin on March 17, 1861, at the same time the United States was beginning a civil war that would tear that country apart, the Kingdom of Italy, a liberal, constitutional monarchy promising freedom of the press, speech, and worship, was formed. Venice was added in 1866, but Rome, despite the efforts of Garibaldi, remained under French control until 1870, when Napoleon III withdrew his troops. Finally, in July 1871, Rome became the capital of a united Italy, a brand-new country with an ancient culture.

The 1848 revolution destroyed the career of Luigi Duse, Eleonora's grandfather. Accused of making fun of the Venetian blockade during performances at his theatre in Padua, Luigi protested his innocence, but when he attempted to bring his company to Venice to perform, he was refused a theatre. His public in Padua abandoned him as well, and because he continued to pay his company when they weren't performing (a practice his granddaughter would perpetuate with her companies), he lost an enormous sum of money.

In the early years of the twentieth century, Eleonora Duse inspired the American slang word "doozy," meaning "a stunning example, a wow." The name Duse (pronounced Doo-zay), however, is originally French, and means "demon" or "spirit"—a fitting name for a family of wandering actors. Apparently the first of the Duses to become an actor, Luigi was born on January 15, 1792, into a middle-class mercantile family in Chioggia. A fishing port town on the Adriatic, some twenty sea miles south of Venice, Chioggia, like Venice, has canals, arched stone bridges, and beautiful churches. Unlike Venice, however, the streets of Chioggia radiate out from the main square in a sensible herringbone pattern. After a visit to Chioggia, Henry James admired the delicate beauty and splendid complexions of the women, and he described the men as "almost as handsome as the women; I have never seen so many good-looking rascals." Good-looking Luigi Duse was something of a rascal, since he defied his father's wishes and left his job in a pawnbroking shop to devote himself first to amateur theatre in Chioggia and Padua before joining a professional troupe. Ambitious and gifted, after a year of gathering experience touring, he formed his own theatre company.

Acclaimed for the naturalness and spontaneity of his acting, Luigi specialized in Goldoni and Gozzi comedies. He also invented a jovial rascal of a commedia character he called Giacometto. In Venice, where he acted for about fourteen years, Venetians spoke not of attending the theatre but of going to see *amico* Duse. On a visit to Venice, George Sand and her lover Alfred Musset saw Luigi perform Giacometto. Sand ranked Luigi's artistry higher than that of the best French comedians. In 1834, Luigi built his own theatre, the Teatro Duse, in Padua. Popular with the poor students of Padua, who loved his comedy and his generosity in allowing them to pay for their tickets with flowers, salami, or even onions, Luigi enjoyed great success until 1848, when, perhaps because of his habit of improvising satiric asides to the audience, his comedy was misinterpreted, and he was charged with anti-Risorgimento beliefs. Even the students turned against him. He lost his theatre in Padua, and it was renamed the Garibaldi Theatre. He died in Padua on January 25, 1854.

Luigi left four sons, Eugenio, Giorgio, Alessandro, and Enrico, who all became somewhat mediocre actors. Eleonora Duse never knew her grandfather, who died before she was born, but she kept his red velvet waistcoat all her life. His example linked her to the glorious past of the commedia dell'arte—the only professional theatre tradition based entirely on the art of the actor. "My grandfather was humble," Duse said, "but he had faith in his art. Without faith no one makes art."

Alessandro Duse, Eleonora's father, 1880s

Duse's father, Alessandro, had little faith in acting. He was a mild-mannered man who wanted to be a painter and had studied art briefly in Venice. When Luigi Duse insisted he become an actor, Alessandro lacked the will to stand up to his father. The old man was a perfectionist with an explosive temper—traits that would resurface in Eleonora. Once, when Alessandro was a young actor, he spoke the curtain lines of a play without the proper timing and destroyed the effect. An enraged Luigi, who was watching from a theatre box, roared, "Asino!" The audience recognized the old actor, and when they applauded and called for him, Luigi mounted the stage and took a bow, upstaging his son.

After Luigi's death, his son Giorgio inherited the Giacometto character and struck out on his own. Alessandro united with his unmarried younger brother Enrico, his uncle Federigo (brother of Luigi), and the actor Giuseppe Lagunaz to form a troupe. When Alessandro married Angelica Cappelletto, she became an actress in the company. The troupe had its base in Chioggia and Venice, but they toured constantly between towns looking for new audiences at fairs and market days. It was a way of life that hadn't changed in centuries. The troupe piled their sets, costumes, and props on a cart and walked along behind it. The completion of railroad lines in the late 1850s, connecting

Milan with Venice, and with various branches in large towns throughout northern Italy, made traveling more convenient, not only for itinerant actors but for other poor people who could ride cheaply in third class.

Shortly before Eleonora was born, the Duse-Lagunaz troupe traveled, probably by train, between Venice, which was controlled by Austria, to an engagement in Vigevano, in lower Lombardy, which was part of the Kingdom of Sardinia. A city of about fourteen thousand, noted for considerable trade and connected by rail to nearby Milan, Vigevano presented a good opportunity for the troupe to find a new audience. Alessandro and Angelica Duse found a room at the Inn of the Golden Cannon close by the beautiful piazza designed by Michelangelo. At 2 a.m. on Sunday, October 3, 1858, their daughter was born. Their first child, a son, had died at birth, and their joy at the birth of a healthy girl is evident in the lilting, liquid names they gave her—Eleonora Giulia Amalia.

AS SHE LOOKED BACK on her childhood from a distance of sixty years, Duse pondered a question: "Where did you come from?"

"From the great suffering heart of a woman," she decided. The death of her son had left Angelica Duse with a grief so great, Eleonora recalled, her mother would suddenly leave the house and stand outside staring forlornly at the sky. Angelica was young, probably in her twenties, and her father, Alessandro, was thirty-eight when Eleonora was born. Eleonora was extremely attached to her mother. The "small hand" of her mother held her "tightly, tightly, always next to her," she recalled. In photographs taken when Eleonora was a girl, mother and daughter look strikingly similar—the same dark hair, widely spaced black eyes, and dangling earrings, which lend a Gypsy-like aspect to their somber expressions.

Knowing her daughter must join the family enterprise and become an actor, Angelica encouraged Eleonora's intelligence and imagination. Early on, she had recognized "magic gifts" in her daughter. "Self-sufficient" with an empathetic imagination, Eleonora saw life in everything around her, including chairs and ordinary household objects. "In their silence they held a great enchantment for me," Duse remembered. Hour after hour she would talk with them and "they seemed to listen, patiently, to me, who asked no reply—and my Mamma found it *right* and dreamlike this speaking to those who haven't the possibility of replying."

Speaking onstage for the first time, though, frightened her. Just four years old, Eleonora played Cosette in a dramatization of Victor Hugo's *Les Misérables*. Her father held her hand and told her the words. Too young to know how to cry on cue, Eleonora burst into tears when another actor whacked her

Eleonora with her mother, Angelica, 1863

on the legs to make her cry. "Don't be afraid," her mother told her. "You know that it's only pretend."

From April to May 1862 at the Teatro Malibran in Venice, the troupe presented *The Count of Monte Cristo* and other standard nineteenth-century melodramas about starving orphans, abandoned foundlings, and wicked seducers who leave young girls with "*frutto della colpa*"—an illegitimate child. Along with her mother's and father's, Eleonora's name appeared on the bill, which changed daily, and there were many opportunities to use the girl in the popular melodramas. At the Teatro Malibran, Eleonora could also have seen performances of her grandfather Luigi's famous Giacometto character as well as Carlo Goldoni plays like *The Servant of Two Masters* and *La locandiera.* The following year, March 1863, when the Duse-Lagunaz troupe crossed the Adriatic and played at the Nobile Teatro in Zara on the Dalmatian coast of Yugoslavia, Eleonora's name was listed as part of the company.

In addition to performing, the actors were responsible for cleaning the theatre, creating and maintaining their costumes, and, of course, rehearsing and learning lines. There was pressure to find new audiences, which meant constant travel. Sometimes they were able to find a theatre to play in; other times they resorted to tents. From the time she learned to walk, Eleonora trudged along behind her mother holding on to her skirt. Sometimes they hurried "aimlessly from one house to another," Duse recalled, and they would find themselves "at dusk in another town," where they would know no one. Roads in northern Italy in the 1860s were rutted and frequently muddy, thieves were a constant worry, rented rooms cold and drafty with bug-infested beds. The food, often just grilled polenta or bread with a piece of fruit, a "poor meal counted out coin by coin," Duse wrote, kept her thin and hungry.

It was a grueling and lonely life for a child. Years later, she told her daughter Enrichetta she wished no child to suffer as she had. "I know what hunger is," Duse said, "and what it means to see night approaching when shelter is uncertain." When she was not needed in the play, she waited alone in her parents' room, and because candles and lamps were expensive, she usually sat in the dark. Sometimes she grew so frightened she climbed up to the roof, where she at least had the light from the stars. There were no other children for Eleonora to play with in the troupe, and she made no friends in the towns they visited.

Once, when the Duse troupe arrived in a small town in Piedmont, Eleonora saw a group of girls playing merry-go-round, "disheveled, laughing and shouting, unrestrained in the wind." Standing outside the spinning circle, Eleonora longed to be a part of their fun. "Dazzled by the hum, by that rotating fly wheel. Ah! To enter there!" Gathering her courage, she stepped inside the circle, and suddenly the little girls became aware of her, "their shouts silenced like a flock of sparrows when they are frightened." The girls stopped their play and stared at the intruder. Eleonora ran to her mother, who was sick in bed, but "so beautiful and so sweet," and Angelica comforted her sobbing daughter.

Angelica Duse always lived in Eleonora's memory as a kind of ministering angel, her one sustaining comfort. If their room didn't have a fireplace, Angelica was there with her warming hands, rubbing her daughter's cold feet. She taught Eleonora how to nurture an abandoned bird and how to free it. While Alessandro Duse seems to have been somewhat distant, even living apart from his family at times, Angelica gave her daughter faithful, unconditional love and encouraged her curiosity and independence. A highly sensitive, observant child, Eleonora also had a mnemonic gift for physical details, colors, images, sounds, and emotional states.

When did she first feel the calling to become an artist? Like Thomas Mann's Tonio Kröger, she felt it "early, horribly early." What Kröger calls a "gulf of ironic sensibility," a feeling of being different, of being set apart, of feeling alone, she, too, felt when she was quite young. When she was twelve, Eleonora and her mother lived in a little two-room house in Bagni di Lucca in Tuscany near a river. During a flood, Eleonora walked across the river bridge and watched as a girl about her age, "not seeming dead, but unconscious, inert like a small branch that the water had carried with it," was pulled out of the water. She was "very, very pale," Duse recalled, "with her arms dangling . . . bare feet, a ticking petticoat, a triangular handkerchief embroidered with little colored flowers knotted on her breast." When the mother of the little girl appeared, all the other women gave way. "And the mother called her, many times she called her, with all the names of the heart," Duse remembered. "Then she picked her up in her arms and held her to her neck and tried to go back up the hill, almost as if to distance herself from the lethal water— out of breath, panting, exhausted and frightened, panting like a poor wounded beast, without seeing the road anymore."

"At that time," Duse said, "my mother, who was there among the crowd, holding my hand firmly and with a heart more ready than all of the women that surrounded her, pushed her way forward and offered her hospitality to the woman." The peasant woman, "with her Death in her arms," entered their house and laid her daughter on Eleonora's small bed and then sat down next to her. While Eleonora watched, the two women took off the girl's wet clothes with great difficulty, and a little later, when "all was useless," they dressed her in one of Eleonora's dresses, "kissing her and decorating her with kisses, crying together, whispering, as if the little girl slept." For Eleonora, seeing the dead girl wearing her clothes, "already saved, blessed with a bunch of flowers on her chest," was like looking in a mirror. In that moment, Eleonora began "to look, to guess, to understand." She realized the inevitability of her own death, the precious precariousness of life, and she developed a consciousness of humanity's fate. Even her Art, which she always capitalized, would not be enough to assuage the desolation of this knowledge.

PERHAPS ELEONORA was born with an empathetic imagination, but it was certainly nurtured by the ready heart of her mother. Guided by her mother and father and by her own observations of other company members,

Rachel, the French actress and
international star, died in 1858,
the year Eleonora Duse was born.

Eleonora also learned about acting. For the most part, nineteenth-century
acting was bombastic and exterior, and actors, who performed a different play
every night, depended on the prompter to remind them of their lines. Published acting manuals, which taught basic techniques of oratory and posing,
were available, but it's highly unlikely a working company descended from
Luigi Duse, one of the finest actors of his time, would have felt the need for
such a manual. Italian actors with roots in the commedia dell'arte had a gift
for natural speech quite different from the academy-trained actors of the
French and Scandinavian theatre, who declaimed their lines and moved to set
rules. Henrik Ibsen noted actresses in Norway "always swooned . . . on the
left of the stage and always with a handkerchief in their left hand," while Italian actresses fainted naturally. Acting, at this time, however, was primarily a

Italian actress and international star
Adelaide Ristori as Lady Macbeth, 1860s

pictorial art, and actors routinely studied paintings and sculpture and practiced attitudes and poses in front of a mirror. In the first years of the twentieth century, when she played *Phèdre* in London, Sarah Bernhardt, who always
remained rooted in the nineteenth century, stood and posed sometimes for as
long as thirty seconds before changing position, moving from pose to pose in
a rhythmic progression.

Italy lacked a national theatre, but it had an unbroken line of great acting
beginning with the Roman Roscius in the first century B.C., to the sixteenth-
century's commedia dell'arte pioneer Isabella Andreini, the first professional
actress of the European stage. In the nineteenth century, Italian opera tours
prepared the way for the international theatre careers of Tommaso Salvini,
Adelaide Ristori, and Ernesto Rossi. The passionate acting style of the Italians
was markedly different from the cooler, more declamatory style of the French
theatre as represented by Rachel. Salvini, noted for his Othello, terrified his
Desdemonas by his murderous violence. Ristori acted the great tragic roles of
Lady Macbeth, Mary Stuart, and Medea with a pictorial larger-than-life emotional style. A London critic of her Medea called it a mixture of realism and
idealism that bordered on the ridiculous. When Ristori describes the "infuriated action of a leopard destroying its victim," he wrote, "she goes through all
the process of rending limb from limb; when she calls to mind the horrible

picture of her dying brother collecting in his hand the blood flowing from his wound and flinging it in the face of his murderers she seems to be actually collecting clotted gore and actually flinging it." This kind of pantomimic pictorial style combined with lavish scenery and costumes was designed principally for international audiences who might not understand the language but relished melodramatic spectacle.

When she was a girl, Duse saw Ristori play the famous sleepwalking scene from *Macbeth*. Ristori revised Shakespeare's play to enhance her own role as Lady Macbeth. This was a common practice in the nineteenth-century theatre. Playbills of the time often broke down the play scene by scene, and actors raced through or cut the minor scenes to arrive at the big emotional scenes where they could make dramatic "points." Eleonora recalled Ristori wore a crown and acted with a composed, classic dignity. In between phrases, Ristori emitted a "light snoring sound." Duse's reaction? "When I returned to my house," she said, "I felt an overwhelming urge to straighten my room."

Armed with the self-confidence and mocking sarcasm of rebellious youth, Duse was not intimidated by the great Ristori. Like all innovators in art, Duse would follow her own path and speak with her own true voice. Perhaps her artist father trained her eye, but for the most part, as she was for the rest of her life, Duse was self-taught. She learned acting by doing and relied on her own imagination and responses. Before performances, she liked to find a place where she could be alone. On one occasion, she found a flax field dotted with statues. "I would go from one to another and stay a while as though I were paying a visit," she recalled. "But I always stayed longest with the mutilated ones as though I were instinctively trying to comfort them." In her imaginative play with the statues, she became both actor and audience, studying what effect they had on her as an observer. She felt pity for one statue in particular that had lost the arms to support a basket of fruit on its head. "When I close my eyes," Duse said, "I can see its stone face and the sun changing color as it shone through the stalks of flax as though through green glass . . . From that time onwards, in the most impassioned moments of my work on stage, images from remembered landscapes have always come to me."

When Eleonora was about twelve or thirteen, Angelica Duse became ill. It's not clear if her illness was cancer or tuberculosis, but she was in and out of hospitals. At that time the Duse company re-formed and combined with the Rosaspina family, which included eighteen-year-old Carlo. Seeing an opportunity, the company exploited the talents of Eleonora and Carlo, teaming them as the lovers in a series of plays, including *Romeo and Juliet, Francesca da Rimini, Pia de Tolommei,* and *La trovatella di Santa Maria.*

Eleonora in her early twenties.

A young, nubile woman surrounded by men has always been good box office. As the only female in all-male casts, Eleonora played the lead in Carlo Marenco's tragedy *Pia de Tolommei*, a standard in Ristori's repertory, and in the charming comedy *La trovatella di Santa Maria (The Foundling of Santa Maria)*. Eleonora also acted the title role in *Gaspara Stampa*, a piece based on the life of the Italian poet, who was desperately in love with Count Collaltino. "I remember the sound of my voice which was still feeble when I forced it in big speeches, because someone behind the scenes hissed at me that I should shout louder, louder," Duse said. "There were so many things that my young, inexperienced soul did not know or understand, and I do not know what painful instinct led me to find the tone of voice or the shrieks that were to move the wretched audience who provided our daily bread. Ten hungry people were torturing me because I was a means of livelihood." After a performance, food seemed too heavy for Eleonora to swallow, and she felt a kind of "confused nobility" in her humiliation. "Perhaps it was the obscure presence of the strength that was to develop in me later, that difference and special quality that Nature had bestowed on me," Duse recalled. "The first lines of my art were developed in that state of agitation, exhaustion, feverishness and revulsion, when my senses had become what I might describe as malleable."

Eleonora schooled herself by reaching out to her audiences and adjusting to their response, and by trying out the different effects she called up from her past, from her observations, from her study of the script, and from her imagination. Her musical, slightly nasal voice conveyed subtle nuances of meaning. Her face, with large dark eyes, clear complexion, high cheekbones, mobile mouth, and dazzling white teeth, was not conventionally beautiful, but her facial expressions, responsive to every fleeting thought, were free of convention, and thus beautiful with quivering, spontaneous life. Later, critics would describe Duse's passion and sensuality, writing of the "Venetian seduction of every movement of her slender body." In these early leading roles, just as her own sexuality and desires were awakening, Eleonora responded to her audiences and they to her like an ardent lover. Sometimes, she recalled, she succeeded in "communicating a great shudder to the spectators through the pure power of silence."

Perhaps her early success and her sensual rapport with audiences gave her confidence, because Eleonora never seemed to have suffered from debilitating stage fright. Why should she? The theatre was her natural world. She also felt a tremendous sense of importance in becoming the primary box-office draw. It was both a heady and terrifying responsibility for a young girl. "Only my mother took pity on me," Duse recalled, "and suffered the same torment with me and knew how to hold me in her arms and stop my ghastly trembling and weep with me, comforting me."

In May 1873 when she played Juliet in the arena of Verona, she was fourteen and had ten years of acting experience, including two years in major roles. Just as Shakespeare's Juliet changes from a carefree girl into a suffering, mature woman, Eleonora, too, had matured into a young adult. The state of grace she achieved that day was not a lucky accident. It was the result of years of study and work and experience. One has to be ready to receive grace, and she was prepared.

In September of that same year, Eleonora was in Tuscany, and her mother was in a hospital in the port city of Ancona on the Adriatic. There was "a great knocking at the door of the house," Duse recalled. It was a telegram with only two words: "Mama dead."

Angelica Duse had died alone in the hospital. Everything was silent, Duse wrote, "except a sound like something was broken in the air—a silence, all an emptiness." Submerged in his own grief, her father, then fifty-two, became more remote and withdrawn. Eleonora, who would turn fifteen on October 3, grieved alone. She walked in the countryside, "away, away, from the women, so alive and so different" from her mother. Unable to afford a new dress, she wound a strip of black cloth at her neck. "Why don't you cry?" one of the women in the troupe demanded. "Why don't you dress yourself in mourning? What a heartless daughter! If my mother died, I would sell myself to dress in mourning clothes."

Eleonora clung to her mother's picture and never showed it to anyone, preferring to keep the image all to herself. No longer did she have the "desolate and dear solitude of mother and daughter," but just the "perennial disorder of houses, of trains, of theatres, of damned people." She still felt warmed by the "faithful love" of her mother, but she was alone. No one waited for her, no one looked for her, no one wanted her. "At night, silent crying, and by day the sleepiness of tired hearts!" she wrote. "That semi-drowsiness of those who are in too much pain."

AFTER THE DEATH of her mother, Eleonora was despondent. The world seemed to her a "broken shell." More than anything, she wanted to see her mother again, and to see her again, she said, "there was nothing to do but die." With adolescent self-absorption, she dramatized her suffering, but her agony was real. Her father dismissed her depression as the *smara*, a dark Venetian mood that descended like a fog bringing weariness with the world, irritation with herself, and restless rebellion against those around her. Her father didn't comfort her, and Eleonora had no girlfriends, no one to confide in or console her. Instead, she looked with envy at a young girl who passed her in the street. She imagined the girl had "parents [who] speak to her with sweetness . . . someone who receives her and embraces her."

Angelica Duse seems to have been the force that held the Duse troupe together. Following her death, the company disbanded. Yearning for closeness and connection, Eleonora turned to her art, "always my refuge and my only consolation." From 1874 to 1878, Duse moved from company to company. Her father acted minor parts, and Duse, no longer the leading lady and the center of attention, played supporting roles.

Hired as *seconda donna* by the Brunetti-Pezzana troupe for the 1875–76 season, Duse refused to accept the line readings given to her by the leading actor Luigi Pezzana, who had toured with Ristori and who was famous for his flamboyant portrayal of the Count of Monte Cristo. Frustrated by Duse's insistence on speaking the lines the way she thought and felt them and by her use of silences to communicate meaning, Pezzana shouted, "What makes you think you're an artist?" Duse would not budge. Angrily, Pezzana informed her she lacked the "figure and voice and intelligence for acting." Duse left his company.

Duse's early successful experiences playing leading roles with her family's company had given her the confidence to defy authority. She also possessed an unshakable sense of self, which was her mother's legacy to her. The death of her mother turned her inward to her own resources. Eleonora had no one to place restrictions or to enforce societal conventions; no one to tell her no or to be a good girl. Her manner was abrupt, direct, even rude at times. Like her grandfather Luigi, Eleonora had a huge ego and faith in her own art and judgment. Despite humiliation and outright dismissal, she resisted stubbornly all attempts to force her into an acting style she found false.

On the broadest level, Duse's rejection of the prevailing acting style was a rebellion of youth against age, of innovation against tradition, of the individual against the group, and the future against the past. She sensed there was more to acting than beauty frozen into a pose. She sought to evoke the quivering wordless emotions of the body and to express the quickening agitation of thought with no separation between the two, her goal being not to please or capture the audience, but to connect and create with them.

Mature beyond her years in her work, in her life she had the healthy desires and the impulses of a passionate young woman. Years later, she told her voice coach Henry Russell that after a performance she had roamed the streets of Turin. "It was because I needed love! I was seeking love," she said. "The thought of returning to my lonely room was impossible. So I walked and walked, still looking for love, until dawn broke and fatigue compelled me to seek my bed." Wandering around the streets of Turin in the middle of the night, at a time when an unaccompanied woman could be arrested as a prostitute, was certainly reckless and probably dangerous. Another time, Duse arranged to meet a man after a performance. When she returned to her hotel to wait for an hour, she fell asleep on the sofa and didn't wake up until 1 a.m. "The fact that I overslept myself proved that I did not love him," she told Russell, "and I broke off everything between us."

Duse was determined to distinguish herself professionally; she remained aloof from other actors. She saved her flattery and charm for those who could advance her career. In the first three months of 1878, she and her father changed companies four times. She was hired by the Ciotti-Belli-Blanes company, and, in the age-old tradition of the theatre, she got her first break in May 1878 when Giulia Gritti, the star, became ill, and Duse took over Gritti's roles for a time. After seeing Duse in several productions in Rome, an important critic, the Marquis Francesco D'Arcais, predicted she would have a brilliant future. He noted, almost as if he were rebutting Luigi Pezzana, that among all the young actresses of Italy, Duse, then nineteen, was the only one who had the figure, voice, and intelligence to become a great leading lady.

While struggling provincial companies like the Duse troupe performed mostly classics or Italian plays, the Ciotti-Belli-Blanes troupe was prosperous enough to afford the translation fees for new French plays. To the dismay of Italian writers, the French dominated novel and play writing in the nineteenth century. Italian plays, it was said, were like Italian wine. They didn't keep or carry well, "but consumed on the spot, they have a wonderfully real and sound flavor." French theatre, like French wine, traveled well, had a long tradition, and was made with art and discrimination. Theatre was a booming industry in France, and often served as the colorful background in contemporary novels. Leading French actors and playwrights used sophisticated publicity techniques to manipulate the popular press, and drama critics wielded enormous power. Government theatre censors limited their expression, but French playwrights Emile Augier, Alexandre Dumas *fils*, and Victorien Sardou wrote realistic plays about current social problems, focusing on money, class, marital infidelity, and the role of women. Their plays appealed to both the aristocracy and the rising middle class and prepared the way for the work of Ibsen, Chekhov, and Strindberg.

Victorien Sardou, one of the most successful playwrights of the French boulevard stage, wrote tightly plotted, five-act plays with strong female characters. His plots often depended upon implausible situations and remarkable coincidences. George Bernard Shaw called the audience's love for Sardou plays "sardoodledom."

In May 1878 in Rome, Duse played the leading role of Marcella in Sardou's *Borghesi di Pontarcy*, which had opened in Paris just a few months earlier. Since Duse traveled constantly and had no contact with educational or religious institutions, the books she read, the plays she acted in, and the characters she played became her reality and her introduction to manners and values outside the insular world of the theatre. Tellingly, Duse was often cast as an independent, outspoken young woman with a slightly stained past but with a good heart and high intelligence. According to the critic of *L'Arte Drammatica*, writing on May 27, 1878, Duse as Marcella received prolonged applause because "her way of acting is the truest and most natural that can be imagined."

IN LATE OCTOBER 1878, Duse, then twenty, and her father traveled with the Ciotti-Belli-Blanes company to the ancient city of Naples, a "paradise inhabited by devils"—a town overlooking the most beautiful bay in all of

Director-actor Giovanni Emmanuel,
late 1870s

Italy yet under the shadow of Vesuvius, an active volcano. The cultural center of the south, with some dozen theatres and many flourishing newspapers, Naples teemed with violent, exuberant life. Elegant hotels, smart cafés and beautiful museums contrasted with slum rows of tall houses where colorful, ragged laundry dangled from crooked iron balconies. Under constant threat from Neapolitan fever, the people sought sunshine and fresh air and practically lived in the streets, lighting candles on every corner for the Madonna, dancing the tarantella, gambling every week in the public lottery, and eating pizza made with garlic and strong cheese. There was constant, unrelenting noise—the pealing of church bells, the rattling of carriage wheels and pounding of hooves on rough lava stone, the banging of tambourines, and a cacophony of voices—beggars demanding alms, babies crying, masters berating servants, and indolent young men shouting over their cards. This turbulent southern city on the Tyrrhenian Sea was a world away from the northern Adriatic serenity of Duse's familiar Chioggia and Venice.

On November 7, 1878, soon after her arrival, the most important newspaper in Naples, the *Corriere del Mattino*, founded and edited by journalist and man-about-town Martino Cafiero, welcomed the Ciotti-Belli-Blanes troupe and "the beautiful Miss Duse, an artist of style and grace." Duse also caught the attention of thirty-one-year-old actor and theatre manager Giovanni Emmanuel, who saw her play Maia in Emile Augier's last play, *I Fourcham-bault (The House of Fourchambault)*, which had premiered earlier that year in Paris at the Comédie-Française. When the leading lady, the *prima attrice*, Giulia Gritti (cast as Maia), once again became ill, Duse, the *seconda donna*, was ready to replace her at the opening of *I Fourchambault* at the Teatro dei Fiorentini.

"I had to act for days and months in roles I hated," Duse recalled, "to obtain the sacred prize of being able to breathe in a part I felt and loved." Feeling and loving the part were essential, but Duse also craved the leading role. She knew to become a *prima attrice*, she needed a showy and sympathetic part to bring her to the attention of the critics. The character of Maia was just that.

Augier wrote plays that reflected the society he knew, which means he wrote about sex, money, marriage, and movement between social classes. All these themes are embodied in the character of Marie Letellier, known as Maia in the play, who has been taken in by the Fourchambault family. A "bit free in her manners," Maia is dark and exotic, half-Creole, and poor. "You are so thrillingly alive!" young Blanche Fourchambault tells her. "I was merely a doll before I knew you; I feel that in your presence I am becoming a young woman, too."

Giovanni Emmanuel was moved and excited by Duse's performance, and went backstage to meet her. "She was an actress who gripped your heart and crushed it as if it were a handkerchief," he recalled. Since Duse's company, the Ciotti-Belli-Blanes troupe, was booked at the Teatro dei Fiorentini only until late December, Emmanuel saw an opportunity to create a resident company headed by himself, with the veteran actress Giacinta Pezzana as leading lady, and Eleonora Duse. Emmanuel also offered a job to Duse's father, and both Duses decided to quit the Ciotti-Belli-Blanes troupe and settle in Naples with Emmanuel's company at the Fiorentini.

The Sannazzaro Theatre was a major competitor of the Teatro dei Fiorentini. They announced on January 21, 1879, that their new season would have 256 performances with 50 brand-new plays presented by five major Italian touring companies, including the Ciotti-Belli-Blanes company starring Giulia Gritti and Eleonora Duse. Not to be outdone, the Fiorentini boasted three days later that they would give "296 performances with 59 brand-new plays" with a permanent company of Giacinta Pezzana, Giovanni Emmanuel, and Eleonora Duse. In a battle that played out in the newspapers, the Ciotti-Belli Blanes troupe threatened to sue Duse for breaking her contract. The Fiorentini countered they had resolved the problem of Duse with a 5,000-lire payment penalty. Finally, on February 8, 1879, in a letter to *L'Arte Drammatica*, Duse fired the last shot, writing that her contract with Mr. Ciotti and Mr. Belli-Blanes had been liquidated with a payment of 3,100 lire. Duse stayed at the Fiorentini, and Ciotti-Belli-Blanes found another *seconda donna.*

The publicity and controversy were good for everyone. The critics, like Edoardo Boutet, then just twenty-two, saw their own reputations balloon and proclaimed Naples as a major theatre center. The merchants and theatre owners counted their money. Duse, who had been the central object of desire for two major theatres, saw her importance and visibility enhanced. Also, at the Fiorentini, she had the opportunity to work with Giacinta Pezzana, an independent, strong actress in her late thirties, and with the innovative Giovanni Emmanuel, who did not stifle Duse's individuality.

During April and May 1879, the Teatro dei Fiorentini presented more than fifteen different plays in repertory—a tremendous workload for the actors. Critics in Naples had an opportunity to see Duse in a variety of roles both classic and modern. In *Oreste*, by Vittorio Alfieri, which opened on April 26, 1879, Duse played Electra in a body-revealing tunic of coarse plain wool. To play Ophelia to Emmanuel's Hamlet, she gathered her thick dark hair into two long braids, unraveled the threads from the lace collar of her white dress, and carried a bouquet of flowers. Wearing white costumes cut simply to reveal her uncorseted body and using flowers as a prop would become Duse's signature in many of her roles. During one performance of *Hamlet*, after Ophelia's mad scenes in the fourth act, Duse received five curtain calls. "Is it Miss Duse's fault if she is an Ophelia to be painted?" one critic asked. "An Electra to be sculpted?" The critics speculated that it must not have been easy for such a young woman to win applause from the demanding Neapolitan audiences, but she triumphed because of "the great love that she brings to her art" and by her "spontaneous emotion." In *Oreste*, for example, her violent fury as Electra overwhelmed the audience. Other critics raved about her grace, her beauty, her artistry, and described her as "completely modern."

Duse played a modern young woman and began her long association with the work of Alexandre Dumas *fils* when she acted in *Le Demi-Monde*, which was first produced in Paris in 1855. This brilliant play, which firmly established the reputation of Dumas *fils* after his early success with *La Dame aux camélias*, offers a rare glimpse of a European half-world that no longer exists, but still reverberates.

Dumas *fils* had firsthand experience of that half-world. Descended from a black slave-girl, Dumas *père* suffered from racial prejudice, but his son endured the stigma of illegitimacy. Raised by his unwed mother (Dumas *père* acknowledged his son when he was seven), Dumas *fils* had enormous sympathy for unmarried mothers and illegitimate children and championed divorce and paternity laws. Dumas *fils'* love affair with a courtesan inspired his most famous work, *La Dame aux camélias,* which shocked audiences with the notion that a prostitute could know true love. *Le Demi-Monde* demonstrated that without divorce laws, women who had been dumped by their husbands were relegated to a half-world of other adulterous women who were forced to become scheming sexual predators to find another husband.

In *Le Demi-Monde,* Duse played Marcelle, a fresh-faced young woman who speaks clearly and directly like a man, despite the fact that she is the protégée of an older woman who paints her eyebrows and lashes and touches up her cheeks with rouge, something no "decent woman" would do. Marcelle is good, but she isn't naïve. When asked if she is well, Marcelle replies, "Well, I'm sorry to say when a woman is always well, no one is interested in her." Without resorting to makeup and subterfuge and with no advantages other than purity and common sense, Marcelle/Duse wins the ultimate prize in a French play of this period—marriage to a rich man.

According to Olga Signorelli, Duse's confidante and early biographer, Eleonora herself was also pure and virginal at this time. She was blessed with a blemish-free complexion and lovely natural coloring. She had no need for theatrical makeup, and was proud she didn't have to powder and paint to hide pimples and imperfections. Duse set herself apart from the class of women who used makeup. "I am bourgeois, completely bourgeois," she insisted to her friend Count Giuseppe Primoli, a Roman aristocrat, whose mother was a Bonaparte princess. Of course, this was nonsense. In claiming to be bourgeois, Duse was elevating herself from the class she had been born into. Actually, Duse was in the process of climbing into the highest and most exclusive class of all—that of a world-class artist.

Onstage, Duse gave free rein to passion and sensuality, but confronted with amorous young men at the stage door who wanted to make a conquest of Naples's hottest young actress, she "bristled like a porcupine" and shrugged off their honeyed words. Offstage, she found it advantageous to adopt the outer manifestations of the middle class. Her bare face glowing, she usually wore dark colors, wrapped herself in a gray shawl, and hurried through the streets of Naples ignoring all the attention and exaggerated bows of her admirers. Her artistry had earned her newspaper columns of eloquent praise from prominent writers and critics, and she had no interest in the juvenile stammerings of local Don Juans.

When Matilde Serao, a young woman who worked in a Naples telegraph office and wrote stories and articles for the local newspapers, offered her friendship, Duse accepted eagerly. Their friendship was formed at a time

Italian writer Matilde Serao, 1880. Her
conversation sparkled with such intelligence
and wit that writer Paul Bourget described
her as "Dr. Johnson in a balldress."

when they both were struggling to succeed and needed to lean on each other.
For the first time since the death of her mother, Eleonora had a female confidante and a woman's advice and encouragement.

Then twenty-two, two years older than Duse, the daughter of a patrician
Greek mother and a weak Neapolitan father, Serao grew up poor in Naples,
where she "used her elbows" to get ahead. Barely five feet tall, plain and
plump, with dark hair and eyes, Matilde was devoted to her sick mother and
supported her shiftless father. While she grubbed at the telegraph office,
Matilde worked on a novel, cultivated friendships with prominent families, and used her intellect and charm to win over newspaper editors. Serao
observed and wrote about the world around her—the sunless slums of
Naples, the bonds of female friendship, the mania for the state lottery, and
the blind passion a young girl felt for her seducer. Serao would become one
of Italy's most prolific and honored writers, publishing over forty volumes of
fiction, hundreds of short stories, and thousands of pages of journalism. At a
time when men dominated journalism, she founded four major newspapers
and a literary magazine. Her fiction, part of a larger Italian literary move-

ment called *verismo*, aimed to give artistic and truthful expression to objective reality.

She was filled with enthusiastic life, as if she had been born from a "burst of laughter and a ray of sunshine," wrote Count Primoli. Serao, like a doting older sister, guided Duse through the literary, intensely masculine world of Naples. Serao taught Duse practical techniques of ingratiating herself with prominent families, and the art of utilitarian flattery and self-promotion, which Duse would use on society leaders and critics for the rest of her life. While Serao never seems to have wavered in her sisterly devotion to Duse and worked for years as Duse's unpaid publicity agent, Eleonora, demonstrating the prejudice of her northern Italian roots, wrote later that while Matilde was "fundamentally good," she lacked depth and was "superficial," like most Neapolitans.

Duse recognized Serao's worth, however, and always called on her in moments of great need. Once, during one of Duse's bouts with illness, Duse told Matilde, "If I die, I know you will say one word of truth about me." Serao loved Duse, especially her "exquisite and sweet" voice. "No one could pronounce my name like her," Serao recalled.

Matilde did not hesitate to use sex and feminine wiles to get ahead. She had many love affairs, but she pushed herself forward with a man's will. Meeting the exuberant Matilde Serao was a turning point in Duse's life. As a rising young theatre star in Naples, Duse had beauty and talent, but living in a country where "who you know" is all-important, Duse lacked contacts with important people outside the theatre. Unschooled and intellectually insecure, Duse read voraciously and honored writers.

For Duse, after years of loneliness and struggle, being with Matilde was not only useful, it was fun. It was probably Serao, her first woman friend, who introduced Duse to Martino Cafiero, her first lover. Cafiero had befriended Serao and published her writing in his newspaper the *Corriere del Mattino*. Most newspaper writers used pseudonyms, and Cafiero was "Mario" and Serao was "Tuffolina" and "Chiquita." Cafiero and Serao called Duse "Nennella," which roughly translated from the Neapolitan dialect means "little baby." In the myth of Duse, recounted by all of her biographers, Cafiero is portrayed as a calculating seducer, and Duse cast in the role of helpless innocent. The myth mimics old-fashioned melodrama and stereotypical views of male-female relationships, but the reality of the relationship of Cafiero and Duse was closer to modern *verismo*.

When she met Cafiero in Naples, Duse may have been an adorable "Nennella," but she was also twenty years old and self-supporting, and while her knowledge of the world was limited, she certainly had experienced life. Doubtless Duse could have had her pick of handsome young men as lovers.

Martino Cafiero, the lover Duse chose, however, was almost twenty years older than she. Unattractive, with a receding hairline, bushy eyebrows, a sharp nose, and a drooping, straggly moustache that hid his mouth, as editor of *Corriere del Mattino*, Cafiero was an important figure in Naples. He was active in politics and prominent in society, and organized balls, festivals, concerts, and assemblies. Under his leadership, the *Corriere del Mattino* published the best young Italian and French writers. His success with women was legendary and because of his ugliness was much wondered at. One of his friends explained that Cafiero charmed women with his caressing and flattering manner.

Cafiero had written of her in the newspaper as the "true Ophelia," and Duse believed he understood her. When Cafiero appeared at the stage door, Duse did not send him away. Ironically, Duse, who had the actor's power to express the inexpressible and to communicate with audiences without words, worshipped writers, and Cafiero caught her attention with the power of his written words. Cafiero's interest in Duse stimulated others to write about her as well. Her name appeared often in the *Corriere del Mattino* and in other newspapers.

DURING THE SUMMER OF 1879, Duse's company at the Teatro dei Fiorentini was filled with turmoil and dissension. The public was tired of the old repertory and grumbled about the lack of new plays they had been promised. When the company presented *Othello* at the Teatro dei Fiorentini in late July 1879, Edoardo Boutet criticized the lack of direction and unity. "The actors showed off with spasmodic convulsions, without science, without awareness, squawking, howling, mooing," wrote Boutet. "All contributed to the poor effect and even Miss Duse . . . and this hurts us to say because we care so much about her and her artistic talents turned her Desdemona of the fourth act into Goldoni's Mirandolina."

Possibly Duse was simply too happy in her love affair with Cafiero to play the doomed Desdemona, but Duse and her company were also concentrating all their energies on their upcoming production of Emile Zola's new play, *Thérèse Raquin*, adapted from his earlier novel. Castigated by some critics as filth, the play had flopped in Paris, but there was much interest in Italy in Zola's writing, which Cafiero had introduced to Naples in the *Corriere del Mattino*.

"The past is dead," Zola had written. Using methods adopted from science, Zola wanted to force the naturalist movement upon the theatre. "We must look to the future and the future is the human problem studied within the bounds of reality," he wrote. "It is the abandonment of all legendary tales;

Emile Zola, 1880s

it is the living drama of characters and their environments." Technical theatre capabilities and techniques had advanced as well, revolutionizing the theatre, and moving it toward realism. In 1879, for example, the Teatro dei Fiorentini replaced the dark and smoky old oil lamps with new gas lighting, which provided more flexibility and more illumination. The box set, with its solid walls and doors, created an environment for the world of the play. *Thérèse Raquin* takes place in one large room, which serves as both bedroom and parlor. The audience peered as if through a keyhole through the "fourth wall" of the box set into a dingy world decorated with shabby furniture.

In four acts with seven characters, *Thérèse Raquin* is a chilling drama with an elegant, classic structure. Coerced by Mme. Raquin, Thérèse has married Mme. Raquin's son, the spoilt and weak Camille, whom Thérèse serves with slave-like obedience. Thérèse subsequently falls in love with the artist Laurent, who is painting Camille's portrait. Thérèse and Laurent murder Camille and make his death appear as a drowning accident. They marry, but they are haunted by their secret. When Mme. Raquin learns the truth about the murder, the shock paralyzes her except for her unblinking eyes, which she uses to torture Thérèse and Laurent. At the end of the play, Mme. Raquin regains her movement and power of speech and says she will watch as Thérèse and Laurent tear themselves apart with remorse. The lovers then drink poison and die at the old woman's feet.

Duse acted the title role of Thérèse. For the first time since she had played Juliet at fourteen, she had a huge, complex, and challenging role. The play begins in the drab Raquin home on a summer night. Laurent is painting a portrait of Camille, Mme. Raquin (played by Giacinta Pezzana) clears the dishes, and Thérèse/Duse sits, motionless. Thérèse's first lines consist merely of yesses and nos and repressed emotions. When Thérèse is left alone with her lover Laurent, she transforms into a joyous, passionate woman. Because she is the daughter of a wild African chief, Thérèse, in keeping with Zola's theories of heredity, acts on her passion. Throughout the play, Thérèse/Duse passes through a world of feelings, ranging from inactive boredom to passion to joy to disgust to remorse to screaming fear, and finally to suicide. Overpowered with emotion, at the end, the audience sat stunned and silent, unable to applaud.

The critic Edoardo Boutet, who attended the opening on July 26, 1879, wrote that the evening was an unforgettable triumph. Everyone, from the stagehands to the old doorman, Boutet said, knew when they saw Duse act they had seen something extraordinary. Duse sought to replace pictorial, declamatory, stereotypical acting with her own individual, modern style. While lesser actors used gesture to emphasize words, Duse used gesture and her body to communicate what words could not. "When I must express violent passion, when my spirit is gripped by pleasure and sorrow," Duse said, "I often am silent, and on stage I speak softly, barely murmuring." Duse believed an actress "must live her art, not comment on it," and she rarely discussed her technique, although she once advised a young actress: "You have to show your heart."

Unlike Adelaide Ristori, who always had immense dignity onstage, Duse fully accepted her physical self and was not afraid to show the ugliness of tears, the awkwardness of anguish, or the urgency of sexual passion in the characters she played. Like the *verismo* writers, Duse believed truth was more important than beauty, and she found a physical, outward expression of the character's innermost thoughts and feelings. Duse's un-made-up skin was remarkably responsive to her emotional states—one moment flushing pink with excitement and in another revealing the paleness of fear.

Years before Stanislavsky set down his ideas on sense memory, Duse drew on her own feelings, memories, and emotional history to reveal the characters she played. The sometimes reckless abandonment of her movements indicated Duse was perfectly at home onstage, with no gate between response and reaction. She spoke quickly and musically, using pauses, repetitions, interjections, and sighs to break up the lines. She sought to portray women as sensual human beings—women who touched. Duse's seemingly spontaneous gestures, like caressing her leading man's cheek or touching his hair or body, without self-consciousness or formality, expressed a kind of easy sensuality that was fresh and true and most important, new, to audiences used to rote gestures. Duse's sexual audacity onstage cannot be underestimated. Much of her early success using an acting technique, which she called "showing her heart," can also be defined as pure sex appeal.

Also, the timing of Duse's first triumph was crucial. The technical advancement of gas lighting, which increased onstage illumination, allowed the subtleties of Duse's acting to be fully seen and appreciated. Since Duse carefully read her notices, the positive critical responses that emphasized her spontaneity, her modernity, her boldness, and her naturalness also served to reinforce the innovative artistic choices she was making.

With her success in Naples, Duse also began that unique relationship with the public experienced by all great stars. In addition to her creation of a character in a particular drama, Duse, in a private rapport between herself and her audience, also created another drama and another character in counterpoint—the continuous drama of herself, the character that would become known as La Duse.

WHILE DUSE WAS PERFORMING *Thérèse Raquin* in the fall of 1879, she was living a real-life drama that sent her spiraling through an arc of emotions experienced by some of the characters she had played. Duse had fallen in love with the writer and editor Martino Cafiero, and she had become pregnant. Later, Duse told the story of her romance to Count Primoli, who took notes of their conversation, which he gave to Dumas *fils* as a subject for the play *Denise* he wrote for Duse. Martino Cafiero also wrote of his affair with Duse and reproduced her letters in a roman à clef published in the *Corriere del Mattino*. "I love you, I believe you," Duse wrote to Cafiero. "If you knew how many times I repeated to myself this same word, all yesterday, all night. A word that is necessary to us women: love!"

Despite the success of *Thérèse Raquin*, the season at the Teatro dei Fiorentini had been financially disastrous. At the end of 1879, Giacinta Pezzana signed a contract as *prima attrice* with the distinguished actor-manager Cesare Rossi, whose Compagnia della Città di Torino leased the Teatro Carignano in Turin and was considered the best theatre company in Italy. Unaware of Duse's pregnancy, Rossi invited her to join the company as *seconda donna* and promised her she would play the important parts not taken by Pezzana. Duse signed the contract, she later told Count Primoli, "as one signs an I.O.U., that we know we cannot meet, and which, at the hour it falls

Actor-manager Cesare Rossi, 1880s

due, we wipe out with suicide." Although his company was full, Rossi also made room for Alessandro Duse as a general actor. Rossi paid father and daughter an annual salary of 7,250 lire. Acting as her own press agent, Duse wrote to *L'Arte Drammatica* about her new position and asked them to announce the news in the journal.

Duse's departure from Naples was difficult. Cafiero turned aloof and cold and showed no sign he intended to marry her. "Things won are done," Shakespeare's Cressida teaches, "men prize the thing ungain'd more than it is." Desperately in love with Cafiero and sexually in thrall, Duse pleaded with him, "Save me from this frightening enemy that follows me and oppresses me. Save me from the solitude of my silent room."

From Turin, hundreds of miles to the north, where Duse continued to act and hide her pregnancy from the company and her father, she wrote again to Cafiero in Naples. "Listen. I swear to you—I don't know how I can find the courage. I wait for your letter, I waited for your telegram before I left . . . I don't know how I can live like this—how I can find the courage."

Duse contemplated suicide, but she continued to pour out her feelings to Cafiero, who ignored her pleas. "Speak to me," she wrote, "with truth, with sincerity . . . like a man." As her pregnancy progressed and she could feel the baby move, she grew more desperate. "For me, nothing," she wrote. "But think, think of what is in me that is yours. Oh Martino, Martino! Is this love! Is this—a father?"

One day as Duse walked downstairs on her way to the theatre, her father looked at her and exclaimed, "So it's true." Alessandro Duse simply put his head in his hands and left. Resigned, Duse went to the theatre and acted, but she imagined her desperate father and wondered if he had deserted her as well.

At this time in Italy, a woman's family protected her honor. A man who refused to marry the woman he had impregnated could be killed with impunity or challenged to a duel. Alessandro Duse, who should have demanded Cafiero marry his daughter, did nothing. Of course, Alessandro Duse, then sixty, was a weak old man with no social position, no money, and no powerful friends, while Cafiero was rich, socially prominent, and an accomplished duelist. To Alessandro's credit, he realized if he deserted Eleonora she would have no one. After aimlessly wandering the streets of Turin, he returned to the theatre and met his daughter at the stage door. He offered his arm. They exchanged just a few words. "How many months?" he asked.

"Seven," she replied.

At the end of May, Duse and her father moved south with the Cesare Rossi company to Pisa. On June 6, 1880, the newspaper *La Gazzetta di Pisa* announced Eleonora Duse was ill and could not play. Since Cafiero would not marry her, to save Eleonora's honor, the birth of her baby had to be kept secret, and the baby disposed of anonymously. In Italy, illegitimate children were called *figli di colpa*—children of guilt. During the nineteenth century, unmarried pregnant women were forced by the Catholic Church and by civil authorities to give up their babies and place them in foundling homes. Illegitimate children living with their unwed mothers, it was believed, were an insult to public morality.

By the mid–nineteenth century in Italy there were twelve hundred baby depositories scattered throughout the country. Rotating "wheels" were set up in churches so that babies could be left anonymously—a method often abused by married couples who found themselves with too many children to support. This system protected men, who were not identified and not held responsible, and punished women, who suffered the full burden of responsibility. An unmarried woman was given no other choice. In fact, if the woman left her baby anywhere but the wheel or foundling home, she could be imprisoned for five years and publicly flogged.

Duse continued to act until her ninth month. She recalled the knowing looks of the young men in the theatre boxes who looked at her swollen stomach as if they were waiting until it was empty so they could fill it up again. Cafiero did not send her any money, but fortunately, Duse had been able to save 1,000 francs. Since it was believed midwives and wet nurses who lived in the country were healthier, Duse went to the farm home of a midwife in nearby Marina di Pisa. The midwife would protect Duse's privacy, see that the baby was baptized, and deliver the baby to a foundling home with the required payment. If there was no payment, Duse could be forced to serve as a wet nurse in the foundling home for two years, and perversely, as a wet nurse to other babies, not her own.

There was no public identification or documentary evidence of Martino Cafiero as the father or Eleonora Duse as the mother. From the viewpoint of both the church and the state, the baby simply had no parents. The logic was that the family structure in general would be destroyed if a woman accused a married man of fathering her illegitimate child. Of course, Cafiero was not married and free to wed, but Italian men, married and unmarried, continued to be protected from paternity searches until the First World War.

Years later, during a visit to Marina di Pisa, Duse told Romain Rolland that when her life was in upheaval or in crisis she returned to the same spot in Marina di Pisa, a "sweet strip of sea." Henry James felt the same way about the place. "If I had lost my health, my money, or my friends," he wrote. "I should go and invoke the Pisan peace . . . [it] may be a dull place to live in, but it's an ideal place to wait for death."

Sometime in early June 1880, at a farmhouse in Marina di Pisa near where the River Arno meets and mingles with the sea, Duse gave birth to a boy. Still hoping Martino Cafiero would acknowledge his son and give him his name, she named the baby Mario after Cafiero's pseudonym. She had a photograph made of herself with the baby in her arms and sent it to Cafiero. He returned the photograph with the word *"commediante"* scribbled across it, a sneering reminder that he considered her no better than a whore. It's unclear how long the baby lived, days or weeks, but the boy died in infancy, and Duse felt culpable. Years later, writing of this painful episode with a careful detachment, Duse spoke to herself: "Your salvation was one—only one, that which was not granted to you—and the love that illuminates, the house that hides . . . you asked and ask pardon."

Duse felt guilty and ashamed. Her culture did not allow her to feel any other way. The world shared the opinion of Dumas *fils'* Marguerite, who says in *La Dame aux camélias*, "And so, whatever she may do, the woman, once she has fallen can never rise again. God may forgive her, perhaps, the world never." In Italy in 1880, a woman who had a child out of wedlock felt shame and dishonor and brought shame and dishonor on her family. Also, if her baby was weak or moribund, the mother was blamed, and Duse felt responsible for the death of her son. In *Denise*, the play written for her a few years later by Dumas *fils* and based on Count Primoli's notes, Denise/Duse leaves her baby to be suckled by a wet nurse who does not give the baby a mother's loving care. Wet nurses sometimes neglected foundlings to nurse their own children, or their milk quality was poor, or they had syphilis. Like Duse's Mario, many of these babies died. In contrast, fifteen years earlier in France, Sarah Bernhardt was allowed to keep and raise her illegitimate son because she lived in a country with greater tolerance. Italian civil law supported the religious policy, stating paternity searches were to be allowed only in the case of violent rape.

While Duse was recovering in Pisa, Martino Cafiero visited her and wanted to have sex with her. Duse refused him, and he left in a rage. A grieving Matilde Serao, whose mother had died a few months earlier, arrived in Pisa from Naples to sit with Eleonora hour after hour. It was a time, Duse recalled, when she lived all in darkness, "dark, dark . . . fainting, sick, and agonizing." Hidden under her clothes, Duse wore a gold locket containing two tiny rose leaves she had taken from the ground where her son was buried. This keepsake, along with a photograph of her mother, Duse kept with her always. It must have comforted Eleonora to remember that her mother Angelica, too, had lost her first child, a son, and had borne her loss with silent courage.

Helped and consoled by Serao, who cared for her with maternal solicitude, Duse was able to return to work in Cesare Rossi's company. Later, Duse thanked Rossi for his help and kindness, and in a rare burst of bitterness against her father, she said, "I turn to you as I would have to my father, if I had had the fortune of having a good and intelligent one who would have protected my youth . . . and my life."

At twenty-one, her youth was over. Duse did not practice or belong to any religion, but she believed Il Signore—Jesus Christ—was a real person who had lived. Inscribed on her stationery at this time were Jesus' words from the Beatitudes: *Beati qui lugent quoniam ipsi consolabuntur* (Blessed are those who sorrow, for they shall be consoled).

Two

D USE'S PHYSICAL RECOVERY, both from Cafiero's desertion and the birth and death of her son, took months. She carried the psychological and emotional scars for the rest of her life. She drew energy from the characters she played, who, she said, consoled her. She read about French actresses Rachel, Aimée Desclée, and Sarah Bernhardt, and imagined the outline of her future. Duse wanted to maintain privacy, however, and sought to keep the public and her relatives ignorant of her personal life.

Writing to his brother Enrico in December 1880, Alessandro Duse reported that Eleonora had recovered her health, but she had been close to death. He warned Enrico not to mention Eleonora's troubles because it would upset her. The following year he and Eleonora planned to stay with the Rossi company. Alessandro would keep the same pay and position, but Duse would move up to *prima donna*, since Giacinta Pezzana wanted to leave and form her own company. Alessandro also attempted to clear Duse's reputation. Some actresses allowed themselves to be kept by "uncles" or "cousins" in exchange for sexual favors, he wrote, but Eleonora made her way on talent alone.

Less than a year after her involvement with Cafiero, Duse began thinking about marriage to Tebaldo Checchi, an actor in her company, who had begun courting her and buying her gifts. Checchi, then thirty-six, played small but important parts like the First Player in *Hamlet* and the comical bore Grivet in *Thérèse Raquin*. He was tall and good-looking, with expressive eyes and thick black hair. He had a reputation as a ladies' man, and was vain about his well-groomed, waxed moustache, which he sometimes reluctantly shaved off for the roles he played. He was a native of Naples, and dressed in the garish style of southern Italian men, in colorful waistcoats and flamboyant cravats, and sported a brilliant diamond on his little finger.

Tebaldo Checchi, Duse's husband, 1880s

Checchi had observed Duse's love affair with Cafiero in Naples and its aftermath, and he felt sorry for Duse, who was "alone and sad and with an impossible father." His affection, he said, soon turned into serious love "for the first time in my life." According to Checchi, he had been warned Duse was "a fantastic woman, who never knows what she wants, and won't do anything in art because she is half crazy." Duse's friends disputed Checchi's motives and gossiped that it was self-interest, and Eleonora's promotion to *prima donna*, that had sparked his attentions. Although he had been raised in an acting family, the Neapolitan Checchi had little else in common with Duse. Still, while Duse did not love him, he offered protection at a time when she felt particularly vulnerable. Cesare Rossi, who cared for Duse like a father and wanted to guard his investment in the twenty-two-year-old actress, urged her to marry Checchi. He argued that marriage would save her from the inevitable, harassing attentions of other men. Marriage offered social respectability and protection from the danger of too much freedom. Facing the responsibilities of leading actress in the Rossi company while providing for herself and for her father, Duse accepted Rossi's advice and Checchi's attentions. Tebaldo also had literary ambitions, which attracted Duse—by the spring of 1881 they were lovers.

Duse became *prima attrice* in March 1881 when Giacinta Pezzana left the company after she had failed in the Turin premiere of Dumas *fils'* play *The Princess of Baghdad.* The play had also flopped earlier at its Paris premiere. The French audience hissed it, the critics panned it, and Dumas swore he would never write another play for the Comédie-Française. The play needed, Dumas felt, "some beautiful passionate Italian woman [with] a certain individuality and temperament." Apparently Duse agreed with him. Despite Pezzana's failure, or perhaps because of what Duse had learned from watching the older woman in the part, she convinced Cesare Rossi she could succeed in the role of Lionette where Pezzana had failed.

The Princess of Baghdad is a cross between a fairy tale and middle-class melodrama. Falsely accused by her husband of adultery, Lionette, the daughter of an Arabian prince, decides to run away. Her six-year-old son stops her and begs her to stay. When her husband confronts her, Lionette fervently proclaims her innocence, saying, "I swear it!" In playing the moment, an intuition came to her "spontaneously," Duse said later. Lionette/Duse looked at her husband and said the line twice. Realizing her husband still didn't believe her, she held their son in front of her, placed her hand upon his head, and vowed again, "I swear it." Dumas *fils* included Duse's changes in later editions of his play. Duse recognized the flaws in the script, but she empathized with Lionette and found humanity in the role. In choosing material, Duse was drawn first to the woman she would embody. She tended to refer to plays not by their titles, but by the names of the women she played.

The Rossi company moved to Venice, where they performed from March 5 to April 13, 1881. This most theatrical city, where every street and canal offered a new scene, had only four theatres. Playing in familiar Venice in the lovely Teatro Goldoni (instead of the shabby Teatro Malibran, where she had played as a girl), in front of warm and indulgent Venetian audiences, Duse triumphed. Cesare Rossi had put together a brilliant company, but his genius was in pairing Duse with Flavio Andò. The thirty-year-old Andò was Sicilian, with black eyes, thick black hair, a curving moustache, a chiseled, handsome

Flavio Andò, Duse's leading man, 1880s.
Duse remarked that he was beautiful but dumb.

face, and the body of an athlete. "Imperious, manly, noble" onstage, Andò acted with intensity and passion, recalled theatre critic Renato Simoni, but Andò was most of all "an artist of love."

Venetian critics liked the Rossi company, particularly the work of the "beautiful, sympathetic, and elegant" Eleonora Duse. In *The Princess of Baghdad*, "Duse has had a true triumph," one said, playing Lionette with "true artistic intuition." The company also repeated their Turin success with the Sardou farce *Divorçons (Let's Get a Divorce)*. Critics agreed that Duse, who deserted her would-be lover to run off with her husband at the end of the play, was "slim, nervous, flirtatious" and enchanting.

The play is amusing fluff, but the issues of divorce and the role of women were hotly debated in France and Italy. Lying beneath the surface of the Dumas *fils* and Sardou plays is a fear of the unbridled sexuality of women, a sexuality that had to be carefully controlled. There was no divorce in Italy, and women had few rights. A woman could marry at fifteen or be seduced with impunity, but she was not allowed to manage her own money until she was twenty-one. If she married, her husband controlled the finances, and she could not even give money to a needy friend without her husband's permission. An unsigned editorial in Turin's *Gazzetta Letteraria* argued this system should be changed because a woman, while absolutely different from a man, "is equal to a man." When Duse had turned twenty-one in 1879, she managed her own money, paid her own debts, and ran her own house. "I no longer command," her father said. The freedom she had enjoyed for two years would be sharply curtailed when she married.

WHEN THE ROSSI COMPANY moved to Rome in May 1881 and played at Rome's best prose theatre, the Teatro Valle, the discriminating and vocal Roman audiences acclaimed Duse as Lionette in *The Princess of Baghdad.* Impressed with the quality of the company and with Duse, Adelaide Ristori, the reigning tragic actress of the Italian stage, asked the company to perform with her at a benefit for L'Accademia Filodrammatica Roma. The play she chose was Giacometti's *Madre e figlia (Mother and Daughter).* The critic of the *Capitan Fracassa,* acknowledging that the creaky old play was not a masterpiece, devoted his attention to the elegance and splendor of the event, which included the presence of Queen Margherita and Roman high society decked out in their spring finery. He did note, however, "la signorina Duse was unsurpassed."

The event carried no particular significance for Ristori except as a way to raise money for her pet project. For Duse, though, playing the daughter of fifty-nine-year-old Ristori suggested the possibility of inheriting Ristori's place in the Italian theatre. After their first meeting, Duse initiated a flattering, almost obsequious correspondence with Ristori. She sent her photograph to Ristori, and asked for one of Ristori's in return, to serve as "a memory—an inspiration—a protection." Ristori replied that most of her photographs were packed, but she sent one of herself as Lady Macbeth. Before appearing with Ristori in June 1883 in Rome at the Quirinale Palace in front of the queen and king, Duse wrote asking Ristori for advice on proper etiquette and help with her costume.

Ingratiating herself with Ristori served two purposes for Duse—as the Marchesa del Grillo, Ristori was influential at the highest level of society, and she was also one of Italy's most honored artists. Celebrated around the world, Ristori excelled in classic tragedy. She had vanquished the great Rachel in Paris and dazzled Londoners (who called her the "Italian Siddons") with her English-speaking Lady Macbeth, which she would act opposite Edwin Booth in America in 1885. Born in Venice in 1822 into a theatre

Onstage, Duse often rejected conventional
"feminine" postures, 1882.

family, Ristori, like Duse, had begun acting as a girl. In 1847, Ristori married
the Marchese Giuliano Capranica del Grillo, which gave her entry into
Roman society, her own salon at the Piazza Capranica, and friendship with
Queen Margherita, but it did not stop her from acting. She refused, however, to perform in plays she considered immoral. For this reason, she
never played *La Dame aux camélias.* "Art was my second life after my family
love," Ristori wrote. "But the art I speak of is that of my own time—as
it was understood by us . . . not this art of modern tendencies, based on
neurosis."

WHEN SHE FIRST acted with Ristori, Duse, who was building a career playing modern, neurotic women, had just become pregnant with Tebaldo Checchi's child. They did not marry until September 7, 1881, when she was over five months pregnant, which suggests some indecision, or perhaps Duse was waiting to see if the pregnancy would proceed. In November 1881, Duse wrote her father that her health was not good. Standing on her feet for hours at a time rehearsing and playing love scenes and physically demanding farce was exhausting but necessary. Just as the Duse-Lagunaz troupe had depended on her when she was fourteen, the Rossi company counted on her presence as the *prima attrice* and the primary box-office attraction, and she worked until the last two weeks of her pregnancy. Duse assured her father, "Tebaldo is full of affection for me." Alluding to earlier problems with Checchi, who often left her alone to pursue an active social life, she told Alessandro that Tebaldo had changed totally and "doesn't go a step without me."

On January 7, 1882, in Turin, Duse gave birth to a girl. "It is today that I had my Enrichetta," she scribbled in pencil in a note to Alessandro Duse, sounding happily relieved after the delivery. "At the moment I'm writing you the little one has left with her father for a small town nearby. Everything went well. I'm writing you from bed but I feel fine. My Enrichetta is darling and healthy as a flower and is my benediction—I ask your benediction—I asked her Grandmother Enrichetta to protect my little creature. My father—what consolation—what sweetness—that small creature—kisses to you."

In 1882, it was not unusual for a mother to send her baby off to live with a wet nurse, particularly for an actress afraid of losing her figure. According to Alessandro, Duse was critically ill for several weeks and unable to care for her baby. Her relationship with her daughter would be radically different from the close bond she had enjoyed with her own mother. Perhaps to placate Checchi for the disappointment of not producing the hoped-for son, Duse named their daughter Enrichetta Angelica, giving her the first name of her husband's mother.

"I can't wait to be well," Duse wrote Alessandro. "Hoping to see my little angel—puttina! Cara! Cara! I think of nothing but her in my soul. She is so beautiful—she has a tiny, tiny mouth, blue eyes and curly hair like her poor grandmother Enrichetta. (Tebaldo told me)—because every night when we are alone Tebaldo talks always about his poor mother. I love her as if she were still alive and now that I have made her the protectress of my Enrichetta. Dear Papa, what a love this is—Kisses."

When her father worried about her health and about gossip that Checchi was "an unfeeling man, incapable of family happiness," Duse told Alessandro

Duse with her daughter, Enrichetta,
about age three, c. 1884–85

she was still anemic, but getting better, and she loyally defended Checchi.
In any theatre company, there are jealousies, conspiracies, and shifting
allegiances, and the Rossi company was no exception. "Incapable of family
happiness," though, is a harsh charge. Duse would soon learn that marriage
had not changed man-about-town Checchi into a devoted husband and
father. A caring husband understood when his wife was sexually unavailable
because of illness, pregnancy, or childbirth, but Checchi admitted later his
relationship with Eleonora was more that of a lover than a husband.

The birth of Enrichetta coincided with and competed with Duse's work
and rising fame, and Duse would always be deeply ambivalent about motherhood and family. Years later, though, she looked back on Enrichetta's birth as
a turning point. Almost as if she were narrating pictures from her past, Duse
described herself at this time: "The young woman is reencouraged—a baby
girl is placed in her arms, a little girl all hers. Her little one is so tiny and
brings back to her heart much pity, and grave anguish to have given life to a
creature . . . pity and duty once again give her strength. Youth allows her
illusion, tenacity, ardor of action, to act!=And the day of illumination was

hers. The drabness of life, tediousness of environment, hatred of the theatre, misery of work, all disappear=Here she is self-sufficient, an interior ray radiates her soul—no more alone and lost but a dear hand in her own."

From the beginning, Duse marked Enrichetta as her responsibility, not Checchi's. The "dear hand in her own" was a pretty image, though rarely reality. During Enrichetta's early years, she lived with a family in Turin, probably the home of her wet nurse. The necessity of supporting Enrichetta and ensuring her future became a convenient excuse for Duse's desire to work, and a way to avoid the more traditional duties of a mother.

IN LATE FEBRUARY 1882, the Rossi company vacated the Teatro Carignano and Duse cleared out her dressing room to make way for Sarah Bernhardt. Turin was just another stop on Bernhardt's grand tour of Italy, Greece, Austria, Hungary, Sweden, England, Spain, Portugal, Belgium, Holland, and Russia. "People spoke only of her in town, in the salons, at the theatre," Duse recalled. Bernhardt's reputation, fueled by a massive publicity campaign, preceded her. Heads of state treated her like a favorite courtesan, showering her with jewels and gifts—a Venetian fan from King Umberto of Italy, a diamond brooch from Alfonso XII of Spain, an antique cameo from the Austrian emperor, Franz Joseph. "What these royals received in return for their generosity is a matter for speculation," write Bernhardt's biographers Arthur Gold and Arthur Fizdale, "but it is generally thought that an exchange of favors was traditional."

Sarah Bernhardt opened in Turin playing the doomed courtesan Marguerite in *La Dame aux camélias*. The thirty-eight-year-old Bernhardt supervised every aspect of her productions, including choice of repertoire, publicity, set design, and the construction of her elaborate costumes. She was not as gifted in casting or direction, however, and she surrounded herself with mediocre actors. She knew, of course, the audience had come only to see her.

Styles in acting change, and Bernhardt and Duse couldn't have been more different. While Bernhardt was a genius, it was the genius of a rare, extravagant personality coupled with an academy-trained theatre technician who always remained firmly in control of her life and her art. Duse was inspired, however, by Bernhardt's sheer power and pioneering example. "She came with her great halo, her well-established, world wide reputation," Duse recalled. "It was a deliverance! There she is! She acts, she triumphs, she awes, she goes away . . . much the way a big ship leaves a wake behind . . . A woman had done that! And, as a consequence, I felt liberated. I felt that I had the right to do what I wanted . . . something other than what was being imposed on me."

Sarah Bernhardt, late 1880s

Bernhardt's decorative, romantic acting—Edmond Rostand called her the "queen of posture"—based on the elegance of her sculptural movement and the beauty of her golden voice, was enormously popular, financially lucrative, but already old-fashioned. Her specialty was death. "No one knows how to die like Mme. Sarah Bernhardt," said the critic of *La France*. Thin, with long arms and expressive hands, Bernhardt had a highly theatrical style, particularly suited for melodrama, and this theatricality extended to her propensity for male roles, including Hamlet, L'Aiglon, and Lorenzaccio. "I do not prefer male roles," she said, "but I do prefer men's brains."

Bernhardt's attitude toward women, which shaped her characterizations of women, was an attitude shared by men and the nineteenth-century culture. A woman was a thing, decorative, exquisite. As a professional woman, Bernhardt behaved like a man and granted herself the privilege of a brain, a soul, and a unique personality, but she did not extend that same privilege to the women she played. Offstage, a woman who lived freely and unrestricted, onstage, Bernhardt exerted iron control, presenting theatrical creations designed to awe, to dazzle, and to overwhelm her audiences.

Critics saw that the younger Duse's acting was a direct challenge to Bernhardt's. Later, the press characterized Duse and Bernhardt's rivalry as a kind of world-class sporting event of battling divas. By the time she saw Bernhardt perform, Duse had begun to shape her own acting aesthetic. Still, she attended all of Sarah's performances that March, and she had a priceless opportunity to "shop" Bernhardt's performances for ideas and insights, and to test her own choices against Bernhardt's. It's tempting to wonder, for example, if Duse's celebrated refusal to make grand entrances, choosing instead to enter naturally and in character, was in part a reaction to Bernhardt's equally celebrated attachment to grand entrances.

Following her Italian tour, Bernhardt moved on to Russia, where she was observed closely by Anton Chekhov, a twenty-one-year-old medical student, who wrote comic pieces as "Antosha Chekhonte" for Moscow humor magazines. In his articles about Sarah, Chekhov made fun of her publicity campaign and her carefully crafted image. "In America she performed miracles," he wrote. "She flew on her journey through a forest fire, fought Indians and tigers . . . gave 167 performances [and] the total sums of the box-office receipts were so long that no professor of mathematics could read them." While celebrity seekers who had come to see the sacred monster swooned in the audience, Chekhov refused to succumb to her dominating presence. "There were brief passages in her acting which moved us almost to tears," he wrote. "But the tears failed to well up only because all the enchantment is smothered in artifice." Many Russian critics, eager to promote Russian art and throw off French dominance, agreed with Chekhov. They were disappointed that Bernhardt's mask of celebrity never slipped out of place to reveal the woman beneath. It's a familiar argument, and the resolution depends upon which extreme one prefers in the theatre—the disturbing disarray of truth and inner life or the dazzling spectacle of pretty lies and brilliant surfaces.

Sated with the spectacle of Bernhardt both on and off the stage and surely envious of all the money she was earning, Chekhov vowed, "I won't write any more about her even if the editor pays me fifty kopeks a line. I'm written out! I quit!" Chekhov kept his pledge. Ten years later when he saw Duse act, he marveled at her art. He didn't know Italian, but he claimed to understand every word she spoke.

WHILE DUSE'S BIOGRAPHERS have maintained that Duse avoided publicity, she understood that privacy itself could become publicity. Actually,
Duse shared with Bernhardt a genius for self-promotion, but Duse's methods
were subtler. She aspired to become a great artist and to become recognized as
a great artist. "An artist without the help of the press and the cooperation of
the good critics can do nothing," Duse wrote. At the beginning of her career,
Duse acted as her own press agent. In letter after letter to critics and writers,
she made them her confidants, allowed them to see her working process,
reported her earnings, asked for advice, used them to promote her work and
to establish her persona as a devoted, mysterious artist. There is nothing more
flattering to a critic than to receive a personal letter from a star allowing a
glimpse into the sanctum of art. Duse's gift of flattery was a trait shared by
most Italians, who breathe flattery, one writer observed, as "one breathes the
scent of violets in woods in the spring." Duse's manner and her writing were
disarming and heartfelt, and even when she blatantly asked the critics to publicize her latest triumph, none of them ever accused her of self-promotion or
of creating an image.

Duse's letters, like so many letters written by actors who want to be heard
as well as read, are filled with dashes, dots (unless they are ellipsis points
enclosed in brackets, all dots in Duse quotations in this book are her own),
capital letters, exclamation marks, heavy, multiple underlinings, blank spaces,
and abrupt changes in tone and subject. Duse's forceful voice, her repetitions,
her inventive syntax, her pauses and angry tirades expressed by well-placed
exclamation marks reflect the rhythm of her speech. She often complained
about the difficulty of writing and communicating with language, but she
was a gifted writer and wrote thousands of letters.

In a letter to theatre impresario Ernesto Somigli, who also edited a theatre
magazine, Duse said to prepare her roles she studied the text in the original
French. "Then I can appreciate the tone of it better and go more deeply into
them." Her professed admiration for Somigli had "opened up new horizons,"
she wrote. "I am faithful to you and totally committed to my work. You know
how ambitious I am!" She enclosed six newspapers. "You could do me an
enormous favor," she said, "by giving these reviews some prominence in your
journal, which I consider an excellent publication and likely to replace *L'Arte
Drammatica.*"

During a brief vacation at Marina di Pisa in the summer of 1882, Duse
talked to the drama critic Antonio Fiacchi. The Italian newspapers had been
full of the glamorous Sarah Bernhardt's tour through Italy. Some had com-

pared Duse to Bernhardt, and that fact was clearly on her mind. When she had played Bologna, she told Fiacchi, she overheard some women talking who had arrived early at the theatre and had seen her walking to the stage. "That's Duse! That's her!" one said. Another woman scoffed, "That little woman . . . she's not much to look at!" Duse admitted she did not look like a typical leading lady, but she was determined to follow her own nature. "We all have different natures and everyone expresses emotion in their own way," she said. "Wouldn't you agree?" she suggested to the critic.

Except for *Scrollina*, by Achille Torelli, and a few other Italian plays, Duse played a French repertoire similar to Sarah Bernhardt's, but she didn't like being compared to Bernhardt. All the noise and stir about Bernhardt threatened to suffocate her. "I must study," she said, "and free myself from this distraction." She wanted the roles she created to be hers alone, in "sentiment, in soul, in expression, and in concept." Duse was competitive, and proud of her unexpected "wild" success as Césarine in Dumas *fils' La Femme de Claude (The Wife of Claude)*, a play that had failed in France, a script even Sarah Bernhardt had shunned. Dumas had written Césarine for the late Aimée Desclée, who dreaded playing it. Césarine is promiscuous, adulterous, a traitor to her country, a ravaging she-demon capable of destroying society, her family, and her husband. At the end of the play, just as Césarine is handing over secrets to a German agent, her husband calmly shoots her. Dumas admitted he had created the character as a symbol. Without legal divorce, Dumas argued, what was a man to do if he were married to an evil woman who betrayed him and refused to reform? "Kill her" is the play's answer. "When I forgave *La Dame aux camélias* I was accused of rehabilitating a loose woman," Dumas *fils* complained, "and now, because I do *not* forgive *La Femme de Claude* I am told that I am preaching murder."

Césarine is "the part that I *love* most in my repertory," Duse told Enrico Somigli in December 1882. The character (and the play) was a success with audiences and critics, but so were the other characters Duse played at this time, like the frivolous, spoiled Gilberte in *Frou-Frou*, an early precursor of Nora in *A Doll's House*. Gilberte, nicknamed "Frou-Frou," wants to become a human being but instead she dies pathetically, misunderstood by those around her who refuse to take her seriously. As Lydia in Dumas *fils' La visita di nozze*, Duse won "resounding, crazy applause." To Gennaro Minervini, who had compared her to Bernhardt in the part, she said she had never seen Bernhardt act it. Duse drew on her own history and feelings of humiliation, anger, and pain when playing Lydia, who had been deserted by her lover, who married another woman. When the man returns to Lydia and wants to have an affair, Lydia/Duse responds with "Pouah," an expression of disgust. In notes in the script, Duse reminded herself to stand straight and remember all

In *La Femme de Claude*, c. 1882–84

the feelings of a dead love, knowing that the man had never truly loved her. "I feel that I have understood Lydia," she said. "I did not faint . . . but I felt my whole face contorted with the emotional strain."

During the early 1880s, when Duse was establishing her reputation throughout Italy, reviewers in Venice, Rome, Florence, Bologna, Turin, and Milan noted, almost without exception, how different she was from other actors, and they remarked on her wild passion. Critics lingered over descriptions of her sensuous mouth, languid eyelids, nostrils that flared in anger, caressing fingers, and supple body. In one short play, *Luna di miele*, she kissed her leading man, Flavio Andò, full on the mouth, a kiss that lasted almost a minute. In *La Dame aux camélias*, instead of kissing Armande Duval chastely and traditionally on the forehead, her Marguerite kissed him on the lips, as if she were drinking him in one last time. After seeing her perform in Rome, Luigi Capuana, in his review of *La Femme de Claude*, called Césarine/Duse an "artistic personification of the beast." He compared her to a writhing serpent,

In *Frou-Frou,* 1882

a leaping panther, a cunning enchantress with "terrible smiles," and a woman who wanted to live "unrestrained by fate." One felt, he wrote, "the powerful hand of a master in that character . . . to which Duse lent all the richness of her artistic talent. For this reason, the stolidness, the woodenness of the other characters went unnoticed."

Césarine was a wild, rebellious character so powerful she had to be gunned down like a dangerous animal. Actors love the freedom of playing a great villain, and Césarine's nature touched a chord in Duse. She, too, was rebelling—against Cesare Rossi, who controlled the choice of her repertory, against the restrictions of marriage and motherhood, against the narrow confines of her sex, and against acting conventions.

Two years after she saw Bernhardt in Turin, in a letter to the critic Francesco D'Arcais, Duse explained her feelings about acting and the women she played. She wrote that even though she sometimes felt it was "strange" and "unseemly" to "advertise her feelings" when she acted, "I use everything that I pick up in my memory and everything that vibrates in my soul." "Acting?" Duse continued in the letter. "That ugly word! If it were only *acting*—I feel that I have never known and I will never know how to act! Those poor women in my plays have so entered my heart and my head that while I do my utmost to make them understood to those who listen to me, almost as if I wanted to comfort them, it is they that have slowly wound up comforting me! How and why and when this tender and affectionate interchange, inexplicable and undeniable, started happening between these women and me . . . would be too long, and also too difficult to explain exactly. I don't care if they've lied, betrayed, sinned or if they were born perverse—provided I feel that they have wept—suffered for lying, betraying, or for loving . . . I stand on their side, *with* them and *for* them and I dig and scavenge not because I crave suffering, but because *feminine compassion* is greater, more concrete, sweeter and more complete than the grief that men are used to allowing us."

DUSE EQUATED her acting process with the mysterious process of falling in love. Just as there was no one way of loving, there was no one way to make art. In her opinion, the love that "wiped out every will, every urge, every trace of intelligence," was the "most true, but certainly the most fatal . . . so it is in art—that sometimes it's revealed like the expression and expansion of a soul." Duse fell in love with her characters, and audiences and critics fell in love with her. Bolognese critic Oreste Cenacchi, in a long article in the *Gazzetta Letteraria* in December 1883, wrote, "It would be an exaggeration to say that Duse performs every part to perfection, but she's on her way to doing so because she loves her art more than the applause of the public." While Duse's interpretation of her characters may have been "the last word for the public," he noted, Duse would never be content and would reach for a "high ideal of perfection."

Joseph Schürmann, Sarah Bernhardt's impresario, saw Duse perform in Turin. He was unimpressed with her untidy coiffeur and Italian features, but he thought her face became beautiful when "betraying some emotion." After observing her act Césarine, though, and finding her equal to all the other greats he had seen, Schürmann invited her to sign with him for a European tour. Duse wisely said no. No one abroad would be able to understand her, she believed. "I need time to perfect my art," she told him.

In the early 1880s, the task of perfecting and promoting her art consumed Duse. After her initial joy at the birth of Enrichetta, Duse seemed to have little interest in her daughter. A family in Turin took care of the child while Duse was traveling and working. The real world—her daughter, her marriage, her friendships—took second place to her ephemeral life in the theatre. Still, just as she captivated audiences, Duse enraptured her friends, both men and women. Eleonora was her "dearest friend," who had an "irresistible fascination," Serao wrote. "If I were a man," Serao effused, "how much I would love her, without end!"

Serao had moved from Naples to Rome, where she worked on the Roman newspaper *Capitan Fracassa* along with her future husband, Edoardo Scarfoglio, and Gabriele d'Annunzio. Serao had published her second novel, *Fantasia*, in 1882. She was an intimate of Count Giuseppe Primoli, known as Gégé to his friends. Although Rome was the capital of Italy, it lacked the financial and artistic clout of Milan. As an international social capital, however, Rome reigned supreme. Few Roman palaces were open to writers and artists, but Count Primoli opened his elegant palazzo near the Tiber to a fascinating group of artists. Paul Bourget found his characters for his novel *Cosmopolis* at Primoli's salon and dedicated the book to him. Primoli's friends included Henry James, Gabriele d'Annunzio, Giuseppe Giacosa, Giovanni Verga, and Proust, but he was particularly close to Serao. After the death of Primoli's father, Serao "was good to me like a sister," Primoli wrote, "like my poor mother would have been. She came to me in the evenings, spent time with me although her time was very precious."

Primoli looked and lived like a Renaissance prince. His eclectic decorating taste—encompassing both ancient and modern art, thousands of books, heavy, overstuffed furniture, Renaissance chests, and beams painted with quotations—had a profound influence on the young d'Annunzio, who later copied Primoli's ornate style. Witty, charming, an excellent listener, a gifted amateur photographer, and a connoisseur of art and of people, Primoli collected artists and made himself useful to them. Roman aristocrats did not frequent the theatre, which was considered a lesser art to opera. When Primoli saw Duse perform for the first time, he thought her the true interpreter of his friend Dumas *fils*' plays, and he returned again and again to the theatre. He had met Duse through Serao, and during Duse's performances in Rome in 1883, Primoli sent his carriage for her, sang her praises to Dumas *fils*, and like almost all of Duse's friends, fell in love with her and enlisted in her campaign to become a world-renowned artist.

Count Primoli, Duse's great friend
and ardent fan, 1880s

Primoli's friend, the playwright (and later Puccini's librettist) Giuseppe Giacosa, who lived and worked in Turin, also fell under Duse's spell. Nicknamed "Pin," the short, plump Giacosa, who was eleven years older than Duse, was married with three daughters, but he and Duse saw each other often in Turin. It's not clear if they had an affair, but in his letters to Primoli about Duse, Giacosa sometimes sounded like a rejected lover. When Duse starred in his play *La sirena* in Rome in October 1883, their arguments over casting disrupted rehearsals. Giacosa's play flopped, but Duse earned applause and glowing notices for her intelligent, natural performance. Giacosa called Duse the "stormy lady" and complained to Primoli that she was a sulky prima donna ruled by her senses.

Giacosa feared the prima donna, but he loved Duse the woman, even though he admitted he talked to her only about art and theatre. Like most of Duse's friends, with the exception of Matilde Serao, Giacosa disliked Tebaldo Checchi. As Duse began moving into intellectual, literary circles dominated by northern Italians and Roman aristocrats, the Neapolitan Checchi became more and more of an embarrassment to her. Giacosa thought Checchi vulgar and stupid, and wished Duse could free herself from him. Checchi pocketed Duse's earnings and claimed to manage her career, but he was rarely seen with her, except onstage. Duse told Count Primoli she spent most of her nights alone.

BY THE END OF 1883, Duse shared directing and producing responsibilities with Cesare Rossi. When Duse did not perform, or when Rossi presented himself in an old warhorse of a play, box-office receipts fell dramatically. Italian companies were often criticized for failing to produce new Italian drama, and Giacosa urged them to premiere Giovanni Verga's first play, *Cavalleria rusticana*. Set in Verga's native Sicily, the stark, naturalistic tragedy of passion and death couldn't have been more different from the bourgeois dramas of Dumas *fils* and Sardou. Duse had originally suggested to Verga that he dramatize his short story. She wanted to produce the play, but Rossi did not want to risk his money on an unproven Italian work and said no. Giacosa then approached Flavio Andò, who was Sicilian like Verga, and Andò promised he would get Rossi to do the play if Verga gave up his first evening's income and provided the costumes. Verga agreed.

Cavalleria rusticana opened in Turin on January 14, 1884, with Duse in the role of Santuzza, Tebaldo Checchi as Alfio, and Flavio Andò as Turiddu. Although the three leading characters were uneducated peasants, their romantic entanglements echoed the most sophisticated French drama. Turiddu had been in love with Lola, who during his absence marries Alfio. Turiddu has an affair with Santuzza, but then betrays her with Lola. Pregnant with Turiddu's child, an enraged and jealous Santuzza tells Alfio of Lola's infidelity. Alfio challenges Turiddu to a duel, and Turiddu is killed.

Advance word and an article by Giacosa about his friend's play had generated interest in the work, and when the curtain rose at the Teatro Carignano, every seat was occupied. The audience saw a painted backdrop of an authentic Sicilian village, a town square, a church, a garden wall, and a cactus hedge. Duse appeared in a blouse of yellow and brown striped muslin and a turquoise skirt with a white mantilla hiding her face. (According to measurements Verga took of Duse, she was about five feet three or four inches tall with a twenty-two- to twenty-three-inch waist.) At the end of the play, the audience erupted into applause for Duse and cries of "Viva Verga!"

Giovanni Verga, 1890s

calling again and again for the author. Despite its successful premiere and Verga's introduction of naturalism into the Italian theatre, the play did not have a wide success until it provided the libretto for Pietro Mascagni's opera of the same name.

The play was an ensemble piece, but Duse was singled out for her performance. Eugenio Torelli-Viollier, the critic of the *Corriere della Sera*, who saw Duse for the first time, reported she was an artist of the first order. Duse's Santuzza, he wrote, was "always restrained and simple . . . and created such powerful emotional effects that she made the audience tremble and cry." Although she urged them on the rest of the company, Duse's working methods and extensive preparation including character research, detailed analysis, and emotional recall, were not shared by the other actors. Even the gifted Andò was "still too much of an actor," Verga believed.

AT THE BEGINNING of March 1884 the company left Turin for a tour of Trieste, Padua, and Milan. Duse enjoyed the sun and sea air of Trieste, but she spent a sleepless night after she had "a phenomenal fiasco" in *La Dame aux camélias*. Apparently, Duse had suffered an off night. "The public is always right," she said, "therefore I have to look inside myself for the reasons why my Marguerite does not work." She complained about women in the audience who boldly seated themselves on the stage. "This window, so fragile, that is the theatre, shatters more often than it holds together," she said, expressing a truth shared by theatre people throughout the ages.

In Padua, inspired by thoughts of her grandfather Luigi Duse, who had triumphed there, she conquered as well. Duse wrote a letter of thanks to the director of *L'Euganeo*, who published the letter. The letter was typical of the kind of letter Duse wrote to critics, presenting herself in the persona of La Duse, a kind of mystical priestess of art.

Dearest Gueltrini,

... *It's over!* ... but the fear was great ... but the success was even more consoling ... *It's over!* ... and now I feel more *complete.*

For these first three performances ... I was so absorbed I didn't even see myself ... or the public. I don't know! I have acted without being really conscious of myself—with a vision ... strange — ungraspable — ineffable — a figure — white — serene — high — consoling — the vision of art.

It's over, and I return to my friends. [...]

If my old grandparents lived sadly ... and almost abandoned in their last years in that place—I have rediscovered all their youth—and I have erased the melancholy memory that I had before coming. What would you have me do? Home is always home! And where our grandparents have lived—and died—one returns slowly ... —against one's will ... on tip-toe ... so as not to disturb ... not to wake up ...

Let's put sad things to one side. I am grateful and happy ... and smiling at everything. [...]

E. Duse-Checchi.

Duse had won audiences in Naples, Rome, Bologna, Florence, Venice, and Turin, but the true test was Milan, the most prosperous city in northern Italy, with the country's most important newspaper, the *Corriere della Sera,* and the undisputed music capital of the country. The Goths, who had taken the city from the Romans, called it "Mailand," the land of May. The centerpiece of the city is its dazzling white Gothic cathedral with a roof of 135

Duse, c. 1884–85

soaring spires. Just a few steps from the cathedral is "Milan's drawing room," and probably the world's first indoor mall, the Galleria Vittorio Emmanuele, filled with elegant shops and topped by a stunning metal and glass roof and center dome. Nearby, housed in a neoclassical building, is La Scala, the most prestigious opera house in the world. Duse's company would play from May 3 to May 21 at the Teatro Carcano on the Corso di Porta Romana, on the opposite side of the cathedral from La Scala. Founded in 1803, the Carcano divided its schedule between theatre and opera, and was noted for its perfect acoustics and the highest theatre prices in town.

Instead of opening in an Italian ensemble piece like *Cavalleria rusticana*, Duse and her company opened with *Fédora*, by Sardou, a melodrama originally written for Sarah Bernhardt, a showcase for a *prima donna*. According to the critic of the *Corriere della Sera,* all the people who regularly attended the theatre were present as well as the most important people in Milan, who did not attend the theatre except under exceptional circumstances. In this case they were there to see and judge a rising new star.

The curtain rose, and Duse appeared as Princess Fédora wearing a Japanese-cut costume of dark red velvet and shrimp-colored satin with enormous tulle sleeves; her thick, dark hair was pulled into a knot on top of her head. Immediately there was a battle between those members of the audience who wanted to applaud her and others who hissed for silence. Used to heavily painted actresses, the critic of the *Corriere della Sera* noted Duse looked pale. Once, when asked why she didn't wear makeup, Duse said, "*Fiamma tinta, fiamma spentà*"—Tint your flame, you snuff it out.

Surprised and somewhat disconcerted at first, the critic thought she looked bizarre and unconventional. Duse didn't strike sculptural poses; "she was a modern creature," the critic decided, "charged with electricity, hot and vibrant from head to toe." At the end of the first act, uncertain what to make of her performance, the audience did not call Duse to the stage, and she shut herself in her dressing room. Disturbed by the "murmuring resistance" of the audience, Duse cheered up when a friend looked in and told her to "take heart," that when she had stepped onstage she had achieved a "*successo di brutezzà*"—a brutal or killer success, which Duse took to be a good omen.

In the second act, she wore a black velvet gown adorned with gold and jet. Gradually, as the audience and the critics grew used to her subtle and original method, which eschewed convention and "every excess, every bloodcurdling scream, every violent action," the applause began. The end of the play received a magnificent ovation. Arthur Symons, who saw Duse perform *Fédora* several years later, wrote that Duse "becomes the impossible thing that Fédora is . . . there is a scene in which the blood fades out of her cheeks until they seem to turn to dry earth furrowed with wrinkles . . . certain blind caresses with her fingers as they cling for the last time to her lover's cheeks, her face as she reads a letter, the art of her voice as she almost deliberately takes us in with these emotional artifices of Sardou."

Seeing Duse for the first time and struggling to describe her impact, one Milan critic found her nature complex, "a little mysterious," and difficult to analyze. The critic concluded that he couldn't explain it, but Duse somehow created a "sympathetic communication, a spiritual current, between herself and the public."

Theatre was an art Duse made *with* the audience, not *to* them. For her, it was an act of love leading to a state of grace. In her case, the rhythm was always the same—sensuality evolving into spirituality.

Word of Duse's triumph quickly circulated, and most performances at the

Teatro Carcano were sold out. Her Césarine was called a "symbol of feminine perversity." In *Divorçons*, her voice was likened to pearls, gold, and crystal, and she was praised for her comedy. Even when she appeared in a small part in the third act of an Italian play, the critic said he had "never seen in the theatre anything more gracious or more perfect." Worn out with superlatives and the repeated effort of reporting noisy ovations, the critic of the *Corriere della Sera* resorted to hyperbole: "Duse is the greatest living artist, truly original and new, she breaks with conventions and disturbs the public."

The public clamored for seats to her *serata* on May 14 when she was to play Marguerite in *La Dame aux camélias*. The theatre was sold out, and men bought most of the tickets. Certain boxes contained five men, a reporter noted, and an indeterminate number of other men crowded in the shadows to see Duse in the flesh. After every act, Duse received call after call, but in the fourth act, when Armande, played by Flavio Andò, throws money in Marguerite's face, Duse stopped the show. Many in the audience had seen Bernhardt in the role and knew that Bernhardt immediately burst into violent theatrical sobs at Armande's actions. Duse reacted as a woman, not a *prima donna*. She stood and looked at him in puzzled, silent disbelief. Could this be the man she loved? And then she sank down onto the sofa murmuring "Armando! Armando! Armando!"—words she added to Dumas's script. There was a "hurricane" of applause, and the audience threw so many bouquets the stage was covered in flowers.

After the performance, Duse was honored at a dinner in the grand salon at Caffè Cova. Cesare Rossi, Flavio Andò, and Tebaldo Checchi had all been invited, but Checchi was conspicuously absent. Apparently the only woman present, Duse sat between Gaetano Negri, the mayor of Milan, and forty-two-year-old Arrigo Boito, author, poet, composer of the opera *Mefistofele*, and the most famous man there. Earlier, Giuseppe Giacosa had written to Boito wondering if he had seen Duse act. "What do you think of her?" Giacosa had asked. Dressed in a gown of crushed green velvet, the twenty-five-year-old Duse moved through the candlelit salon, the tables laden with white linen, heavy silver, and fragrant camellias. Champagne was served, and an orchestra played. She talked to Giovanni Verga, and to Eugenio Torelli-Viollier and Boito, who both asked for a photograph. In her soft green dress, Duse looked young and spring-like amidst the older, bearded, and mustached men in their stiff, dark evening clothes.

On May 25, three days after Duse left Milan to return to Turin, Boito wrote thanking her for the photograph she had given him. It was just the one he had wanted. He said that after she left, he and his friends Luigi Gualdo and Giovanni Verga had fallen to the ground with their noses pressed to the floor. The message was clear—she had felled them. In a P.S., he wrote, "You

Sarah Bernhardt as Marguerite in *La Dame aux camélias*. Bernhardt played Marguerite for decades and in hundreds of performances repeated the same gestures and intonations with clocklike regularity. Duse saw her play Marguerite three times with unvarying precision and later described Bernhardt as a "wonderful mechanism."

Duse in *La Dame aux camélias*. Verdi regretted that he had not seen Duse play Marguerite before he wrote *La traviata*. "What a beautiful finale I could have written with this crescendo of Armandes that she found . . ."

are not obligated to answer." Unwilling to release Boito from her spell, on the last day of May, Duse did answer in a teasing letter giving him the task of finding her a little present, perhaps a photograph, "something that *speaks*," to fill a corner in her room. "Ah! *Prima Donnas!!*" she sighed. A few days later, Boito replied to her "adorable" letter and said he had found nothing fragile enough to send her. Instead he spoke in a four-line poem written in red ink on a May calendar, playing with the idea that in French the word *"mai"* was May, but in Italian, it meant "never." "Words are made to play with," he said.

Duse reveled in her power and achievement. After years of touring, she had captured Italian audiences. She felt "reinvigorated—young—confident" in her art.

"I will make art, always!!!" she exclaimed to D'Arcais. "I will go to America . . . I will go to Spain. I will go to Vienna. I will go . . . I will go . . . I will take my name as far as I can—I will keep my heart more hidden than a pebble in a well—One word alone—great—infinite—Art—"

FOLLOWING HER MILAN APPEARANCE, Duse returned to Turin to rehearse a new play by Giacosa at the Teatro Carignano. After just one rehearsal, she became ill. Tuberculosis was suspected, but it is more likely she was exhausted and bored with the familiar routine of Turin after dreaming of the world. Plus, the illness gave her an excuse not to do Giacosa's new play, which seemed to have been rushed into production to take advantage of Duse's success. Her doctor ordered fresh air and rest, and Giacosa suggested she go to the Piedmontese mountains. He found an isolated house for her and Checchi in Brosso, not far from his own villa.

After just a few weeks in the pure mountain air her lungs and her eyes, irritated by the gaslights of the city and the stage, began to recover. "I feel reborn," she said. Calling themselves the "three Romeos," Boito, Gualdo, and Giacosa visited her there. These three men, who were all intimate friends, would serve her, advise her, and court her.

During her vacation, Duse maintained her correspondence. She wrote to Adelaide Ristori and sent good wishes for her journey to England. "With all the devotion for the artist—and the respect for the woman," Duse said, "you were like (if you will permit?) a . . . mamma—to me." At the end of the summer, she and Checchi moved to a small chalet he had found on Lake Maggiore. She felt well enough to leave the mountains for a quick trip to Turin to see Enrichetta. Also, Duse wanted to "drink . . . a little music." She "couldn't miss" a performance of Boito's *Mefistofele.*

Most of the time, she told Count Primoli, she wore a blue cotton dress and

Two of Duse's "three Romeos," Giuseppe Giacosa (left)
and Arrigo Boito (right), 1880s

a white straw hat, and did nothing but "breathe the mild and perfumed air."
She sat in her blue drawing room and gazed at the green mountains, she
played like a girl with a kitten, but thoughts of work intruded. "I know that
when I leave this peace," Duse told Primoli, "I must return to *work;* the work
that was always my refuge . . . and my only salvation. I know that I must
work, work, work." And there was another reason to return to work,
Enrichetta "my little girl, so dear," had great need of material support.

　　During her vacation, Duse claimed she didn't read any scripts, but she did
read newspapers, and there was a stir about Dumas *fils'* new play. Reporters
had asked her about rumors that it was intended for her. Duse was mortified
that Dumas might think she was participating in gossip. Like the extremely
private Verdi, Duse loathed chatty theatrical publicity. It made her ill, she

said. Filled with dreams of success, Duse concealed those aspirations when writing to Primoli. Although she had sent Dumas *fils* newspaper clippings of her Milan engagement (publicity *she* could control), she wanted him to think of her as an artist, not just another striving actress. She begged Primoli to tell Dumas she had never spoken to journalists about his play. "When you are convinced that I don't love the theatre but adore only art," Duse said, "then you can with good conscience grant me this favor that I ask of you."

IN OCTOBER the company finished their season at the Teatro Carignano, and moved to Rome. "*All* the Roman public is well predisposed for Eleonora and her repertory," Matilde Serao wrote Giacosa. She also told him that after months of battling cholera Martino Cafiero, "the most Neapolitan of Neapolitans," had finally died. When Checchi heard of Cafiero's death, he decided to leave Rome. He knew Duse had loved Cafiero, and he thought his presence would be irritating to Eleonora. He asked Matilde to stay with her. Duse sometimes did not write to Serao for months, and while Matilde was hurt by her friend's neglect, she kept her home filled with photographs of Eleonora, promoted her career, and was ready to offer sympathy whenever it was required. Serao spent a day and a night with Duse, who was sobbing and distraught. She relived her love affair with Cafiero and remembered the sound of his voice calling her "Nennella." Serao consoled her and advised her that her husband, Tebaldo, was a "good man." Duse felt differently.

In early January 1885, Duse had had enough. In a letter to Checchi, written in slashing pencil strokes, she said she was ill and seeing her doctor. The carnival of Rome was going on, but "she didn't give a fig." She had taken financial responsibility for her daughter because she "had no other protector in the world." Then, as if responding to a comment by Checchi, she demanded, "Are we married? Frankly, I don't trust it anymore. It's painful for a wife to confess this, but I don't have faith anymore . . . I don't like women who are criers and complainers who accuse their husbands to excuse themselves . . . But my heart and my head and an infinite number of events for over a year have disillusioned me so much about my husband—I confess that if I had followed him I would have died of a heart attack. I don't want to go on and on about my virtues but for five years—I was silent—silent—silent. A lifetime . . . my husband certainly does not know the hearts of women and certainly has never known or understood me. Here is a woman who for five years has worked like a dog (and I am not a dog!)* A woman—who every year—had—a birth—or a miscarriage—pleurisy—or pneumonia that

*Duse uses the word *cagna*, which means bitch, whore, or bad actress.

threatened her life—and who continually as soon as she was well always went back to work—and with that work, tiresome, and beyond all my forces—it was my husband who in the company of belles and young women who made me work, saying 'Do it. Have courage.—this way you'll make a dowry for the child.' That work produced in 2 years a dowry worth almost *100,000 francs!*"

Duse underlined 100,000 francs three times and ended the letter abruptly with no signature. She was sick, pregnant, and worn out. The company had been rehearsing *Théodora*, by Sardou, a spectacular, plot-heavy melodrama set in sixth-century Istanbul. Written for Bernhardt, the play is completely ridiculous but does offer an opportunity for lavish costumes and sets. At the end, Théodora poisons her lover by accident, and then, as the curtain falls, she waits to be strangled with a scarlet cord. Duse thought it was "theatrically coarse." She was excited, though, about Dumas *fils'* play, *Denise*. Dumas had confirmed the rumors that he had had Duse "foremost in my mind" when he wrote the play, and he wanted her to premiere the script in Italy. The plot was a familiar one to Eleonora. A young girl is seduced, becomes pregnant, and has a child; the child is given to a wet nurse, and the child dies. Later, the girl meets a decent, kind man who wants to marry her. She confesses her sin. He marries her anyway. This banal story, which was, of course, Duse's own history, seemed shocking in 1885—not that a woman would get pregnant out-of-wedlock but that a decent man would marry such a woman.

On January 3, 1885, Count Primoli, who had told Dumas *fils* Duse's personal story, read the play to her at his house in Rome. "You can well understand how her heart was beating," he wrote to Dumas. "The first act . . . charmed her, but she was waiting for her part. The second interested her, but—she was still waiting. She said nothing, but I understood what she felt; a great admiration for the play but regret to see Denise kept in the wings . . . but then came the confession scene—the scene upon which the whole piece hinges—one of the most beautiful scenes you have ever written. I was sure of its effect. She remained breathless; her color changed; from her staring eyes tears fell on her cheeks. She got up suddenly at the life-like details about the dead child. She bit her handkerchief, and was compelled to hear the end of the speech behind a screen . . . she dreamed of creating, without even learning the lines, this ideal and loving creature . . . whose life it seemed to her she had lived."

The next day Duse wrote to Primoli and to Dumas, "How the atmosphere of *Denise* purifies!" The death of Martino Cafiero, followed by a play that revealed and purged her feelings of guilt and culpability, had a powerful effect on Duse. If she could be forgiven through art, perhaps she could forgive herself.

As Denise, 1885

A few days later, a rehearsal of *Théodora* was cancelled because Duse had collapsed. In a dramatic letter to Dumas, Primoli described her ordeal. Duse's "illness" was caused by the complications of a miscarriage. Primoli visited her room and found her lying in a blood-drenched bed. Her eyelids were closing, and she opened them again only by a sheer effort of will. "She didn't want to die," Primoli wrote to Dumas. "She wanted to be Denise first." Doctors entered and left, discouraged. "One of them was even cynical enough to say he would come back to declare her dead, or sign the death certificate," Primoli reported. "Duse heard him and summoned up her force to push him away and fell back down in a pool of blood." Eleonora held on, but the next day, she felt life escaping her. Everybody around her was going mad, Primoli said. Her husband was "tearing his hair out." Instead of isolating his wife, Primoli wrote, Checchi allowed her friends and acquaintances to come into her room. "If she gets back up," Primoli said, "I fear she will be forced to act until she falls. In a few days she will once again be back on the stage unless she goes down between the boards." Finally, when Duse was able to open her eyes, the first thing she did, Primoli told the playwright, was to ask for a copy of Denise's confession to keep her company.

As Primoli had predicted, Duse returned to work at the Teatro Valle in early February. A company of thirty-four actors depended on her for a livelihood. Advance publicity orchestrated by Serao and Primoli—articles about Duse, Dumas *fils*, and his new play—filled the newspapers. *Denise* opened on March 3, 1885.

"There's Denise," Primoli murmured when he saw Duse. She wore a "soft and chaste" gray dress "with long straight folds which mysteriously half open and seem to hold a secret," a dress that molded her "figure in all its purity." Except for Denise's confession in the third act, the critics found the play talky and repetitious. Duse thought the first two acts were "heavy," but her scene in the third act, describing the death of her baby, "worth the whole play." Her baby was beautiful, Denise/Duse says. "He seemed to understand. He smiled at us. He moved his little hands and feet. We gave him everything he needed, but this wet nurse didn't love him. He wasn't taken care of the way he would have been by his mother . . . so he died. He looked at me on the point of dying. This poor little one."

After seeing *Denise*, the critic of the British magazine *The Atheneum* reported Duse "has broken with the whole tradition of Italian acting with which the English public is familiar as seen in Madame Ristori . . . It would be more accurate, perhaps, to say that she has broken with all dramatic tradition . . . her method—and even nature has a method—does not admit even the possibility of pose . . . her stillness is absolute." At every performance, Primoli said, Duse could not stop her tears, and she "might have tired the public had it not been carried away."

Primoli, too, had almost been carried away by Duse. In a romantic gesture, Duse had sent him a bouquet of violets and a letter with just one word—Denise. "I seem in love," he wrote Giacosa, who had been worried about Primoli's infatuation with Duse. "I assure you however, that my only love, my only occupation is my mother . . . in my heart there is the same difference between her and the rest of the world as there is between Duse on the stage of the Teatro Valle and the rest of the troupe. But I do care for the diva, only in a way that isn't very good for me . . ."

Duse cultivated her friendship with Primoli—his social position and connections were invaluable. To Primoli, she was "La Diva," and with him she used an elevated tone and rarely gave him details of her mundane working life. Duse used another tone entirely in a letter to Louisa, an actress friend, written during a rehearsal break for *Denise*. The company had introduced Sardou's *Théodora* into the repertory. The play ran six hours, and except for the acting of Duse, which was "unsurpassed," wrote the critic of the *Capitan Fracassa*, the production was six hours of misery.

"You can't imagine what this Theodora is," Duse wrote Louisa. "The work is baroque, but I've had another success. Yet I assure you that after the performance I wept with exhaustion. My costumes are magnificent and I resemble a madonna—without the halo. In the scenes in which I'm disguised as the poor Mirta [. . .] I felt completely at ease and said the words of love tenderly—and wept with Mirta [. . .] The success was all mine, and it upsets me that this laryngitis hinders my rehearsing. Denise is my greatest success. I can't tell you how deeply the audience is moved in the third act [. . .] Oh, this art consumes my life, yet is a source of strength. I couldn't live if I didn't have art. I'll rest as long as the doctor prescribes it, and this leisure doesn't bother me except in those eternally long nights. Then Froufrou and Cesarina and Santuzza and Margherita dance in my head and make my lips and hands burn with impatience. [. . .] I'll say nothing of the troupe except for Tassinari, who recites well and is pretty, the rest of them would do better to keep silent. Not a one who understands, who resonates. Last night in Froufrou I was so sad and acted so well. You know that I'm not saying that out of vanity, not when acting means suffering. I'm writing you during the breaks in the rehearsals [. . .] If you could see how lamentable this stage is! I can't tell you what sadness has overtaken me. A revulsion that almost tastes like disillusionment. At what? You will ask. Mainly . . . at nothing in particular. I assure you that the only moment of relief is when I feel that sleep has me in its grasp, and the most revolting moment is when I awake. I'd like a sea journey, in order to live 20 days alone [. . .] breathing fresh and wholesome air that will renew body and soul [. . .] Life is tiresome. Farewell. They keep interrupting me."

Duse's self-absorbed single-mindedness and her dismissal of the other actors in a company considered the finest in Italy, including the gifted Flavio Andò, may not be particularly attractive traits, but they are an indication of the size of her ego, her unwavering belief in her own talent, and her commitment to an artistic ideal that took precedence over every other aspect of her life, including her child.

AT THE END OF APRIL 1885, Duse and the company sailed from Genoa for South America. Her husband, Checchi, kept to himself in his cabin, reading, he claimed, a thick German book about South America, but the twenty-nine-day voyage was not the restful trip Duse had envisioned. She had her own spacious stateroom, but an opera company was on board, and between the "trilling of the tenors and the toe tripping of the ballerinas" there was no opportunity for quiet or solitude. Plus all the other passengers, the "poor devils" speaking a jumble of languages all with "empty little brains" left her exhausted.

On May 1, just a few days after their arrival in Montevideo, the company opened with *Fédora*. Advance publicity had been good, and the theatre was full. Garibaldi had fought for the independence of Uruguay, many Italians had emigrated there, and Duse found a receptive audience. The persistent, nosy press, though, irritated her. When she was asked for dates and personal information, she rebelled. "What does it matter where I was born, how I have lived, how much I have despaired, how much I have believed in art?" she said. "All this is vulgar when reproduced in the newspapers—and without interest for the public." Shortly after their arrival, her already strained relationship with her husband erupted into open warfare. When Tebaldo Checchi attempted to meet with journalists on her behalf, she told him she would handle them. Checchi's clumsy, obvious attempts at press relations infuriated her. Duse's idea of publicity was on another plane from Checchi's. Before her departure for South America, Duse had met in Rome with Adelaide Ristori, who had toured South America, and Ristori had given her letters of introduction, including one to Dom Pedro II, the emperor of Brazil. "Do you think that I couldn't have done this without you?" Duse now asked Checchi. "I'm tired of hearing that it's always you." After this exchange, the couple stopped speaking.

On June 22 the company arrived in Rio de Janeiro, and Duse checked in at the Hotel Vista Alegre. Press coverage of her arrival was light. The newspapers were consumed with the "great scandal" of a local duel involving the writer Valentim Magalhães. Still, the huge theatre was packed for the first performance of *Fédora*. The constant murmuring of the audience disturbed Duse, and she felt "weak and tiny." It was a "complete fiasco," she thought. The Brazilian critic Artur Azevedo, however, who saw her that evening, became her champion in Rio.

The next performance was *Denise*, given to a sparse audience, but Duse felt that even though Denise lacked the elaborate costuming of Princess Fédora, she was able to connect with the audience. Concerned and distracted by the illness of the second male lead, Arturo Diotti, who was just four years older than she and devoted to her, Duse closed her head and heart and "the boat began to move a little . . . slowly," she said. The huge theatre seemed smaller. "I wept, and made them weep," she wrote Matilde Serao. Sitting in a box close to the stage, Artur Azevedo was transported by her performance. "Dumas made Denise," he effused, "and Deus made Duse."

Suffering from yellow fever exacerbated by overindulgence—too much food, especially fruit, too much drinking, and staying out all night—Arturo Diotti died on June 28. Duse and the company were devastated over the loss of the attractive young Diotti, but adhering to theatre tradition, they continued to perform with a substitute. "You see how we replace?" Duse said. "What a sad thing!"

In performance after performance in Rio, Duse earned accolades from the critics and from her audiences. Her leading man, Flavio Andò, was extremely popular as well, and his elegant beard and moustache even started a fashion, "barba á Andò," among Brazilian men. Both Cesare Rossi and Flavio Andò became sick for a time with mild cases of yellow fever, and Duse, knowing audiences paid to see her perform, carried the burden of the company's success on her shoulders.

The critic Azevedo wrote that he had never seen an actress who moved him so much. On July 1, Azevedo reported he had found an unsigned poem, written in pencil on the back of a playbill in the theatre. He published the poem, a hymn of praise to Duse, which everyone believed to have been written by Azevedo himself. Other reporters joked about Azevedo's "passion" for Duse, but he was not alone. The critic of the *Gazeta de Noticias* observed that one doesn't need to know Italian to understand Duse. "It is not even necessary to hear her—one just has to see her onstage."

Duse chose *La Dame aux camélias* for her benefit performance in Rio on Friday, July 17. The theatre was packed with Brazilian society, including Emperor Dom Pedro II. At the close of the third act, Dom Pedro called Duse to his box and gave her a heavy gold bracelet. At the end of the play, Azevedo stepped onstage and gave Duse a camellia and then recited a poem he had written for her. The writer Valentim Magalhães, who had survived his duel, followed Azevedo, and gave Duse a copy of the journal *A Semana (The Week)* printed on silk and filled with literary tributes to her. He then recited verses he had written. Two other poets also stepped onstage to intone their verses in praise of Duse's dark eyes and amazing art. As is usual in these situations, the critics and writers, while lauding Duse, were also using the opportunity to enhance their own reputations.

After the recitations, families that had banded together presented Duse with gifts, which included a star made of pure white diamonds, a brooch of diamonds and Brazilian emeralds, and a box of gold and silver. Her South American impresario gave her a huge star with golden flowers, and a hair ornament of gold and diamonds. Other gifts included a Brazilian flower made of gold and velvet, a watercolor of Rio, the letter *E* formed in pearls and gold, and over sixty bouquets of flowers.

A few days later, Duse thanked Artur Azevedo for his words at her benefit and confided to him that during "times of triumph when the audience acclaims me and ennobles me, my satisfaction would be incomplete if the image of my daughter doesn't accompany me [. . .] I associate my daughter with all my pleasures and all my sorrows."

One of the sorrows, of course, was Enrichetta's father. By mid-August, the couple had decided to separate. Checchi, then forty-one, planned to leave the theatre company entirely and stay in South America. In a letter to the critic D'Arcais, Checchi presented his reasons for their separation. Even though he was angry with the critic for not responding to his earlier letters, Checchi wanted to give his side of the story before gossip got back to Italy. According to Checchi, Duse owed everything to him. He had paid her debts, bought her clothes, promoted her career, turned her into a lady, and had saved her from death three times. His wife was drunk on success, Checchi said, and influenced by "false friends" and by "unhealthy readings" of the lives of Rachel, Desclée, and Bernhardt. Duse had a restless character that always needed "something new and bizarre, some emotion, and with my tranquil good health I couldn't give her this. With me, life was flat, monotonous, solid bourgeois." What she did to him was shameful, Checchi said, but "with crazy people, young people, and drunks you don't get angry." He concluded on a conciliatory note, perhaps remembering he was writing to a friend and admirer of Duse. "If she believes that she can be happy by herself, may God bless her and give her many long years of happiness, I will not be the one to disturb her and I don't wish her any ill."

What had Duse done to Checchi? According to most early accounts, including Olga Signorelli's biography of Duse, the couple separated during the Rio engagement because Duse had a passionate but short love affair with Flavio Andò. There are no love letters, no written evidence of such an affair, and it seems unlikely. The two actors had been working together for five years. Their rapport and passion onstage were evident, but the time for a blazing love affair, and there probably was one, would have been at the beginning of their association. Sexual jealousy does not appear to have motivated Checchi. He had not been faithful to his wife, and they had been estranged and distant for some time. In his letter to D'Arcais, Checchi also suggested Duse had no one else and would be alone. What Duse and Andò did have was a strong professional relationship. Their success together both in Italy and in South America gave them confidence, and at this time, they decided to leave Cesare Rossi's company, join forces, and create their own company. This decision, of course, had a profound effect on Checchi and other company members, who naturally were worried about their own future. By September 7, 1885, back in Italy, Cesare Rossi's son Alessandro was already looking for actresses "without Duse's craziness" to replace her. "Don't worry yourself about the Duse affair, with her ingratitude, with the dirty dealings of that Sicilian Andò, who under the veneer of a gentleman is a ham actor and a crook," Alessandro wrote his father.

It's not surprising that in 1885 an ambitious woman who wanted to be independent and manage her own company and own affairs would be called crazy. Checchi couldn't dominate his wife, and in losing her, he lost access to her income. Checchi's decision to remain in South America, however, seems a radical response to a marital separation. Checchi didn't give specifics to D'Arcais about Duse's "shameful" treatment of him, but during a performance in South America, Duse had opened the bodice of her costume and scornfully exposed her naked breast to her "pale and disconcerted husband." The message was primitive but clear—My body, my life, belongs to me.

Duse's lifelong antipathy for Checchi was based on more than his meddling with her career. Circumstantial evidence suggests Duse brought pressure on Checchi to remove himself from the theatre and her presence entirely. In the company were two lovely sisters, ten-year-old Emma Gramatica and thirteen-year-old Irma Gramatica, who were both close to Duse, and who would go on to long and successful theatre careers. Years later, Emma told a reporter that during their stay in Rio, she "decided to commit suicide" by making herself sick from eating too much fruit and spending the night outdoors, two behaviors that had led to Diotti's death. She didn't succeed. She also didn't give the reason for her suicide attempt. Later, the actor Ciro Galvani, who toured with Duse for years, although he wasn't on the South American tour, said Duse had caught Checchi in bed with Gramatica. With Emma? he was asked. "No! Not with Emma! With Irma," he said.

Checchi told D'Arcais it was a "mad impulse" that made Duse banish him from Italy. There was no legal reason to force Checchi to abide by Duse's "impulse." It's reasonable to believe, however, Duse banished him and had the moral authority to banish him, not because she was having an affair with Andò but because her husband had defiled a child.

Through all the turmoil of the South American tour, Duse kept a photograph of Adelaide Ristori close to her and looked to the older woman as an example of courage and inspiration. On August 25, Duse poured out her thanks to Ristori in a long, rambling, heartfelt letter. "I look at your photo-graph—that looks at me—and says to me: Work."

Duse's first foreign tour established a pattern in her relationship with the public—her unexpected and unfamiliar art first provoked resistance, followed by acceptance, quickly followed by adulation. The critics' reviews praising her performances validated the audience ovations.

"Today I'm conscious that I've won a *victory* with my art in this faraway place," Duse wrote in October 1885. "But what hard work—what sadness in these days [. . .] Art . . . *and the life of the theatre* . . . God, what an abyss between them!"

Three

D URING HER VICTORIOUS SOUTH AMERICAN TOUR, Duse felt "a sadness without a name that gnaws at me." She might have listed the bitter parting from her husband, the death of her friend and colleague Arturo Diotti, the guilt she felt over the separation from her daughter, and the pressure of her first foreign tour with the daily routine of rehearsals, performances, public appearances, and press relations.

Onstage she escaped into her art, but offstage, as she would throughout her life, she sought to "untie my heart"—to talk out her problems. In Buenos Aires, she turned again to Cesare Rossi, then fifty-six, the protective father she never had had. Duse loved and supported Alessandro Duse, who had retired the year before and moved to Venice to paint, but they had little contact. Although Rossi disliked the "immoral" themes of the new French plays and Duse resented Rossi's control and stinginess, they remained cordial and even affectionate with one another. While Rossi complained about the caprices of *"prima donnas,"* he knew they still had months left to work together. Duse was his star attraction, and he was a kind man who genuinely cared for her. In a note to Rossi, Duse thanked him for dispelling her doubts and lifting a great weight from her mind.

"When I am in the theatre," she told him, "among these *strangers,* I make myself strong by *pretending to be serene*, but in this moment . . . alone . . . here in the house . . . with many thoughts, *with all the responsibility of my daughter* . . . all weighing on me . . . I must thank you for your consoling words today [. . .] for calming my spirits and my thoughts."

The company returned to Italy at the end of November 1885. They played at the Teatro Valle in Rome, where Duse was reunited with Matilde Serao and Count Primoli. In late December, the newspaper *Capitan Fracassa* reported Tebaldo Checchi had written from Buenos Aires he wouldn't return to Italy and would no longer be an actor. He also told the newspaper that when he had married Duse, he had been rich and had used all his money for her career. He claimed he was alone, without a job, and penniless. On Christmas Day 1885 Duse fired off a cold letter of correction to the newspaper. She characterized herself as an artist and a woman who was alone and helpless. She disputed Checchi's assertion of a lost fortune, and wrote that, while the management had made money in South America, she had many debts to pay, including those left by her husband. "Art—and determination—will help me," she wrote. "Art . . . that was—always—in every grave moment—the protection—the sweetness—the refuge—the smile . . . of my life . . ."

The story and Duse's letter were picked up by Milan's *Corriere della Sera*. Noting there had been much speculation about the cause of the split between Duse and Checchi, the true reason for the separation, said the unsigned story in the *Corriere della Sera*, was the "incompatibility of their characters."

DURING LENT IN 1886, the company played Venice. If some performances hadn't been cancelled because of her "blessed voice," Duse reported, her earnings would have been "phenomenal." Audiences and the critics accepted her as "half-Venetian" and at the last performance there, Alessandro Duse proudly watched his daughter act in a theatre crowded with people and filled with flowers. From there the company crossed the Adriatic and played at the Teatro Communale in Trieste. By April 1886, the company was exhausted and fractious, and the performances suffered. Duse pushed Rossi to do new plays, and he resisted, unwilling to take the risk, especially with scripts he considered corrupt. "Rossi can't understand," Duse complained, "that I'm not some chattel, but a person."

As usual, when she was going through emotional storms, she also became physically ill. Duse's recurring malady, which usually struck following a long tour, affected her voice and her lungs. At this time, she also had heavy, painful menstrual periods. Just before the onset of her period, she was depressed and irritable, and during the first few days of her cycle, she took to her bed and performances were cancelled. Illness or the threat of illness has always been a powerful weapon of divas—it was a weapon Duse wielded time and again, sometimes because she was legitimately ill, and sometimes simply because she had learned the theatre wasn't sold out. Experience had taught her the truth of the line "when a woman is always well, no one is interested in her." The scarcity of her performances—often she played just three times a week—contributed to her mystery and increased the public's desire to see her. Emotionally and physically, though, Duse was exhausted, and her doctor and fan, the eminent physician and senator Dr. Jacopo Moleschott, ordered her to rest for the summer.

After picking up Enrichetta in Turin, Duse retreated to a cottage in the little town of Varazze, on the sunny gulf of Genoa. There, living between olive trees and "the beautiful sea . . . the eternal sea," Duse played like a girl with her four-year-old daughter. The theatre, though, and the future were constantly on her mind. To compensate for her lack of education, she read constantly, searching for new material and new ideas. She corresponded with D'Arcais and begged him for news from Rome. "How can I explain," she wrote, "that every time I leave the theatre, and when I return to it, I'm overcome by that same old, ominous fear." She joked that perhaps the funeral bell might soon be ringing for her, but "it would be too early," she said. "As a woman—for myself—I need to work 6 more years—and as a mother—10 more years—to assure the future of my little girl who belongs to me."

Throughout her life Duse rarely spent more than a month settled in one place—the gypsy life of an actor was too ingrained. After weeks of relaxing by the sea, she grew bored and restless. Her treatment required both sea and mountain air, and she asked the ever obliging Giacosa to find her a place in the mountains. "A great laziness weighs on me," she wrote him. The only idea she had in her head was "*Healing for work.*" Giacosa found her a house in Biella, north of Turin. Breathing the fresh air of the mountains, surrounded by greenery, watching Enrichetta run through the meadows, all made her so happy she even invited Cesare Rossi to spend a day with her to enjoy the peace. Rossi, who was no fool, knew Duse's moods were as changeable as Venetian weather. He didn't accept her invitation, but he did send her the 1,000 lire she had requested.

IN LATE FALL 1886, Duse finally convinced Rossi to produce two "immoral" new plays: *L'Abbesse de Jouarre*, by the French historian, critic, and author Ernest Renan, and *I portineria (In the Porter's Lodge)*, by Giovanni Verga, a gritty working-class love triangle set in Milan. The Rossi company opened both plays at the Teatro Valle in Rome.

Prices were raised for the opening of *L'Abbesse de Jouarre* to take advantage of the curiosity aroused by the philosophical work. Duse played an abbess sentenced to death during the French Revolution. With her in prison is a man she had loved before she entered the convent. Believing they are going to the guillotine the next morning, the lovers sleep together. The man is executed, but the abbess is spared. Pregnant with his child, the abbess marries a Republican officer to give her baby legitimacy. The play and Duse were applauded, but D'Arcais advised her "not to confuse a book with the theatre." Renan, who hadn't expected a commercial production of his difficult, verbose play, wrote Duse a letter of gratitude, calling her an "artist of genius." Duse kept the play in her repertory and led the way for pioneers like André Antoine, who opened his Théâtre-Libre in Paris in 1887. When he asked Renan for permission to present *L'Abbesse* at the Théâtre-Libre in 1888, Renan said, "The success of the play in Italy was due entirely to the efforts of a single actress, Mme. Duse, a woman of great intelligence." He would grant permission to do the play only if Antoine could find a French actress equal to Duse. Antoine immediately sought out Sarah Bernhardt, just back from an American tour. Antoine saw his theatre movement as a battle, a fight that had already been won "by the naturalists in the novel, by the impressionists in painting, and by the Wagnerians in music." He outlined his vision for the theatre to a fur-draped Sarah lounging on a chaise. Duse, the famous Italian actress, Antoine said, had played the role to great acclaim in Italy, and the role of the abbess would challenge Bernhardt's great genius. Do you know about this Duse? Bernhardt asked an old lady in the room. "Ah yes!" the woman said, "Duse— not really worth much." Content with her proven box-office hits and secure in her genius, Bernhardt refused Antoine's challenge.

Verga's *I portineria*, which had failed earlier in Milan, received critical raves in Rome. The two-act play was so real, wrote critic Eugenio Checchi, that the audience didn't interrupt the play to applaud, but kept the most religious silence. The somber drama failed to draw audiences, however, and Duse dropped it from her repertory.

While writers mostly used spiritual, even religious terms to describe Duse's presence in her last years, during her twenties, thirties, and forties, and in fact, for most of her career, critics like Suner, of the *Fanfulla Domenica*, celebrated her sensual physicality. Even taking into account the overheated prose of much nineteenth-century criticism, when describing Duse, male critics often wrote swooning tributes. Suner, for example, in a long article lingered over every part of her body—her cascading, tangled hair; her transparent olive skin; her rosy lips, which became moist in the ecstasies of love and sparkling in anger; her caressing hands; her elegant figure moving quickly and gracefully; her gestures rippling like the surface of the sea; and her very being pulsating with profound emotion. After this outburst, Suner concluded Duse's genius would lead to a rebirth of Italian drama.

Verga, Giacosa, and other Italian playwrights knew with Duse starring in their plays, they had a better chance of success with audiences that preferred the opulent sets, pretty costumes, and polish of the popular French plays. While Duse continued to perform Verga's poetic *Cavalleria rusticana*, she didn't like the narrow confines of *verismo*. She aimed for a transformation of life, not an imitation. For this reason, after rehearsing Luigi Capuana's dialect play, *Giacinta,* she decided not to produce it, which depressed the financially strapped Capuana so much he considered suicide. The newspapers criticized her harshly, saying she didn't have the right to refuse the work of such a respected artist. "My art belongs to me," she answered. Playwrights shouldn't base their work "on the personality of an *actress,*" she believed, but should be *"guided by art alone."*

When a young, bitter playwright complained to her about critics, Duse didn't betray any of the trade secrets she used in dealing with them, such as cultivation and flattery. Sounding older and wiser than her twenty-seven years, she chided the author: "What a child you are! One lives in a world of frogs, and you don't want to let them croak! [. . .] Go your own way, don't look back! Don't dirty yourself with what the so-called critics will say. Let them all burst! [. . .] Time builds and destroys for all. [. . .] Think only of finishing your work—that is everything."

Duse gloried in her work. She explained to D'Arcais her break with Rossi was irrevocable, and soon she would be her own boss. She felt *lavoro,* work, was the "greatest power in the world." There was no woman, she believed, who after experiencing the efforts and rewards of work, as she had, would not defend that work with vigilance and tenacity.

IN JANUARY 1887 the Rossi company, which was on the brink of splitting up, performed at the Teatro Manzoni. Opera-loving Milan audiences were known for their disdain of the theatre, but the *Corriere della Sera* reported that when Duse performed, elegant men in evening dress crowded into the theatre and erupted into a "frenzy" when they saw her. Duse had grown friendly with the writer Luigi Gualdo, an intimate of Arrigo Boito's. Because of his penchant for formal attire, Duse dubbed him "Gilet Bianco" (white waistcoat). Gualdo visited Duse at her house and attended all of her Milan performances. "Every evening," Gualdo said, "she forces an audience which is basically hostile to applaud furiously and lick her feet."

"Of all the actors," wrote one critic, "Duse is the only one who knows how to give a character human nature as well as a symbolic nature." As she had done in her earlier appearances there, Duse worked her magic on the skeptical Milan audiences. After seeing a month of her performances, the *Corriere della Sera* critic wrote, "All of our public is in love with this actress, whose success is truly extraordinary."

The biggest lovefest in Milan at this time, however, was at the world premiere of Verdi's *Otello* at La Scala on February 5, 1887. With a libretto by Arrigo Boito, *Otello* was Verdi's first new work since *Aida,* written in 1871. After months of intense and extremely secret preparations, Verdi, assisted by

As Goldoni's Pamela, 1880s

Boito, had directed his own rehearsals. On the day of the opening, crowds filled the streets shouting "Viva Verdi!" La Scala was sold out, but Giacosa had arranged for Duse's ticket. Throughout the performance, the ecstatic audience interrupted the opera again and again with applause and acclamations. At the curtain call, Duse watched as Verdi brought Boito onstage to accept the ovations. When Verdi, his wife Strepponi, and Boito left the theatre, a mob unhitched the horses to their carriage and pulled the carriage down the street toward the Grand Hotel. Boito thought the crowd had gone crazy. In an effort to restore order before the second performance of the opera, the management of La Scala wrote an open letter to the public begging them not to disrupt *Otello*, but to hold their reactions until the end of an act or the end of the opera.

When Duse played in Goldoni's *Pamela* a week later, Arrigo Boito, Franco Faccio (the conductor and Boito's close friend), Verdi, and Strepponi shared a first-row box at the Teatro Manzoni. The white-bearded Verdi sat in the back of the box, hidden from the crowd, and the audience respected his wish there be no ovation for him. When Eleonora was a little girl, her mother had taken her to see the Villa Verdi at Sant'Agata. Duse, however, was more interested in Arrigo Boito, the man who sat next to Verdi. During an intermission, the Verdis and Boito visited Duse backstage. When they parted, Boito and Duse clasped hands, smiled at each other, but didn't speak. On February 20, 1887, just over a week later, they became lovers.

After their first introduction at Caffè Cova three years earlier, Boito and Duse had exchanged a few notes. Duse had thought of Arrigo often, but the May poem he had sent her, ending in "never," had disturbed her. Duse typically ransacked letters for meaning in the same way she analyzed scripts. What did that "never" mean? "I cannot give myself if love does not absolve me," she told him. But whom did she love? She didn't really know him.

Slim, with gray-green eyes, a trim beard, and a high, scholarly forehead, Boito, like Duse, was a celebrity. While Duse's career was still young, Boito, then forty-six, was nearing the end of his. The son of an Italian painter and a Polish countess, he was a distinguished writer who moved in the highest social and literary circles. He was not married but was involved with a mysterious aristocrat, a beautiful but ailing woman named Fanny. During his youth, Boito had been wild and impetuous, part of a bohemian group of Milanese writers who had challenged tradition and wanted to remake Italian art. Wounded by the humiliating failure of his opera *Mefistofele*, based on Goethe's *Faust*, at La Scala in 1868, Boito worked on another opera, *Nerone*, all his life but lacked the confidence to finish it. He is known primarily for writing *Otello* and *Falstaff*, two librettos that stimulated Verdi to return to composition. By a strange coincidence, Boito's collaboration with Verdi on *Otello* had almost been derailed by Martino Cafiero, Duse's former lover. Cafiero had published a report quoting Boito as saying he wished he had composed *Otello* instead of Verdi.

Boito apologized and Verdi forgave him, but the old genius shrewdly analyzed Boito's character. "He has much talent, he aspires to originality, but he proves rather odd. He lacks spontaneity and he is short of melody; many musical qualities."

IN 1887, with Flavio Andò, Duse started a new professional life as head of her own company, the Compagnia della Città di Roma. At the same time, Duse imagined she could start over her personal life with Boito. She felt young, girlish, four years old. "I am made of Arrigo," she exclaimed early in their affair. "Look at me! Look at me!" she told him. "I feel the heat of love, while I write you—all my youth, all my virginity, is yours . . . God!" Dante's *La vita nuova (The New Life)* became their much quoted talisman. Their correspondence, contained in one enormous volume edited by Raul Radice, is a

Arrigo Boito, Duse's lover and Verdi's librettist,
late 1880s

vivid, loving, angry, sometimes silly, and often painful record of their relationship.

Onstage Duse could forget herself and transform drama into transcendent
life. Offstage she thought about herself constantly and dramatized her everyday life. "I did the first, tiniest, most enormous act of the day," she joked to
Boito in one letter. "I got up." When she wasn't performing or rehearsing,
Duse spent much of her time alone. A voracious reader, she carried trunks of

books with her and wrote letters. The hundreds of pages she wrote to Boito reveal that the same qualities of acute observation and analysis Duse brought to her work, she also turned on herself and Boito. Sometimes she referred to herself in the third person, balancing this grandiosity with self-mockery and irony.

During the summer of 1887, when Duse's company played Sicily, Boito joined her in Palermo. Even though it must have been difficult for the fastidious Boito to live in such close proximity to what he called the "corruption" of the theatre, their love survived this first trial of traveling together. In August, they vacationed together with Enrichetta in a mountain town north of Bergamo. Contemptuous of the bourgeois dramas in Duse's repertory, Boito urged her to aim higher. To this end, during their August "honeymoon," he worked on an adaptation of Shakespeare's *Antony and Cleopatra* for her. A snob, like many of his contemporaries in the world of opera, Boito looked upon theatre as an inferior art. While urging her to improve herself as an artist by doing Shakespeare, Boito also told Duse her birth into the theatre was her "original sin." If they were to live together, Duse had to retire from the theatre. In the euphoria of love, Duse agreed. She planned to work for two more years, save her money, and then quit acting. Boito wanted to spare Enrichetta from the damnation of her mother's profession, and he promised Duse they would all live together—"three heads at one window"—not in stony, masculine Milan but in watery, feminine Venice.

During the first year of their affair, their letters were filled with baby talk and pet names like Bumba and Bumbo, Zozzoletta and Zozzi. Often, Boito seems overwhelmed by her passion. He casts himself as both her lover and her teacher. "I give you all of me," he wrote, but he also urged her to be calm and offered self-improvement advice. Their differences can be clearly seen in their writing styles—Boito ordered his precise sentences into neat paragraphs while Duse jumped from thought to thought, her sentences sprawling across the page and running up and down the margins of the letters. His letters, except for occasional outbursts of passion and creative wordplay, often sound flat, while hers sing with emotion, images, texture, and details—Arrigo's toothmarks on a cigarette, the slant of sunlight through her shutters, the ticktock of a clock like the beating of her heart, the smell of incense in a Venetian church, the stink of Neapolitan streets, the ivory brush and tortoiseshell box on her black bedside table, his letters tucked under her pillow.

When Duse played Genoa in September and October and Turin in November 1887, she wrote letters to Boito almost daily. The letters are striking in their frankness. As she did in her acting, she kept nothing back. She loved him. She wanted him. Her child, Enrichetta, who was with her, loved him. Believing Arrigo's promises, she hired a lawyer to try to obtain a legal

separation from Checchi, who had returned to Italy for a visit. When Checchi asked to see Enrichetta, Duse, in a curt note, gave him permission to see
her from three to five on November 10.

Checchi had threatened to take Enrichetta from her as well as any money
owed to her, which increased Duse's anxiety and need for support from Boito.
"Where are you?" she wrote him. "No more—no more two houses—but
one—with me—with me . . ."

She did have some doubts about Arrigo's commitment. She asked him
once if he had been obligated to hide the photograph of her he kept by his
bed. She knew that every fall Boito vacationed on Lake Como with the
Milanese aristocrat Donna Vittoria Cima, who also happened to be a close
friend of Boito's lover, Fanny.

Boito was conservative and protective of his social position and of his ties
to Fanny, and insisted his relationship with Duse be kept secret even from her
close friend Matilde Serao. With typical northern prejudice, Boito didn't like
the Neapolitan Serao. He thought her writing was rambling and her manners
were vulgar. In addition, she wrote for newspapers and couldn't be trusted.
Duse promised not to embarrass him or do anything to create gossip. At
Boito's urging, she read Dante and Shakespeare. She even stopped writing to
Serao. Filled with loyalty and love for her "Nennella," Serao accepted Duse's
failure to write regularly with stoic grace. "She's so important," Serao told
Giacosa, "that I think it's petty to expect that of her."

Duse resented the fact that she wasn't allowed into Boito's aristocratic circle, but his closest friends, Giacosa and Gualdo, who knew about the affair,
became her friends. They often served as Boito's surrogates. When Arrigo was
unavailable, the fat Giacosa and the thin Gualdo, like two faithful knights,
provided advice, comfort, and amusing distraction. Duse was closer to the
novelist Gualdo, who was handsome, and had the manners of a diplomat.
Giacosa's friendship, on the other hand, had ulterior motives—he had
romantic feelings for her, plus he wanted her to do his plays.

Although Duse thought Giacosa's script *Tristi amori (Sad Loves)*, which
had failed in an earlier production in Rome, was flawed, she produced and
starred in it as a favor to him and Arrigo. Duse played Emma, a character who
sacrifices romantic love for maternal love. The play opened at the Teatro
Gerbino in Turin on November 30, 1887. Giuseppe Depanis, in *Gazzetta Letteraria*, praised Duse's understated, deeply felt performance. She revealed
Emma's soul, he wrote, with "a glance, a gesture, a silence." The opening-
night audience applauded enthusiastically, but they were probably responding to the onstage passion of Duse and Flavio Andò, who played her lover.
The play failed to win larger audiences, and Giacosa soon moved into the
more lucrative business of writing librettos for Puccini.

FOLLOWING THE OPENING of *Tristi amori*, Boito stayed on in Turin with Duse for several days. After paying a huge enrollment fee of 1,000 lire, on December 1 Duse placed Enrichetta, who would be six years old on January 7, in an exclusive boarding school outside of Turin. When she saw Enrichetta dressed in her school uniform, "it seemed to me that she was no longer mine," Duse said. During the first week, Enrichetta cried and cried for her mother, and suffered under the school's discipline. Duse felt guilty at leaving her there. "We will take the sweet little girl with us, eh?" she asked Boito. "She has shown much character and strength."

As some of the sexual excitement and curiosity of a new love wore off, Boito began to reveal impatience with Duse's suffocating neediness and her volatile emotions. "Now is the time for work," he advised. Alone in his Milan study, Boito had little understanding of the pressures Duse faced as director, producer, and star of her own company. Sometimes she didn't have time to write him, and he complained about "dying" letters.

Duse packed her twenty-seven trunks, and the Compagnia della Città di Roma moved to Rome to play at the Teatro Valle. From there, Duse wrote to Boito about money worries, about two female servants cheating her, and on Christmas Day 1887, she moaned, "I feel old, I feel old . . . strange and alone—alone alone like a dog." The trip had been miserable. Rome was humid and hellish, filled with gossip and annoying reporters. She hated the popular Sardou plays. Her maid didn't want to cook. Matilde Serao had a scoundrel for a husband and was miserable in her marriage. Count Primoli, who didn't have to work, had nonchalantly lost 200,000 lire, while, at twenty-nine, she felt her own shoulders curving under the strain of work.

Boito pictured himself as a romantic lover. When he received a letter from Duse, he slit open the envelope with his mother-of-pearl knife, carefully counted the pages, and then began reading. Boito's fantasy of a playful, sparkling correspondence and love affair with a glamorous actress had transformed into the reality of a messy relationship with a demanding, driven woman with a small child, a woman who told him more than he wanted to know and asked more of him than he was willing to give.

Except for a brief visit to Rome, Boito remained at a safe distance from all this turmoil, supposedly working on his opera *Nerone*. There was no question of their living together until she gave up her work. Boito didn't respect her work, what he called a "fiction of life." When he read a "vulgar" newspaper interview with Duse, which described her crying, flinging herself around the room, and revealing confidences to a reporter, he said, "You don't need these journalists." This counsel could only have reminded Duse of her husband

Checchi's attempts to advise her about the press. Her reply to Boito doesn't survive; in fact, only two of her letters to Boito are extant from 1888, but whatever she wrote prompted Arrigo to call himself "Asino!" (Ass!) in a cringing apology, which was marred only by a further slap at her profession. "Pass, you pure one, through the corruption of your strange destiny . . . I know who you are."

Sadly, neither one of them really knew the other.

"One year we have lived in a dream," Boito wrote on February 20, 1888. "One year exactly." The honeymoon was over.

WHILE BOITO PLEADED with Duse to read his letters more simply, she dug through his letters for meaning, for "tone," and looked between the lines for what was not said. "I know well the sense of every word!" she asserted. Obsessed with keeping their affair secret, Boito didn't like meeting in cities. He knew so many people, he said, he would be sure to be recognized. He drew up elaborate plans and absurd schedules for their rare meetings, going so far as to count the steps to a private hotel entrance and to specify the number of times she should knock on the door. He wasn't married, and she was separated from her husband, who lived out of the country. What did he fear? The truth, which Duse sensed, was that despite all Boito's protestations of love and lofty talk of art, he was ashamed of her because she was an actor, and beneath him in class and education.

In late March, Duse forwarded Boito an excited note Enrichetta had written to her about their upcoming meeting in Venice. The message was unmistakable. *Enrichetta and I will be together in Venice. If you are serious about "three heads at one window," you will join us there.* In mid-April, Boito met them in Venice and entered their "little world" at the Palazzo Barbarigo on Santa Maria del Giglio. It wasn't a happy visit.

A few days after he left, the forty-six-year-old Boito attempted to cure Duse's depression by advising her to say a litany of thanks for all she had: "29 years, a beautiful, good daughter, and fruitful work and . . . you add the rest." The rest, apparently, was up to her. When she gave up her work, Boito said, he would keep his promise. "Your work can't support the force of life in all its truth," he wrote in May.

Was Boito playing with words, or was he serious about asking Duse to choose between her art and him? Over and over, he called her his *piccoletta*, his black-haired "little girl" with ivory skin. He wrote to her like an affectionate, controlling father. *Don't throw your money away,* he advised. He was urging his *piccoletta* to leave the theatre, while actor-manager Duse was planning a production of his adaptation of Shakespeare's *Antony and Cleopatra*, a production that would cost her company 9,000 lire—a fact she casually slipped into a letter. It is likely Boito was never serious about living with her and Enrichetta. Forcing Duse to make the impossible choice between him and her art would insure he would never have to disrupt his quiet, well-ordered life and his daily meetings with his close male friends in Milan so that he could live *en famille* in Venice.

Perhaps Duse accepted this as well. "This morning, at the first hour of dawn," Duse wrote Boito from Venice on March 31, 1888, "the supreme power spoke to me of what I must do in my life; I bowed my head . . . and I said = *So be it* ="

DUSE FELT AT HOME in Venice. The city looked like a gorgeous theatre set decorated with fading marble *palazzi,* gliding black gondolas, bright-sailed Chioggia boats, and shabby hidden piazzas all reflected in the shimmering mirror of the canals. Unlike the exclusionary social world of Boito's Milan, the freer, more cosmopolitan Venetian society embraced Duse. Katherine de Kay Bronson (Mrs. Arthur Bronson), an American from Boston, lived in Venice with her daughter Edith in the Casa Alvisi overlooking the Grand Canal. In *The Aspern Papers*, Henry James immortalized her as the kindly and savvy Mrs. Prest. Blue-eyed with chestnut hair and bold enough to smoke cigarettes, Mrs. Bronson made herself useful to artists. She was a close friend of James's and had been a patron to Robert Browning, who had stayed at her palazzo in Venice, and also at La Mura, her home in Asolo. She and her daughter Edith befriended Duse and provided introductions and womanly warmth. Duse was also welcome at the Malipiero Palace of the German Princess Hatzfeldt, where Duse met Countess Sophie Drechsel and Matilde Acton. The widowed daughter of an Austrian general, Acton, like Matilde Serao, was intelligent, outspoken, and "hated everything that was false and sentimental." Both Matildes were devoted to Duse. Acton's thick, black hair, which she wore in braids, her refined profile, and the shape of her mouth reminded Duse of her mother Angelica. She observed Acton at every opportunity and imitated her dress, her manners, and the graceful movement of her hands. Tutored by Acton, she also began a serious study of French.

Acton introduced Duse to her former lover, the Russian Count Alexander Wolkoff, who was also known by "Roussoff," the name he signed to his paintings. Roussoff was the kind of man who liked women and kept his former mistresses as friends, even giving them painting lessons. He was married to an Englishwoman, lived in the Palazzo Barbaro-Wolkoff on the Grand Canal and supported himself by selling large watercolors in London and Paris. When he met Duse, Wolkoff was in his late forties and ravishingly handsome.

He later dazzled and terrified the poet Rilke with his "indescribable moods and astonishing contradictions." A brilliant conversationalist and friend of Tolstoy (whom he thought "a complete idiot"), Wolkoff had also been a frequent guest of Richard and Cosima Wagner's at their home in Venice. After Wolkoff met Duse, he dashed off a courtly letter praising her "fine and sensitive nature" and her "beautiful and sweet face." Duse had confided her fears about providing for her daughter's future, and he offered advice. "Love *something*," he said, "do not always love *someone* . . . Make up your mind to travel, for in foreign countries you will have a cultivated audience. I am sure that your successes abroad would do you good from every point of view." Do not forget, he told her, "that I am sincerely devoted to you and that you can count on me everywhere and always."

Meanwhile, as Duse continued her tour, Boito sent her news of his meticulous plans for their summer holiday. Understanding Boito's almost pathological need for secrecy, Giacosa had found Il Castello di San Giuseppe, a former convent of the Barefooted Carmelite friars, some sixty miles west of Milan near Chiaverano in Piedmont. "The place is beautiful," Boito wrote, "and not as isolated as it seems," although to get there required a twenty-minute walk uphill. The address was Chiaverano in Ivrea, but Boito warned Duse not to put the name of the convent on the address. People had learned to unite their names, he wrote, but if he and Eleonora were careful they could elude curiosity.

Boito's elaborate precautions to avoid publicity appear ludicrous, but he felt he was taking prudent steps against a booming popular press that produced gossip instead of hard news. In his work with Verdi, Boito had learned to be discreet and secretive. Unscrupulous reporters, with their inside sources in theatres and telegraph offices, wrote whatever sold papers. Even though Boito hated newspapers, like everyone else, he needed something to read on the train. On July 4 on the train to Ivrea, he read a report that Duse planned to leave at the beginning of August for a tour of Germany and America. He wrote to her the next day wondering why she had failed to tell him the painful news.

The newspaper report proved to be a rumor. When her tour was finished, as usual Duse suffered from her recurrent lung problems, and she traveled to Roncegno in the Dolomites to stay at the Hotel dei Fratelli Waiz for a water cure. She arrived in Ivrea on August 12 and stayed with Boito until August 30. Inspired by the ambience, or by a personal erotic fantasy, Boito gave his *piccoletta* a new name during their time together at the convent. He called her *chierichetto*, altar boy.

"It's true, Lenor," Boito wrote from San Giuseppe on September 1, "the one who stays behind is sadder than the one who has departed." "My *chierichetto*, my poor *chierichetto*, tell me about your health," he asked. Duse had left to continue her theatre tour, before playing a two-month season in Milan, where she would premiere his *Antony and Cleopatra*. Although Boito met Duse briefly in Livorno and Pisa, he didn't join her in Milan as he had earlier promised.

Duse opened her Milan season in October. Again, the theatre was sold out for her performances, and the reviews were filled with praise. On November 14 the *Corriere della Sera* announced Duse would present *Antony and Cleopatra*, translated and adapted by Arrigo Boito. A few days later, perhaps hoping Boito would read the article, Duse told the newspaper the rehearsals of *Antony and Cleopatra* had made her "very tired."

In fact, she was overworked and furious. In preparing a role, Duse needed long periods of solitude, time to think about the character and fully imagine it. She and her company were rehearsing *Cleop*, as she called it, while performing every night. *Cleop* was Duse's title for Boito's truncated adaptation of Shakespeare's masterpiece. Her copy of *Cleop* was dense with notations in Boito's small, neat handwriting as well as her own blue-penciled changes, cuts, and corrections. Because Boito stayed in San Giuseppe, she wrote him long, time-consuming letters, one twenty pages long, filled with questions about the production, the costumes, and the script, questions that could have been answered easily if Boito had simply moved home to Milan and attended rehearsals. Duse had hired Alfredo Edel, who had created the costumes for *Otello*, to design *Cleop*, but Boito had to approve every detail. "Help me be able to work," Duse pleaded. Instead, Boito wrote letters filled with encouragement about the lofty intellectual environment in which she lived—"Do it your way," he advised generously, "Always your way." Then, not trusting her, he pointed out "the serpent of the old Nile is not a *prima donna* of melodrama."

When it became clear Boito wouldn't be joining her, Duse snapped at him. "You are you and do what you please" and "You're so out of things." Still, Duse was a young woman, not the godlike Verdi. Boito's aversion to the theatre ran deep—he even had nightmares about a theatre filled with vulgar people and an angry Duse. Clearly, he was fearful of her in full diva mode. "*Coraggio,*" Boito wrote to her, but he couldn't overcome his paralyzing fear of self-exposure. She needed him, but he needed to hide even more. Bored with Sardou and the rest of her reliable but lucrative repertory, Duse had the courage to risk the finances of her company and her own stature as an artist on an unproven translation. Knowing the papers had already announced that the play was his work, Boito still asked Duse not to put his name on the

As Cleopatra, late 1880s

playbill. The subtext was clear. I don't have faith in my work. You're on your own. He didn't attend the opening to offer her moral support, which sent an even more painful message to Duse—he didn't want his aristocratic Milanese friends to see him with her.

The result was predictable. Despite a gorgeous production and elaborate costumes, the play failed. After one additional performance, which didn't sell well, Duse replaced it with *La Dame aux camélias*. Boito had cut some of Antony's part and many important scenes. The reviews excoriated his translation, but the response to Duse's performance was mixed. The critic of *Il Secolo*, comparing her to tragedians like Ristori, felt Duse "didn't have the figure or the voice for great characters." The critic of *Il Sole* disagreed. Duse's variety and diversity of expression were unsurpassed, he wrote, moving rapidly from "love, hate, fury, wildness, pride, tenderness, desperation, and triumphant certainty." Another critic said Duse's Cleopatra was simply *La Femme de Claude* in Egyptian dress. In portraying Cleopatra as a human being, Duse was rejecting the pictorial acting style of Ristori and Ernesto Rossi. A few months earlier, she had been appalled by Rossi's false, overblown performances in *King Lear* and *Hamlet*. In transferring her modern acting style to a classic character, Duse stimulated a debate among Italian critics. But the real judgment on *Cleop* would come in later performances when Duse had time to get over her anger and develop the role.

On November 23, the day after the opening, Boito wrote a long letter to her accepting all the blame for the disaster. His adaptation was too brief. He had failed Shakespeare, and he had betrayed Lenor. Everyone would know, he said, that it was his fault. He hadn't seen the play in performance, but he offered to make changes in the script. He also blamed the failure on the "inebriation of the last two years." He wanted to see her. "Tell me that you don't hate me," he wrote. Three days later Duse wrote him a short cold letter. She was exhausted and didn't want to see him. When Duse was safely in Florence, Boito finally came down from his mountain to Milan. On December 5, he wrote her with the news that the "all-wise" Verdi had seen her performance and had been moved by it.

FOR DUSE, the failure of *Cleop* had been "enormous, phenomenal, absurd," the most humiliating flop of her career, which was probably why she was determined to turn it into a success. Sales for *Antony and Cleopatra* in Florence were good, but her performance was still unfinished, and the critical reception was mixed. Her company moved on to Naples. From there she wrote to Giacosa, who had criticized her for attempting Shakespeare. "If you've ever regretted that you've treated me badly," she said, "here is my new address. You've got the people you love with you [. . .] In the evening when I light my large lamp, I feel that there are empty places around the lamp . . . so write to me."

Boito wrote to her constantly. "What do you want?" he asked. "When?" Before the Naples opening of *Cleop*, he wrote, "This time the battle of Shakespeare must be won. It is NECESSARY." Again, the play failed. Duse's other performances, though, were well received. Her performance in *Fédora* was noted in the *London Daily News* as well as the *New York Times*, who called her "Bernhardt's Italian Rival," although more space was given to her costume of white brocade embroidered with delicate flowers, cut low at the neck, with half-sleeves of lace, a long, white boa, and two diamond solitaires.

After weeks of punishing Boito with silence, as soon as Duse needed him, she reached out for his help. On February 25, 1889, Duse wrote Boito she was happy to have received his telegrams. She explained that she had been ill and had given only four performances in February. With time on her hands, she wrote him long letters. Apparently, she had forgiven him both as a writer and a lover. "I love you with all of me," she said. "I have a fear of satiating you with love and with lamentations."

"The heart of my good Lenor will live under my hand," Boito assured her. Stay tranquil, he soothed. Duse's weakness posed no threat to Boito, and he responded to her like a compassionate yet distant father. He asked her to tell him everything, constantly assuring her of his love and concern. To cheer her up, he sent her a glass prism like one he kept on his desk. "If you put it in the sun it dances and moves like a living thing," he said.

"I will lift the veils," Duse wrote Boito on March 15, "and we will speak." Her depression was not only psychological but physical. As Boito knew, for years she had experienced heavy bleeding during her menstrual cycle, but it had grown worse, and her doctor feared she would hemorrhage. For the past several months, she had lived in fear and pain. Her gynecologist, Dr. Ottavio Morisani, had decided to treat her heavy periods as well as a fungus infection with a cycle of cauterizations, which were designed to destroy the thickened endometrial lining of her uterus. The treatments, which were spread out over several months, involved cauterizing the walls of her uterus with a red-hot iron. If these treatments failed, a hysterectomy, her greatest fear, was the only remedy. "I would no longer be a woman," she said. "I would disgust myself." Most of all, she wouldn't be able to feel or express herself as a woman. "I would be a woman eunuch," she despaired.

Meanwhile, she still had to lead her company, and with Alberto Buffi, her administrator, and Flavio Andò, she plotted the Compagnia della Città di Roma's future work. She asked Boito about Egypt's climate, and she contemplated a tour of Russia and wrote to Alexander Wolkoff asking for his assistance. He replied that she surely didn't need help, "provided that her health was good and that she could bear the horrible climate." He promised to contact his society friends in Russia, who would do all they could to help her. She worried about Enrichetta in Turin. Matilde Acton had attempted to see the girl, but since she wasn't a family member, the school wouldn't allow her to visit. Duse was also concerned about her father in Venice, who had been upset by newspaper reports about her illness. Matilde Serao visited and brought her new baby, but mostly Duse was alone with nothing to do except write letters, read books Boito sent her, and follow theatre gossip.

When she read an announcement that Giacosa was writing a play in the style of Sardou for Sarah Bernhardt, she was incredulous. "Does he have a fungus on the brain?" she wrote Boito. "Ask him if he wants me to send him Dr. Morisani."

"It's true," Boito replied. "The Hebrew seductress has seduced our friend."

For seven months, from February 1889 through August 1889, Boito responded to a deluge of letters from Duse with kindness, humor, and concern. He was working on the libretto of *Falstaff* for Verdi, but he listened to her rages, sympathized with her boredom, and shared her fantasies. "I'm a *chierichetto*," she wrote. She would cut her hair, wear a black skirt, and a white blouse, and would go to the convent to live with him. "Will it please you?"

She used her letters to Boito like a daily journal. She was thin and tired, and sometimes the blood rushed to her head, and she became furious. "What a beast I am!" she raged, and then the act of writing the letter calmed her. "Come here," she invited, "wrap yourself around me." Her illness revolted her. "Women are made badly," she said. At times she convinced herself she didn't need him. "I must work," she exhorted herself. "I will help myself." Then, angry that he hadn't come to see her, she asked him not to write. "What could you say that I don't know?" Her frustration was caused, she wrote, by the "impossibility at the moment of two destinies." Finally, Boito visited her for a few days in mid-July. After he left, she wrote a letter singing with joy. "Arrigo, Arrigo Arrigo! Ammmmmore amore!" She held the letter to the lamp and sent it off "hot hot."

JUST AFTER A TRIP to Paris and London, Matilde Acton had joined Countess Sophie Drechsel at Tegernsee, a popular resort area in the mountains of Bavaria. For two weeks, Acton had been in "a state of high excitement," and on July 12, 1889, she took the Drechsels' boat out onto the lake, "gave a great cry, threw herself into the water, and was drowned." A few days later, Duse read the news. She was devastated. Acton had been her feminine ideal. Acton's lover had "taken away his protection," and she had killed herself.

"I have believed myself capable in some moments of a similar thing," Duse said. Duse berated herself that even though she had loved her friend, she hadn't been able to help her. "I recall her one evening among many," Duse told Boito. "We were going out of her house. She was so sweet in the simple way she dressed in the evening—and she said as we walked, 'how fine the air is this evening' . . . 'I had no children!' . . . and we left it at that. She went off to see people, and I went back in to write you. I saw her disappear toward the palazzo, and the town street, quiet, tranquil—at a slow, effortless walk—Poor thing! She wore a little chain, like mine, underneath, on her breast. She had it hidden there; no one understood her, none of the people there!"

The chain Duse wore held the gold locket containing the dried rose leaves from the grave of her dead son. Acton's death haunted Duse. Matilde didn't have the reasons Duse had to live, Boito counseled. "You have me," he said, "and you have your daughter."

IN LATE SUMMER, the treatments ended, and Duse was healthy enough to join Boito for a few weeks in San Giuseppe. While they were there, Boito continued to work on *Falstaff,* his secret project with Verdi. In August, accompanied by Enrichetta, Duse returned reluctantly to Naples for a checkup with Dr. Morisani. After the preceding seven months in Naples, she was sick of the sun, the mosquitoes, the chaos of the bazaar, and the foul streets lit with glaring electric lights. Enrichetta got on her nerves, and Duse tried to amuse her. "*I swear* to you I love that child," Duse wrote Boito, "but I have some moments . . . —when I just can't stand her!"

In September, she returned Enrichetta to her school in Turin and resumed her own work in Milan. Boito was out of town making his annual visit to Donna Vittoria Cima and presumably seeing Fanny as well at Villa d'Este on Lake Como. Giacosa and Gualdo kept Duse company, and she asked Boito not to come and see *Cleop*. She detested him, Lake Como, Donna Vittoria, and everyone around him. A friend had offered to show her the cathedral at Como, but "I couldn't do it," Duse said. It would have made her suffer too much to know Boito was nearby and behind doors that were closed to her.

When her company played Sicily in October, she complained she was acting in front of brutes and stupid people. The city noise was overwhelming, the sirocco made it difficult to breathe, and the harsh electric light in the theatre, which had replaced the softer gaslights, irritated her eyes. She had no news, nothing that deserved telling. "There are those in the world who can live next to you!" she told Boito. "That is the true gift—that is the true grace—"

She sent letters to Boito at Sant'Agata, where he worked with Verdi on *Falstaff*. After Boito left, Verdi forwarded one of Duse's letters to him, and Verdi's handwriting next to Duse's looked, Boito said, "like a lion's paw on a swallow's wing." After changing her filthy, noisy Palermo hotel for another one, Duse cheered up. She also met the Marchesa di Ganzeria, who introduced her to Marthe, a young Parisian woman, who would act as Duse's companion during her upcoming tour to Egypt. Duse had been reading Pascal's *Pensées*, and she philosophized about herself. "It seems to me," she wrote Boito on November 10, 1889, "that two people have been born within me— one—the one that you have loved - = the other - the one who has to make her own way! There was a time I felt such a sweetness in the thought of wrapping myself around you—but now, I understand that it is not possible. I will help myself! Never fear—Work——work - I'm behind in so many basic things, but by learning them I will help myself."

Yet, at thirty-one, Duse depended on Boito and was still "afraid that you won't like me." Distance and their long separation, though, had increased her passion. "Make love to me—violently, madly," she wrote. In mid-December, Boito met her in Naples for a brief visit. On Monday, December 17, 1889, she and her company arrived in Alexandria, Egypt.

"NEW PAPER, new ink, new pen, and new life," Duse wrote to Boito on December 19 from Alexandria. "I swear that when I need, absolutely need to, I find the courage."

Crossing the Mediterranean had been rough. Duse never suffered from seasickness and had little sympathy for her fellow passengers. "Pigs," she called the sick, terrified men and women who fell to the deck praying and swearing. As usual, she remained aloof from her acting company, the "tribe." The French actor Coquelin was on board, but Duse spent most of her time talking to a group of French priests. One handsome young priest in particular charmed and impressed her. "He had chosen his life," she wrote, "and he had faith in his choice."

At the head of her own company, Duse, too, had chosen a path to take her name "as far as I can," a vow that she had shared with the critic D'Arcais five years earlier. D'Arcais believed, however, "Duse had committed a grave error" in taking on the moral and financial direction of her own company. Afraid those responsibilities would distract her from "the study of her art," he also criticized her for going on tour just to make money. "Work provides money," Duse asserted, "and money is nothing other than independence, that most sacred and adorable thing."

Under British protection, Alexandria was a thriving port city with about a 25 percent foreign population. Duse drew her audiences mostly from the large contingent of Italian and English residents. The French colony was "hostile," she reported. Applauded and honored by the locals with gifts and ovations, she earned about the same for a performance here as she would have received in Italy, which meant that the company would barely make a profit.

Her impressions of Egypt were colored by her disappointments with the box office. She hated everything. Alexandria was a filthy, poverty-stricken bazaar filled with ignorant people who sat around "squatting and smoking from morning until night." She even took exception to the harmless Egyptian fez, which she saw men wearing in cafés, in churches, in paintings, in the theatre, in the water closet, in the sky, and in "every place," she ranted. "That fez grates on my nerves." The humid climate disagreed with her; she and most of her company got mild cases of influenza; because of the unreliable mail service, she went for days without letters; and she missed Arrigo, Enrichetta, and her father, who was old and alone in Venice.

The company moved to the "delicious air" of Cairo, with the pyramids in the distance, and opened with *Cleop.* Her long study of the play and the time to rehearse had begun to pay off. The reception was good for Cleopatra in her home country, and Duse's dark mood lifted. With Marthe, her young Parisian companion and theatre-struck fan, she practiced her French. They ate dinner together, and Marthe would sit by her bed, hold her hand, and read to her or vividly describe Paris scenes. "What a young and vital place it is," Duse said. "How one envies that happiness!"

At the end of February the company left Egypt for a four-month tour of Spain in Barcelona and Madrid. When she arrived in Barcelona, Duse wrote Boito, "I am a man—(I don't say it to boast) and I have courage and strength—and GOOD SENSE—more than you can imagine—and I have a child that needs me! And you? = You don't need me—no—I feel it—"

Busy with the libretto for *Falstaff,* Boito was also distracted and concerned for his friend Franco Faccio, who was dying from syphilitic dementia. Boito spent a great deal of time with Faccio, and his letters to Duse became shorter and more abrupt, less sensitive to her emotional storms, which Duse, of course, quickly perceived. When Boito suggested they meet in Marseilles, she replied, "I don't have the strength, the good cheer, the health, or the time for such a trip." She stopped writing him for a week, and then apologized and explained. She compared herself to a rabid dog; sometimes the blood rushed to her head and she was overcome with disgust and impatience. Boito joined her briefly, but the reunion was troubled. Following his visit, he wrote that she was "strange."

"*I'm strange,* you say?" Duse replied. "In Barcelona you called me a name that wasn't mine—"

Boito refused to give up Fanny. While he promised he, Duse, and Enrichetta would have a life together, that life was always in some nebulous future, when Duse had stopped working. The hundreds of letters they wrote to each other couldn't bridge the chasm that separated them.

"Art is not worth a single tear," Boito told her. "It's life's great enemy."

For Duse, art *was* life. To stop working, to stop making art, would be death. "I've accepted Russia and America—all—I will accept everything," she said.

ALTHOUGH SHE COMPLAINED about the backward Spanish "swine," the Spanish tour was enormously lucrative and an artistic triumph. For two weeks of work she earned more than a month's work would have yielded in Italy. Tickets for her sold-out performances were scalped at three times their price, and the critics wrote valentines. "She speaks without violence," wrote *El Globo,* "she does not shout, she does not adopt studied postures." The critic for *El País* reported, "When she cries, she genuinely cries . . . the public goes from surprise to surprise . . . her naturalness has no rival."

Her companion, Marthe, returned to Paris at the beginning of May. Duse occupied herself with sightseeing in Madrid. She attended several bullfights, dodged the attentions of a persistent Spanish gentleman who brought her strawberries, and walked in Retiro Park, the only place where "there is a little green." One evening when it was too hot to perform, she went for a stroll with the beautiful daughter of a friend. "It's so sweet," she wrote Boito, "to have a 15-year-old girl on your arm. So sweet."

She spent hours at the Prado Museum, where she studied the paintings as well as the people looking at the pictures, storing up details and impressions. She noticed people liked narrative works best—just like theatre audiences who wanted the familiar five acts with a death, she complained. "The public *(pigs!)* like plot, the *story*, in the picture! Nothing else! They can go to hell!!"

A cholera epidemic struck Spain at the end of June and emptied the theatres. The company hurried to leave the country before a quarantine was imposed. Duse didn't like traveling with her "tribe," and decided to leave them and stop in Paris before going on to Turin. She wrote to Luigi Gualdo in Paris and asked him to be her escort—"with him the hours will be less long," she said. Incognito, she went with him to the Comédie-Française. Afterward, Duse ridiculed the French national theatre. The men "were all hacks," she said, and the actresses "painted dolls," a view she shared with her rival Sarah Bernhardt.

Once, driving past the stage door of the Comédie-Française after a matinee, Bernhardt noticed a large crowd had gathered. She stopped and asked why all the people were there. They're waiting for the actors to come out, she was told. "What for?" said Sarah. "To hiss them?"

Gualdo also took Duse to Marly to meet Dumas *fils* at his home. Gualdo called Duse the "great neurotic" and Dumas the "great skeptic." When they met for the first time, they played the roles of great romantics. When she saw the old author, who had written *Denise* for her, Duse burst into tears. After her visit, as her train pulled out of the station, Dumas held up roses he had cut from his garden and forgotten to give to her. Just in time, she reached from the moving train and grabbed them. When she was safely on a subsequent train to Turin, Gualdo wrote to Giacosa that Duse "is like Paris because her climate is the most changeable in the world." Just between us, he added, there may be complications with the "Russian," suggesting Duse had confided in him about her friendship with Alexander Wolkoff.

AFTER VISITING ENRICHETTA briefly in Turin, Duse rested at a hydrotherapy spa before joining Boito for a few weeks at San Giuseppe. They both were preoccupied and tired. Boito and Verdi were also completing *Falstaff*. In

Alexandre Dumas *fils*

addition to preparing two new plays to add to her repertory, Duse was finalizing plans for her Russian tour.

In September, Duse returned to Barcelona for another short, lucrative season, and Boito made his usual visit to Donna Vittoria Cima on Lake Como. Duse punished him by not writing for a week. When she did write, her letters were short. She spoke of herself as "Lenor" with self-distancing irony, supplying the pauses, so Boito could catch her tone. "Lenor . . . is down," she said, "—and only Lenor can help Lenor." When she returned to Turin to play a season at the Teatro Gerbino, Boito remained in San Giuseppe suffering from a cold. Again, he didn't see her performances of *Antony and Cleopatra*, but this time the play was a hit. "Last night I worked," Duse wrote Boito. "I had 7 lives in my body, in my voice, and, I swear, my hairs stood on end so I could have counted them all just like I felt my blood trill."

Boito was delighted with the success, and couldn't help indulging in a little schadenfreude over the failure of Sarah Bernhardt's *Cléopâtre*, by Sardou, which premiered in Paris on October 23, 1890, Bernhardt's forty-sixth birthday. Like Duse, Bernhardt was preparing for a long tour, and the competitive Bernhardt wanted to imprint her own image on the classic character. Bernhardt painted her face, lined her eyes with thick black, and even colored her palms a "terra-cotta red," so that onstage if "I catch sight of my hand it will be the hand of Cleopatra." When the slave brought her news of Antony's marriage, she stabbed him and then destroyed the set, ripping the Egyptian draperies and smashing vases and goblets. For her writhing death scene, she used a live garter snake, which inspired the French singer Yvette Guilbert to add a number to her concerts called "Sarah's Little Serpent," in which the snake, faced with Sarah's emaciated body, dies of malnutrition.

RESPONDING TO the public's constant demand for new work both in Italy and on her upcoming tour, Duse met with Marco Praga, then twenty-eight, to hear his new play, *La moglie ideale (The Ideal Wife)*. Praga met with Duse in her apartment. Like many actors who tour, Duse had transformed her surroundings into her own personal and familiar world. She covered ugly and unfamiliar furniture with her own fabrics and cushions and decorated her rooms with fresh flowers, favorite books, and mementos.

Often effusive in her writing, in dealing with actors, authors, and businessmen, Duse eliminated social niceties. "Sit there and read," she commanded Praga. She sat with her elbow on the table and her head in her hand and fixed her eyes on him. Too afraid to look at her, Praga read the first act and then waited for her to speak. "Good," Duse said, and told him to rest for five minutes and read the second act. After he read the third act, Duse talked to him for hours, about other plays, actors, and their mutual friends Giacosa, Boito, and Verga. When he was sufficiently relaxed, Duse told him that Giulia, the "ideal wife" in Act I and II, disappeared in Act III. "You see, Praga, if I had to act the play as it is, I would have to find another actress for the third act." Praga went back to his hotel and feverishly wrote a new third act, which he said was "dictated" by her. He sent it off and waited. The next evening he went to the theatre. "I've read it," Duse said. "It's fine." Rehearsals started a week later. Praga stood in a corner and watched Duse explain his text and demonstrate the "correct inflections and appropriate movements and gestures." It was "sheer joy," he recalled.

La moglie ideale opened in Turin on November 11, 1890. The play revolved around a love triangle, but Praga fashioned a satirical twist—Giulia, the ideal wife, is also an ideal mistress. When her lover deserts her to marry someone else, Giulia refuses to succumb to romantic passion. She continues the role of the perfect wife. The themes of betrayal and loyalty, marital hypocrisy, and most of all, the role of the intelligent and duplicitous Giulia appealed to Duse.

The opening-night audience in Turin roared their approval. Like most audiences, they enjoyed seeing their own lives reflected onstage. Wearing the latest Paris fashions, Giulia/Duse was a modern woman, "a woman that we all know," wrote one critic. At the end of the play, Giulia, the only woman in the play, is trapped in a world of men and governed by their rules. From beginning to end, little has changed.

THE SECOND NEW PLAY Duse added to her repertory was Henrik Ibsen's *Casa di bambola (A Doll's House).* In her continuous search for a writer who could speak for her, Duse had read Ibsen in French translations. Ibsen's plays, with their deceptively real surfaces underlaid with metaphor and symbolism, excited her as an actor, an impresario, and as a woman. Ibsen's plays questioned the very foundations of society and the relationship between men and women. "It's the soul not the drama that he tries to give us," Duse believed.

Ibsen never saw his greatest interpreter act in his plays, but she was the kind of actor his plays required. In Munich on January 31, Ibsen had attended the world premiere of *Hedda Gabler* with Marie Ramlo acting the title role in the traditional, declamatory manner. The play failed. Four years earlier, he had advised a young actress: "No declamation! No theatricalities! No grand mannerisms! Express every mood in a manner that will seem credible and natural. Never think of this or that actress whom you may have seen. Observe the life that is going on around you, and present a real and living human being."

Boito had dismissed Ibsen as "an old Norwegian pharmacist." They pretend to enjoy him in Paris, he told Duse, but "it's not possible that you like him." Duse knew Boito had been wrong before. He had advised Puccini against *La Bohème* and didn't bother to come to the opening of Verga's *Cavalleria rusticana* because he thought it would fail. Duse disregarded Boito's opinion.

It's logical to assume that as Duse worked on the character of Nora in *A Doll's House* and analyzed Nora's struggle to become a human being, she drew parallels with her own life. (Ibsen liked to point out the character is called "Nora" because it's the affectionate, childish diminutive of her real name, Eleonora.) In November and December 1890, while she was preparing *A Doll's House,* Duse and Boito wrote short letters and saw each other only briefly. Duse's pet names—*piccoletta, chierichetto, bumba*—disappear from their correspondence. Boito had failed her as a man and as a writer, and from

Padua, just before she went to perform in her grandfather Luigi Duse's theatre, Duse wrote him, "I work—I think of nothing but *working*." When Boito proposed a short, secret visit to Venice, Duse told him, "I prefer nothing to a little." "Don't write to me," she said, and to make sure he obeyed, she didn't enclose her address. "Lenor knows how to write words that cause suffering," Boito responded.

In December in Venice, Duse visited her friend the Countess Sophie Drechsel and "untied" her heart. She also had long talks with Alexander Wolkoff. They shared their grief over the loss of Matilde Acton, and Wolkoff advised her on her upcoming tour to Russia. With Wolkoff, Duse also milked the role of a helpless artist who didn't understand business. "Try to keep an account of, and write down, your expenses," he advised. "For the present, you must think of nothing but making money, so as to have a reserve. If you fall ill, what on earth will you do with your company?"

"Yes, yes," Duse smiled. "You are right."

"By the nature of that smile," Wolkoff said, "I saw that if left alone without being continually looked after by some devoted friend, she would always remain without a cent." Never mind that Duse and her administrator Alberto Buffi had been managing her finances for years—Duse longed for someone to take care of her. She knew Wolkoff's Russian contacts and his friendship would be invaluable. Also, he had been Matilde Acton's lover and friend, and Duse enjoyed his conversation and his company. Wolkoff scathingly dismissed Boito as mediocre, both as a man and as an artist. How could a man who had the love of a woman like Duse love another? he asked her.

On February 9, 1891, at the Teatro Filodrammatici in Milan, Duse presented *A Doll's House*. She had given her audiences Giulia, Praga's "ideal" wife; now she presented them with Nora, a wife and mother who evolved into a genuine human being. The two characters, even their names, represented the two women Duse felt herself to be (her name, of course, was Eleonora Giulia)—one who wanted the safety and security of a man's protection, and the other who wanted to fulfill her own destiny. Duse asked herself and her audiences, which woman was "ideal." *A Doll's House* was a daring professional choice, economically smart (ticket prices were doubled), and a personal, defiant gesture aimed at Arrigo Boito. She wasn't his *piccoletta* or his *chierichetto* or his *bumba*. She was a thirty-two-year-old woman, his equal, and determined, she told him, "not to waste one more day of my life."

At the premiere, despite muttering disagreement in the audience during the final discussion scene between Nora and Torvald, the *Corriere della Sera* called Duse's performance "perfection," and *A Doll's House* a "great artistic event" and a "true triumph," not of applause but of "intimacy and of deep feeling."

As Nora in Ibsen's *A Doll's House*. Duse wore a heavy
necklace holding the Helmer household keys,
the chain to her domestic life. Early 1890s

Psychologist Laura Hansson saw Duse play *A Doll's House* a few years later. Duse entered as Nora, wearing a faded, red blouse, "a pale, unhealthy-looking woman, with a very quiet manner," Hansson wrote. "She examines her purse thoughtfully, and before paying the servant she pauses involuntarily, as poor people usually do before they spend money." She sat on the floor and played with the children, "without any real gayety, as grown-up people are in the habit of playing when their thoughts are otherwise occupied." Hansson observed that Duse "has the dreadful sensation that a human being has nothing but minutes, minutes; that there is nothing lasting to rely on; that we swim across dark waters from yesterday until tomorrow."

FROM MILAN, Duse's company moved to Rome for a brief season before traveling to Russia. In Rome, Count Primoli introduced her to Sabatino Lopez. "My God," she said, looking him up and down, "not another play-wright!" When one of her performances was cancelled, Lopez went to her hotel and asked if she would meet with him. Since Lopez was also a theatre critic, Duse seized the opportunity to add another advocate to her art and invited him to her room and asked him to talk to her for an hour. They spoke of the books Duse was reading—Tolstoy, Dostoevsky, and Ibsen. When Duse talked, Lopez savored the enchantment of her voice, "slightly nasal, yet incomparably sweet, insinuating, and caressing, so seductive that I closed my eyes to continue to feel all her charm."

Duse also met Velleda Ferretti in Rome, part of "*your* circle," she told Boito. "I didn't like her much—and if I saw her again I'd be bored, and if I saw her a lot I would end up hating her the way I hate everything around you [. . .] How I detest all of you! It makes my blood boil."

When Boito suggested he travel from Milan to Rome to say good-bye, Duse replied, "I don't need to kiss you, to revive love. No . . . no—the anguish is deeper—and *doesn't come from the lips.*" She had a lot to do, she told him, performances of *A Doll's House,* business appointments, and Alexander Wolkoff, just back from a trip to Cairo, was in town for two days and wanted to introduce her to the Russian colony in Rome. "I promised *Wolkoff* that I'd *come out of my shell,*" she said. If Boito had scrutinized Duse's letters as carefully as she read his, her emphasis would have been perfectly clear.

At first, Duse told Wolkoff she couldn't love him, but as their affair pro-gressed, she grew to love him, mostly because she needed him, and he loved her. Her affair with Wolkoff would consist of infrequent meetings and dozens of letters and telegrams from January 1891 until November 1892. Unlike her liaison with Boito, her relationship with Wolkoff would remain secret and completely unknown to Duse biographers. Except for a few, Duse's letters to Wolkoff were destroyed, but his letters to her were discovered in 1986 in a travel bag packed in cartons belonging to the Austrian Countess Christiane Thun-Salm. Duse had given them to Countess Thun-Salm for safekeeping before one of her American tours and had never picked them up.

Boito and Wolkoff, both in their late forties, were Duse's lovers and teach-ers, but their love and their teachings couldn't have been more different. Duse had idealized Boito both as an artist and a man, and he had fallen from his pedestal. While Boito had contempt for the theatre, Wolkoff gloried in her

Artist Alexander Wolkoff,
Duse's Russian lover

work and her celebrity. Boito excluded Duse from his aristocratic circle, and the married Wolkoff welcomed her into his world in Venice, Rome, and Russia with generosity and warmth. Boito didn't help Duse with her work and didn't want to hear about vulgar business details. Wolkoff eagerly offered his financial expertise as well as his public relations skills. With Boito, Duse had clung to the hope of a home and family, but Wolkoff scorned such a bourgeois dream. That kind of life, he said, "is constructed to kill love." Duse's talent placed her above "stupid, brutal and hypocritical society," Wolkoff instructed. "In my imagination I see you great. Above the wretched masses of the little ones. There where others would be touched—you have made a mortal leap above them." Wolkoff made no promises of a shared life. His intentions were clear—a wonderful love affair for as long as it lasted. Their Roman holiday "was like a dream," he told her. "Each minute, each movement, each silence—like an entire life in two days."

"Love! Love!" Duse wrote to Boito from Rome, then stopped herself. "*No*—it's wrenching heartbreak—."

Distance, new scenes, and fresh faces are time-honored antidotes for heartbreak, but for Duse there was only one sure remedy—*lavoro*. "I want to meet my work with all my strength." With her "tribe" of twenty-three actors (nine women, including the young Emma Gramatica, and twelve men, plus her leading man Andò and her first "Romeo" Carlo Rosaspina) and all the paraphernalia of the theatre—sets, furniture, props, costumes—her suitcases, and trunks of books, Duse boarded the train that ran "straight for Munich and Berlin," with no stop in Boito's Milan. After a day's rest in Berlin, the Compagnia della Città di Roma traveled into Russia and their first engagement, at the Maly Theatre in St. Petersburg, the Venice of the North.

Four

"TODAY I AM STILL very tired from the journey," Duse wrote Wolkoff when she arrived in St. Petersburg. "My health is good and my mind is clear, only I find the world too big, and *life too useless.*" Wolkoff had arranged for an apartment for her and her maid, "two beautiful rooms and they are so warm!—so warm!" Duse exclaimed. "One must be an Italian to realize the great joy of a room in which one does not continually shiver." "Thank you for your goodness to me," she told him. "You don't know how much of my courage I owe to you." She had bought a little book "where I shall enter *all my expenses*. But if money goes," she teased, "what is the good *of writing it down? What is the good* of giving oneself all that trouble?"

Duse's company opened in St. Petersburg on March 12, 1891, with *La Dame aux camélias*. Although she was promoted as a famous actress in her short biography, which was distributed along with her photograph at the theatre, she was unknown in Russia. Duse knew St. Petersburg primarily from Tolstoy's novels. A port city on the banks of the Neva River with spacious streets and canals, the city also had a large Italian immigrant population, mostly involved in the arts and architecture.

When Duse opened her season, audiences had their choice of art and entertainment—Ciniselli's Circus, operas from Italy and France, an Austrian theatre company led by the brilliant young actor Joseph Kainz, and a French company headed by Lucien Guitry, the most handsome young leading man in Paris. On opening night, Duse looked out at a half-empty theatre.

St. Petersburg would set a pattern for Duse's conquest of other cities. Advance sales would be slow and the first performances sparsely attended. Then, through word-of-mouth and reviews, by the end of her stay, audiences would clamor for tickets. Alexey Suvorin, the editor of *The New Times* and the most important critic in St. Petersburg, observed that life was Duse's

school. "Her simplicity is the fruit of extreme complexity . . . She doesn't ges-
ticulate or declaim . . . she creates her characters, makes them live with a simplicity never before seen on the stage," Suvorin wrote. "She justifies every
slight gesture or movement with interior motivation."

Suvorin's friend Anton Chekhov, who blamed the recent failure of his play
Ivanov on bad acting, wrote to his sister after seeing Duse on Monday, March
16, in *Antony and Cleopatra*: "I don't understand Italian, but she played so
beautifully that I had the feeling that I understood every word . . . I've never
seen anything like it. Watching Duse, I was overcome by depression from the
thought that we have to form our reactions and taste on such wooden
actresses . . . Looking at Duse, I realized why the Russian theatre is such a
bore."

Believing actors can "learn something even from the worst Italian
ranters," Joseph Kainz, then thirty-two, accompanied by Hermann Bahr, an
ambitious twenty-seven-year-old Viennese critic, saw Duse on Tuesday,
March 24, in *La Femme de Claude*. Bahr, part of Jung-Wien, a literary circle
that included Hugo von Hofmannsthal and Arthur Schnitzler, recalled during the performance, "Kainz clutched my arm and gripped it hard . . . quite
unprepared, without warning, without the slightest idea of what to expect,
suddenly to be caught up by Duse . . . suddenly to be confronted with Duse,
to see Duse for the first time—what that means is beyond any power of
words to express."

Later, when Bahr returned to Vienna, he found the words for his response
and published the article in the *Frankfurter Zeitung*. Throughout his life as a
critic, playwright, director, and theatre theorist, Bahr, like many critics who
wrote about Duse, would use her art as an inspiration and a springboard to
shape his own aesthetic. During his career as a writer, he moved from roman-
ticism and naturalism into mysticism and symbolism. He divided actors into
two types—those who transformed, like Duse, and those who played only
themselves, like Sarah Bernhardt. Later, he would link the transformative
power of the actor to his theory that to remain modern one had to stay flexible and in tune with the time.

On a night off from performing, French actor Lucien Guitry saw Duse in
Antony and Cleopatra. "From the moment she entered the stage until the curtain fell," he said, "she played everything, because for her it was impossible
not to play all." While many actors at this time hurried through a play and
stopped at important scenes to make dramatic points, Duse did not, Guitry
recalled. "In the last act . . . a slave presented to the Queen of Egypt, who was
seated on a heap of cushions, a little basket of exotic flowers. Under these
flowers was the asp . . . Quite simply she took the asp in one hand, and with
the other she opened her bodice, then threw the serpent on her breast, closing

again her dress with both hands. This action took about two seconds, but in that short space of time there was a long monologue which one could not have written in ten pages—regret, dread, memories of the past, hope, the possibility of escaping from her fate, the vision of her tomb, the funeral procession. 'What does the asp do? It moves . . . Is it going to sting? Is this a happy thing? Is this deliverance?' . . . And then suddenly the sting, a swift look of agony, a shudder . . . It is the end; she is dead."

From March 12 to April 29, Duse gave twenty-one performances in St. Petersburg of twelve plays—Boito's adaptations of *Antony and Cleopatra* and *Romeo and Juliet*, Goldoni's *Pamela* and *La locandiera*—and eight other plays were divided between Sardou and Dumas *fils*. *La Dame aux camélias* and *Antony and Cleopatra*, with four performances each, were the most popular. All of her performances in St. Petersburg were successful, but "my greatest success here," she wrote Wolkoff, "was with my representation of Cleopatra." She also thanked Wolkoff for introducing her to various society ladies who had been good to her. Duse is a perfect artist, Princess Wolkonsky told Wolkoff, and "as an individual pre-eminent! To see her play is an incredible enjoyment . . . and I love her for life!"

St. Petersburg society and the Italian community turned out for Duse's benefit on Wednesday, April 22. She chose to play *Romeo and Juliet*. The evening ended in torrents of applause and a stage covered with flowers. Duse was presented with a stream of gifts—the usual bouquets, jewels, a crown of gold from the Italian colony, but also a most unusual world globe made out of plants—the north was moss, the south was laurel leaves, and at the equator, twelve white *E*s encircled the globe, symbolizing "the immortal E. Duse embraces the world." Afterward, the street to her hotel was covered with flowers.

As she had with Boito, Duse bombarded Wolkoff with letters and telegrams as a way of untying her heart and comforting herself. "You know Lenor," Wolkoff counseled, after receiving one of her long letters, "do something. Occupy yourself with something and you will be content. Write about your life. Your impressions. A novel. A novella. Whatever you want. Your work in the evenings is not enough. Read something proper not always these dumb novels. Read for eg. the letters of Wagner and Liszt. It was the last favorite book of M. [Matilde Acton] . . . You're so original and clever. It will do you good and then we'll read it together in Moscow . . . I kiss your feet, nothing more—not even your knees, just your feet." After receiving a furious letter from Duse accusing him of saying he wasn't coming to Russia, Wolkoff struggled as Boito had with her intense scrutiny of his every word. "But no," he explained, "it's just that I'm not free now. How did you understand this sentence?" After a flurry of expensive telegrams, they arranged to meet in

Moscow in May. "I press you to my heart, Eleonora," Wolkoff wrote. "Don't make me too mad from happiness."

On May 4, Duse opened in Moscow at the Korsh Theatre with *La Dame aux camélias.* Just as opera fans went again and again to see Verdi's *La traviata* (based on *La Dame aux camélias*) and discussed the merits of Adelina Patti and Nellie Melba, who sang Violetta, theatre audiences in the late–nineteenth century saw the Dumas *fils* play many times and relished comparing the performances of Bernhardt and Duse and others who attempted the part. Duse's genius was in rethinking and redefining a role that had belonged to Sarah Bernhardt. Since Bernhardt, who was fourteen years older than Duse, was also on a world tour at this time, critics often compared the two women. "She doesn't restrict herself to acting a Parisian," wrote one critic. "She gives us a woman. She reads between the lines of Dumas's script and plays a character deeper and fuller than the one created by Bernhardt." Moscow's most important critic, Vyacheslav Ivanov, said, "I've never seen such excitement in a Moscow theatre. For the first time I understood how poetry could be transformed into the most pure and authentic reality."

A young actor and director, Konstantin Alekseiev, then twenty-eight, who had taken the stage name Stanislavsky so as not to embarrass his wealthy, bourgeois family, made a practice of studying foreign actors. In 1891, when Duse performed in Moscow for the first time, Stanislavsky had just begun directing plays. He had been heavily influenced by Germany's Duke of Saxe-Meiningen Company, which had toured Russia in April 1890 performing Shakespeare and Schiller. The Saxe-Meiningen Company emphasized ensemble playing (with particular attention to integrating extras and crowd scenes into the action), historically accurate sets and costumes, and well-timed lighting and sound cues. The productions ran with precision, but the acting was nondescript.

Stanislavsky had been particularly impressed by the acting of Ernesto Rossi and Tommaso Salvini, part of an earlier generation of Italian actors, but when he and his young contemporaries saw Duse, they realized she was different. What Stanislavsky yearned to replicate in the acting of Duse and Salvini was a "physical freedom, in the lack of all strain. Their bodies were at . . . the inner demands of their wills."

Stanislavsky envied actors like Salvini and Duse, "but not a single artist will ever betray his secrets," he realized.

"If there is no great master near you whom you can trust," Ernesto Rossi told him, "I can recommend only one teacher."

"Who is he?" asked Stanislavsky.

"You yourself," Rossi replied.

From May 2 to May 20, Duse gave only nine performances during her first

Stanislavsky in 1898

appearance in Moscow, but her influence on Stanislavsky was incalculable. Along with Stanislavsky, two student actresses, Nadezda Smirnova and Marina Krestovskaja, returned again and again to study her. They were struck by Duse's ability to communicate without words, her freedom of movement, her sensitive use of props, her lack of makeup, and her "strange costumes." Made of soft fabrics like silk, chiffon, and fine wool, her clothes rippled and flowed over her body. In *La Dame aux camélias*, she wore only different shades of white, and without a corset, she could "curl up like a cat" on the sofa, or stretch full length with her arms over her head, even cross her legs like a man. On her unpainted face, Smirnova said, every fleeting expression and color of emotion could be clearly seen. Krestovskaja, who saw Duse act many times, said, "her best performance was always the one she gave 'that day' . . . and there was always something new and unexpected."

After one performance, overcome with emotion, Krestovskaja remained in her seat close to the stage. An Italian actor came out and told her Duse would like to see her in her dressing room. "Why were you crying?" Duse asked in French. "Because you're leaving," Krestovskaja said.

Duse in Russia, 1891

"I'll return soon," Duse replied. After learning Krestovskaja was an actress, Duse told her to write if she ever needed help. When Duse left Moscow, Krestovskaja accompanied her to the railroad station. Give your mother my thanks and gratitude, Duse said. Why? asked Krestovskaja. "For permitting her daughter to accompany an actress!" Duse said. Throughout her life, Duse would reach out to women, particularly to cultivated women and to young actresses. Her shame over her exclusion from society as a child had left her with a hunger for acceptance into a society that had rejected her. All her life, she would strive to elevate her profession to a high and respected art.

Once, years later, Colette saw Duse in Rome accepting homage from a crowd of admirers. "She did not smile, but presented her brow to them as though it were a defensive wall; and the little nose, offended now, was quivering with disdain. 'Look,' the Italian woman with me whispered, 'look what a *lady* she is!' " Offstage, Duse swathed herself in cloaks, veils, and gloves, usually in dark colors. Once, when she thought the young Russian Krestovskaja's street clothes were too flamboyant, Duse advised, "An actress must not attract attention when she's not on the stage . . . an actress must pass through life unobserved."

STILL, WHEREVER SHE TRAVELED, Duse attracted attention. Wolkoff joined her for a tour of Kharkhov, Kiev, and Odessa in southern Russia during June. Again, she was greeted with cheering audiences, standing ovations, stages covered with flowers, and extensive newspaper coverage. At the railroad station in Kharkhov, a crowd gathered around her and a young man asked how Duse took hold of people, "by the heart, the mind or the soul?" Wolkoff translated the question. Duse told him to answer for her. "Madame takes hold by all three," Wolkoff replied.

In August, Duse vacationed with Enrichetta in Tegernsee with Countess Sophie Drechsel, who was helping find Enrichetta a school in Germany. From Bayreuth, where she saw a performance of Wagner's *Parsifal,* Duse wrote Boito about the problems she was having with a teary, sulky, nine-year-old Enrichetta, who recoiled from every new face. She had always used sweet words with Enrichetta, she claimed. Sometimes she wondered if she should be firmer with her, but she simply wasn't capable of it right now. "The joys of motherhood!!!" she exclaimed. "How people who've never been through it love to sing about it! Incredible!!"

Despite the close and loving ties she had had with her own mother, Duse was not a good mother to Enrichetta. The pain of the fictional women Duse played was more real to her than the anguish of her flesh-and-blood daughter. Separated from her mother for months at a time, Enrichetta suffered from

Enrichetta, about age nine, c. 1890

loneliness and emotional neglect. Duse had been a self-sufficient child who enjoyed the constant physical presence of her mother, and she couldn't understand her daughter's need. From Enrichetta's birth, when she had been packed off to a wet nurse, then to boarding school, mother and daughter had had long separations and never formed a strong bond. Duse justified her separation from her daughter as a way to give Enrichetta an education and turn her into a lady while removing her from the "taint" of the theatre. Consumed by her drive to take her art around the world, Duse didn't have time for a daughter, who was growing up and thus was a constant reminder to Duse of her own age.

With Boito there had been a slight hope for a different kind of life, with a man to take care of her and Enrichetta, but that hope seemed to have vanished. From Turin on October 12, 1891, Duse wrote Boito a cryptic letter.

"Yes—" Duse wrote, "above every thing—It was more than life." There's a tone of regret and loss in the letter, and no hint of her relationship with another man. "What I've passed through in these months!" Duse said. "I know that I was dying." Perhaps she and Boito met after one of her performances of Giacosa's *La Signora di Challant* at the Teatro Carignano, but in 1892 and 1893, which overlaps with her love affair with Wolkoff, Duse and Boito were estranged, and there are no extant letters between them.

IN LATE DECEMBER 1891, since her first Russian tour had proved financially and artistically successful, Duse, accompanied by Wolkoff, returned to Russia. Again she played at the Maly Theatre in St. Petersburg. "One day when we were looking from the window of the hotel," Wolkoff recalled, "we saw a man drawing a coffin along on a little sledge. 'My father is dead!' Duse cried. 'I know it!' On the same day, and with sorrow in her soul, she had to play. Then she received the letter."

Alessandro Duse had died in his sleep in Venice on January 11, 1892. Performances were cancelled for three days while Duse mourned her father. "I had never seen such agony of sorrow; her cries and tears never ceased," Wolkoff wrote. "She remembered her childhood, her youth, the modesty and humility of her father—his life of poverty and his passion for her."

"Well, what is the use of speaking of it?" Duse said. "Not to have him any more!—I alone know what I have lost."

For her final performance in Moscow, Duse played the role her Moscow audiences liked best, Nora in *A Doll's House.* Years later, Duse advised a young French actress on playing the role. Duse's notes to the actress revealed her own preparation, and her ability to turn action into metaphor. As Nora, Duse wore a heavy chain necklace, which held the household keys, a symbol of her life as wife and mother. "Take it slowly, don't hurry and you'll soon find yourself on the edge of the stage, look straight ahead, your eyes, no longer sad and tormented, no longer searching for anything but for yourself within yourself! So then, slowly, if you like, take off your beautiful earrings, slowly, without moving, take off your necklace too, I'll send it to you, and undo the knot that holds your self together, your life, holding your length and breadth."

Of all the great Noras he had seen, the critic Maurice Baring recalled, the "image of Nora that remains with me to this day is the infinitely disillusioned face of Duse, the desperate irony of her disenchanted voice, expressing an irony beyond all bitterness, when Torvald, realising that he is safe in the eyes of the world, cried: 'I'm saved!' and she quietly said: 'And I?' "

TÄNCZER, A VIENNESE IMPRESARIO, had read Hermann Bahr's article about Duse, and he had noted her artistic and box-office success in Russia. He convinced Duse to bring her company to Vienna for four performances at the unfashionable Karl Theatre. Duse, of course, would have preferred to play at Vienna's Burgtheater, which was considered the finest theatre in the German world. But she was unknown in Vienna, which had a flourishing theatre and cultural life. As usual, she opened with *La Dame aux camélias*. Only the first rows of the theatre had been sold, and, as she had at her first performance in St. Petersburg, Duse looked out on many empty seats. Bahr's article and word-of-mouth, however, had brought some important critics and writers to the Karl Theatre.

Everyone in the Karl Theatre that first night felt a witness to something new, critic Hugo Wittman recalled. "A new sun had risen on the stage itself," he wrote. "Duse possessed a peculiar—I might say physiological—quality I could never explain. When she had to produce a supreme effect . . . she drew a sort of misty veil across her features, and it seemed as if her hair stood on end and her face was half obscured by the fog of her inner emotion. God knows how she did it . . . it was unstudied, absolutely natural . . . a histrionic gift from heaven that she had disciplined and developed by incessant practice and made exquisitely responsive to the mood she would express, to every shade of feeling, until it was a perfect instrument in her hands. Yes, that was modern art . . . yet entirely free of any modernism . . . whoever seeks to be modern—merely modern—ceases to be an individual, and certainly ceases to be an artist."

While Wittman saw modern art in Duse's acting, Hugo von Hofmannsthal compared her Vienna debut to the ancient Great Dionysia in Athens. Duse had a profound, almost religious, influence on the eighteen-year-old Hofmannsthal, who had excited Vienna two years earlier with his first published poems. "Duse struck chords in us only rarely touched by an artist, and then only by one who tears himself wide open," he wrote. "She interprets what is between the lines of the play . . . With a trembling of her lips, with a movement of her shoulders, with a modulation of her voice, she paints the evolution of a decision, the swift untangling of a chain of thought, the interior psychological-physical event that precedes the formation of a word."

Today, of course, this kind of acting—thinking the thoughts of the character and revealing inner life through the body—is the goal of all serious actors, who have been trained in methods inspired by Duse's pioneering work. Duse's art, while it shaped theatre acting in the twentieth century, was also important in developing a technique that was necessary for film.

Duse's acting, like the film acting of Chaplin, Pickford, and Gish, transcended national boundaries. "For her the whole world was the same," remarked the impresario Joseph Schürmann, "the same theatre, the same audience. Audiences in tears everywhere, and the people suffered along with her." As Schürmann suggested, Duse's audiences, despite the differences of language, culture, class, and geography, *were* all the same to her. Her style was "ourselves," observed one critic. "It's our era, our tense, weary high-strung, groping, restless age."

It was almost as if the zeitgeist had willed her into being. In refusing to wear wigs and makeup and corset, Duse stood metaphorically naked in front of her audiences. At the same time Freud was developing his theories of the unconscious, and Ibsen was exploring the unconscious in his plays, Duse was giving flesh to those ideas onstage. The era's harsh new electrical lighting illuminated every nuance of her acting, which was startling, disturbing, new—artistic and erotic. Her tears and her rare, melting smile pierced the heart. Beneath our surface differences, Duse believed, we share a common human core, and she communicated that truth through the medium of the theatre and the women she portrayed. Her acting never went out of fashion because it addressed the big questions—What does it mean to be alive? Who are we?

Duse projected exquisite subtlety into a theatre audience of thousands. Acting is being, Duse believed, and art like hers required intensive study, imagination, and concentration, and for this reason she always had contempt for actors who relied on intuition and inspiration of the moment. "This is how I work in my room," Duse explained to the French actress Georgette Le Blanc. "I construct the entire character in my mind, and it's there, in silence and solitude, that I bring it to life. Sitting in an armchair or lying in my bed, eyes closed, I evoke the whole role, the whole play. And what I want to avoid more than anything else is repetition."

"She lived her role with such truth that there seemed no distance between the soul of the heroine she was playing and the deepest part of her own soul," Le Blanc observed. Yet, Duse's "double self"—the character she played and the persona of "La Duse"—were always present. "Even when she appeared to completely forget her own individuality," Le Blanc reported, "I always sensed that mysterious current of sadness that emanated from her and that anguished me to tears."

Critics and other artists marveled at Duse's ability to reinvent the character and not repeat herself night after night. Once, asked if she always played a role in the same way, Duse said, "Naturally, I have a general picture of the role, but the details change depending upon my mood and the sensations of the day."

Duse's success in Vienna was her first European triumph. As her acting matured, she also solidified her La Duse persona, which set her apart even more from her great rival, Sarah Bernhardt. Paul Schlenther, a theatre director and drama critic, observed Duse closely during her Vienna performances. Since Duse refused to give interviews, he told his readers, he didn't know "whether she is silent or talkative, whether she is 'nice,' to whom and how long she has been married, what skeleton she keeps in her closet and what are her favorite dishes. Outside of her roles I have seen her only when, at the close of each act . . . the continuous roar of applause made the curtain rise again and again, and she stood before us, holding the hand of her associate Andò . . . her slight shoulders wrapped in a cloak (her favorite garment), her lithe figure leaning slightly to one side . . . No self-conscious smile of thanks, but on the other hand, no naïve joy in success . . . at times, with an upward movement of her long, delicate hands, she would run her fingers, as she is fond of doing while acting, through her wavy black hair, which she invariably wears drawn up in a simple Grecian knot." In other words, La Duse refused to beg for applause like a common little actress or even to accept accolades as her due like Bernhardt. Wrapped in her cloak of mystery, La Duse preferred to remain unknowable.

In all of her roles, Schlenther observed, even in the hollow Sardou plays, Duse brought something human into the theatrical sensationalism. "And the shades of her emotion are evident," he said, "even when she turns her back to the public." The final impression Schlenther took away from every one of her performances was "A human being!" His exclamation mark is telling. Anna Karenina, Madame Bovary, Dorothea Brooke existed in novels as complete human characters, but in 1892 to present a woman as a human being onstage was revolutionary.

Schlenther was also describing a sea change in the history of acting. Bernhardt was always aware of herself as an actress being watched by an audience. Bernhardt's technique, which had turned Sardou's melodramas into box-office bonanzas, was at odds, however, with the new dramaturgy. Bernhardt never acted Nora in *A Doll's House,* for example, but she and Duse both played Magda in Hermann Sudermann's *Heimat (Homeland),* called *Casa paterna* in Italian and *Magda* in English. Later, Bernhardt admitted she had tried many times to succeed in the role, but she had always failed. It was one of Duse's great triumphs. In the last decade of the nineteenth century, when Duse acted Sudermann's play, she embodied in her performance and her interpretation of the text a radical new view of woman.

TALL, WITH AN ENORMOUS, cartoonish beard, Sudermann had begun writing short stories after his first trip to Italy in 1889. His third play, *Magda,* which dealt with the difficulties faced by a woman with a profession in a patriarchal society, enjoyed productions around the world and is considered Sudermann's best work. Magda, a famous opera singer, returns to her home after a long absence. She wants to reconcile with her estranged father. Years earlier, though, she had a secret affair with Herr von Keller, a local aristocrat. When Magda became pregnant, Keller abandoned her, and Magda raised the child on her own. Her father and her former lover both are willing to accept Magda, but at a great price. Keller says he'll marry her, but only if she gives up her child. At the end of the play, when her father demands she submit to his authority, stop working, and marry her former lover, Magda rebels. "Do you know whether I am worthy of him?" Magda says. "Do you know whether he was the only one—." The father shouts "Harlot!" grabs a pistol to shoot her, and then has a seizure and dies. Clearly, returning home for an independent woman is fraught with peril, but instead of being punished for her actions, symbolically at least, Magda kills the men who try to repress her.

When Duse played Magda in Berlin in December 1892, Sudermann was in the audience. "My Magda comes to life," he enthused to his wife. "Try to imagine an ideal Magda and then add thousands upon thousands of little surprises and insights . . . The scene with her father sent a chill through everyone in the audience, and the death scene, which was a miracle of understatement, defies description."

On December 4, 1892, in response to Sudermann, who had written her a congratulatory note, Duse pointed out the gap between her life and his fictional Magda. "Your Magda has worked 10 years?" she said. "The woman who writes to you has worked 20. The difference is enormous, if you take into account that unlike Magda this actress is counting the days until she can leave the theatre. Magda lived at home till 17. The woman who writes to you had nothing like this. At 14 she was put in long skirts and told 'You must act.' That's a big difference between us. Besides, Magda is your creation and belongs to you, the other lives and wears clothes like everybody else. But she is scrupulous to thank you because it was thanks to your *Casa paterna* that she has the duty to perform tonight." Like Magda, Duse also had been abandoned by a lover and had had an illegitimate child, but Magda had raised her child, while Duse's son had died—another difference. Duse seemed to be asking Sudermann, Where's my life? Where's my story? Who will witness my struggles?

AFTER FIVE YEARS of hard work and responsibility, the pressures of running her own company were beginning to tell on Duse. "I've had enough— more than enough—of the Theatre," Duse confessed to her friend and advisor Alexandre Ouroussov, a Russian lawyer and critic, on December 1,

1892. "I hope I can give it up next year." She had written to him for advice about a potential lawsuit, and she outlined her situation. "I'm in a very selfish phase of my soul," Duse explained to Ouroussov, "because this damned Theatre has so worn down my true sensitivity that I no longer suffer for anyone, and this is a vileness that eats at me—and if I'm unable to love anyone in this low world, I prefer to leave it as soon as possible. 'Before dying I would like to do some good.' But how—and where—there's the rub. All is falsified around us—and everything that makes us act and speak is only self-love! This is not enough—how can we get out of this blind alley? How to overcome the nausea that 'charity' instills in my soul. I know not, and I'm uneasy. As for business, I will tell you that apart from the 19,000 rubles which I have placed you know where, I have nothing set aside for my daughter."

After Russia and Vienna, she hadn't worked from June to October 1891, but she still had to pay her company. She also had spent 15,000 francs (and another 150,000 francs "have flown away!") to furnish an apartment for herself in Wolkoff's house in Venice, which was most likely the "charity" she was referring to in her letter to Ouroussov. Wolkoff's children had moved to Russia, leaving the top floor of his house available. When Duse wasn't on tour, she lived in the Wolkoff palazzo in an apartment with a separate entrance.

In 1893, Wolkoff painted Duse in watercolors. In one portrait, clearly the work of a worshipful lover, the head and shoulders view is lovely but not soft. Wolkoff wanted "above all to reproduce the unique expression of her eyes." No background detracts from Duse's strong, bare face and half-closed eyes, which radiate strength and power. She looks down on the viewer with a melancholy, all-knowing, yet decidedly intimate expression.

DESPITE HER CLAIM to want to give up the theatre, Duse continued her campaign to conquer the world city by city. Impressed with Duse's box-office earnings in Vienna and Berlin, the impresario Tänczer, in partnership with Americans Carl and Theodor Rosenfield, quickly arranged a tour for her in the United States. When she arrived in New York in January 1893, Duse was shocked by the "confusion of streetcars, motor vehicles, warehouses, skyscrapers" and wanted to return to Italy. The Rosenfields were savvy producers, and had booked Duse into a New York season that prior to her arrival, one critic wrote, "was so barren of promise." Edwin Booth, the greatest American actor of the nineteenth century, who had played Iago to Salvini's Othello and Macbeth to Ristori's Lady Macbeth, was worn out and dying.

In striking contrast to the publicity hoopla generated by Sarah Bernhardt's first visit to America in 1880, Duse slipped quietly into New York on her first visit and checked in to the Murray Hill Hotel. There *was* a publicity

Duse as her lover Wolkoff painted her

campaign on Duse's behalf, but it was so subtle the public believed Duse was a great artist above such vulgar manipulation. When a reporter who spoke Italian followed Duse into her hotel elevator, she turned on him: "Sir, I do not know you, neither do I wish to know you. I have received no callers up to now, and my desire is to receive nobody. On Monday night I shall appear in public, and I will be seen upon the stage. Away from that I do not exist." The reporter, naturally, published an account of their meeting. Duse's novel policy of restricting reporters' access created a sensation and resulted, of course, in curiosity and even more coverage of her acting.

Her society friends also worked behind the scenes, and society opened its doors to Duse—the same doors it had kept closed to Sarah Bernhardt for "fear of being tainted by her old-world depravity, her being a Jew, and her shameless love of publicity." Duse's Venetian friend Katherine de Kay Bronson had arranged for Duse to meet her sister, Helena de Kay Gilder, wife of Richard Watson Gilder. The Gilders were at the pinnacle of New York social and artistic life. Richard Gilder, a close friend of President Grover Cleveland, was the editor of *The Century Magazine.* His sister Jeannette Gilder was a brilliant journalist and founder of *The Critic,* and had been the first in her circle to shed the hoop skirt and wear a man's shirt and coat. The Gilders hosted informal Friday receptions at their Clinton Place home for prominent New York friends and for visiting artists like Paderewski, Kipling, and Sargent. Mingling with the people who controlled the press was much more effective than talking with mere reporters.

The Gilders' daughter Rosamond, who later became the editor of *Theatre Arts Monthly* and a noted theatre scholar, described the bond between her mother and Duse, who communicated in French: "It was as though twin souls had met and spoken." Duse would form many such intimate friendships. Even though she had come from abject poverty and Helena Gilder from wealth and privilege, each woman had something the other one wanted—Duse longed for a stable home and family life, and Helena Gilder envied the free life of an artist. Duse "came and went in my mother's house," Rosamond Gilder remembered, "a lovely, graceful figure of trailing lines and bubbling laughter. She appeared at odd hours and in every possible mood, strolling in for a cup of tea at two o'clock in the morning, spending an afternoon curled up in the corner of the library sofa, or a morning playing with the children in the nursery."

American audiences saw Duse for the first time on January 23 at the Fifth Avenue Theatre at Twenty-eighth and Broadway. Although *A Doll's House* had been announced, Duse performed neither it, *Antony and Cleopatra,* nor *Magda* during her American tour. The American theatre and American audiences were decades behind Europe, and Duse relied on her old French repertory and a double bill of *Cavalleria rusticana* and *La locandiera.*

As usual, she opened her tour with *La Dame aux camélias,* and even though New Yorkers had seen the play countless times, Duse won them over with her acting and with the ensemble direction of her company. The critics noted the absence of "points," those conventional aria-like moments which Duse gave up to achieve something deeper and truer. She had worked out the blocking and the detailed, telling moments that told the story of the play visually, revealing the drama as a whole, not just separate incidents, which is, of course, modern directing. Flavio Andò was also praised as "the first actor we have seen who acts Armand Duval as a real man, and not a milk-sop . . . a man whom it was possible for Marguerite Gautier thoroughly to love." Traditionally, actresses called attention to Marguerite's first appearance by crossing from up center to down center stage between two rows of carefully positioned party guests. Duse, instead, simply appeared among the party guests who were grouped naturally. The death scene usually took place in a large comfortable chair placed in the center of the stage, but Duse/Marguerite died, critic Alan Dale reported, "in the arms of Armand, in an unstudied attitude . . . her head dropped, her hands opened loosely, her arms relaxed their tension, and by the simple force of gravity she fell. It was horribly real, terribly impressive. There was nothing of the theatre in it." Dale was wrong; it was consummate theatre, but of a different sort than he had seen before.

Audiences were provided with a printed synopsis of the plays, but her Italian, Dale wrote, "is infinitely more intelligible than our mother tongue as it is spoken by nine actresses out of ten." Dale also hailed Duse's lack of vanity. She "cried and looked ugly . . . she made her nose red, and her eyes grew heavy and sore, her skin took the unpleasant red tint of the weeping woman." When she played the unhappy, tragic Santuzza, she looked haggard and emaciated, but on the same evening, she played the comic, charming Mirandolina in Goldoni's *La locandiera*, and, in an exception to her no-makeup rule, added a touch of rouge to highlight her transformation. Duse's methods are "new to us yet," wrote Alan Dale. "They surely cannot be without their permanent effect upon our stage."

Confronted with a new kind of acting and without a concerted publicity effort to tell them what to think and how to evaluate Duse, critics referred again and again to the "mystery" of her art. "There are mysteries about this Italian woman," noted the *New York Times*. "Perhaps the safest decision to reach is expressed by saying that she is always of the age and always of the beauty demanded by the roles she plays." Actors turned out to observe Duse's technique, and many of her audiences were "composed of two elements," reported the *New York Recorder,* "the professional people who were there to see Duse and those who went to see the professional people who went to see Duse."

Duse performed only three to four times a week, which contributed to her mystery. Duse's technique, which "does not permit me simply to 'play' my parts, but much against my will, forces me to suffer with the beings I represent," took too much out of her to play the usual eight performances a week. She spent her off-days with the Gilders or cloistered in her hotel. Since she didn't have an entourage, Duse used her friends to run errands and comfort her whenever she demanded. "Madame, I need you," Duse wrote in a typical note to Helena Gilder. "I cannot move from my bed today—and I *must* talk to you. Will you be so good—will you answer my prayer—will you come to me today at any hour you wish? I have something I want to ask of you, and also I want your advice [. . .] Please answer—and what is more, please answer *quickly* for the Impresarios are waiting my answer, which depends on yours—and they will not let me alone."

In mid-March, Duse and her company moved west to Chicago. Duse wrote playful, chatty letters to Helena. "You write to me—you say: 'Well—

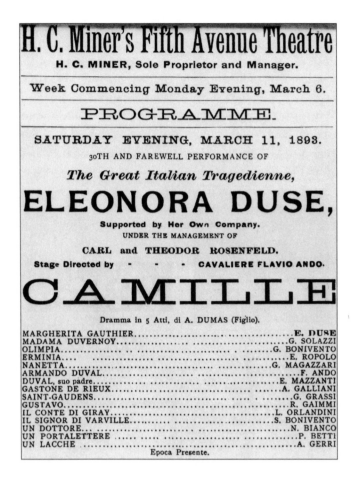

H. C. Miner's Fifth Avenue Theatre

H. C. MINER, Sole Proprietor and Manager.

Week Commencing Monday Evening, March 6.

PROGRAMME.

SATURDAY EVENING, MARCH 11, 1893.

30TH AND FAREWELL PERFORMANCE OF

The Great Italian Tragedienne,

ELEONORA DUSE,

Supported by Her Own Company.
UNDER THE MANAGEMENT OF

CARL and THEODOR ROSENFELD.

Stage Directed by   -   -   -   CAVALIERE FLAVIO ANDO.

CAMILLE

Dramma in 5 Atti, di A. DUMAS (Figlio).

MARGHERITA GAUTHIER	E. DUSE
MADAMA DUVERNOY	G. SOLAZZI
OLIMPIA	G. BONIVENTO
ERMINIA	E. ROPOLO
NANETTA	G. MAGAZZARI
ARMANDO DUVAL	F. ANDO
DUVAL, suo padre	E. MAZZANTI
GASTONE DE RIEUX	A. GALLIANI
SAINT-GAUDENS	G. GRASSI
GUSTAVO	R. GAIMMI
IL CONTE DI GIRAY	L. ORLANDINI
IL SIGNOR DI VARVILLE	S. BONIVENTO
UN DOTTORE	N. BIANCO
UN PORTALETTERE	P. BETTI
UN LACCHE	A. GERRI

Epoca Presente.

how goes it?' Well? Well!—I die and that's all. 'eh'—'What?'—'how?'—'why?'—Say no more! I DIE! Two words—two syllables—and all is said. Let's talk no more about it. If you knew what it was like to suffer from Nostalgilder—that most exasperating of diseases—worse than influenza—you wouldn't dare ask me how I am. DO YOU WANT ME TO PERISH? Well, then-no-no-NO. Not here—I beg of you. I DIE Voila!"

In Chicago, Duse received an enormous amount of publicity praising her for not seeking publicity. Chicago men wore fedora hats to *Fédora*. Duse ordered some new dresses from a Chicago dressmaker. They came with stiff linings, and she sent them back. "Your crinolines wobble too much," she said. "I can't control them. Take them all out and use the softest silk you can get for lining."

Duse didn't care for Chicago and thought the Chicago World's Fair "awful" and the buildings "horrible." She also missed her new friend. "Bankrupt yourself and come to Boston!" Duse wrote to Helena. "Remember that life is short. When will you find another Duse? Well, then? Ruin yourself— come to Boston!"

Helena Gilder left her husband and children in New York and joined Duse in Boston for her brief tour there. Boston critics were impressed with the company's swift dialogue. Sometimes several people spoke at once, with no waiting between cues. *La Dame aux camélias* proved to be the most popular production. Duse/Marguerite also surprised her audiences "by the appealing naturalness of the camaraderie of the final hand grasp and shake which she made to follow her last passionate embrace." Several critics reported Duse's practice of touching and caressing her acting partner with little unconscious movements. This technique, which Duse used throughout her career, was similar to her occasional use of wordless vocalisms in place of dialogue.

H. T. P. Parker, the critic of the *Boston Transcript*, compared her to Sarah Bernhardt. "Beyond doubt Duse has the greater versatility," he wrote. "Her art is the finer, the more subtle, the stronger and the more pervading in its grasp of well-nigh every detail, psychological or physical . . . She is not tall, though the strong lines of her shoulders and hips give her slight body a certain dignity of carriage. Her arms are notably long, with large hands, that seem to possess an uncanny power of suggestion . . . She seems to trust not at all to inspiration or to the impulse and chance of the moment. Every word seems to have been spoken, every gesture, every movement of the features, every device of quiet byplay seems to have been planned from the start as detail."

During her first American tour, her reviews were overwhelmingly positive. The *New York Herald* reported it was Duse's "latent power that perhaps constitutes the greatest charm of her work . . . We feel that the woman has given vent to only a part of the tremendous passion, anger or grief that fills her." Despite the glowing reviews, there were some empty seats at Duse's performances, which were attended primarily by fashionable society, actors, and Italian-Americans. Conservative, middle-class American audiences still found her repertory morally offensive. Also, Duse was Italian. Sometimes, the press reflected the prevailing prejudice against Italians, who at this time were at the bottom of the social scale. "For giving us Eleonora Duse," wrote the *New York Dramatic Mirror*, "we can forgive Italy for the organ grinders, the mafia, and for Burt Haverly's 'Banana Song.' "

The abyss between the life of the theatre and her art continued to plague Duse. She felt like a slave to the public, to the playwright, and to her own temperament. In a note to Helena Gilder before a performance, Duse wrote, "It is evening. The hour of departure—the hour of memories, of prayers. One

Duse as Mirandolina. In acting Goldoni, Duse urged her
company to play with "Brio! Brio! Brio!"

must hide everything and go to work. May God keep my daughter and every
woman from such an existence!"

On April 22, 1893, Duse sailed for England. "I bankrupt myself to tell you
that I love you," she cabled Helena on May 20 from London. "We think of
her as Duse of the Beautiful Hands," Rosamond Gilder wrote later, "among
the figures of dramatic legend." During her stay in New York, the Gilders had
commissioned a cast of Duse's right hand, almost as if they wanted to own
and preserve a piece of the elusive actress. Duse's relationship with the Gilders
was typical of many relationships she would have with "civilians" over the
years. As long as her "civilians" were useful to her, she would shower them

with attention, notes, and affection, but when she grew tired of them or they weren't necessary to her, she would forget them and they would disappear from her life, almost like a play she had grown tired of performing. "Still," said Désirée von Wertheimstein, who later lived with Duse and observed this behavior, "in spite of their unhappiness, not one of them would have wished to forgo the joy of knowing her."

"IF I DON'T LIVE *outside* the theatre," Duse claimed, "I don't know how to create art."

For almost two and a half years, she had devoted herself to work and needed a respite, but her first London appearance had been announced and the tickets already sold. When she arrived at the Savoy Hotel in London, she was exhausted. After dealing with a "thousand things," she escaped for a day into the green countryside. She also postponed her London debut for several days while she adjusted herself to the new city and the theatre climate.

London was enjoying a brilliant theatre season. Oscar Wilde's *A Woman of No Importance* had opened in April at the Haymarket; Ellen Terry and her acting partner, the distinguished Henry Irving, played their familiar Shakespeare and melodramas at the Lyceum Theatre; and Ibsen's new plays were introduced to London audiences in rotating repertory at the Opéra Comique with productions of *Rosmersholm*, *Hedda Gabler*, and *The Master Builder*. The actor-manager Herbert Beerbohm Tree starred in *An Enemy of the People* at the Theatre Royal. Duse saw the trend and added *A Doll's House* to her London repertory, which also included *La Dame aux camélias*, *Fédora*, *Cavalleria rusticana* and *La locandiera*, and *Divorçons*. Her only miscalculation was in booking Boito's adaptation of *Antony and Cleopatra* on Shakespeare's home ground.

When Duse acted *La Dame aux camélias* in London, Ellen Terry "rushed on the stage . . . and fell weeping into her arms." In her mid-forties, Terry belonged to another generation and the grand, pictorial acting style of the nineteenth century. Moved by Terry's warmth and affection, Duse reached out to her as a woman and artist. "You have given me both pain and pleasure," Duse wrote. "*Pleasure* by means of your art which is so sincere and noble . . . *Pain* because I feel a deep sadness in my heart when I see a beautiful and generous female nature give its soul to art—as you are doing—when it's life itself, your very heart that speaks so tenderly, mournfully, nobly, *under* your acting."

Terry always kept a copy of Wolkoff's 1893 portrait of Duse in her bedroom at her cottage at Smallhythe Place in Kent. Under the image, Ellen Terry wrote, "*There is none like her—none.*"

Ellen Terry in Shakespeare's
The Winter's Tale, 1906

William Archer, the British critic and Ibsen's translator and champion, considered Duse "the most absorbingly interesting actress I ever saw." Archer, of course, would have been predisposed to her simply because she chose to perform Ibsen. Experiencing Duse's freshness after Bernhardt's artifice, Archer wrote, was like "passing out into the fresh air from an alcove redolent of patchouli." He hated Boito's dry and prosaic adaptation of *Antony and Cleopatra*, and could see "nothing in the least voluptuous" in Duse's Cleopatra. The professional and personal heat between Duse and Andò had cooled, and Archer was disappointed in their lovemaking. Kisses that had once lasted as much as a minute were now, according to Archer, mere birdlike pecks.

Actually, Andò was growing restive, and Duse was bored with her limited repertory. On May 12 she wrote a long, conciliatory letter to Cesare Rossi and suggested a future collaboration. Suffering from her recurrent bronchial problems, she was also depressed because her physician, Dr. Moleschott, had died on May 20 in Rome. Although her first London performances had been successful, her debut was overshadowed somewhat by Arthur Pinero's answer to Ibsen, *The Second Mrs. Tanqueray*, which introduced the incandescent performance of newcomer Mrs. Patrick Campbell as Paula Tanqueray, yet another fallen woman who commits suicide to atone for her sins. Although William Archer predicted the play wouldn't run, it enjoyed an enormous success and made Stella Campbell a star. Duse would add it to her repertory as well.

"I HAVE WORKED years and years—all of my youth," Duse wrote Count Primoli after her London tour, "and now I want a long vacation." She returned to her beloved Adriatic and the "tranquility and pure air" of Venice, to her apartment in Wolkoff's narrow sixteenth-century palazzo. From the large Gothic window at the front of the house she enjoyed a marvelous view of Venice and the Grand Canal, and from the back of the house she gazed down on a walled garden of luxuriant green plants and flowers.

After a few months' rest and a visit to Switzerland with the Wolkoffs, in November she traveled to northern Europe, fulfilling engagements in Vienna, Berlin, and Munich. Once again, she succeeded with audiences and with young artists and intellectuals. The overwhelmingly positive response to Duse, particularly in northern Europe, indicates, of course, the popularity and power of her acting. But the reviews and articles also had another purpose (as they do today)—of promoting the writer's own aesthetic. For example, the German playwright Gerhart Hauptmann, then thirty-one, who won the Nobel Prize in 1912, called Duse "art personified." "Her greatness lies in not wishing to create or represent a character," he wrote, "but in incarnating the

The Wolkoff palazzo in Venice

soul of the character, from which that character acquires shape and outline. This is the secret of the modern tendency in art." Change the pronoun and Hauptmann might have been describing himself. Underlying all of his work, which moved from naturalism into symbolism, is compassion for human suffering. The same concern guided Duse. She called it "the secret voice" that spoke to her heart, "an echo of the pain of the world."

On New Year's Eve 1893 in Berlin, her own pain consumed her. After completing some final engagements, she planned to dissolve her company and join forces with her old collaborator Cesare Rossi and his company. Her almost decade-long partnership with Flavio Andò was coming to an end, and he was moving to another Italian acting company. On December 31, 1893, after a silence of twenty-seven months, Duse wrote to Boito. Her furious

Duse loved the city where she had spent much of her youth.
"Always my heart was in Venice," she said.

outburst reads more like a dramatic monologue than a letter. Alone, depressed, feeling sorry for herself, yet proudly wanting Boito to understand what the last eight years had cost her, she defiantly untied her heart.

> And if it's the last day of the year that I write—so be it. I regret little of it.
> Another 32 days, and it's over.
> I needed to scrape my bread together—and I did, and she who lives after me will find bread and a humble house—
> They thought I would lose my way—No—but it's so miserable that we can't help each other in this world.
> Everyone for themselves—there's a rule to live by!
> But it's over! And tonight I need to *shout* that I've worked—and it's over!
> From 1886 to today I've worked. Who helped me? No one, and everyone—but now it's over!

Another 32 days, another 4 cities, then I'll go off to the end of the world!

Meanwhile tomorrow I leave here.

Whoever has lived in PRISON, will understand! Whoever has lived in darkness, underground, without death's oblivion, will understand! It's over!—Whoever has lived bound hand and foot, biting the gag and not screaming—will understand, yes, if tonight I shout, it's over, it's over. And, after 32 days I'll go to the end of the world!

This is all, there's *nothing else* I want to say—Eleonora

Duse often couched her powerful aspiration to impress her art on the world and her need to seek Dionysiac abandonment in the more socially acceptable terms of earning a living for herself and her daughter. Boito accurately read her subtext and the "nothing else" and wrote and asked her to forgive him. Duse replied that she had never meant to reproach him. "Nothing but blessings," she said.

In Munich, on January 31, Duse gave her last performance with her Compagnia della Città di Roma. On the evening of February 4, while she was in Milan making legal and financial arrangements for Enrichetta's future, she went to find Boito. He wasn't home, and his house was dark except for a light at the door. She didn't dare go up to his studio, but she tapped at his window. "How could I come back, how could I go on living and not do it," she wrote him. She was leaving Milan, because "I couldn't live here one more hour!" then added, "If I live, perhaps— . . ." After reading her letter, Boito added his own bitterly ironic words and a Dante quotation to her letter: "Anytime, any place. Whenever, wherever, and however Lenor wants. Amen. *In her will is our peace.*"

In February, Duse vacationed with Wolkoff, his wife, and their daughter in Egypt. Wolkoff hired a boat to go up the Nile, and Duse relaxed on deck, watching the sailors and listening to them sing. Feeling ignored, Wolkoff complained Duse wasn't interested in any of the sights or in nature. Duse had already been to Egypt and seen the pyramids. Also, her love affair with Wolkoff, which had been founded on her need for his help with her first Russian tour, was over. With ruthless practicality, Duse did not break off their friendship. According to Wolkoff's friend Hermann Graf Keyserling, Wolkoff had "that unique unselfishness that gentle Russians often show when they are in love." Wolkoff continued to help Duse even though she had ended their sexual relationship. "Sometimes he was found sleeping at her door," Keyserling wrote.

The prospect of reconciling with Boito filled Duse's thoughts while she vacationed in Egypt with the Wolkoffs. "Is it still possible?" she wrote Boito on February 15. "Will we ever be able to stop deceiving ourselves?" Duse still fantasized about a man to protect her and Enrichetta. "It was beneath your hand that I had desired to die," she said, "—in a house that might have been ours—that was remote and peaceful—and in the most complete humility."

At the same time she was writing Boito, Duse was negotiating contracts and conferring with Cesare Rossi about rehearsal schedules and choice of repertory for a six-week season in London, followed by another European tour. Duse's timing in drawing Boito back into her life is telling. Since her infatuation with Wolkoff had ended and there was no possibility of a future with the married Wolkoff, once again Duse flirted with the idea that maybe Boito would commit to her as a woman and as a working artist. Onstage, Duse experienced an intense, intimate communion with her audience, and she longed for the same communion—knowing and being known—in her personal life. In early April, Boito and Verdi were in Paris to prepare for the premiere of *Falstaff,* and Duse met Boito there for a few days. "I felt the flame reflicker," Duse admitted to Boito, "but little enduring joy and little sweetness. There was still a world between us!"

On May 7, she opened in London with *La Dame aux camélias*. According to William Archer, the question on everyone's lips in London—"Well, what about Duse?"—had been answered with "As great as ever." Following the headiness of her first-night success and the sheer exhaustion of the preparations for it, Duse was too agitated to sleep. At thirty-five, she felt her youth was over, and she wanted to take charge of the life remaining to her. She stayed awake all night and into the next morning writing a long letter to Boito. "You love me! I love you! No—no—We won't speak of anguish!" She had always refrained from discussing details of her working life, which Boito considered vulgar, but now, "YOU MUST know all that!" she said. She told him of her disappointment with her new company. "What scum! They make up their eyes, they powder their cheeks—they wave their hands and flap their mouths—and think they're translating life. It makes me sick to my stomach." Of course, Duse was partly to blame, since she had hired the "scum."

Although Duse was fond of Carlo Rosaspina—her former "Romeo," who replaced Flavio Andò—unfortunately Rosaspina was a merely competent actor, without Andò's stunning good looks, work ethic, and exceptional talent, and the burden of carrying the plays fell more heavily on her. Also, sixty-four-year-old Cesare Rossi, whom she had counted on for support both artistically and administratively, lacked strength and confidence and was proving insufficient. She was also unhappy with the "absurd" contract she had signed.

"You have struggled less than me to earn your living," she continued to Boito. "You have lived (yes, perhaps in anguish—poor Arrigo) but you have always had a house. I had to make do with a back room and I'm a woman."

Two days later, on May 10, Duse wrote Boito another long, thoughtful letter. She recalled the failure of *Cleop* and their inability to tell each other the truth about it. "I'm telling the truth, when I say that I would like to *live* still by this love, but to live requires pride and humility on both sides. Truth, truth is needed, the only remedy! The remedy that protects the dream, the ideal, the reality of these two lives, that want to be joined— . . ." She told him she would never go back to the way it was before. Although she didn't mention Boito's Fanny by name, she asserted, "My life is worth as much as that other woman's. But you never thought, or feared, that I could die because of all this—and so you forced me to leave you—and so you could lose me again— I could go away—without suffering—now—if I had no more hope!" Enrichetta needed her, and she needed help with Enrichetta. "Help me help her," she begged. "Help me *protect* our life, not destroy it. Help me feel that I'm reborn the *only* one on your path—if you desire to walk beside me on that path until the end of life." She apologized if "I've said badly what I wanted to say." Still, the act of allowing herself to speak freely was healing. "Now I'm more tranquil," she concluded.

Her tranquility was short lived. Tebaldo Checchi, who had moved to the south of England, where he worked as Argentina's consul at Newport, was in London. He threatened to seize the money she had set aside for Enrichetta, and Duse believed he was spying on her to find evidence to gain custody of Enrichetta. She warned Boito it wouldn't be safe for them to meet in London. Checchi must also have been curious to see Duse onstage, particularly since she was an international celebrity. She wanted him out of her life, and she couldn't bring herself even to write his name. "Why does death exist," she wondered bitterly, "if it's not ready to take Rocambole??" [This was the name she called Checchi—an ironic reference to the worthless comic hero of *Les Exploits de Rocambole*, a popular series of French novels.] Even the envelopes Checchi used revolted her. "That handwriting, that red seal with the engraved sign of the zodiac (charlatan!), all the disgust—all the infecting filth sticks to me." Duse knew she must defend Enrichetta, "who is innocent—and save her life. But she weighs on me like a black thought, like something oppressive and gloomy!—Pouah! I'm disgusted with it—I write your name on this white paper: ═Arrigo═ and start my day again!" When Boito sent her advice about handling Checchi, Duse dismissed it as impractical. "Strange thing," she told him, "You, the person that I *love the most*—and can obey *least*— strange thing."

IN HER SIX-WEEK LONDON SEASON, Duse gave only twenty-three performances, playing about four times a week. She also played Mirandolina for Queen Victoria in a command performance at Windsor Palace on May 18. In contrast, when Sarah Bernhardt played London, she gave twenty-three performances in three weeks. On June 14, when Duse gave her last performance of her London season as Marguerite in *La Dame aux camélias*, she "swept her audience away in a whirlwind of emotion and enthusiasm." William Archer speculated Duse may have been "stimulated by the presence of Sarah Bernhardt, who then saw her for the first time."

On June 15, Duse and Boito met again briefly in Paris, where Boito was getting ready for the Paris premiere of *Otello*. Duse was jealous of Boito's relationship with Verdi. She complained that Verdi was an old magician who made everyone (including Boito) sing and dance to his tune. Boito could not have been pleased with Duse's assessment of *Falstaff*, which she had seen in London. "God, Arrigo—forgive me," she wrote, "—but it seemed such a . . . melancholy thing, that *Falstaff.*"

Actually, Duse couldn't respond to Verdi's happiest opera and Boito's most sparkling libretto because she had just read *The Triumph of Death* by the thirty-one-year-old Italian poet and novelist Gabriele d'Annunzio, and she was delirious with excitement—either not caring or unaware of how her words would sound to Boito.

"And yet another thing! That *diabolical—*divine *d'Annunzio.'* That book— I have finished it—Ahi! Ahi! Ahi!!!—Each of us . . . poor women—think that it's *she* who's found all the words—That *diabolical* d'Annunzio knows them all! [. . .] I would rather die in a *ditch* than fall in love with a soul like that. All the great *test* of courage, all the great virtue of *bearing life* . . . all the enormous anguished sacrifice of *life* and living is destroyed by that book. No! no! no! *Despise* it, but neither *Falstaff—*neither d'Annunzio—I mean—no—I *detest* d'Annunzio, but I adore him.—"

Like so many other readers of the best-selling novel, Duse was swept away by Giorgio Aurispa and Ippolito Sanzio, two doomed lovers, who find themselves together one early morning in a gondola on the Grand Canal and later lose all consciousness of the outside world as they make wild, rapturous love at Venice's Hotel Danieli.

In his novels, d'Annunzio celebrated sensuality, including the pleasures of oral sex, wrote graphically about infanticide and patricide, dramatized the struggle between men and women, and shocked readers with a decadent indifference to human suffering. While other novelists were peeping "like schoolboys through the crack of the door," Edwardian novelist Arnold

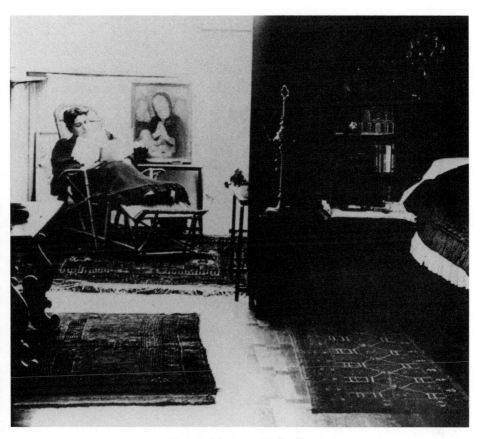

Duse in Venice at Wolkoff's

Bennett observed, d'Annunzio was an adult, "who can deal with an Italian woman."

Following her London tour, in September 1894, Duse returned to Wolkoff's house in Venice. That fall Count Primoli visited from Rome and photographed her in her apartment stretched out in a chaise lounge reading a book and standing up in a gondola in the Grand Canal. D'Annunzio was in Venice to meet with his French translator Georges Hérelle, and perhaps it was Count Primoli or Angelo Conti, the art historian, who arranged a meeting between Duse and d'Annunzio.

Duse was greedy for new impressions and sensations. Just as her ancestors in the commedia dell'arte had manipulated multiple scenarios with various characters, Duse, too, was adept at creating new lines of action when an old plot was wearing thin or lacking in interest. When new characters entered, the old ones were relegated to supporting roles and bit parts, or sometimes they just walked offstage. When she met and talked with d'Annunzio that September, she was casting for a new leading man in her life.

D'Annunzio used women as muses to inspire his work, and he transformed the raw material of his love affairs into brilliant prose. His current muse, Maria Gravina Cruyllas di Ramacca, a married Sicilian princess, had become a demon who "wishes to possess me entirely, like an inanimate object, and whom I no longer love," d'Annunzio told Georges Hérelle. With Maria Gravina he had a daughter, Renata, called "Cicciuzza," and he had three sons with his estranged wife. *The Triumph of Death* was based on his tempestuous love affair with yet another woman, whom he had discarded.

At their first meeting Duse and d'Annunzio talked of art and the theatre. Duse thrilled to discover a man and a writer who seemed to know all the words. According to d'Annunzio, Duse wrapped him in "an endless web of flattery." Subtle flattery was a gift he shared with the actress. "To hear oneself praised with that magic peculiar to d'Annunzio," Isadora Duncan recalled, "is, I imagine something like the experience of Eve when she heard the voice of the serpent in Paradise." With his receding hairline, pointed beard, and sharp, barbed moustache, d'Annunzio looked like Mephistopheles. Less than five feet six, he was about the same height as Duse, and she could look directly into his large, intelligent, gray-green eyes. He had bad teeth and a weak chin, but "when he talks to one he loves he is transformed to the likeness of Phoebus Apollo himself," Duncan said.

"I see the sun," Duse wrote to him after their meeting, "and I thank all the good forces of the earth for having met you." In equating d'Annunzio with the life-affirming and light-giving sun, she had overlooked that d'Annunzio had given the sun a dual role in *The Triumph of Death*—it is also a source of deadly heat and blinding cruelty.

Five

A S IF SHE WERE PREPARING for a new role, Duse imagined her love affair with d'Annunzio before she lived it. Love affair, though, is too limiting a phrase. It was also an artistic collaboration, a union of evenly matched opposites, and a literary creation. D'Annunzio coveted Duse's fame and especially her gift of expression, which transcended words, and she envied his ability to create worlds with words on a page. Nonfiction accounts, including d'Annunzio's *Il fuoco (The Flame),* his roman à clef published in 1900, have been written about their union, as well as novels, an opera, and a movie.

Years later, Duse told biographer Olga Signorelli about their first tryst, which was most likely in the fall of 1894 in Venice. Duse had just read *The Triumph of Death,* and their encounter mirrors the meeting of the characters Giorgio and Ippolito. After d'Annunzio and Duse were introduced, they couldn't sleep and wandered separately and alone around Venice. D'Annunzio took out a gondola and just as the sun was rising, he stepped out of the boat and faced Duse. It's perfectly plausible either d'Annunzio or Duse might have arranged such a rendezvous. Just like Giorgio and Ippolito, their love nest was Venice's most romantic hotel, the pink, palatial Danieli. "I have found harmony," Duse said. "I have felt your soul and discovered mine."

ALMOST FIVE YEARS YOUNGER than Duse, d'Annunzio was born on March 12, 1863, in the gritty fishing town of Pescara on the Adriatic Sea in the Abruzzi, the ankle in the Italian boot. Even today northern Italians are prejudiced against those who come from this poor, rugged area, but d'Annunzio honored his birthplace. "When I find myself amongst strangers," he wrote, "isolated, different, wildly hostile, I sit down, cross my legs and gently shake

Duse in Venice, c. 1894–95

my foot, which to me seems weighty with that ground, that bit of earth, that moist sand, it is like the weight of a piece of armour—an iron defence."

D'Annunzio was sent away to an elite Jesuit boarding school near Florence when he was eleven. He excelled academically, but his Tuscan classmates ridiculed his rough Abruzzese speech. After years of reading the classics out loud, he developed a flexible, caressing voice devoid of any accent. At fifteen, he pawned his grandfather's gold watch to pay for a visit to a brothel, and at sixteen published his first book of verse, *Primo vere*. He was ambitious and shrewd. To advertise the second edition of his poems, he faked a press release to a Florence newspaper informing the world, "Gabriele d'Annunzio . . . some days ago (5 November) on the Francavilla road, fell from his horse and died on the spot. The new edition of his *Primo vere* is expected daily." Other newspapers picked up the story and sales soared.

Like Matilde Serao, d'Annunzio moved to Rome, where he wrote society

Gabriele d'Annunzio, late 1890s

and gossip columns for Roman newspapers, continued to publish poetry, and ingratiated himself with fellow writers and Roman high society. At twenty, he eloped with a duchess, Maria Hardouin, blonde and beautiful and only nineteen. Her parents disapproved of him, but she was pregnant and in love.

When Duse played Rome in the early 1880s, d'Annunzio attended her plays and observed her from a distance. Once, after a performance of *Théodora,* he glimpsed her "pallid face" through the window of her carriage. She knew of him through their mutual friends Matilde Serao and Count Primoli. Duse read the novels he had published in the 1880s, including *Il piacere (Pleasure),* about the decadent world of the Roman aristocracy, and *L'innocente* (later made into a chilling movie by Visconti). In 1892, d'Annunzio gave her his *Roman Elegies,* inscribed "To the divine Eleonora Duse."

Literary talent and celebrity had always attracted Duse. She had hoped Boito would be the playwright she had longed for, but he had proved disappointing both as a writer and as a lover. She had grown tired of her familiar repertory, and she urged d'Annunzio to try writing for the theatre. Her union with the flamboyant d'Annunzio, whose scandalous affairs were the talk of

Italy, seemed a betrayal of the conservative, retiring Boito. When Boito wrote to her in Venice and asked if he could see her in Milan in late October, Duse said no. Without explanation, she asked him to destroy all her letters, "every trace of me." Soon after, she rethought this hasty decision—perhaps her tryst with d'Annunzio would be just a passing fling—and said she would be able to meet him. She asked him not to destroy anything until they had spoken. Her strategy with Boito was similar to her dealings with Wolkoff—she would distance herself from him but not cut him off completely.

Accompanied by the British writer Laurense Alma-Tadema, Duse left Venice in October to resume her German tour with the Cesare Rossi company. Duse often took female friends with her on tours. Laurense "possessed an astonishing gift for conversation, which was invariably interesting and often brilliant," and since Duse didn't socialize with her actors, having an understanding, intelligent friend with her alleviated the isolation and boredom of the road. Also, since actresses were still considered a half step away from courtesans, friendship with a "lady" was another way for Duse to elevate her profession into a socially acceptable art form.

Laurense, then thirty, was just a few years younger than Duse, and with her thick, dark hair, dark eyes, and broad, high cheekbones, she looked as if she could be Eleonora's sister. The daughter of the famous painter Sir Lawrence Alma-Tadema, Laurense moved in royal social circles as well as the art and theatre world of London. A few years earlier, when her father painted the portrait of the musician and Polish patriot Ignacy Paderewski, Laurense had fallen in love with Paderewski. Unfortunately, he loved someone else, but Laurense learned Polish, translated his songs, and was his devoted friend.

Although Duse continued to be popular with German audiences, her tour of German cities was mismanaged, which made her furious. The tour had coincided with the holiday season, when "everyone is taken up with that idiotic Christmas tree!" Laurense kept Wolkoff informed of their progress. "I am afraid she only writes to you when she is in one of her crises and at moments of great difficulty, so that you do not realise her normal state," Laurense reported.

Also, Cesare Rossi's acting company irritated her. After Cesare Rossi's poor reviews in London that summer, Duse had politely dismissed the old man but had continued with his actors. "I beseech these wretches," she complained. "Nothing, nothing works, nothing elevates them. [. . .] My own exactitude, my lucidity in the performance, all the accumulation of 10 years of work, nothing is respected by these poor devils. For them, acting is like playing at lotto—it's chance. I get angry and tense from my head to my feet every day [. . .] not one intention is understood, not a single tenderness is shared. It's agony!" One uncultured "Neapolitan thug" of an actor, who was "pretentious from his necktie to the melodramatic interpretations of the words," repelled her in particular. She longed for a refined and intellectual ambience. It's better, she decided, "to be alone than accompanied by the wrong people."

She parted from the company in mid-December. "I blessed them also," she said, "especially for the pleasure of never seeing them again."

DUSE COULD NOT BE as ruthless with Boito. From Genoa, on Enrichetta's birthday, January 7, 1895, she wrote Boito, "except for kisses," he didn't know her at all. "Nothing is possible, nothing can be said between us!" Perhaps remembering his promise of "three heads at one window," she called him "an ambiguous creature." His mysterious Fanny had died from her long illness, but Boito was unwilling to offer any commitment to Duse beyond what he had already given. Did you ever "really read" my letters? she asked him. The only thing left for her, she wrote, was "to pick myself up and carry myself on my own back and go down the road." "I'll do it," she promised. "So be it. Addio. So be it," she repeated, sounding like one of Dumas *fils'* women. She didn't sign her name to the letter, as if she were disappearing from his life.

But, of course, she wasn't. She couldn't have written so many letters to Boito if she hadn't derived some kind of pleasure from the correspondence. Judging by their rare meetings, they enjoyed their epistolary love affair more than the real thing. Duse needed someone to watch her live, someone to spill out her thoughts to, and their bond would not be easily broken.

Although angered by Boito's "ambiguity" and his lack of passion, Duse still loved him, and her feelings vacillated. "Don't promise anything Arrigo!" she wrote on January 11, 1895. She was overwhelmed with work and asked him not to come to her. Yet on February 2 from Venice, she changed her mind—perhaps they could have a life together. "Do you see me?" she asked. "Inside?" On the other hand, she feared if they saw each other it would be off-key, the way they had been in Paris. Boito agreed to a meeting, "provided Lenor is Lenor." Stung by his criticism, Duse blamed the theatre, which was becoming more and more "my malediction" and turning her into "A PRIMA DONNA."

Onstage in the familiar fiction of art—her natural world—she was relaxed and true, but offstage she sounded increasingly tense and histrionic. When Boito wrote that she had seemed more "tranquil" in February 1895 during her visit to buy *chiffons* at the House of Worth in Paris, she snapped at him. André Antoine's Théâtre-Libre was "true," she said, but the rest of Parisian theatre was a "world of puppets." Paris was a "banal" city where everyone lived on pastries and bonbons, a diet she loathed. How could she be tranquil? she asked Boito. "Whatever gave you that impression?" she said. "Did I *lie* when I wrote to you?—No. Well, certainly, I don't know how to write, since I like to believe that you know how to read [. . .] My heart is swollen with a thousand inexpressible things!"

D'Annunzio was also in Paris at this time, staying at the Hotel Meurice. He had sent a note to Duse, calling her "my dear friend." He enclosed his photograph. "I have a thousand things to tell you," he wrote, "a thousand things to ask. I will come tomorrow between 5 and 6 . . . I think of you this evening. If I dare, I would come and look for you." Did they see each other in Paris? In a letter to Boito, Duse told him she was spending the day where "there is a large park—lighted lamps—and one person full of words—."

AFTER PARIS, Duse continued her tour into Holland and Belgium. The impresario Joseph Schürmann had finally convinced her to sign with him. Wealthy and well connected, Schürmann knew how to handle temperamental stars. He had managed Adelina Patti, Sarah Bernhardt, and Benoît Coquelin. Deeply suspicious of all impresarios, Duse trusted Schürmann enough to say that at least he wasn't a thief and his lies always had an element of truth. Still, he annoyed her by referring to Bernhardt and Coquelin as her "illustrious predecessors."

Boito was tired of reading about endless theatre problems, and asked her to stop sending him such anguished letters. Furious, Duse kept silent. "I've done it!" she declared on March 19, 1895, four weeks later. "But the heart is a strange thing, Arrigo, that if you cut out the agony—the best part is lost." She claimed she wasn't bitter anymore. "Poor Arrigo!—You are you—You can't change—and neither can I." The *prima donna* prevailed and defiantly continued the letter with pages of laments. Surrounded by "imbeciles," she was sailing in "high seas without a rudder." Carlo Rosaspina, who had replaced Andò, was of that "race of true ham actors" who rely on "inspiration" and "intuition." Even the weather was depressing—rainy, cloudy, and cold. "In all reality, and tranquility," she concluded, "I affirm, that death is preferable to the life I live."

A few weeks later from Brussels, like an impetuous adolescent, she had changed her mind again. She didn't want to write to him after all—"All the words have already been said between us."—and pleaded with him not to force her to do so. Her performances had received ovations and critical success, and as usual, when this happened, she adored wherever she was, and so she praised Brussels as "the loveliest city in the world."

During her stay, Duse met the young actress and singer Georgette Le Blanc, who had a house in Brussels. An older friend of Le Blanc's had warned her Duse was capricious and it took a long time to gain her confidence. Duse was especially tender, though, with trembling young actresses of any nationality who came to look and to worship. Duse invited Georgette to her hotel. When Georgette arrived, Duse staged a striking picture. She lay in bed; her glossy black hair framed her face and flowed over her pure white, cassock-like nightgown. "I hate lace and feminine lingerie," Duse explained. The true beauty of her face, Georgette recalled, was her "burning eyes. Black eyes like dark flames."

Duse showed Le Blanc love letters she kept under her pillow, but Duse said she didn't believe in love anymore. "Everything is dying," Duse announced. "To love is already no longer to love." Le Blanc sensed Duse hated growing older. "All I have of joy is entrenched in doubt and despair," Duse confessed. When they said good-bye, Duse caressed the younger woman's hair. Georgette, who was barely out of her teens, was in the spring of her life. At thirty-six, "I'm in the summer," Duse told Georgette, "and summer is so close to autumn and that is the end."

DUSE LONGED FOR A VACATION, but she had to earn enough to pay her company while she rested. After Brussels, she returned to Germany for a series of performances to fulfill her contract there with Joseph Schürmann. Although he had advised her to tour in Italy, Duse decided instead to go to London in June for a three-week engagement at the elegant Drury Lane Theatre, which could accommodate twenty-five hundred. The twelve-hundred-seat Daly's Theatre in Leicester Square, flashily decorated with Cupids blowing bubbles made of electric lightbulbs, had booked Sarah Bernhardt for June. Unhampered by the inferior Rossi company, and performing with her own well-rehearsed actors, Duse would finally confront the "divine Sarah." This first opportunity for a direct comparison between the two divas might have gone unremembered except for the presence of George Bernard Shaw, who had just been hired to write theatre criticism for *The Saturday Review.* Shaw wanted to write for the ages. He believed dramatic criticism should serve high art, and not just advertise entertainments.

After seeing Bernhardt and Duse perform, "I will shew what criticism is," Shaw said to himself and proceeded to write what is still considered one of the finest essays ever published about the art of the actor.

> *On their physical appearance:* Madame Bernhardt has the charm of a jolly maturity . . . and her complexion shows that she has not studied modern art in vain. . . . She paints her ears crimson and allows them to peep enchantingly through a few loose braids of her auburn hair. Every dimple has its dab of pink; and the finger-tips are so delicately

incarnadined that you fancy they are transparent like her ears, and that the light is shining through their delicate blood-vessels. Her lips are like a newly painted pillar box, her cheeks, right up to the languid lashes, have the bloom and surface of a peach; she is beautiful with the beauty of her school, and entirely inhuman and incredditable . . . The dress, the title of the play, the order of the words may vary; but the woman is always the same. She does not enter into the leading character; she substitutes herself for it.

All this is precisely what does not happen in the case of Duse, whose every part is a separate creation. When she comes on the stage, you are quite welcome to take your opera-glass and count whatever lines time and care have so far traced on her. They are the credentials of her humanity; and she knows better than to obliterate that significant handwriting beneath a layer of peach-bloom from the chemist's. The shadows on her face are gray, not crimson; her lips are sometimes nearly gray also; . . . But Duse, with a tremor of the lip which you feel rather than see, and which lasts half an instant, touches you straight on the very heart; and there is not a line in the face, or a cold tone in the gray shadow that does not give poignancy to that tremor . . . The truth is that in the art of being beautiful, Madame Bernhardt is a child beside her . . . Duse produces the illusion of being infinite in variety of beautiful pose and motion. Every idea, every shade of thought and mood, expresses itself delicately but vividly to the eye; and yet, in an apparent million of changes and inflections, it is impossible to catch any line of an awkward angle, or any strain . . . She is ambidextrous and supple, like a gymnast or a panther . . .

On their interpretation of Magda: I doubt whether any of us realized, after Madame Bernhardt's very clever performance as Magda on Monday night, that there was room in the nature of things for its annihilation within forty-eight hours . . . And yet annihilation is the only word for it. Sarah . . . did not trouble us with any fuss about the main theme of Sudermann's play, the revolt of the modern woman against that ideal of home which exacts the sacrifice of her whole life to its care . . . In fact, there is not the slightest reason to suspect Madame Bernhardt of having discovered any such theme in the play; though Duse, with one look at Schwartze, the father, nailed it to the stage as the subject of the impending dramatic struggle before she had been five minutes on the scene . . . Sarah Bernhardt played [the scene in which Magda's former lover appeared in the third act] very lightly and pleasantly . . . the peach bloom never altered by a shade. Not so with Duse. The moment she read the card handed her by the servant, you realized what it was to have to face a meeting with the man . . . He paid his compliments and offered his flowers; they sat down; . . . Then a terrible thing happened to her. She began to blush; and in another moment she was conscious of it, and the blush was slowly spreading and deepening until, after a few vain efforts to avert her face or to obstruct his view of it without seeming to do so, she gave up and hid the blush in her hands. After that feat of acting I did not need to be told why Duse does not paint an inch thick. I could detect no trick in it; it seemed to me a perfectly genuine effect of the dramatic imagination.

On the audience's reaction to Duse: To say that it left the house not only frantically applauding, but actually roaring, is to say nothing; . . . But there really was something to roar at this time. There was a real play, and an actress who understood the author and was a greater artist than he.

ON A NIGHT OFF from performing, Sarah Bernhardt went to Drury Lane with her friend Gabrielle Enthoven to see Duse's Magda and offered her own opinion in a pun. *"Elle n'est pas une actress elle est une femme divigne."* "She isn't an actress, she's a woman of the grapevine" is the literal translation—in other words, an ordinary, earthy woman— *"divigne,"* far beneath the "divine" Sarah.

"Sarah was an actress and gloried in the fact," Enthoven wrote. "Once when I was waiting in the wings for her at the end of a play when she had torn our hearts to ribbons—she came up to me and said, 'I have been thinking we will have an *entrecotte* but lightly cooked, don't you think?' I was also in the wings when Duse came off. She had been acting in *La Femme de Claude* and the tears were streaming down her face." Enthoven believed Duse's greatness "was in part her sublime simplicity . . . and her unconquerable spirit when at work. Nothing she did was ever good enough—'Learn, learn,' she said to me, 'one must be continually learning.' "

After reading Shaw's review (which Laurense had translated), Duse composed a letter of thanks. Flattered by her letter, Shaw bragged about it and poked fun at himself in a letter to Ellen Terry. He had received a missive from Duse's "Secretary of State" [Laurense Alma-Tadema], he wrote Terry. "The Signora Duse . . . permitted herself for a moment to betray a consciousness of the Press, and even to thank me. I was prodigiously pleased; but what I want to know is, does she corrupt every critic in the same way . . . ?"

Even though she didn't play every night, Duse became more and more exhausted as her London run progressed, plus she suffered from painful neuralgia in her face and chest. She had been working continuously for almost a year. Public and critical response to her third London season had been over-whelmingly positive, but as Shaw realized when he went back to see her, she sometimes "misses fire." Performing Magda, "being frightened, or imagining herself ill or what not," Shaw confided to Ellen Terry, "[Duse] had steeped herself in morphia, & was visibly swimming in it. Result—all the great passages escaped her . . . and yet it was a great performance. She played for all she was worth at that moment; and it was more than enough for anyone who had not seen the sober performance."

ON JUNE 22, 1895, a notice appeared in the literary supplement to *Le Figaro* that Gabriele d'Annunzio intended to write a new book about Eleonora Duse. An avid reader, Duse probably read the announcement or heard about it from one of her friends. Her estranged husband, Tebaldo Checchi, read it. A few days later Checchi wrote a fawning letter of protest to d'Annunzio. The three-page letter, written in calligraphy as elegant as d'Annunzio's own, argued, "We will leave aside the husband, the customary butt . . . but what about the daughter? . . . for, dear Gabriele, you will have poetized your heroine . . . with all the colours of your brilliant palette; yet there will always remain the common and vulgar fact of a wife who deceives her husband." It's not known if d'Annunzio answered the letter, but he had no intention of writing about Checchi's relationship with Duse.

While Duse recovered from the exertions of her long tour, d'Annunzio sailed to Greece on a yacht belonging to Edoardo Scarfoglio, the husband of Matilde Serao. Called *Fantasia,* after one of Serao's novels, the ship had a crew of ten and a cook. D'Annunzio invited Georges Hérelle to go along, and the straitlaced Frenchman was shocked by d'Annunzio's and Scarfoglio's behavior. Hérelle had hoped to devote some time to work, but d'Annunzio preferred to sunbathe in the nude, tell pornographic jokes, visit prostitutes, and ignore all the sights. Actually, d'Annunzio was absorbing experiences and later would turn even the most trivial episodes of the trip into poetry and dramatic scenes. D'Annunzio returned to Italy filled with inspiration, including an idea for a tragedy called *La città morta (The Dead City),* based on his visit to the ruins of Mycenae.

The lovers met in September in Venice, again at the Hotel Danieli. "Sacred to Love and to Grief," d'Annunzio noted on September 26, 1895. Unlike Boito, who wanted Duse to give up acting, d'Annunzio honored her profession, envied her power over audiences, and was greedy for information. *Il fuoco* was already taking shape, and he filled notebooks with records of their conversations, her memories, and physical descriptions. He shared with her his ambition to write grand plays and create a theatre worthy of them—a great open-air amphitheater like the ancient Greek stage. Duse would give flesh to his words and carry his plays around the world.

The simple act of seeing Duse step into a room and observing the movements of her body inspired a frenzy of creativity in d'Annunzio. In a passage in *Il fuoco*, d'Annunzio described her improvising his idea for a scene in *La città morta*. "He gripped her hands and, without realizing, he hurt her. She did not feel the pain. They were both intent on the sparks generated by their joint energies. The same electric vibration was racing along their heightened nerves . . . A profound shudder went through him, as though he were participating in a miracle." For both of them, the act of creation was more exciting, more satisfying than sex.

Duse believed she had found the dramatic poet who would complete her. "You will help me, no?" Duse wrote to d'Annunzio. "Oh—the blessed strength—here it is! You throw yourself back into my arms, which is my art, and you make me worthy of it!—How can I tell you the *thanks* I feel inside me!"

Duse didn't ask for a commitment from d'Annunzio. She knew he was married with three sons and had a daughter by his current mistress, who still shared a home with him. Don't write to me, Duse instructed, unless your heart tells you to. "Don't lie to me—you have no duty toward me, no obligation—*never* do it—[. . .] I will help myself." And to help herself, Duse explained, she would throw herself into a sea of work and drown there. "In the evenings when I work—I throw myself in, and only you know, only you can comprehend all the *twists and turns* that my soul and body make to form an *expression* of art!—And I need to invent an inexorable control—*harmonizing oblivion with memory.* The most divine thing—and the most grueling profanity."

Duse and d'Annunzio saw each other in Florence in October. They both knew Carlo Placci, a patron of the arts in Florence. At his house d'Annunzio met Duse's friend, twenty-four-year-old Giulietta Gordigiani, an aspiring concert pianist and the daughter of Michele Gordigiani, a Florentine painter. Duse had met Giulietta in 1888 and had grown close to the young woman and her family. Tall, slim, and attractive, Giulietta was high-strung and intelligent. In d'Annunzio's *Il fuoco*, Duse is the great tragedian Foscarina, and Giulietta is transformed into Foscarina's dearest friend, the young singer Donatella Arvale. D'Annunzio is Stelio Effrena, a writer, kind of a Nietzschean "superman" who dreams of creating a great theatre and who desires both Foscarina and Donatella.

In November 1895 in Venice, d'Annunzio performed his first public speech, a tribute to the beauty, history, and art of Venice, at the inaugural Venetian international art exhibition, which is known today as the Biennale of Venice. D'Annunzio reproduced this speech almost verbatim in the opening pages of *Il fuoco*. When he met Duse, d'Annunzio had decided to write for the theatre, and at his first public performance in Venice he was guided by the presence of Duse, his muse and mentor, who initiated him into the theatre.

In anticipation of his debut, d'Annunzio suffered stage fright, and Duse soothed him, flattered him, and directed him. Just before d'Annunzio (as Stelio) delivered his speech, Duse (Foscarina) gave him her traditional opening-night blessing: "May light shine upon you, Stelio!" D'Annunzio imagined the audience as a monster, "a gigantic creature with thousands of eyes," the women's jewels looking like "shining scales that rippled out towards the darkness." He saw Duse/Foscarina standing apart, and admired the beauty and purity of her unadorned throat and naked shoulders.

During his speech, d'Annunzio experienced what some actors feel during performance. For a moment, he forgot his lines and "the light of his thoughts went out like a torch blown out by the unconquerable wind . . ." As he spoke, he marveled at the actor's double self: "Whilst his mind coiled and uncoiled so vigorously in that continuous rush of words, he still kept a strange capacity for observing what was going on around him that was almost a separate faculty of material observation." And he noted that "in the communion between his own soul and the soul of the crowd a mystery was happening, something that was almost divine . . . And it seemed to him that his very voice was gradually acquiring increased power."

As he looked over the audience, d'Annunzio imagined an infinite number of crowds, "in great theatres . . . cheering wildly at the sudden glory of an immortal speech." Again, he observed Duse/Foscarina with "her body ripe from many encounters, weighty with voluptuous awareness. He saw her now as the marvellous instrument for his new art, the woman who had made great poetry plain to him . . . He felt bound to her not with the promise of pleasure, but with the promise of glory."

D'Annunzio's speech ended with an image of sexual intercourse, of Venice abandoning herself to a god. There was a "great burst of applause," and the "audience breathed out their delirium in the shout to the man." Afterward, Duse/Foscarina and Giulietta/Donatella, "confused in a blur of whiteness," came to greet him. Throughout the book, d'Annunzio conflated the image of the two women—Eleonora and Giulietta—almost as if they were older and younger versions of the same self.

Celebrity and worldwide fame are powerful aphrodisiacs, and with "orgiastic sensuality," in *Il fuoco* d'Annunzio imagined Duse's "trembling, captivated audiences . . . her unknown lovers," and he fantasized about making love to her "right after a successful performance, when she was still warm with the breath of the crowd, soaked in sweat, panting and exhausted . . . yet needing to be taken, to be shaken, to be bent backwards in the final spasm, to receive his violent seed, to sink finally into a dreamless stupor."

D'Annunzio equated his artistic outbursts, his poetic eruptions, with the spurt of his semen. Writing and sex were means of domination, and he recognized the suffocating, inebriating effect this had on his lovers. In *Il fuoco*, when Duse/Foscarina is with her lover, she "seemed to lose touch with her own life and to be moved into a kind of intense, hallucinatory fictitious life where it was difficult even to breathe."

At the beginning of their affair, Duse and d'Annunzio idolized one another—adoring what they saw of themselves in the other and what completed their selves. The author saw his ideal interpreter, and the actress saw her ideal writer. They both possessed vivid, self-dramatizing imaginations; mesmerizing voices; hunger for sensual experiences and intellectual challenges; a need for intensity; and a shared dream of art.

In the fall and winter of 1895–96, they spent time together in Venice, Florence, and Milan, and they "honeymooned" at Marina di Pisa, where Duse had lost her son in 1880. *Il fuoco* suggests the reason she was drawn back to Marina di Pisa—because Duse/Foscarina wanted a son by d'Annunzio/Stelio. "It is only fair," she says in the book, "that new life should come from my body, since I have given my master the gift of myself." Duse, then thirty-seven, didn't get pregnant, probably a result of her gynecological treatments a few years earlier. There would be no son, but Duse and d'Annunzio exchanged vows to formalize their artistic collaboration. Duse called it "the promise of Pisa," where "a silent *pact* was signed between us," and d'Annunzio gave his "promise to my art."

In early 1896, Duse's art took her to Vienna and on a brief tour of Scandinavia. "You will smile now," she wrote from Stockholm. "I found some violets under the snow, *living*, LIVING, and tranquil, as if they were in a greenhouse." D'Annunzio knew how to read her metaphors, and violets became her flower, a symbol of awakening. After seeing him in Florence, Duse wrote from Paris on January 18, 1896. "Your touch is still on me—but the road *is there*, and it must be taken." She connected the feelings she had for d'Annunzio with the transcendent grace she felt in her acting. "I would like to DISAPPEAR, all, all, all!—Give all of myself, and melt. It would be to you and for you, for the great work—the *work* that you have called *'joyous* and *fruitful.'*"

Duse was referring to the plays d'Annunzio planned to write, but except for the title he hadn't written a line of his first play, *La città morta*. Instead, he was working feverishly on *Il fuoco*, "a book of passion." At the end of the book, Duse/Foscarina sailed for America to earn money for their theatre. "The nomadic woman armed herself with courage and prepared her *viaticum* for the journey," d'Annunzio wrote. "On the table in front of her were her familiar books, some with corners of pages turned down, others with notes in the margins, some containing leaves or flowers or blades of grass between the pages . . . all her favourite little things were laid out before her . . . all made holy by revered memories, animated by some superstitious belief, touched by the finger of love or death."

ON FEBRUARY 6, 1896, Duse arrived in New York on the *Majestic*. Irma Gramatica, in her early twenties, who had acted with Duse for the last nine years, traveled with her, but the rest of the company followed a week later. Joseph Schürmann, Duse's American producers, and a *New York Times* reporter met the boat. Wearing galoshes, a macintosh, a veil, and a rain hat, Duse managed to look "vibrant" to the *New York Times* reporter. Schürmann escorted her to the Holland House. Although Schürmann had turned away advertisers, including one enterprising dentist who wanted Duse to promote his false teeth, an ophthalmologist put up posters around town of two huge eyes—one laughing and the other crying—and guaranteed he could make anyone's eyes look just like Duse's. Billboards on streetcars hailed the appearance of "Eleonora Duse The Passing Star."

Duse refused to be interviewed except to grant an interview to a female reporter to explain why she wouldn't be interviewed. As usual, this created a flurry of attention. When the reporter accused her of lacking respect for the press, Duse appealed to her as a woman. "We women must stick together and help each other," she said. "I ask you to please ask your colleagues why a worker who works all day, after finishing his job, has the right to rest at night; while I, who work all night, cannot enjoy being alone during the day?"

Before opening in New York, Duse traveled to Washington, D.C., for a brief engagement there. On the day she left, she wrote d'Annunzio. She missed him and when she had woken up, she imagined him speaking to her on a street in Asolo. In her hotel room, she created a kind of portable altar, framing his words and placing them with a vase of flowers by her bed. She asked about his work. "You are on high," she concluded.

While she waited for d'Annunzio to write plays for her, she presented the top hits of her repertory—*La Dame aux camélias* and the Italian double bill of *Cavalleria rusticana* and *La locandiera,* and her new production of *Magda.* Her Washington appearances were a huge success. Along with Supreme Court justices and other government officials, President Grover Cleveland and the first lady attended all of her plays, filled her dressing room with chrysanthemums and roses, and invited her to a tea at the White House. Later on the tour, after Thomas Edison saw her perform, she visited his laboratory in New Jersey, and he recorded her voice on the phonograph. (The recording has not been found.) In her letters to d'Annunzio, Duse doesn't mention these distinctions or the success she's having. She's lonely, having trouble sleeping, and finding excuses for d'Annunzio's failure to write. "God, it's so easy to write a short letter and free yourself from obligation. I thank you not to do this."

In late February 1896, when Duse opened at the Fifth Avenue Theatre, Sarah Bernhardt was just completing a month's engagement at Abbey's Theatre. Bernhardt had wisely dropped *Magda* from her New York repertoire, and the only role they shared was Marguerite in *La Dame aux camélias*. Duse opened with it, but she played it only four times. Her most popular performances were *Magda* and the Italian double bill—she performed both twelve times.

The attitude of the critics who compared Bernhardt and Duse can be summed up by a headline in *The Illustrated American* under three photographs of Duse: "Eleonora Duse, the Italian actress whose perfect art has made Bernhardt's artifice seem mean and paltry." The critic's characterization of Duse's "perfect art" was influenced by the fact that at thirty-seven—fourteen years younger than Bernhardt—Duse had the more youthful face and figure. Also, as an Italian woman, she was assumed to be hot-blooded and passionate. While critics, mostly male, wrote high-minded panegyrics to Duse's art, she moved them on a more basic level with pure sex appeal. The New York audiences agreed with the critics. Duse's box-office returns for *La Dame aux camélias* exceeded Bernhardt's.

Duse appealed to men, but as her international fame increased, she also attracted legions of devoted women fans. During her New York stay, Duse played a benefit of *Pamela* for the city's kindergartens, which further endeared her to women. Whenever she left the theatre, women waited to catch a glimpse of her. They bought her photographs and picture postcards, pasted news stories about her into scrapbooks, followed her career, and lived vicariously through her.

Years later, the writer Helen Gansevoort Mackay, who had seen Duse in New York, described what Duse had meant to her as a girl and offered a rare glimpse of Duse's preparation. "I managed to steal week by week from my grandmother's writing desk and escape from school and go in secret to all of Eleonora Duse's matinees," Mackay recalled. "I would get a place always in the front row, in a corner opposite most of her entrances . . . Often the seats beside me were taken by two elderly women who told me they did not come to see the play, only to see the Duse as she was herself . . . I saw the stage badly, but could see her, waiting for her cues in the wings. She sat with her head bent, a cloak around her shoulders, not speaking to anyone, looking at nothing. She was there always much too soon for her calls . . . Her black hair waved from her forehead heavily. Her face was not symmetric, one eye lid drooped and one corner of her mouth. In that was the strange part of her beauty. Watching her as she waited, I came to know some small gestures she had, of turning her head away from people who spoke to her, of lifting one hand and letting it fall again, as if she were asking herself a question and giving up the answer . . . At her cues she threw off the cloak, stood up, and came on the stage awkwardly, a little dazed, as if she did not know what people were thanking her for in their applause. Then she became the heroine of whatever play it might be, and gave, through some imagined woman, all that was deep in herself. She took applause after the play as if she were grateful but very tired, as if all her gift had been given and she could not even remember what it had been anymore."

Mackay later became a close friend of Duse's, but when she was a girl, "I never thought of trying to know her. It was not necessary. She was in my days as I made the story of them. I traveled the world with her . . . When she left, she was still with me."

IN EARLY APRIL the company left New York for engagements in Boston, Philadelphia, and New Haven. Duse had refused to play Chicago. In Boston, she became ill, suspended performances, and wrote d'Annunzio a long, anguished, self-dramatizing letter. During the weeks while she was in New York, Duse hadn't written to him, except a telegram saying "work-work-work," but she complained of the unspeakable suffering caused by his silence, forgetting she had asked him not to write. Most of d'Annunzio's letters to Duse were lost or destroyed by Enrichetta, and it is not known if he wrote to her regularly at this time. Since Duse wanted immediate responses to her telegrams and letters, his "silence" may have lasted only a few days.

Duse used letter writing as a release for feelings, which means she often wrote, as Laurense Alma-Tadema pointed out, when she was upset or depressed. Time after time in her letters to her lovers, Duse complained of her suffering and of the enormous anguish she endured that made her long for death. "How is it that I can write today?" she asked d'Annunzio. "Is it perhaps because the heart is like the sea—I don't know—I don't know anymore—I swear that I don't know anymore—" she repeated. Duse loved to play the role of the suffering woman. This is not to say she didn't really suffer or feel pain at the moment of writing—she possessed a powerful imagination.

She presented a less histrionic view of the suffering caused by love, though, in a letter of advice to an actor friend she wrote around this time. "So be courageous and good, again and always again. This word 'again' is the word we need most, because it means so many things: 'again' means patience, it means courage, it means struggle, it means forgiveness, it means love and sur- render. [. . .] I hope and wish that my words may lead you into each other's arms and that you will resume your lies [. . .]" Involved in simultaneous relationships with Boito, Wolkoff, and d'Annunzio, Duse loved and lied. D'Annunzio, of course, was a master liar who lied with impunity to his wife, his various mistresses, and most of all to his creditors.

In early May, Duse ended her tour in the United States. The morning before she left New York, she visited The Players Club in Gramercy Park. The beautiful space dedicated to actors impressed her. She met with the members and spoke in honor of the Players' founder, Edwin Booth. Duse's second American tour was artistically and financially successful and established Duse as a cult figure among her American fans. It would be decades, however, before provincial America caught up with Duse's new art and her portrayal of women as human beings. The conservative *New York Tribune*, shocked at Duse's scandalous repertory, offered her some parting advice. When she came back to the United States, she should "consign Magda to a lunatic asylum and Camille to the graveyard, and come back with a repertory of fresh and decent plays."

DUSE RETURNED to her apartment in Venice and a reunion with d'An- nunzio, who was there soaking up the atmosphere while writing *Il fuoco*. On a quick trip to Paris to see Giulietta Gordigiani, Duse dashed off a short letter to d'Annunzio. Since she wasn't having a crisis or feeling lonely or isolated, Duse's letters to him become shorter and less passionate at this time. Also, she was preoccupied with decisions about money and work. She rejected d'An- nunzio's first proposal for a meeting, but "Venice seems possible for a million other reasons that I don't have time to tell you." Instead of rushing back to Venice, though, she planned to stop in Basel, where it was "tranquil and green."

In August, Duse traveled to Milan to meet with Joseph Schürmann and her administrator Ettore Mazzanti about future work and to confer with lawyers. Boito was out of town, vacationing in the mountains, and Duse vis- ited him there. "The strongest is the loneliest," she wrote to him after her stay. "The loneliest is the strongest." The visit had not gone well, but Duse avoided discussing it. "I would like to write you many things that I feel and don't know how to say, but my head hurts, and I have the trunk, or rather, *two* trunks to pack."

She moved to Rome in mid-September to begin rehearsals with her com- pany. On September 30 she wrote to d'Annunzio professing to tell him the "truth!" He had asked her to stage *La città morta* that November. Months earlier, with Count Primoli, d'Annunzio had woven what he called "a frightful conspiracy" for the play's performance. With Primoli's help, he had contacted Sarah Bernhardt, who had accepted the play, which had yet to be written, for production at her theatre in Paris. In the contract, he restricted her to performing the play in France. He offered Duse the Italian rights and proposed she present the play in November. Duse was too much of a professional, and too wary of unproven new plays, to sign a contract for a play she hadn't read. Instead, she resorted to the traditional delaying tactic of smart producers. "The truth is," she repeated, "that today I don't have the two actors or the actress that the play requires." She didn't mention the expense involved in mounting a new production. Actually, d'Annunzio's play, unlike most of Duse's repertory, was an ensemble piece with four major roles, two women and two men. With Carlo Rosaspina and Irma Gramatica and herself, Duse had three of the roles covered, and just needed a strong young male lead for the other role, but d'Annunzio wanted well-known stars for the roles. A few weeks later, when she invited d'Annunzio to read the play to her in Rome, he declined—for a good reason. He hadn't finished it.

In the meantime, she added Pinero's *The Second Mrs. Tanqueray,* a proven hit that required a female star, to her repertory. She had promised d'Annunzio she would cancel all her engagements out of the country and remain in Italy to find the actors who could present his play. An Italian tour fell through when she learned that rival managers refused to rent her their theatres. Undoubtedly prodded by Schürmann and needing to earn money, she broke her promise to d'Annunzio and decided to return to Germany and Russia.

Giulietta Gordigiani joined her in Rome and planned to travel with her to Germany. Duse adored the young woman, but she was not happy about d'Annunzio's interest in her. Duse had no illusions about d'Annunzio's sexual fidelity, but she was jealous of his bold attentions to her friend. It's likely Giulietta told Duse about d'Annunzio's attempt to seduce her in Florence in early October. Giulietta had spent a "beautiful day" with d'Annunzio on October 4, and they had gone on a "peaceful walk." It's "vile to pretend to love when you're not in love," Giulietta told him. "If you love me I don't love you because love doesn't mean the same thing to you as it does to me and so my duty is to ask you this question—would you, could you, consider me as your little sister and excluding any other thoughts—and *for always?* Under these conditions our union could be eternal."

Believing the correspondence between Duse and d'Annunzio stopped after Duse learned he had signed a contract with Sarah Bernhardt to produce *La città morta,* previous biographers of Duse and d'Annunzio have concluded the couple were estranged for months because Duse felt betrayed by her lover.

In fact, the correspondence didn't stop, and Duse was more upset with d'Annunzio's interest in Giulietta than about his contacts with Bernhardt. D'Annunzio acted deviously, but predictably, in his attempt to secure a first-rate production for his script. Although both Bernhardt and Duse wrote to him claiming to be excited and thrilled about the opportunity to present his work, their actions contradict their words. Both stars were hesitant to stage d'Annunzio's ensemble play. Georges Hérelle had translated *La città morta* into French, and Bernhardt had promised d'Annunzio she would arrange everything for an immediate production, but she didn't produce it until 1898, and Duse would take even longer. Ironically, the "frightful conspiracy" d'Annunzio had woven really had only one victim—himself. He learned just how powerless a first time playwright is when confronted with two powerful stars who also are producers with an eye on the budget.

IN MID-NOVEMBER 1896, Duse and her troupe left for Berlin. D'Annunzio came to Rome to say good-bye and to wish her well. "I left almost against the will of my heart," Duse told him, addressing him as "dear soul." Later, in his notebook, d'Annunzio wrote that in Duse's "sad step" away from him, he heard the rustle of laurel leaves. Duse often struggled in letters for words to express her thoughts, but onstage and offstage she had a genius for turning action into metaphor. "She had tied a hair round each of my fingers as I talked with her, close beside me," d'Annunzio recalled. "I was tied by five hairs and I began to feel the hurt as if the five hairs were five chains . . . She does not release me and says, 'Break them! Snap them! . . .' The hairs break but the knots remain round my knuckles . . . She takes my hand thus ringed with sharp pain. I feel her tears falling. An obscure anguish binds us, fibre to fibre . . ."

Since Giulietta, much to Duse's disappointment, had decided not to go with her to Russia, Laurense Alma-Tadema joined them in Berlin and accompanied Duse to St. Petersburg and Moscow. Sometimes her women companions irritated her, but they provided valuable support. Duse managed a large company, which included making decisions about repertoire, casting, sets, costumes, scheduling, advertising, plus directing the plays and preparing her own roles. All this required an enormous amount of energy and stamina. Since she was the star and the box-office draw, the constant financial responsibility for the company rested on her shoulders. To compensate, her daily life was made as easy as possible. Her loyal maid, Nina, who had served her for many years, drew her bath, dressed her, brushed her hair, washed her clothes, mailed her letters, packed and unpacked her trunks, coaxed her to eat, undressed her at night, and put her to bed. Her women friends ate with her, walked with her, ran her errands, wrote letters for her, and listened to her laments. Duse called them her "guardian angels." In return, the women traveled the world, met interesting people, lived in the reflected glow of her charisma, and even inherited her lovers.

It was probably during this tour to Berlin that Duse introduced Giulietta to Robert von Mendelssohn, an amateur cellist, who was related to the composer Felix Mendelssohn. With his brother Franz, Robert controlled the Mendelssohn bank in Berlin. Like most of Duse's friends, Robert had fallen in love with her. He transferred his affections to Giulietta, and in 1899 they married.

During her Berlin engagement, Duse arranged for Enrichetta, who was attending school in Dresden, to visit her. She hadn't seen her daughter for six months. Duse had visited her in Dresden in June, when Enrichetta had been ill with lung or bronchial problems. To Duse's relief, Enrichetta, who would be fifteen in January, was healthy. Duse wouldn't permit her daughter to attend any of her performances. On the last night of Enrichetta's stay, Duse allowed her daughter to sleep with her and "the dear little thing cried . . . and curled herself up next to me."

DUSE'S PERFORMANCES in Berlin were a great success, but instead of crowing over her triumphs, she complained to Boito about her huge expenses and her inability to save money. In other words, she couldn't retire just yet. When she arrived in St. Petersburg, "the cold knocked her to the ground," but her reception by the critics and the sold-out crowds at the Maly Theatre was warm and effusive. Sudermann's *Magda* proved popular with the Russian audiences, who hadn't seen it before.

As usual, success cheered her up, and her letters to Boito from Russia contain fewer laments. She explained that she had to switch to another pen, and "it's impossible to *speak* of misery with a *goose* pen." Her audiences in St. Petersburg wondered why she didn't perform Shakespeare—a nudge to Boito, who had promised to translate *As You Like It* for her. "I want to *see you*, soon, soon," she exclaimed. When her tour concluded in St. Petersburg, she asked Boito to meet her, perhaps in Berlin, where "you would make love to me and hold me tight and close all night."

Boito must have smiled at Duse's criticism of her absent "angel," Giulietta, who was bombarding her with letters "HERE, three or four a day!!" and expecting Duse's immediate response. Giulietta was preparing for her professional debut as a concert pianist in Florence, was filled with anxiety and doubts, and completely absorbed with her own problems and her own personality. Doesn't she understand I have work and responsibilities? Duse asked. *"If there's no silence, there's no work!"* Laurense, her other "angel," was sick with influenza during most of their time in St. Petersburg and wasn't much help.

Offstage, Duse spent her time reading, writing letters, taking long walks, and window-shopping. In an elegant St. Petersburg shop, she found two beautiful pearl earrings, "like two large tears, like two exclamation points!" She had made something of a fetish of never wearing jewelry. D'Annunzio admired the artfulness of her choice, which made the beauty of her bare skin stand out in contrast to other women who covered themselves with jewels. Boito detested anything flashy, impractical, or expensive. With Boito, then fifty-four, Duse could play a teasing girl, a girl dependent on his advice. She bought the pearl earrings, wore them once, and then put them in a box. She asked Boito to "baptize" them and give her permission to wear them. "They change me a lot and *accent* my face," she said. Plus, they made her smile when she looked at herself in the mirror. "Of course, I know that I didn't need to buy the pearls," she sighed, imagining his disapproval, "but . . ."

Duse caught a cold in St. Petersburg that developed into influenza by the time her company arrived in Moscow. She also suffered from a return of the facial neuralgia that affected one side of her face. Steam baths and hot-water treatments didn't cure her, and all of her Moscow performances were cancelled. Her doctor ordered her to find a warmer climate. On her way to sunny Genoa and the Ligurian coast, she stopped in Vienna on February 12. She wrote to d'Annunzio, "dear soul," at the Grand Hotel in Rome. "Hold my hand tightly," she wrote, "and tell me about yourself." She had received his telegrams, but she longed to "rehear his voice" in a letter he had promised.

When she arrived in Genoa, she found instead of sun a violent wind whipping through the palm trees, drenching rain, and a torrent of telegrams, letters, and contracts flooding in from all parts of the world. Boito had sent her *Rosalinda (As You Like It)*. She thought it was weak; maybe they could try to do it, but it would probably be a waste of time. "The days pass and I decide nothing," she said.

In search of sun, she moved to Santa Margherita. On March 2, she wrote letters to both d'Annunzio and Boito. She padded her letter to Boito with a long quotation and a list of troubles—she had spent two days in bed because of her period, and she was besieged at her hotel with requests for autographs and photographs. She told d'Annunzio, who was in Rome, nothing of her problems; instead she worried about him. "What is it that troubles you?" she asked. "I still have hope for you. What is it that bites? I remember an evening of profound honesty on your part . . . also a profound promise in myself that never again, never again, would any misunderstanding, any egoism, separate me from that memory. Why don't you believe me? . . . Speak to me again and give me 'Città Morta.' [. . .] The heart, it *knows* you," she concluded.

DURING MARCH 1897, as Duse made her way south toward d'Annunzio and Rome, she was moving emotionally farther and farther away from Boito. Her liaison with him had been a dead end, but her relationship with d'Annunzio promised to fulfill a dream Duse shared with other theatre artists around the world. More and more, she felt "everything that is disgraceful, low, dumb, dubious, lacking all grandeur, in these unworthy tours that are undertaken on the basis of profit." She admired André Antoine's Théâtre-Libre in Paris, Jacob Grein's Independent Theatre in London, and Otto Brahm's Freie Bühne in Berlin. The ambition she shared with d'Annunzio, though, was much greater than the creation of a little avant-garde theatre. Their love affair and their artistic collaboration, perhaps unique in the history of the theatre, united a major poet and novelist and experimental first-time playwright with an international star of the commercial theatre.

D'Annunzio read *La città morta* to her, and on March 28, 1897, Duse signed a contract for the Italian rights. She enclosed the contract in a letter to the Florentine attorney, Adolfo de Bosis, who was acting as producer. The signatures were a "lie," she wrote. "Everything cannot be foreseen or said, perhaps, in a case like ours, but time will thank you."

At the same time, Joseph Schürmann was negotiating for Duse's first appearance in Paris. Bernhardt heard about the negotiations and invited Duse to play at her theatre, the Renaissance. Sarah's magnanimous gesture was much applauded. Duse accepted the favorable terms, but she was apprehensive about her first appearance in Paris, a city that considered itself the world capital of art. Eventually, every artist who desired greatness had to reckon with the city that had the highest alcohol consumption of any city in the world, the liveliest cabarets, the most beautiful fashions, the most rigorous critics, and half a million spectacle-loving theatregoers who bought theatre tickets at least once a week.

With Schürmann's, Primoli's, and d'Annunzio's assistance, Duse prepared her attack on Paris. One of Duse's greatest achievements as "La Duse" was her convincing portrayal of an artist without ambition who cared only for art and nothing for publicity. "You'll see how I know how to follow you and precede you!" she declared to d'Annunzio. "We'll guide the crowd who know nothing."

Most likely assisted or edited by Matilde Serao, Primoli wrote an article for *La Revue de Paris*, which "guided" opinion and Paris's perception of Duse.

The article was actually a brilliant press release shamelessly flattering Sarah Bernhardt, the superior taste of the French people, and the genius of French writers. Primoli prepared the audience for Duse's repertoire, which included three of Sarah's plays, and a new play by d'Annunzio. Since Bernhardt held the French rights for *La città morta,* Duse wouldn't be able to do it, and she asked d'Annunzio to improvise some poetic verses for her. D'Annunzio thought it was a mad idea. So write me the role of a madwoman, Duse countered. In ten days in April 1897, d'Annunzio wrote *Il sogno d'un mattino di primavera (The Dream of a Spring Morning).*

In addition to preparing his puff piece, Primoli also contacted his friends in Paris to secure Duse's warm reception there. He convinced Adelaide Ristori, who had vanquished the great Rachel, to write an admiring article about Duse as well. Meanwhile, d'Annunzio retreated to the Hotel della Porta in Albano outside of Rome to write his *Sogno.*

While Primoli and d'Annunzio worked, Duse tried to relax in Capri at Villa San Michele, the home of her friend, the Swedish physician and psychiatrist Axel Munthe. Hoping to give herself strength, she began a regimen of strychnine injections. The strychnine, which acted as a stimulant, made her nervous and caused her eyes to swell. While she confessed her problems and anxieties to Boito, in her letters to d'Annunzio, she hid her pain, but her anxiety can be clearly seen in the wild, often incoherent scrawl of her handwriting.

Walking helped relieve her stress, and on one rainy-day stroll, she found photographs of ruins that she sent to d'Annunzio as ideas for the *La città morta* production. "Don't lose them," she admonished. They planned a lavish production to inaugurate their proposed new theatre in Albano. The problem was they didn't have the money to fund it, although d'Annunzio had met with Harold Bennet, owner of the *New York Herald,* about underwriting their scheme and finding other backers.

"When will you give me the dream?" Duse asked d'Annunzio impatiently. She longed to get it into rehearsal, since Schürmann had scheduled her Paris debut for the beginning of June. "I bless your silence because it proves that you're working," she wrote. She admitted she was a beast, and asked him not to be angry with her for bothering him. She explained she was worried because she didn't know anything about the play. She refrained from speaking about love. "I know, I know, I know all the words that I can never say to you. I know them [. . .] I see the road, we can go there, in silence." Of course, it was impossible for Duse to remain silent for long.

After receiving a telegram from Boito, who had heard about her collaboration with d'Annunzio and was deeply hurt, Duse enclosed his telegram in a letter to d'Annunzio. "To live without making someone else suffer!!" she told d'Annunzio. "It's not possible." Boito hated d'Annunzio the writer and the man, and Duse pleaded with Boito to understand her artistic betrayal. "Today a new power is in sight—oh—tell me *how* could I refuse it? [. . .] I'm terrified of resuming my work with the eternal *Dame aux camélias*—my very *mouth*, at this point, refuses to speak *those* words! The boredom, the boredom, that is *deadlier* than any other danger to the artist." Duse desperately wanted Boito's respect and blessing. "Trust me. *Let me have my wings*," she said. "GIVE ME wings. *I will return*—into the palm of your hand!" Boito delayed a month before sending Duse a telegram with his blessing.

Duse reminded d'Annunzio of the sacrifices she was making—she was "putting herself into the flame" for him. "Accept it! Accept it!" she exclaimed. "May the gift not make you sad! [. . .] Tell me that you accept me and you must promise me nothing!" [. . .] "Now smile at me and never more, never more, will I speak to you about myself."

In mid-April, Duse left Capri and moved to Rome to wait for d'Annunzio to finish his play. In a letter to d'Annunzio, Duse described a scene with a Roman cab driver who had disturbed her by mistaking her for d'Annunzio's wife Maria Hardouin. If her story was true, Duse must have encountered the most obtuse cab driver in all Rome. Duse was not only a well-known celebrity, but she was the physical opposite of d'Annunzio's wife. Perhaps Duse resorted to playwriting to say what she wished to say. "This is how certain eyes see," Duse told d'Annunzio. "They see and they don't distinguish. She is beautiful, she is blonde, she is young, and she is yours. She is your *thing*. She belongs to you. I am a poor thing who belongs to no one but myself. But what can I do about it?"

After just a week of writing, d'Annunzio finished *Il sogno d'un mattino di primavera* on April 23, Shakespeare's birthday. Duse joined him in Albano for a few days, and he read the one-act to her. Her reaction to the play was shaped by the sound of it in her lover's mouth. The magic of d'Annunzio's speaking voice was once compared to a violinist playing a Stradivarius. "It was a slow precise voice accompanying the words right to the last vowel . . . the tones rose and fell in an unending stream." D'Annunzio seduced his lovers with the power of his voice, and men fell under his spell as well. Bernard Berenson, Arthur Symons, and Harold Nicolson all commented on the mesmerizing power of d'Annunzio's voice.

In *Il sogno* the lyrical verses reveal violence, raging eroticism, murder, and madness. The sexual desire of the principal character, Isabella, propels the play. It begins after Isabella's lover, Giuliano, has been murdered by Isabella's husband. Isabella spends a night clinging to the body of her dead lover, and his blood drenches her. When morning comes, she is insane. D'Annunzio was fascinated with the sexual appetite of women, and he often endowed (and punished) his female characters with a dangerous, insistent sexuality.

Duse had proven herself around the world in bravura roles in plays that appealed to her middle-class and upper-class audiences. She had also succeeded with Zola's naturalism, Verga's *verismo,* and Ibsen's social realism. D'Annunzio's symbolist script, heavily influenced by Maurice Maeterlinck, with the role of Isabella, a character "beyond life," offered Duse a new challenge and put her at the forefront of the new experimental drama sweeping across Europe and confronting the bourgeois, commercial theatre. The year before, Wilde's *Salomé* had debuted at the Théâtre de l'Oeuvre in Paris, Hauptmann's *The Sunken Bell* had premiered in Berlin, and Chekhov's *The Seagull* had opened at the Moscow Art Theatre.

Intoxicated by d'Annunzio's words, Duse didn't object to the static quality of the script. When d'Annunzio wanted to cut some of Isabella's speeches, Duse objected violently. It would be a "mutilation," she asserted. "I must say everything." "Never, never, never was 'Dream of Spring' more sweet and cruel!" she felt. "You enter the dream, through those words [. . .] Lenor, will say things . . . that no one has heard her say before—and she must be beautiful and all smiling."

Duse left for Paris at the end of April. D'Annunzio didn't travel to Paris with her. He had embarked on a campaign to win a seat in Parliament for the constituency of Ortona a Mare, which included his hometown of Pescara and Francavilla, where he lived with his mistress, Maria Gravina. "When Ariel is not here hand in hand with me," Duse confessed, despite her promise not to write about herself, "all my gaiety goes to the devil! And there is no more youth around me!" Duse knew the stakes involved in her Paris campaign. Yes, she was famous, an international star, but what did it really mean? "Fame, too, is a mask of papier-mâché," Duse believed, "and when you touch it, putrefaction comes out . . . !"

WHEN DUSE'S PARIS repertory was announced, Bernhardt was furious. Duse's company planned to give ten performances of six plays during two weeks in June. In addition to *Cavalleria rusticana, La locandiera,* and *Il sogno d'un mattino di primavera,* the other three plays, *La Dame aux camélias, La Femme de Claude,* and *Magda* were all standards in Sarah's repertory. Where was *A Doll's House,* which Duse had introduced to Italy, Russia, Germany, and Austria? And *The Second Mrs. Tanqueray?*

Duse's decision to confront Bernhardt in Paris acting in her rival's plays was a brilliant decision and would underscore their age difference. Her former partner, Flavio Andò, the best male actor in Italy, had agreed to leave his own company and reprise his role of Armande and act with her in d'Annunzio's *Il sogno*. Also, since Duse was acting in Italian, the familiar plays would be easily followed by the French audience and Duse's acting choices and style, dramatically different from Bernhardt's, would be emphasized. If she failed in these plays, she could always insert her newer plays into the bill as a backup. In fact, *The Second Mrs. Tanqueray* was announced for mid-June but later withdrawn because of the popularity of the other plays.

Before her Paris debut, Duse consulted Jean-Philippe Worth of the House of Worth. The fashion house dressed royalty, aristocrats, actresses, and opera stars but refused to have anything to do with Sarah Bernhardt, who had once ordered five costumes and then had three of them made by a rival house. "To my mind," Worth said, "the greatest aristocrat was one not of noble birth, but of royal soul, Eleonora Duse."

Worth personally designed her costumes, and "she had the rare trick," he said, "of making you see exactly what she wanted. Perhaps she would lead you to a window and pointing to a tree whose leaves were just turning would say, 'I want a dress of that shade of brown'; or going to a vase, she would pull a rose and say, 'Make me a frock the color of that.'"

When they talked about her costumes for *La Dame*, Duse shocked Worth when she informed him she never wore jewelry and didn't have any with her. "But, Madame, in Paris you must wear jewels in this play, for we French could not imagine [it] without jewels," he exclaimed. "We must see some material evidence that Marguerite Gauthier was richly provided for." Worth finally convinced her and lent her a pearl necklace worth about 40,000 francs.

Duse left no record of her first meeting with Sarah Bernhardt, but the Comte de Montesquiou said he introduced them. "It was more like a collision than a meeting," he recalled. "The two women grasped each other so tightly that it looked like a mad wrestling match." Bernhardt invited Duse to sit in her box at the Renaissance Theatre for a matinee performance of Rostand's *La Samaritaine,* a biblical play about a courtesan meeting Christ and then preaching the Holy Gospel to her depraved friends. With exaggerated courtesy, Duse stood up every time Bernhardt appeared onstage and remained standing throughout her scenes. Since Montesquiou was sitting with her, he stood up, too. The audience enjoyed a double spectacle and divided their attention between Sarah posing onstage and Duse popping up and down in her box.

On June 1, 1897, it was Sarah's turn to watch Duse act. Bernhardt was outraged that Duse had chosen to open with *La Dame aux camélias.* After years of playing it, Bernhardt felt the script belonged to her. Duse had vanquished her rival in Russia, Austria, Germany, England, and the United States, but

Paris was the final round. Theatre companies across Italy sent Duse good wishes for opening night. The reputation of Italian theatre and Italian national pride were at stake. For Duse, the stakes were higher than a personal triumph or a victory for Italian art. In a match with Bernhardt, who represented the pinnacle of nineteenth-century acting, Duse represented the revolutionary future.

The Renaissance Theatre was completely sold out. Scalpers had sold tickets for about 500 francs a seat. In her prominent box in full view of the audience, accompanied by her son Maurice and his wife, Bernhardt looked radiant in an embroidered silk gown with a wreath of roses in her bright red hair. Other boxes were filled with French and Italian nobility and actors from the Comédie-Française, including Eugénie Doche, the original Marguerite. In the orchestra seats *tout* Paris was gathered. The critics Jules Lemaître, Henry Fouquier, and the white-bearded dean of French critics, Francisque Sarcey, were also present. Duse's friends were out in force, including Count Primoli; the writers Marco Praga, Roberto Bracco, and Antona Traversi; the beautiful Italian actress Tina di Lorenzo; and members of the Italian and Russian embassies. An American writer, Victor Mapes, was on hand to record his impressions.

At 9 p.m. three loud knocks signaled the play would begin. Bernhardt leaned forward with her chin in her hand, glanced around to check she was being watched, and then stared intently at the stage. When Duse entered without makeup, her abundant hair simply coiffed, dressed in a flowing white gown and her Worth pearls, applause and whispering broke out. French audiences were used to seeing actresses wearing layers of makeup and brilliant jewels. "As the play goes on, her nervousness betrays her at every step," Mapes wrote. "It holds her in an agony, which she tries in vain to dominate. Her voice sounds hollow, her fingers twitch, her whole form is trembling from head to toe . . . Little by little, however, she obtains possession of herself, and she is playing almost as usual before the act comes to an end."

During the intermission, Duse retreated to her dressing room. Count Primoli attempted to see her, but she wouldn't admit anyone. Sarah had not allowed Duse to use her own spacious dressing room and had given her a smaller dressing room, which required her to go outside the theatre on a kind of fire ladder to get to the stage. While Duse prepared for the second act, Bernhardt entertained visitors in her box. According to Mapes, the second act was received better with murmurings of approval, but the third act failed. In the fourth act, Flavio Andò "developed such force and passion that he quite eclipsed Duse, and made the real sensation of the evening." Duse's "exhaustion and despair" gave added poignancy to the deathbed scene. "As the audience filed out," Mapes wrote, "after giving one final look at Bernhardt, there could be no doubt as to the result of the issue. If someone had triumphed it was not Duse."

Duse's friend Roberto Bracco telegraphed an entirely different report to Italy. Duse's art was a triumph of truth and sincerity, Bracco said. After the play, he talked to the writer Georges de Porto-Riche, who called the evening "the most profound sensation I've ever had in the theatre," and the widow of George Bizet gushed, "Oh, your Duse! She is Bizet in prose!"

The French reviews were measured and impartial. Henry Fouquier reported that the audience was the most brilliant he had ever seen, Duse had great talent, and Andò partnered her exceptionally, but he refused to speculate on whether Duse's newer art had triumphed over Bernhardt's established artistry. Sarcey took a few days to write his careful, somewhat hesitant response, but at the end, he confessed to confusion. Duse's presence had gripped him and held him captive, he said, but he couldn't describe how exactly. "I feel that I am not in the proper key . . . *Chi lo sa?* since we are in Italy. It is nevertheless true that La Duse is an *artiste* by race, and, if one insists, a great *artiste*."

A week later, Duse played *Magda*. The French critics didn't care for the German play, but Sarcey declared while Sarah made the play seem idiotic, "La Duse makes it seem almost possible . . . when Sarah played the part, she never allowed us to forget for an instant that she was Magda. With la Duse, we no longer remembered it; and then, as she . . . uttered . . . a powerful outburst of scorn and anger, without ever forcing the note, the tirade against her infamous seducer, the audience was completely captured. Every one was delighted to see so much naturalness combined with such great force of feeling." Before coming to definite conclusions about her talent, Sarcey wanted to wait until he had seen her in her other plays. And, Duse, cleverly, made him wait. Her scheduled performances of *Cavalleria rusticana* and *La Femme de Claude* were postponed because she had caught a cold, probably brought on by stress, anger, and her sensitivity to drafts. She fumed to d'Annunzio about the inconvenience, going from "fire to ice," caused by walking from her remote dressing room, outside across a long fire ladder, and then back inside to the stage.

Still, she continued to rehearse *Il sogno* for its world premiere. Also, Bernhardt had asked her to participate in a tribute to Dumas *fils*, who had died in 1895, and she had agreed. Perhaps intentionally, Bernhardt had scheduled the event for June 14, the day before *Il sogno* opened. Duse played the second act from *La Femme de Claude*, Bernhardt acted *La Dame aux camélias*, Coquelin recited a poem, Tamagno sang an aria, the singer Yvette Guilbert read a monologue, and a bust of Dumas was unveiled. The evening ended with the audience roaring their approval as they saw what no one had ever seen before or would ever see again—Bernhardt and Duse, on the same stage, hand in hand, taking a bow.

Bernhardt didn't attend the opening of *Il sogno*, presented with Goldoni's *La locandiera*. She went to London to work leaving Duse in residence at the Renaissance. Hérelle's translation of *Il sogno* had been published in the *Revue de Paris*, and audiences were familiar with the morbid story. Duse looked spring-fresh in a floating Worth gown of five layers of violet gauze and a satin slip embroidered on the bodice with a circle of green leaves.

According to one French critic, the play, a mediocre poem, was successful because of the presence of an Italian claque. Duse's beauty and artistry received unanimous praise, but d'Annunzio's symbolist poem was called pretentious, infantile, too long, mannered, and insignificant. The fact that an avant-garde play, more suited to a small art theatre like the Théâtre-Libre, had been given a full-scale commercial production by an international star, was significant. Duse's willingness to take risks with an untried play demonstrated remarkable courage. For d'Annunzio, Duse's support and belief were a key source of encouragement, and he continued to write plays.

When she heard about the poor reviews for d'Annunzio's play, Sarah announced from London she would perform *Il sogno*. "What fly is biting her?" Sarcey asked, disgusted with the battle of the divas. "If she wishes to engage in a duel . . . she should take refuge rather in those inaccessible regions which it would seem Duse could never penetrate, and act *Phèdre*."

During the last week of her stay, Duse performed the rest of her repertory, including *La Femme de Claude* and *Cavalleria rusticana*. Again, in the familiar pattern, her acting had a cumulative effect on the critics and audiences, who were beginning to understand her new methods. French actors, precise as metronomes, produced beautiful sounds, and audiences listened to plays the same way they listened to music. Duse's acting required the audience to grow and change with her—to experience the play in a new way. For the first time, they were seeing a woman playing a human being onstage in all her complexity and completeness. "In la Duse we have seen on the stage a woman's nature and an *artiste*'s nature completing each other," Gustave Larroumet wrote in *Figaro*. "She leaves behind her a seed that will bear fruit."

On July 1, the Italian Embassy hosted a formal dinner with a French menu in honor of Duse. *Tout* Paris dined on *aspic de foie gras parisienne, haricots verts au beurre*, and *canard rouennais à l'orange*. François-Félix Faure, the president of the French Republic, professed disbelief Duse hadn't acted in French. "Why, signora, were you speaking Italian?"

Francisque Sarcey wrote an open letter to *Le Temps* asking Duse to give a special invitation-only matinee for her fellow artists. Duse said she would be honored and the date was set for Saturday, July 3. Fifteen thousand requests

Duse (center) with all the stars of the Comédie-Française, 1897

for seats were sent to Schürmann. Since Bernhardt refused to allow her the-atre to be used unless the invitations went out in her name, the performance was moved from the Renaissance to the larger La Porte St. Martin, which held fifteen hundred.

"It was one of the most beautiful houses I have ever seen," Sarcey recalled, "for from top to bottom it was quivering with sympathy . . . there was no artificial commotion; it was expectation, full of security and joy." Duse played *Cavalleria rusticana*, the last act of *La Dame aux camélias*, and the second act of *La Femme de Claude*. The next morning in *Le Figaro*, Jules Huret called the event a "strange and admirable phenomenon—the force and the nobleness of true art. If this gathering of artists was applauding with unanimous enthusi-asm, it was not only because it perceived clearly the genius of la Duse . . . the applause meant even more. It was the unconscious and impulsive translation of their love of their art, the homage they paid over and above the interpreter, to their ideal—to their art thus ennobled before them, which added to their own feelings of pride."

Afterward, the artists rushed the stage to talk to her, to embrace her, to give her flowers, or to shake her hand. Young actors and actresses with tears in their eyes didn't dare to approach her. Suzanne Desprès, a young actress who had taken out a loan to buy a ticket, attempted to touch Duse's sleeve as she passed by. Duse turned, smiled at her, and laughed. She pulled a ribbon from her dress and gave it to Suzanne.

Duse's actors, along with the Italian ambassador, waited until everyone had left to say good-bye. "Go, go; you are free!" she said to her company, kissing and hugging them in farewell. "Thanks, thanks to you all a thousand times!"

The next morning, the actors of the Comédie-Française, whom Duse had privately disparaged as "painted dolls," hosted a farewell breakfast for her on the Bois de Boulogne. Not everyone, though, sang the praises of La Duse. "Now they want to bury me," Sarah Bernhardt complained in a letter to Montesquiou. "All this is bad, including La Duse who has played a shrewd role—Oh how shamelessly shrewd! It's all ugly, despicable. The Italian *artiste* is an underhanded, ignoble creature. Imagine, she didn't even write to thank me or bid me farewell!"

Despite her overwhelming success, Duse was ready to leave Paris, "this prison of a city." She had won, but the battle had been hard fought. The constant intrigue, the condescension of the French, who flaunted their superiority, and her long campaign to prove her art had all been exhausting. Always sensitive about her lack of education and her humble roots, Duse felt, nevertheless, enormous pride in her artistic heritage and the artistry and professionalism of her company.

"I assure you," she told d'Annunzio, "that the mountebanks and buskers who arrive towards evening in our little provincial towns on a cart, with a dog following and a woman always breast-feeding a brat who doesn't look much of a baby, with a shabby, patched carpet, an old costume, and a trapeze like a gallows—well, all that miserable pack deserves more to live than any of those I have seen here these past days!"

Because of "double-dealing," Duse broke a contract to perform that summer in London. "Too long and boring to tell you all," she wrote to d'Annunzio. His letters kept her going—"What joy! Another letter from Ariel. Thank you. Thank you!"—and she longed to get back to him. "When? When will we see each other?" she asked.

The *prima donna* had the world at her feet and thousands of adoring fans, but without Ariel, her bright, fallen angel, she was just a solitary woman. "Advise me," she said. "I feel myself so alone—away from the world."

Six

THE STRESS OF Duse's Paris debut left her exhausted and ill. Her doctors disagreed about her treatment—one advised her to go to the mountains to rest and another urged her to go to the sea.

"Where will I go?" she asked d'Annunzio. "Return to Italy? I need air to live. Switzerland? With the horrible tourists?"

During her few months of "rest" during the summer and fall of 1897, she traveled in Switzerland and Italy, visiting both mountains and sea; rented and furnished a house; managed a company; plotted her next career moves; arranged for her daughter's care; and balanced a complicated love life. "I have strong and tenacious roots to life," she said, "and my strength returns after a brief rest and a little lightening of my load."

When she found herself in a lull, she grew depressed and nervous and felt that her life was sliding away from her. In choosing d'Annunzio as her lover, she was assured of living as intensely offstage as she lived onstage. Judging from the evidence of Duse's self-dramatizing letters to d'Annunzio, she knew her lover watched and studied her with the concentration and perception of an obsessed fan who wanted to discover all her secrets.

WHEN DUSE RETURNED from Paris, she rented a house in Settignano, in the hills northeast of Florence, but she kept her apartment in Wolkoff's Venetian palazzo. According to Wolkoff's friend Hermann Graf Keyserling, Wolkoff "withdrew quietly and with dignity, without saying a single word." Although hurt by Duse's defection, Wolkoff continued to advise her and to irritate her by reminding her to save her money like a good bourgeoise.

Duse christened her house "La Porziuncola," after the original sanctuary of St. Francis of Assisi. Wheat fields, slender Tuscan cypresses, and olive

La Porziuncola, Duse's home in the hills
of Florence, 1898

groves provided an enchanting view, and the grounds blossomed with roses
and orange trees. A cloister-like path led to the double front door covered
with a tangle of sweet-smelling jasmine. Inside, the whitewashed rooms
looked more like the tasteful residence of a dedicated scholar than a famous
diva. Instead of pictures of herself, Duse hung reproductions of classic paintings and portraits of Keats and Shakespeare. She traveled with trunks of
books, and she filled every room of La Porziuncola with books. Above her bed
she suspended a brass balance, the Libran sign of the zodiac, which she always
kept with her.

While her house was being whitewashed, Duse rested in Marina di Pisa
and then played the tourist with d'Annunzio. They made a pilgrimage to
Assisi and the Basilica di San Francesco, the burial place of St. Francis, which
boasts Giotto's extraordinary frescoes of the saint's life. They also spent time

at the seaside in Rimini. During the Middle Ages, Rimini had been ruled by Sigismondo Malatesta. Legend held that in the Malatesta castle of Gradara, the thirteenth-century lovers, Francesca and Paolo, had been murdered by Gianciotto, Francesca's husband. A devoted reader of Dante, d'Annunzio knew the story of Francesca da Rimini and the Malatesta family, and later would draw on the legend for a play he wrote for Duse.

At the moment, though, they discussed their plans to establish a theatre at Albano and inaugurate it with his current script, *La città morta.* With the help of the critic Edoardo Boutet, d'Annunzio had been contacting actors in an attempt to find a suitable male lead and a young female star for his play. Flavio Andò, Duse's former partner, now led his own theatre company with the beautiful young actress Tina di Lorenzo as *prima donna.* To Duse's disgust and anger, Flavio Andò had refused d'Annunzio's overtures. If actors couldn't be found, d'Annunzio knew Duse would continue to tour internationally with her old repertory. D'Annunzio saw his alliance with Duse as a chance to make money, to bring glory to himself as a writer, and to return the Italian theatre to its former prominence. Duse believed her collaboration with d'Annunzio would relieve her from the boredom of her old repertory, bring her the "consolation" of characters written especially for her, and provide Italy with a national theatre.

For the first time in her life, Duse was involved with a younger man. Although she deferred to d'Annunzio's literary genius, because of her wealth, her international fame, and her assured, experienced theatre talent, she was the dominant partner in their relationship, advising, teaching, and leading. She called d'Annunzio lover, friend, son, Gabrioletto, Ariel, dear Soul, and other pet names. D'Annunzio, the man of many words and many lovers, called Duse lover, sister, mother, Ghisola, and Isa.

In *Il fuoco*, he described her variously (and exhaustively) as a lonely, nomadic woman; a great tragedienne; a chalice for his words; the promised woman; tragic muse; the Dionysian woman; a night creature shaped by dreams and passions; a wandering temptress; a bird of prey; a thing he could hold in his fist; a dangerous, threatening thing; his carnal mistress; a prophetic muse with a fantastic imagination; a many-souled, marvelous instrument for his new art; and a creature of perishable flesh.

Of all the phrases d'Annunzio used to describe Duse, there is one significant omission—a person who was equal to him. In his old age he was able to see her as a separate, precious human being, but during the years of their love affair, which, tellingly, were also the highest point of his literary achievement, he saw her as human plunder for his art. In writing about Duse, at times he seemed more in love with his own words than he was with her.

"I want to possess you the way death possesses in the first hour.

(Eleonora)," he confided to his secret notebook. "I want to gather you like a sheaf, like a sheaf of wicker-bound lavender, to brandish you like a banner, and then I want to disperse you, blow on you and spread you out, like the dandelion, spread you to the wind, in all directions, dissolve you in the Great All—Pan—my love . . ."

After their Rimini reunion, the lovers went in opposite directions. Despite the "horrible tourists," Duse traveled north to Mürren to meet Enrichetta at a health spa in the Bernese Alps. D'Annunzio went south to Francavilla to campaign for Parliament and to see his mother, and tried to avoid his sexually voracious mistress, Maria Gravina. (In May, Gravina had given birth to a son, but d'Annunzio suspected her of having affairs and refused to acknowledge him as his own.) "The world," he told his publisher, Emilio Treves, "must be persuaded that I am capable of everything."

D'Annunzio's detractors charged that his run for Parliament was just a means of gathering material for a new book, but in the blazing hot days of August 1897 d'Annunzio tramped through Ortona shaking hands, making promises to constituents, and giving speeches. Calling himself the "candidate of beauty," he spoke to his audience of farmers in lofty language. "The fortune of Italy is inseparable from the fate of beauty, of which Italy is mother," he proclaimed.

ON AUGUST 6, 1897, the day after her arrival in Mürren, Duse scribbled a long, impassioned letter to d'Annunzio. Lying in bed, suffering from a nagging cough and a backache, Duse sounded anything but weak, exhibiting a manic energy. She apologized for her wild, messy writing, and she begged his forgiveness for her insistence on "doing, taking action, helping you." Heady with the thought that at last she had found her ideal playwright (or dizzy with the effects of the morphine and atropine she was taking), she wrote four pages in "one breath"—pages filled with advice, news, flattery, a tirade against Flavio Andò—a flood of words punctuated with exclamation marks, dashes, and dots as she jumped from subject to subject. She was articulate, if somewhat subservient, in discussing their collaboration. "I know well that the artist that executes the *work of art* IS NOT the work of art," she said, "and we actors offend you poets because we interpret (and we betray you) by sometimes insisting on interpreting you our way . . . and yet . . . a good instrument, agile, firm, *responding* to every line, is necessary to a work of art." She wanted to be the responsive "instrument" of his art, but she worried his political ambitions would rob him of writing time. Finally forced to finish the letter because it had become too dark to see, she signed herself "Eleonora."

Realizing she was writing to a man who knew how to "say everything," she wondered if she should rip up the letter, should she send it, would he read it? Then, her eyes fell on a bouquet of mountain flowers that some admirers had sent her along with a letter. "They told me," Duse continued, "that my *art* (!) was for them, their 'greatest consolation.' You see—you see, you see, it's possible, it's really possible to *open the doors*—and I . . . I swear to you that I did it, ennobling those stupid, clumsy plays I have acted till now!" She closed her letter with an image of herself falling asleep using the manuscript of *La città morta* as her pillow. A few days later in another long letter, she described the sweet, shuddering, disturbing intoxication she felt in front of an audience. It was an inflaming fever, which reminded her of another kind of fever. When will I see you again, she asked?

DURING HER STAY in Mürren, Boito asked if she wanted him to come and comfort her. In her letters to d'Annunzio, Duse often sounded like a character from one of her plays or one of her lover's novels—gushing with feeling and alive in the moment. Sometimes she would send him a letter or telegram with just one oversized word, such as AVE! or a word repeated many times. In her letters to her old lover Boito, she was more blunt but still in the moment. No, she wrote from her sick bed in Mürren, she didn't want him to visit. She was ill and grumpy and sarcastic. She didn't have the comfort of "a stupid religion" or any hope of winning over her "stupid nature." "Writing?" she said. "I am here, fogged in, without a rudder, and in high seas." The doctor told her she would feel better soon. "What joy!" she snapped. Boito couldn't inflame her sexually, but he still had his uses. She sent him a note she had received from Enrichetta and asked him to write to her. "The poor girl turns to me, but I'm like her in this moment, more dead than alive, and I can't help her." Suffering from the beginning stages of tuberculosis, Enrichetta stayed for a time with Duse in Mürren, then visited Sophie Drechsel in Dresden. In late September, Duse placed Enrichetta in a sanitarium in Davos-Platz.

To Boito, who had always been her confessor, Duse revealed the truth about her feelings for Enrichetta. "But you can't say everything," she wrote. "Who can you tell, for example, about the sadness, the physical, yes physical repulsion, alas, of a hand that touches you? The heart goes back and forth all day between the desire to help, and the instinct that revolts, because of a word, some minor thing, some *character trait* that reminds you, implacably, of its *origin*.—the father's like that.—in her, and you see him. No—it's horrible! Such sorrows cannot be written down!—"

Writers have rarely dealt with a mother's physical repugnance for her own child. Some mothers certainly have such feelings, but they seldom confess them. It's a taboo subject. One writer who explored the taboo was Ibsen in *Hedda Gabler*. Just as Duse was confessing her feelings about Enrichetta to Boito, she was preparing *Hedda*, which she introduced into her repertory in early 1898. Trapped in a marriage with a man she loathes and pregnant with an unwanted baby, Hedda kills herself and her unborn child. In reviewing her first performances, critics noted that Duse's portrait of the tortured Hedda revealed more than the stereotype of a female demon. She played Hedda as a "human being," wrote one critic, a nervous woman full of "seductive audacity" who "lived and felt." Duse drew on her own experiences in preparing the role, and she also found the universal in Hedda, the tragedy of unfulfilled female nature.

Although appalled by her feelings, Duse couldn't control or overcome her visceral response to even "some minor thing" in Enrichetta that reminded her of Checchi. Duse's rejection of Enrichetta increased as her daughter matured and her features and behavior hardened into adulthood. Duse's dread of aging made the situation even more difficult. Duse prided herself on giving Enrichetta material comfort, excellent medical care, a good boarding-school education, and an assured future—everything she had lacked as a child. But she was unable to give her daughter what Angelica Duse had given Eleonora—an unconditional, physically affectionate maternal love. Duse simply couldn't separate her daughter from the image of the hated Checchi. There's little evidence she worked very hard at overcoming her feelings. Duse often used her friends Sophie Drechsel and Laura Groppallo as stand-ins for a role she should have played herself. Yet because of her desire that Enrichetta have a bourgeois life of social respectability, and since an actor's life was antibourgeois, Duse had no other choice than to place her daughter in boarding schools and with surrogates. Unfortunately, during the time they did spend together, Enrichetta was often ill. Any performer who must depend on a healthy voice and body to work lives in fear of illness and, if possible, avoids anyone, even loved ones, who are sick. Of course, when Enrichetta was healthy, Duse felt less pressure to visit her.

AFTER LEAVING HER DAUGHTER in the sanitarium at Davos-Platz, Duse devoted her energies and attention to her new lover and their artistic ambitions. At times, she overstepped the boundaries she and d'Annunzio had set for their relationship and wrote words she never dared to say when they were together. "I love you—I love you," she said. "This is the only word that my soul cries out." D'Annunzio must have noted this indiscretion, because a few days later she asked his pardon. She had hoped he wouldn't mention it. The pact they had agreed to in Pisa involved more than love—it was a binding contract between two artists to create a new theatre, an open-air theatre on the shores of Lake Albano south of Rome, a theatre dedicated to producing d'Annunzio's plays and starring Duse, who would also lead the campaign to raise the money.

Talking and writing about his theatre, which he hoped would rival Wagner's Bayreuth, was an easy task for the voluble writer, but the process of negotiating with Duse and her impresario as well as other actors and their impresarios, who all had complex schedules and contracts, was frustrating for d'Annunzio. "Oh misery!" he exclaimed about the complications involved in staging *Il sogno d'un tramonto d'autunno*, his new companion piece to *Il sogno d'un mattino di primavera*. When writing his play, the theatre novice d'Annunzio hadn't taken into account that Duse couldn't cast (from her own company) his all-female script, which required ten actresses.

In late October 1897, Duse rehearsed for a tour of Italy and the French Riviera. Most likely to dissuade her from her infatuation with d'Annunzio and his plays, her impresario Joseph Schürmann insisted on accompanying her on the Italian tour. With the exception of Ibsen, her familiar scripts and characters bored her, but they were popular and lucrative. Flavio Andò and his leading lady, Tina di Lorenzo, continued to refuse their offers of collaboration on *La città morta*. (To act with Duse would mean, of course, that di Lorenzo would have to step down as *prima donna*.) D'Annunzio suggested Ermete Zacconi, then forty, an actor-manager, who was considered one of the best actors in Italy. Duse said she and Zacconi were an "impossible combination." While Duse assured d'Annunzio she longed to present *La città morta*, she knew merging her company with another would be a financial and administrative nightmare.

IN EARLY NOVEMBER 1897, Duse introduced Venetian audiences to d'Annunzio's *Sogno*. The critics thought she was lovely, but they dismissed d'Annunzio as a playwright. G. Pozza in the *Corriere della Sera* called the symbolism "obscure" and the play nothing more than a lyrical fragment. Despite the critical reception, Duse kept it in her repertory for a time. "I have refound the harmony," she wrote d'Annunzio. "Oh! bene bene bene benedizione!"

At this time, Anita Vivanti Chartres, a young Anglo-Italian poet and playwright, who was writing a play for Duse, followed her tour and wrote a portrait of her for the *New York Dramatic Mirror*. "Duse's hatred of publicity and newspaper interviews has assumed the proportions of a mania," she noted. In choosing Vivanti to write about her, Duse was, as usual, controlling and manipulating her public persona of "La Duse." Vivanti had ulterior motives as well. She wanted Duse to produce her new play, and she wanted to publicize her connection with Duse to interest New York producers in her own work.

Like modern celebrity journalists, Vivanti made herself a part of the story. "When we were alone together, talking of the play I was writing for her, or discussing modern art, her youthful struggles with poverty, or the world weariness that came to her finally with her splendid success, Duse was herself," Vivanti wrote, "impulsive, eager, passionate, tender, sad. But the mere announcement of a visitor would freeze her into silent hauteur." Some of Duse's visitors were aristocratic women who "frankly expressed their envy" of Duse's freedom and longed to be in her shoes. In Turin, Vivanti reported, Duse spent the mornings driving through the Parco del Valentino looking at "green things." In the evenings, Duse played to packed houses and earned as much as 10,000 francs for each performance. "A stupendous sum of money for Italy," Vivanti wrote. Lest the reader think Duse was greedy, Vivanti noted she was "exceedingly generous." She paid her company when they weren't working and had even given Worth's dressmaker a diamond ring as a tip.

At home, Duse dressed in loose white satin, bundled up her abundant dark hair any which way, never wore corsets, never used powder or paint. "During the days that I was with her," Vivanti said, "we used to sit at opposite ends of the large table sometimes without exchanging half a dozen words, and she used to laugh her approval across to me when I absolutely refused to answer her if she made any attempts at polite conversation." When Duse chose to talk, though, she was "startlingly brilliant." Believing Duse was "the saddest woman I have ever known," with a taste "for the dismal and melancholy," Vivanti was captivated by her charm, praising her as "highly cultured, sincere, brave, and good."

In her portrait, Vivanti glossed over biographical wrinkles, such as Duse's separation from her husband and her adolescent daughter, whom she rarely saw. Vivanti portrayed La Duse as a free, brilliant, independent artist, a woman who made lots of money through her own labor, who was envied by aristocrats, who wasn't a slave to fashion or polite behavior, yet a woman who remained deeply mysterious. It was the image Duse sought to convey to the world—an image that resonated with her female fans—women so devoted and worshipful they would spread their shawls and cloaks onto the street so she could walk across them.

In late December, when Duse played Monte Carlo, Vivanti returned to New York. Although Vivanti reported that the details for the production of her play *Good and Evil*, which she had written for Duse, were settled in Monte Carlo, Duse never produced the play. Vivanti had served her purpose, and Duse and her company moved on to Rome, where once again Duse presented d'Annunzio's *Sogno*. When the play opened at Rome's Teatro Valle in January 1898 on a double bill with Goldoni's *La locandiera*, the audience gave an ovation to welcome Duse (who had last played Rome in 1891), but they refused to applaud d'Annunzio's *Sogno*. The notoriously conservative Roman audience, used to *verismo*, operettas, and farces, didn't care for d'Annunzio's poetic, symbolist drama. Duse was furious with the Roman "barbarians" for rejecting the modern work of her lover and cheering a classic play she was sick of performing. "The boredom, the boredom," she told d'Annunzio, "more murderous than repulsion,—no, no, I don't know how to do it anymore!"

In Rome, she overcame her aversion to reporters and gave an interview to explain her determination to present work the public might not like or understand. During her entire career she had remained true to her own taste and her own acting aesthetic, and in her rebellion she had helped transform the theatre. Now she planned to use her fortune to establish a new theatre to present d'Annunzio's plays. "I've earned some money," she said. "I'll earn some more if I want. What would you have me do? Buy a palazzo? [...] I will die happy if I have done one fine thing, a work of beauty." Those close to her, however, like Matilde Serao and Joseph Schürmann, worried she was risking her finances and prestige. If d'Annunzio wants money, give it to him, argued the practical Serao, but don't do his plays.

Duse didn't listen. "There's only one voice I want to hear," she said.

ACCOMPANIED BY Matilde Serao's husband, Edoardo Scarfoglio, d'Annunzio attended the Paris opening of Bernhardt's production of *La città morta* (translated into French by Georges Hérelle) on January 21, 1898. In this five-character, ensemble play, set near the ruins of Mycenae in Greece, using the unities of time, place, and action, d'Annunzio wove classic legends with a contemporary love triangle involving incest and adultery. When Leonardo, a young archaeologist, uncovers the tombs and the treasures of the Atrides, his sister Bianca Maria, and their friends, the poet Alessandro and his blind wife Anna, all become caught up in the ancient horror. Leonardo falls in love with his sister, Bianca, who is also loved by Alessandro. Many long, beautifully descriptive but undramatic speeches lead to a brutal conclusion. Leonardo murders his sister to free himself from the temptation of incest and to protect Alessandro from committing adultery.

The fifty-four-year-old Bernhardt played the blind Anna, a seer character like Cassandra, who senses the impending tragedy but can do nothing to prevent it. When Anna discovers Bianca's body at the end of the play, in d'Annunzio's stage directions: "She stoops over the dead girl, utterly distracted, feeling about until she reaches the face and the hair, still wet with the death-giving water. She shudders from head to foot at the clammy touch, then utters a piercing shriek in which she seems to exhale her soul. 'Ah . . . I see! I see!' she says, as her sight is restored."

Photographer Helen Lohmann, who saw Bernhardt in the role, recalled that Sarah followed d'Annunzio's stage directions exactly, shuddering and then shrieking, *"Je vois! Je vois!"* When the play opened in Paris, Duse, Matilde Serao, the writer Ugo Ojetti, and a group of friends gathered in Rome at Count Primoli's palazzo to wait for telegrams that reported the audience reactions after each of the five acts.

Duse couldn't sit still. "Her lips were white but her broad Slavic cheeks, the wild part of her anxious features, were flushed red as though with fever," recalled Ojetti. She paced nervously, ran her fingers through her hair, lay for a time with a hot water bottle on her stomach, described Bernhardt's acting in *La Dame aux camélias* as "precise as clockwork," and gave a little speech about d'Annunzio's genius. By the time she left in the early-morning hours, Ojetti noted Duse had ripped all the petals off the flowers in a floral arrangement.

Bernhardt received just a few curtain calls, and although d'Annunzio was applauded and called to the stage, he didn't appear. The French and Italian reviews were mixed. "Sarah contributed immensely to the success despite her artificial, infantile, whining voice," the *Corriere della Sera* reported. "The other actors were mediocre. The sets and costumes were vulgar." Not surprisingly, Bernhardt decided to pull the play from her repertory after only twelve performances, and according to Scarfoglio, d'Annunzio failed to change her mind with a night of lovemaking.

During d'Annunzio's three-week stay at the Hotel Mirabeau in Paris, Duse sent a flood of telegrams. "Ah! The sun? Where are you?" she asked. Finally, she persuaded him to tear himself away from Paris and a full social calendar that Duse feared included various assignations. D'Annunzio joined her in early February 1898 at the Grand Hotel Belle Vue in Santa Margherita, a winter health resort tucked into a thin strip of coast on the Ligurian Sea in northwest Italy.

THE POOR CRITICAL RECEPTION for *La città morta* had disappointed them both, but the box-office failure was especially painful to d'Annunzio. He needed money, and he urged Duse to collaborate with Zacconi and produce *La città morta* as soon as possible. Duse couldn't ignore her own contractual obligations and the financial penalty of suspending her upcoming tour to work with Zacconi, particularly on a play that had just had a widely publicized failure. At the moment, the risk was too great and the costs too prohibitive. D'Annunzio had published *La città morta*, which brought in some income, but the play was not as popular with readers as his novels. "I have read d'Annunzio's *La città morta* the tragedy which was to rival Aeschylus," Bernard Berenson wrote to Isabella Stewart Gardner. "Well it does not even rival Ibsen, and would be happy to approach Maeterlinck . . . Tis a pity for d'Annunzio's talent is enormous."

Duse exhorted d'Annunzio to work on his new script, *La Gioconda*, which had a more traditional structure that kept the *prima donna* at the center of the action—in other words, forget the other stars; if necessary, she could carry the play on her own. To keep him working and happy, Duse created an atmosphere of health, peace, and tranquility. At her home in Settignano and in Bocca d'Arno, close by Marina di Pisa, where she rented a vacation house surrounded by pine forests and wild yellow broom, she had all the things she loved—the scent of the earth, the roar of the sea, sunshine, fresh air, green plants, ripe olives. In March 1898, d'Annunzio joined her, and they established their base in Tuscany.

D'Annunzio leased La Capponcina, a fourteenth-century villa in Settignano, complete with gardens, vineyards, olive groves, and a narrow path through protective hedges that connected the property to Duse's more modest house. As a further sign of their commitment, d'Annunzio severed all ties with his mistress, Maria Gravina. In November 1898, Duse asked Boito to come to her room at the Hotel Hassler in Rome, and she ended their relationship. Although Duse continued to write to him sporadically, it would be years before they saw each other again. After their parting, Boito was haunted by nightmares. "This is greater than death," he wrote in a note he attached to Duse's letters that he carefully saved.

D'Annunzio's mistress had taken most of his personal property in Francavilla, leaving him his stable of horses and his kennel of greyhounds, which he moved to Settignano. In one of the most beautiful passages in *Il fuoco*, he described Duse moving among his bounding dogs, "with lithe undulating movements like the walk of the ancient Venetians, known as the greyhound walk." Duse's ability to transport an audience into a frenzy, d'Annunzio believed, was because she had "a savage sense of life," and "had rediscovered the Dionysian sense of nature in which she lost her human consciousness."

D'Annunzio hired veterinarian Benigno Palmerio to manage the estate while he renovated and redecorated the villa. D'Annunzio's opulent, oppressive decorating style was the direct opposite of Duse's spare, sun-washed taste. Layering period on period in a style which can only be called Dannunzian, he stuffed his home with valuable antiques; oversized, heavy furniture; hanging tapestries; wooden carvings and statues; plaster casts; framed and painted

D'Annunzio at La Capponcina, his home
near Duse's outside Florence, 1898

mottoes; and countless objets d'art as well as the death masks of two of his
heroes, Beethoven and Wagner. His bed was draped in green velvet and on the
headboard was carved "Per Non Dormire." A guest room piled with cushions
was set aside for Duse's use. To pay off his debts (which amounted to about a
quarter of a million dollars) and to fund his extravagances, he set to work on
La Gioconda, worked feverishly on *Il fuoco*, and began a series of poems, called
laudi, hymns of praise to the earth, sea, sky, and heroes. Dressed in a long,
monkish robe, he sometimes wrote fifteen hours at a stretch, interrupting his
labor only for meals and brief rests. The middle finger of his hand deformed
into a stained and horny lump from the constant movement of his pen.

IN 1898, Duse didn't have much time to spend relaxing in Tuscany. She toured throughout Italy, the Riviera, and Portugal. As usual, when the box-office receipts were good and the theatres were full, she was happy, but in Marseilles on March 31, after constant rain kept the crowds away, she was depressed by the "sadness of this room in a hotel." Plus, she was suffering from pain in her hand and was being treated with morphine massages.

Her spirits perked up when she made her debut in Lisbon. She opened with *La Dame aux camélias*, the audience responded with thirty-six curtain calls, and the critics, many who were seeing her for the first time, wrote raves. Duse possessed a "soul of fire in a body of thistledown," wrote one. "Anyone who listens to that voice for five minutes will inevitably succumb to her mysterious sorcery."

In Lisbon, Duse practiced her "sorcery" on Dona Maria Luisa Domingos de Sousa Holstein, the Duchess of Palmella, who arranged for Duse's presentation to Queen Amelia of Portugal. Duse didn't hesitate to exploit her fame and form friendships with important and powerful society women. In return for intimacy with the famous actress, the duchess gave Duse money and gifts of jewelry, including two precious pearls that had once belonged to Madame de Staël. The two women became so close Duse called the duchess "mother."

Duse returned to Italy in May and played the Teatro Brunetti in Bologna, which was renamed Teatro Duse in her honor. All along her tour, Duse sent d'Annunzio telegrams, letters, and gifts. With Boito, who hadn't valued her profession, Duse had suppressed her strong, independent side and often played the role of a needy little girl. D'Annunzio honored, even worshipped, her art and appreciated her ability to make money. He had no qualms about casting her in the traditional male role of breadwinner. With Adolfo de Bosis acting as intermediary, Duse sent him cash. She also gave him two exquisite emeralds. In one note she simply said, "I'm speaking to you of profound love that asks nothing." But of course her generosity carried a price—d'Annunzio was expected to work, to write plays for her and their new theatre.

WHILE DUSE SUPPORTED d'Annunzio's profligate habits, she kept a close watch on Enrichetta's finances. Enrichetta had been released from the sanitarium in Davos-Platz and had returned to school. Duse complained to Laura Groppallo that the girl didn't seem to know the difference between "100 francs or 1,000 francs" and spent money as if it came from an "inexhaustible spring." She asked Laura to speak to Enrichetta about financial matters and advise her to look to her future. In October 1898, Duse was forced to cope with Enrichetta herself. One of Duse's friends had visited Enrichetta at her boarding school in Zurich, and had written Duse the girl was overworked, pale, and ill, and her cough had returned. Since spending the winter in the northern city threatened Enrichetta's life, Duse decided to take her daughter with her on a tour of Egypt and Greece from November 1898 to February 1899.

Even though Duse hired a young Englishwoman as a chaperone for Enrichetta, her daughter's presence brought her "ceaseless pain and anxiety." In need of sympathy, Duse wrote to Boito from Alexandria in late December. Since she had spent everything she had earned, she needed "to remain at the yoke." In addition to securing Enrichetta's future and her own, she also had to raise money to produce d'Annunzio's new plays. She and Ermete Zacconi had finally agreed to a contract in which they would present *La Gioconda* (to alternate with *Le Demi-Monde* and *La Femme de Claude*) on an Italian tour.

On December 24, 1898, d'Annunzio sailed from Naples to join Duse. He arrived in Alexandria weak and seasick, and Duse pampered him with a warm bath, champagne, and according to d'Annunzio, an orgy of imaginative love-making. "When I am above her, in her arms, she caresses my lips and my eyelids with violets."

It was d'Annunzio's first trip to Egypt, and Duse introduced him to the wonders of the pyramids and the Sphinx. In the Khedive Gardens of Cairo, Duse became lost in a winding green maze. As she frantically fought her way through the hedges, scratching her hands in the process, d'Annunzio hid nearby and became aroused by her distress. Before helping her free herself from the labyrinth, he recorded her terror and her shouts for help and used the situation in a scene in *Il fuoco*.

To some extent, all writers are voyeurs, but d'Annunzio was a sadistic voyeur. Clearly, he was interested in just how far he could push Duse. When would she break? His cruelty would reduce Duse to tears; he would watch and then write up the scene. "The warm drops fell at last," he wrote, "but she did not let them flow down her cheeks. With one of those movements that often sprang from her pain, with the unexpected grace of an unfolding wing, she brushed them away, wetting her fingers and spreading the dampness across her temples."

Since Duse knew d'Annunzio was writing about her in *Il fuoco*, a book that she called "expected and poisoning," and since she had read pages of the manuscript, the possibility exists she was "acting" her responses as he watched her. No wonder she felt at times her real life was a fiction. Still, Duse made no effort to stop d'Annunzio from writing about her. She told Lillian and Adolfo de Bosis she had no right to intervene in his art. Sometimes his penetrating gaze frightened her, but she believed he was a genius, and his interest in her was enormously flattering. He knew she feared getting older, and he didn't hesitate to portray her as an aging actress, yet his descriptions of her in *Il fuoco* are beautiful and inspired by love. In one passage, d'Annunzio writes of watching her walk: "He embraced her whole person with his warm gaze: the gracious, noble line of her sloping shoulders, her free, flexible waist above her strong hips, her knees that moved lightly against the folds of her skirt, her pale, passionate face, her eloquent, thirsting mouth, her brow as strong and lovely as any man's, her eyes that lengthened into her lashes, as though moistened by a tear that kept forming and dissolving without being shed, her whole passionate face of light and shadow, love and pain, her feverish energy, her quivering life." What woman could resist such prose?

D'Annunzio's facility with words intimidated Duse. She had always felt insecure about turning her thoughts and feelings into words. Over and over again in her letters, she wrote that she didn't know how to write what she felt about him. "Speaking is one thing," she said, "but smiling at you on paper is another."

Duse confided to d'Annunzio that her whole life had been a "sweet, inexhaustible" tormenting search for a harmony between life and art—for a moment when the two could touch, "barely . . . briefly." With d'Annunzio, she felt there were times when she had found that harmony. As they traveled together in Egypt and Greece, Duse worked and d'Annunzio gathered material. No incident was too small to go unrecorded. Inspired by her appearing suddenly in his room, with a "flash of energy" he described a character in his new tragedy. Her eyes filled with tears, and afterward moved by "profound and sincere emotion," the lovers sat hand in hand.

WHEN THE TOUR ENDED in February 1899, they stayed for a time on the Greek island of Corfu, where d'Annunzio began work on *La gloria*, a new political play. Giulietta Gordigiani joined them there. The relationship between the two lovers and Giulietta was complex. Giulietta seems to have rejected d'Annunzio's attempts to draw her into an affair or into a ménage with Duse, but the three were extraordinarily close. Giulietta was "ours," Duse wrote to d'Annunzio at one point. D'Annunzio relished watching and describing female affection and friendship. According to Duse, he sometimes made love to her "like a woman," not penetrating her with "that fagooootto!" but "sliding" back and forth in a simulation of lesbian sex. In *La città morta* and *La Gioconda*, he wrote about both the rivalry between two women for a man and about the loving friendship between women.

In Corfu with Giulietta and d'Annunzio, Duse said a *"horror"* came over her, "something snapped in my brain," and she didn't dare to speak as "the venom coursed through my blood." D'Annunzio described this rage in *Il fuoco* and attributed the cause to the jealousy of an older woman for a younger one.

"What's wrong with you?" d'Annunzio asked her over and over again in Corfu. "Have you gone crazy?" Not wanting to interrupt his work on his new play, Duse kept coldly silent about her jealousy of her young friend, a jealousy complicated by her own love for Giulietta. Also, on Corfu, Duse felt neglected. D'Annunzio was immersed in work and inattentive, and Giulietta planned to marry the Jewish banker Robert von Mendelssohn, which would end their threesome. Duse felt betrayed.

"It seemed to me I had loved a monster," Duse told d'Annunzio later, in an attempt to explain her overpowering rage. "She—and you—it seemed to me that both of you had been eating my heart, for the last three years! And then you both took another path.—In those days, it seemed to me, *you were going toward* Sicily,—and, she towards the Synagogue.—The horror took me—and the poison *broke* inside. A monster it seemed to me I had loved, in her, whom I had loved so much! For whom I had saved all and to whom I had given all! A monster.—In vain I had loved, in vain, *in vain*! And you worked. Outside in the garden, the flowers were living in dewy peace beside you. How could I dare, then, to say the atrocious thing to you. In the evening you were reading, you were tired, I put you to bed, and I trembled . . . I loved you so much, you two! How I loved you . . . And with that wound, abruptly, numbly, I left for Rome."

DUSE WENT TO ROME to meet with Ermete Zacconi and "smooth away" the difficulties between them. Zacconi had been raised in an acting family, had toured throughout Europe, and was noted for the versatility, intelligence, and scrupulous preparation of his roles. Although not as classically handsome as Flavio Andò, he was good-looking and powerful. Like Duse, he was drawn to the new, modern dramatists—Ibsen, Hauptmann, Maeterlinck, and Strindberg. The two actors had met four years earlier. After seeing him perform, Duse had sent Zacconi a note praising the "perfection" of his art. Zacconi had first seen Duse act in *Fédora* and *La Dame aux camélias* in Turin and had been moved and inspired by her. Duse quickly eliminated their differences by offering him a 50 percent split of the profits after expenses were paid. Since Duse had released her own company, she would join Zacconi's company and direct the actors. D'Annunzio reserved the right to arrange the sets. "The contract honored me," Zacconi said, "and I accepted it." They agreed to begin rehearsals of *La Gioconda* in Sicily.

"So poor deluded Duse has succumbed to that beast d'Annunzio," Isabella Stewart Gardner wrote to Bernard Berenson, when she learned of Duse's decision to present *La Gioconda*. Gardner's perception of Duse as victim to the beast d'Annunzio was shared by Matilde Serao, who tried to counsel Duse against her involvement with the writer. "I swear to you on the head of my children whom I adore to have done all possible to save my unhappy friend from these unpardonable errors of this horrible period of her life," Serao told Count Primoli. "For which I have received this gracious result; she, the great Duse, treated me either hurtfully or with open coldness. Gabriele d'Ann. considers me his personal enemy; and my husband and all his friends treated me like dirt."

While Duse traveled to Sicily, where they planned to open *La Gioconda* before a tour of major Italian cities, d'Annunzio stayed on in Corfu to finish *La gloria*. "Here I am—now—here—alone as always, alone and responsible for every one of my actions," Duse wrote d'Annunzio from the road. As usual, when work was not going well, her health suffered. She couldn't sleep and caught a cold and a cough. The chaos in Zacconi's company distressed her. Because of d'Annunzio's lack of experience, the sets didn't arrive on time, and although she tried to assert her authority and rehearse the cast, there was no time to orchestrate nuance and detail. She also discovered d'Annunzio had been lying to her about the finances. Everyone counted on her artistry and fame to pull them through, but she felt like a freak, she told de Bosis, a bearded lady in a sideshow.

D'Annunzio joined her in Sicily and on April 15, 1899, *La Gioconda* opened at the Bellini Theatre in Palermo. Despite the high prices, the theatre was sold out. Rowdy students from the University of Palermo packed the galleries. The curtain rose and revealed a large room with lovely painted views of springtime Tuscany. D'Annunzio set the scene in Florence and on the coast of Pisa and drew on details of his life with Duse. He dedicated the work to "Eleonora Duse of the Beautiful Hands." A brilliant artist, the sculptor Lucio, played by Ermete Zacconi, has attempted suicide. Lucio is torn between his model and muse Gioconda, and his loyal wife, Silvia, acted by Duse. Silvia nurses him back to health, but he cannot forget Gioconda. Silvia confronts Gioconda in Lucio's studio and lies that Lucio wants to send her away. In retaliation, Gioconda tries to destroy the statue Lucio has created of her. Silvia protects the sculpture, but in doing so her hands are crushed. Her sacrifice saves the art, but at the end of the play, Lucio leaves her and returns to his studio and Gioconda. The play closes on a kneeling, sobbing Silvia, wearing a high-necked, long-sleeved robe, which covers her mutilated hands. Beside her, prostrate and frightened, are two young girls, Beata and Sirenetta. The image is powerful—three females literally and figuratively crushed by the demands of masculine art. Ironically, however, Lucio, supposedly the artist-superman, is not as dramatic or as interesting as the two women.

Gioconda, the artist's willing instrument, and Silvia, the artist's strong caretaker, were both inspired by Duse's relationship to d'Annunzio. The face of Gioconda is never seen, since she always appears heavily veiled. Lucio's description of Gioconda is d'Annunzio's tribute to Duse's acting and his attempt to put into words the transcendent power of a nonliterary art: "A thousand statues, not one! She is always diverse, like a cloud that from instant to instant seems changed without your seeing it change. Every motion of her body destroys one harmony and creates another yet more beautiful . . . The life of the eyes is the look, that indefinable thing, more expressive than any word, than any sound, infinitely deep and yet instantaneous as a breath, swifter than a flash . . . Now imagine the life of the look diffused over all her body . . . Imagine through all her limbs, from the forehead to the sole of the foot, that flash of lightning, like life!"

Duse needed all her acting skill to quiet the noisy and disruptive opening-night audience, which included supporters of d'Annunzio's former mistress, Maria Gravina, a Sicilian princess. Duse won them over, and when the curtain closed at the end of the first-act love scene between Lucio and Silvia, she and Zacconi received eight curtain calls and d'Annunzio three. The critics thought the play morally perverse, but they raved about Duse's saint-like Silvia and the enchanting performance of young Emma Gramatica as Sirenetta.

Less than two weeks later, on April 27, 1899, after only three rehearsals, the company opened—and closed on the same night—d'Annunzio's *La gloria* at the Mercadante Theatre in Naples. It was a debacle. The plot centers on the political struggle between two politicians in contemporary Rome—the conservative Bronte and the demagogue Flamma. (D'Annunzio had foolishly announced he had based the character of Bronte on the conservative leader Francesco Crispi.) In league with Flamma, Bronte's mistress, Comnena (played by Duse), poisons Bronte and then like Lady Macbeth spurs Flamma on to power. Feeling his hold over the people slipping away, Flamma begs Comnena to kill him. She stabs him and then leaves his body to the Roman mobs, who tear him to pieces. D'Annunzio scholars call the play his absolute worst, but they agree it foreshadows Mussolini's political rhetoric and his manipulation of the mob. Mussolini even adopted Flamma's political slogan—"He who stops is lost"—as his own.

The opening-night audience in Naples tried to stop the play and threatened to turn into a mob. A large claque whistled and booed and called out for d'Annunzio's death. Not even Duse's fame and reputation could stop the uproar, and she told Count Primoli later she felt as if she were being slaughtered.

In d'Annunzio's *La Gioconda,* c. 1899–1900

Where was d'Annunzio while she was defending his play? "Me?" d'Annunzio told his friend Scarfoglio, "I was busy raping a nun!" In fact, while Duse was onstage, he had a "quick fuck" in the dressing room of a young actress who played a sister of charity in the play. Duse heard about the remark and the fornication, and she was furious.

Without explaining his own contribution to Duse's state of mind, d'Annunzio complained to his friend Angelo Conti that Duse was unjust, cruel, saw only lies and deceit around her, and had been possessed by a "bad demon that gives her no peace." When *La Gioconda* was received warmly in Venice in May, Duse was still upset with him and with the mismanagement of the tour. D'Annunzio continued to gather material for *Il fuoco,* noting the hiss of her voice; her white, contorted face; her poisonous sarcasm; and the jeering bit-terness of her laughter.

When the tour closed in Turin, Duse wrote a note to Zacconi. "Among all the poverty of the environment, among the errors, among the many injustices of these days, what remains with me *only* in my heart, is the memory of you, dear companion, who was *perfect and noble* towards every attempt at art that we tried to carry out."

While Duse talked of art, others talked incessantly about the Duse-d'Annunzio alliance, which was written up in the newspapers and gossiped about in drawing rooms from Boston to London to Paris to Florence. The popular press printed speculation and gossip as fact. "The Duse's Own Sad Tragedy," announced a headline in the Boston *Record*, purporting to have the latest news from Paris. "She loves, without hope, d'Annunzio, the novel-ist . . . passion is eating her away."

"Have the Duse and d'Annunzio broken?" Isabella Stewart Gardner wrote from Massachusetts to Bernard Berenson in Florence. "Poor Duse! I wish someone would kick d'Annunzio for me."

D'ANNUNZIO TALKED HIMSELF back into Duse's good graces, and they spent the summer in Settignano and on the coast of Pisa. With his "dear, dear companion" and muse at his side, d'Annunzio felt happy and blessed and composed some of his most beautiful poems.

"I love your life, Gabri," Duse said. "Your genius and your soul."

In August 1899, Duse left their Tuscan retreat to return to work. For an extended tour in which she planned to introduce *La Gioconda* to Europe, she joined the company of the scholar and actor Luigi Rasi, who ran a theatre school in Florence. Her old companion Carlo Rosaspina, the character actor Ciro Galvani, and Duse's administrator Ettore Mazzanti were the principal male leads.

Her collaboration with Rasi began badly. The two had little in common. Unlike Duse, Rasi had not been raised in the theatre—he was an academy-trained actor, and his manner toward Duse was extremely deferential and obsequious. Duse thought Rasi "mediocre" and insincere, and believed his company was taking advantage of her. She wrote d'Annunzio she would have to take up her whip to get them in shape. Rasi and his young *prima donna*, Teresa Franchini, wanted to learn from Duse and to study her methods, but Duse kept aloof from the company, and to their disappointment, rarely attended rehearsals. What was new to the Rasi company was old to Duse. On the tour, she was presenting seven of her old parts, including Marguerite,

D'Annunzio at home.

D'Annunzio took this
snapshot of Duse in the late
1890s.

Magda, Cleopatra, and Paula Tanqueray—roles that hardly required further rehearsal.

Teresa Rasi, Luigi's wife, kept a diary of the tour. When Duse did rehearse the actors, Teresa wrote, she was "very gentle and patient." Duse's methods produced results, and the tour received critical acclaim. Duse kept d'Annunzio informed of the tour's progress. At a time when ordinary people used the telegraph office for only the most urgent communications of life and death, she sometimes sent him four telegrams a day. It was a way of keeping her insistent voice in his ear, of reminding him how hard she was working and the sacrifices she was making for him. "Everything is inexpressible," she told him on August 8, quickly followed by another telegram asking for letters, but when she received one, she sniped, "A letter? What is a letter after all?" Once, she dispatched an urgent telegram with just three sarcastic words, "The day passed."

On August 13 from the Grand Hotel in Aix-les-Bains, she moaned that she was unable to hold a pen and couldn't write, but then proceeded to write a long letter. "For you, I have lived, Gabri—these last years." In another letter, she outlined a schedule of work for him. In September and October, he was to finish *Il fuoco* and in November "throw it to the crowd which waits for it," and then get on with writing his new tragedies—"Antigone—Cassandra—Anna."

In September the company moved north to Switzerland, Germany, and Austria. Audiences always greeted Duse with standing ovations, interminable applause, and "bravas," Teresa Rasi said. Observing that Duse played the parts differently at each performance, Rasi noted, "She's certainly not a stereotypical artist."

In Zurich, d'Annunzio joined Duse at the Hotel Baur-au-Lac. The French writer Romain Rolland and his wife, Clothilde Bréal, were at the same hotel, and Rolland, who was awarded the Nobel Prize for Literature in 1915, studied both d'Annunzio and Duse. Rolland admired the innovative beauty of d'Annunzio's writing, but his "public" persona repelled Rolland. The dandyism, the sexual scandals, the "crowd of snobs following him in stunned pursuit . . . and those poor, crazed women who run after him, panting with emotion and desire." Rolland was surprised to find little that was Italian or seductive in d'Annunzio. He looked more like a Parisian, with an "oval-shaped head, brown hair cut very short, a short, pointy, blond beard, a Jewish nose, thick and lumpy, piercing eyes—alert, intelligent, but cold and hard, very different from the portraits of his youth—nothing of a poet, nor of an artist." Rolland's wife, Clothilde, on the other hand, found d'Annunzio quite seductive. "What grief, one would be ready to bear for the love, however brief, of such a poet," she confessed later.

When Rolland met Duse at the Hotel Baur-au-Lac, he was charmed. Dressed in her usual white, Duse sat down by Rolland and snubbed two French actors, Charles Le Bargy and his wife Simone Benda, who wanted to impress her. Perhaps for this reason, Simone Benda later wrote a dubious account of their meeting, in which she described Duse as having a dark, sun-burned complexion and a limp. According to Simone, when she had recited a poem by Hugo, d'Annunzio had fallen at her feet, which sent Duse into a jealous rage. Duse had locked Simone in a hotel room with d'Annunzio, and then cancelled her performances and left Zurich. Rolland reported a different drama. He described Simone as a "mediocre French actress," who had per-formed a long monologue from *Hernani*, and afterward Duse left the room without speaking to her.

Rolland and Duse shared a love of music, and Duse confided in him. "I wake up in the middle of the night sometimes in these hotels," she said, "and I'm terrified. It's unbearable. I have to surround myself and seal myself up in a world of music, to flee, and close my door to the world." In their conversa-tions, Duse told Rolland that d'Annunzio "is never sincere. [...] He's always stiff, he lies, he lies perpetually, he never says what he truly thinks [...] His life is an inn; everyone passes through." Still, she worried about d'Annunzio and asked Rolland and his wife to comfort him and relieve his "dangerous sadness."

Rolland's account of the two lovers in Zurich, their tempestuous whisper-ings, their abrupt and dramatic exits and entrances, reads like a drama—a fact he noted. "Curious thing," he wrote. "Only in the theater is she a good, ten-der, and sincere person—always La Duse (and that is, theatrically, her great imperfection: she is nothing like the roles she plays). In life, she is an actress, in spite of herself, preyed upon by phantom-like passions which she incar-nates on the stage."

In passages describing Duse, Rolland hints at more than a friendship. "She has an exquisite face, a beautiful mouth, from where all her feelings flow del-icately and profoundly," Rolland wrote. For him, above all, Duse was "a face. And this, in the first place, is lips . . ."

D'ANNUNZIO HAD COUNTED on royalties from *La Gioconda* and was annoyed by the company's delay in presenting his script. Duse told him the production wasn't ready and she wasn't satisfied with the sets. Since she was having a financial and critical success with her old repertory, her impresario, Schürmann, certainly didn't push d'Annunzio's risky new work. Schürmann was also concerned about the effect the upcoming publication of *Il fuoco* might have on Duse's reputation and career. She brushed off his concerns.

She had read the book, had authorized its publication, and would not stand in the way of adding another masterpiece to Italian literature. "Besides," she said, "I'm 40 . . . and in love."

The company moved to Lucerne and Berlin, and d'Annunzio returned to Italy, where Duse showered him with telegrams. From July 20, 1899, to October 21, 1899, she sent him 162 telegrams in addition to dozens of letters. In one telegram she wanted to know why he hadn't responded immediately to the fourth telegram she had sent the day before. "*All* I have given you, and said," she wrote, "—my love made of every *love*, of every tenderness, of every strength." Since she had given him everything, the least he could do was respond at once to each one of her telegrams.

Duse's torrent of telegrams seems comically neurotic but also understandable, since she didn't have anyone to confide in on the tour. She did correspond with the Duchess of Palmella, primarily to complain about her health and the rigors of the tour. Since Duse required constant assurance and attention and since she had no intimate friend with her, d'Annunzio received the brunt of Duse's epistolary energy. Also, she didn't trust him, and the telegrams asserted her constant presence. The demon that shakes me, she wrote, is "*the horror of a lie* [. . .] Your genius needs truth."

In Berlin, the company rehearsed *La Gioconda*. "What an interesting rehearsal!" Teresa Rasi wrote. "What discipline! No one said a thing: they hung on every word from her lips! She deserves such religious respect, for all that she does and says."

After she visited Enrichetta, who was at boarding school in Berlin, Duse became ill with a cold, fever, headache, and pain in her hands. Enrichetta attended a performance and sat alone in a box. Teresa Rasi noticed Enrichetta kept her head down and never looked at her mother onstage. Duse also saw Giulietta Gordigiani Mendelssohn, who lived in Berlin, but Duse confided to the duchess that Giulietta had "disappointed" her. Apparently, Giulietta, occupied with her new husband, had not rushed to Duse's sickbed. Speaking as "*your own mother,*" the duchess counseled Duse, "*you must not be discouraged. You must not doubt. You must continue the struggle as you have.* Don't let your immense talent be killed. You know because you're great you will be loved, but even more because *you love.*"

On September 26, 1899, the company presented Boito's *Antony and Cleopatra* at the Lessing Theatre in Berlin. Duse and the Rasi company were acclaimed—it was a true ovation, Rasi recalled.

Duse rarely wrote or spoke of her triumphs or about the Dionysian ecstasy she sometimes felt onstage, but on October 3, her forty-first birthday, she wrote to d'Annunzio about *Antony and Cleopatra*. "*I was beautiful, and I was dignified,*" Duse told him. "You know, that *grace* doesn't come to me often!

But that evening, I had it completely—and afterwards, my voice and my strength were consumed by a deep and dark suffering of love—Art, too, like love, is insatiable and inconsolable, at times."

To confess her joy in performing Boito's play while failing to produce *La Gioconda* was tactless, and d'Annunzio reacted angrily. He scolded Duse for delaying production of his play, and in an interview with *La Stampa*, he insulted Italian actors, saying his plays required an elect company, not a group of buffoons descended from the commedia dell'arte who didn't understand anything new. The article was sent to Rasi, who showed it to Duse and the other actors, who confronted her and asked her to cut *La Gioconda* from the tour. She sympathized with her "companions in art," and quickly wired d'Annunzio and asked him to confirm his vulgar insults. "I haven't seen any journalists for months. It's all a stupid lie," d'Annunzio lied. "Please assure Rasi and his company of my pure faith."

Duse placated the actors, and the *La Gioconda* rehearsals continued. The company moved on to Bucharest. The city was in mourning for a court official, theatre prices were too high, and at first attendance was poor—so Duse, naturally, found it a "stupid and hateful city." What will I do here? she asked d'Annunzio. "There's not a museum. Not a painting! Not even the possibility of music, here nothing." Mostly, she hadn't received any letters from her Gabri. "I, Isa, I tell you that I love you. It's the truth, I have never lied to you." When he did send a telegram, it didn't please her, and she wired back: "Detestable empty reply."

When *La Gioconda* opened, though, Duse received twelve curtain calls and was acclaimed by critics and the leading Romanian actors as a pioneer in modern art. As the tour progressed, Teresa Rasi noted Duse had become friendly and loquacious with the company. "In the wings during *Cleopatra*," Rasi wrote, "she spoke of Shelley of Byron of Christ and Christianity, of paganism!!!" Success cheered everyone up, including d'Annunzio, who joined the company for a few days when they moved to Vienna.

"If you were tied to me . . . ," Duse suggested to her lover in Vienna, but d'Annunzio didn't respond to her hint. Duse knew of his infidelities and wanted an exclusive relationship. Tormented by jealousy, she asked, "Who holds you close? Who do you hold in your arms tonight, while you sleep? How many times have I left you in the caresses of others? This TRUTH! Why?"

The Vienna engagement ended on December 4 with innumerable curtain calls and a rain of flowers onstage. Duse parted cordially with Luigi Rasi, the man she had disparaged privately as a "mosquito." She gave him a leather cigarette case, and too moved to speak, he kissed her hand. As usual, after a long tour, Duse was ill. Suffering from bronchitis, she returned to La Porziuncola to recuperate.

"SOLITUDE IS A GOOD CONSOLER," Duse believed, and she spent many days alone at La Porziuncola, fighting a fever and influenza she had contracted while recovering from bronchitis. Two "inevitable and terrible words: leaving and working" haunted her. "I would like to scream my revolt," she told Boito on February 1, 1900. The world had entered a new century, but she remained mired in the nineteenth-century world of Sardou and Dumas. "I wanted to *found in Italy* (!!!) something that was art and free-wheeling flight toward something that could truly be called art and expectancy of new forces! But nothing was understood. [. . .] *Art of what?*—I've nothing left (what a life!) except the *name* I've made."

Duse had fulfilled her dream of taking her name around the world—in fact, she had become a name, but she hated the constant touring and was made sick by the lack of enthusiasm for d'Annunzio's plays. "We are nomads in Italy," she said. "Our actors have no theatres they can call their own. We are the sport of every wind that blows. A national theatre is necessary to the development of national drama."

Their shared utopian dream of a new kind of theatre, an art theatre opposed to the bourgeois, commercial theatre—a theatre art that like religion would be the salvation of the human spirit—was the real tie binding d'Annunzio and Duse. That philosophy was at the core of *Il fuoco*. After five years of work, in February 1900, d'Annunzio finished the book, and it was published in Italy in March, and soon after translated into French and English.

Il fuoco created a worldwide furor. Supposedly, Sarah Bernhardt returned the book unread to d'Annunzio, shocked (or jealous) at the portrait of her rival. Duse's legions of fans were outraged at what they saw as her exploitation by the writer. Their neighbor in Settignano, Bernard Berenson, called *Il fuoco* "the event of the moment . . . there are exquisite and sublime pages in this filthy book."

Tourists quickly caught on that they could use *Il fuoco* as a sightseeing guide to Venice. Those who read more deeply understood d'Annunzio's achievement in bringing the novel into the modern world by reshaping the very idea of character and narrative and literary vocabulary. It would take almost a century, though, for literary critics to recognize the breadth of his feat. *Il fuoco* is "a novel of acting and aging, of Wagner and Monteverdi and Venice," writes d'Annunzio scholar Paolo Valesio, "a great fresco that inspires, among others, James Joyce and Thomas Mann."

Duse also understood what he had accomplished, and the conclusion of the book carried particular meaning for her. When the book ends, the poet Stelio leaves his life of sensuality behind to devote himself to art. D'Annunzio, too, had promised Duse he would change his life, that he would no longer be the man of pleasure. With *Il fuoco*, d'Annunzio had achieved what Duse had always sought: "You have compressed art into life and life into art," she said.

Angelo Conti, d'Annunzio's close friend who appears in the roman à clef as Daniele Glauro, wrote a review of the book for *L'Illustrazione Italiana*. He echoed Duse's words: "*Il fuoco* is the synthesis of all the life and all the work of Gabriele d'Annunzio, and is the ultimate expression of his mastery and of his anxiety." The true protagonist, Conti believed, was not the poet but the actress who lived and breathed in the book.

IN MARCH 1901, Duse returned to work and a tour to Monaco, Vienna, Berlin, Frankfurt, and London. Everywhere she was received with ovations and critical raves. Duse had entered a pantheon in which she seemed above mortal criticism. On April 13, she played *La Gioconda* at the Burgtheater in Vienna, where she was awarded the Gold Cross of Merit. D'Annunzio was with her, taking notes as usual. When he saw his name and Duse's on the façade of the gray stone theatre, and listened to his words resound in the vast theatre, he felt a "singular sensation!" He noted the presence of the old emperor, who sat "mummified" in a box. "Isa," he wrote, "speaking of the diversity, the dreadfulness, and the fullness of her life in these days, says= Madness is no longer *rich*."

D'Annunzio returned to Italy, where he was again running for Parliament representing Florence. On March 24, he had suddenly changed sides in a *salto di quinta* (switch of wings) from the extreme right to the extreme left, but he was defeated in the election. Actually, d'Annunzio was not serious about his political ambitions, preferring to devote his time to writing and to attending productions of his plays. He also busied himself defending *Il fuoco* from critical attacks. When he joined Duse in Frankfurt in May, she advised him to sneak into her hotel room and avoid some of her friends who had been offended by her portrayal in the book.

The controversy over *Il fuoco* and d'Annunzio's portrayal of Duse as a kind of mythic theatre goddess helped publicize his plays and their collaboration. In London in May and June, Duse played a short season at the Lyceum Theatre. "This is the most monstrous city of all," she complained. The heat, the fog, the crowds, and the gray, sunless days depressed her.

In the evenings, though, at the theatre, she slipped into her natural world. "I felt yesterday," she wrote d'Annunzio after one performance, "(and it's rare for me) the charm and grace of a woman, a harmony between soul and flesh, so ecstatic, orgasmic, and so sweet . . ."

On a visit to London that spring with his father, James Joyce, then eighteen, saw Duse in *La Gioconda*. She had the same powerful effect on Joyce as she had on so many writers. According to Joyce's biographer Richard Ellmann, Joyce "perhaps aspired to be d'Annunzio's successor in her affections," sent her a poem of praise and kept her portrait on his desk. Soon after, when Joyce read *Il fuoco*, he believed d'Annunzio had surpassed Flaubert as a novelist and was profoundly influenced by the Italian writer's lyrical prose.

While James Joyce, London audiences, and critics succumbed to Duse's spell, Max Beerbohm, who was noted for his wit and his caricatures, dared to resist La Duse. When he took the job of drama critic at *The Saturday Review*, Beerbohm had asked to be paid more than his predecessor, George Bernard Shaw. "I have less experience of the theatre," Beerbohm quipped, "and so will find the work more difficult."

Beerbohm dutifully attended Duse's repertoire of plays at the Lyceum. His review was published in the May 26, 1900, edition of *The Saturday Review*— an issue seemingly devoted to bashing modern (and Italian) art. The opera critic declared Puccini's *La Bohème* the "greatest rubbish" ever written; therefore he couldn't waste time criticizing it. The book critic dismissed d'Annunzio's *Il fuoco* as heavy, boring, "form without substance." Beerbohm, without malice and with more wit, continued the theme in his review. "There never was an influence so awe-inspiring as Duse," he wrote. "(Imagine anyone calling Duse 'Eleonora'!). At her coming, all the voices of the critics are hushed. Or rather, they are uplifted in unisonant dithyrambus . . . If a fiery chariot were seen waiting outside the stage-door, no one would be much surprised." Beerbohm refused to bow down before the "demi-goddess." He admitted he saw "power and nobility in her face." He admired "her movements, full of grace and strength." But he was "hostile to her," he wrote. "I can't surrender myself, and see in her the 'incarnate womanhood' and 'the very spirit of the world's tears' and all those other things which other critics see in her. My prevailing impression is of a great egoistic force; of a woman overriding, with an air of sombre unconcern, plays, mimes, critics and public. In a man I should admire this tremendous egoism very much indeed. In a woman it only makes me uncomfortable."

Beerbohm's response to Duse was, of course, comically misogynist, but he also perceived what no other critic had expressed—the sheer force of her will. That will had raised her from the terrible poverty of her childhood to the pinnacle of art and fame. D'Annunzio, who poeticized her will into a myth, understood the tremendous human effort she had made. Duse often exhorted her actors to strengthen their spirits. Yes, she had great gifts, but as she pointed out to Carlo Rosaspina in an acting note, Rosaspina's defects came not from lack of talent but from "an unhealthy, bad will," a sickly spirit lacking a powerful imagination.

Offstage, with her many illnesses and her continual complaints of suffering, Duse sought to minimize her strength to gain sympathy and attention— a technique that worked well with her women friends, who were protective and supportive. With d'Annunzio, however, she was the strong one. Yet there were times when she longed for his support. "Poor me," she sighed from her hotel room in dreary London, thinking of him in sunny Tuscany, where he had "a house, flowers, grape vines, olive trees." She assured d'Annunzio she had a lonely, strenuous life. Jewels and crowns meant nothing to her, she said. She wanted to be with him. D'Annunzio, being himself, was completely self-absorbed, concerned only with his writing, a duel he had fought, and the election he had lost. Upset with his meager royalties from *La Gioconda*, he chided Duse with presenting the play only five times in London. She responded angrily. The Lyceum Theatre chose which plays they wanted, she pointed out. "Every time I have wanted to disappear from you, it has been you who has tied me," she said. "No, No, I don't want to agonize like this! I have silenced love—I alone know. I don't want to suffer like this anymore."

As usual, he coaxed her back. "I don't want your scorn," he said.

"Words! Words! Too many words!" she telegraphed. "Pay attention to the words, Gabri. No more words. That which is will be."

The London tour and their epistolary word battle ended in mid-June. To escape the stifling heat of Settignano, d'Annunzio had rented a villa to catch the breezes from the Tyrrhenian Sea, at a point called Il Secco near Viareggio. He moved his favorite horses and dogs with him as well. Claiming to be disgusted with speaking, Duse joined him there. She rested while d'Annunzio wrote—an ode to the new young king Victor Emmanuel III (who replaced King Umberto I, who had been assassinated by an anarchist), an ode to commemorate Nietzsche, and many lyrical poems, like the exquisite "Rain in the Pinewood." In early 1901, he wrote an ode on the death of Verdi. Like Stelio, his self-portrait in *Il fuoco*, d'Annunzio was becoming the great bardic poet of Italy.

D'ANNUNZIO STAYED ON in Il Secco while Duse worked to raise money for the Italian premiere of *La città morta*, for their new theatre, and, of course, to support d'Annunzio's lifestyle as well as herself and Enrichetta. From

August 1900 to May 1901, Duse was on the road in Switzerland, Germany, France, Spain, Portugal, and Italy. "The ideal of art is our consoler. The only one," she believed.

As long as he dangled an ideal of art in front of her, d'Annunzio knew Duse would remain at the yoke. "My life belongs to you," she told him.

When Duse found herself short of money to pay the yearly rent on La Porziuncola (or more likely needing funding for *La città morta*), she called upon the Duchess of Palmella. "Can I watch you in your impossible agony without trying to help you?" the duchess replied. On February 7, the duchess gave her 23,000 lire (then about $4,000). As a young girl, Duse had learned how to use her voice and body to beg for money. With her wealthy benefactors, she didn't have to beg. The duchess pleaded with Duse to accept the money, and the duchess assured her it would be their secret. Apparently, Duse had also been distressed that she was looking older. "I swear to you," wrote the duchess, playing the doting mother, "you are still *young and beautiful . . . you don't even need a toilette to be great and unique. It suffices to just be you.*"

On March 20, 1901, *La città morta* opened at the Teatro Lirico in Milan. Duse played the blind Anna; Ermete Zacconi joined Duse's company to play Leonardo; Carlo Rosaspina acted Alessandro, Anna's husband; and Ines Cristina played the young virgin Bianca Maria. Bernhardt's production of *La città morta* had been criticized for its ugly sets and costumes. Duse wouldn't make the same mistake. Her production, constructed by Odoardo Rovescalli, with the golden treasure of the Atrides carefully researched and reconstructed by the Instituto Germanico, was visually stunning.

In keeping with d'Annunzio's theory of total theatre, which he had introduced in *Il fuoco*, every aspect of the production—words, lighting, sets, costumes, music, direction, acting—merged into one single art, with no one aspect dominating, including, theoretically, Duse herself. Today, of course, this is common theatre practice, but at the beginning of the century, it was revolutionary. Duse supervised every detail, including the long, flowing wig worn by Bianca Maria, which Duse had especially made in Paris. Worth of Paris designed the costumes, using a color palette of black and white and the linear, fluid lines of Greek sculpture. One of Duse's costumes was a black charmeuse gown embroidered with black and gold and completely lined in white charmeuse. Another costume was ivory crepe de chine with white pearl embroidery and trimmed with jewels and braid.

Lured on for four acts by the ensemble acting, the beauty of d'Annunzio's words, and the gorgeous sets, many in the opening-night audience were revolted by the final brutality. At the end of the play, when Leonardo kills his sister, someone from the gallery shouted, *"Assassino!"* Critics and audiences,

In *La città morta,*
c. 1901–03

though, were astonished by the splendor and unity of the production, which set a new standard for the Italian theatre. Critics also noted a new musicality and tenderness in Duse's voice. D'Annunzio, of course, had written the part of Anna for Duse, and some of the lines carried a personal subtext. "Why have I not had a son?" Anna asked. This motif of the lost son would be a constant in Duse's work, particularly during her last years.

The choices Duse made in playing the final moments, when Anna discovers the body of Bianca Maria, were the clearest possible demonstration of the difference between nineteenth- and twentieth-century acting. Unlike Bernhardt, Duse didn't follow d'Annunzio's stage directions but made her own choices based upon the woman she had created, and she gave herself time to think the thoughts of the character before speaking the words. When Duse as the blind Anna felt the body of the dead girl, her dead eyes, which had been opened throughout the play but not seeing, "slowly became alive." She remained still for several moments while the realization dawned that she could see; then she cried out, a cry "which truly seemed to be the exhalation of her soul so full was it of wonder at seeing, of horror at what she saw, and mingled joy and anguish at the gift of sight coming to her at such a price." It was a cry that "shocked the audience." Then she spoke the lines *"Vedo! Vedo!"* ("I see! I see!") very softly.

FOR THE NEXT FEW MONTHS, the company toured the play to Genoa, Bologna, Florence, Rome, and Venice. "Work—ah! What salvation!" Duse enthused. Her lover followed the tour, but like Boito, he quickly tired of traveling with actors. Buoyed by the success and the profits from *La città morta,* he was eager to finish *Francesca da Rimini* and rush it into production.

After the tour ended in late May, d'Annunzio spent months researching and writing. He consulted medieval historians to insure accuracy in creating siege weapons, costumes, and sets. He and Duse traveled to Rimini again and to Venice, where they met with Mariano Fortuny, who was designing the sets and advising on the lighting and the special effects, which included realistic battle scenes with boiling oil, smoke, and fire. Overwhelmed by the work involved in building the sets, Fortuny withdrew from the project, and Odoardo Rovescalli replaced him two months before the opening.

Duse, too, was having doubts. As producer and financial backer of the project, she had signed some of the twenty-six actors needed for the production, including Gustavo Salvini (the son of the great Tommaso Salvini) and Carlo Rosaspina. Even though d'Annunzio hadn't finished the script, Duse knew it was an enormously complicated and expensive endeavor. She feared Salvini was an unknown quantity and felt Rosaspina lacked power.

Reluctantly, hesitantly, she admitted to d'Annunzio she might look too old to play Francesca, and she worried she might not have the physical stamina to sustain the character for five acts. She wondered if d'Annunzio thought she might be too old as well. "I wouldn't want this thrown in my face by others," she said.

Instead of performing *Francesca da Rimini,* Duse suggested that she continue to tour with *La città morta* and *La Gioconda* in characters she felt comfortable playing. She would work for his art, but at a distance. "Give me the right to decide this last step myself," she said. "My soul is my art." She begged him to think about her suggestion and tell her the truth. Duse also was anxious about funding the production. Again, she told the Duchess of Palmella about her money worries, and the generous duchess responded with cash and loving words. "So forgive your dear mother who loves you like a child and who suffers when she knows you're tormented—it's so little, so little . . . don't say no because it would be such a burden for me."

D'Annunzio needed Duse's name and her money for the expensive project, and he convinced her she wasn't too old to play Francesca. To reassure her, he dedicated the play to her and composed sonnets in her honor. In early October at La Capponcina, in a room fragrant with roses and cyclamen, he read the play to Duse, Gustavo Salvini, Carlo Rosaspina, and the other actors, as well as selected journalists and critics. As Duse listened to d'Annunzio read in his "exquisite, penetrating" voice, from time to time, she left the room. She believed in the poet, but with her vast theatre experience, she must have sensed the static quality of the script. In writing his play, d'Annunzio paid attention to sound and rhythm like a composer writing music for an opera. To suggest the medieval period, he used archaic words in long lyrical passages. Again, he wove together his favorite themes of violence and passion. The characters are taken from Dante, but he had rethought the story and the characters and made them his own.

Set in the violent world of medieval Italian nobility, the play contains the tragic love story of Francesca, who falls in love with the married Paolo, who has come to court her for his brother, Gianciotto. Francesca marries the hideous Gianciotto, but is also desired by another brother, the vicious, one-eyed Malatestino. At the end of the play, the lovers are caught by Gianciotto. Francesca tries to protect Paolo, but they are both stabbed by Gianciotto. The lovers fall together, and Gianciotto breaks his sword across his knee.

The company rehearsed at the Teatro la Pergola, Florence's opera house, for two months. Luigi Rasi and some of his students were involved in the production, and Rasi's wife, Teresa, kept a rehearsal diary. At first, all went well. Teresa found d'Annunzio courteous and affable, and not as eccentric as his reputation. In the beginning, Salvini, who played Paolo, rehearsed alone with d'Annunzio, but when he began to rehearse with Duse, their different methods became glaringly obvious. Salvini, like his famous father, was from the old, declamatory school of acting.

"But why not renew ourselves, do new things, make progress," Duse believed. Salvini acted "as if he's performing in front of an open window!" she said. "What is more eloquent than silence?" she asked. "When we see a person who is still and silent, don't we immediately ask: what's wrong? What's disturbing them?" Despite their different methods, Duse hoped as they worked together they would improve. "We need to satisfy the author," she said.

Meanwhile, the author was overseeing every detail of the production—everything from choosing fabrics to showing Duse how to hold a prop hand mirror. Both d'Annunzio and Duse directed the actors, which led to conflict. D'Annunzio yelled at everyone, including Duse, while Duse's methods, although vigilant and attentive to detail, were more gentle. Duse chided a young actress, Emilia Varini, saying, "You have spoken badly, really badly!" but embraced her to soften the criticism. For her old comrade Rosaspina, who had failed to put enough variety and color in a speech, she didn't need words but simply smiled and gave him two light taps on his arms. To the young woman who played Francesca's sister, Duse was positive and encouraging. "Slower, sweeter," she said, "like that, good, brava!"

Duse became friendly with the young actress Emilia Varini. "In three years, she'll be something!" Duse said. During a break in rehearsal, Duse chatted with Teresa Rasi and asked about her marriage to Luigi. Teresa confided that her marriage was a union both of passion and of aspirations. Duse approved, saying passion isn't enough to unite two people; there must be something "higher, more true, more enduring."

Her attempt to create an enduring art with d'Annunzio was fraught with problems. Worth in Paris sent Duse's costumes to the wrong place, which led to a hassle with customs. "I have to pay heaps of money," Duse said, "and have clothes that are ruined, and who knows when I'll get them." Still, despite her money worries, Duse accommodated d'Annunzio's vision by spending a fortune buying costumes, wigs, and properties, including two valuable antique pens no one in the audience would be able to see. On the other hand, d'Annunzio refused to accommodate the actors. Foreshadowing film technique, he rehearsed scenes out of order and sometimes kept Duse waiting up to thirteen hours to work on a scene. His constant, watching presence onstage and backstage got on her nerves. Once, she yelled, "Go away, you're bothering me!" D'Annunzio responded by seating himself in the wings beside Emilia Varini and flirting with her. Duse retaliated by leaving rehearsal only to return and shoot a scathing look at Varini and stop speaking to her. "I respect his genius," Duse said, "but I wish he would respect my work!"

When the company moved to Rome in early December, the chaos increased. Duse had booked the Teatro Costanzi, between via Nazionale and via Viminale, for the production. The vast theatre usually featured opera and ballet. Puccini's *Tosca* had opened there the year before. The theatre also boasted the latest electric lighting, but at one point, in an attempt to create a shadowy atmosphere, d'Annunzio threatened to smash the footlights if they weren't removed. He shrugged off warnings that the stage would be too dark.

The principal actors—Duse, Salvini, and Rosaspina—all became ill (or pretended to be) and missed some rehearsals. Their absence may have been related to d'Annunzio's habit of inviting the press to rehearsals. While d'Annunzio sought publicity and wanted to turn the production into a media event, Duse believed rehearsals should be private and journalists and critics should not see the mistakes and errors of a work-in-progress, since they would never be able to free themselves from their first impressions. "The stage must be a place of mystery," she said, "which no one can penetrate; what we prepare must come as something completely new."

"All of Rome," wrote one reporter, turned out for the opening on December 9, 1901—politicians, artists, writers, the aristocracy, and the bourgeoisie. An unruly crowd had begun to gather in late afternoon. By curtain time, the audience was volatile with anticipation. It was widely known Duse had spent 400,000 lire on the production (about $80,000 then), which was the most that had ever been spent on a production in Italy.

About an hour into the first act, Francesca/Duse made her first entrance. She wore a wig (to cover the gray strands in her hair) and a gorgeous, embroidered gown. The magnificent spectacle of the sets, ornate costumes, and the lyrical verses of the first act pleased the audience. D'Annunzio was called to the stage three times. Unfortunately, his decision to do away with the footlights during Act II made the stage so dark the audience couldn't see the battle scenes. Plus, smoke poured into the house and some of the scenery collapsed. As the play lumbered forward, the audience, confused and exhausted by the spectacle, didn't know what to do. Cheers and volleys of applause (particularly for a love scene between Duse and Salvini) alternated with boos and whistles and cries of *"Basta!"* During intermission, d'Annunzio cut portions of the fifth act.

When the curtain finally fell, six hours after it had first risen, there were more cheers and more hisses. Backstage, d'Annunzio shook Salvini's hand. Seeing Duse on her way to her dressing room, d'Annunzio grabbed her and asked, "And you, dear, how are you?" Duse's only reply, reported Teresa Rasi, was "an expressive movement of her head."

"Oh, the theatre!!" Teresa concluded in her diary. "What a world!!!"

In *Francesca da Rimini*, c. 1901–03

"Nobody would be surprised if it ended with a revolver," said Adelaide Ristori. Giorgio, Ristori's son, believed d'Annunzio had become Duse's "vampire" and was slowly destroying her "morally, physically, and artistically."

Luigi Pirandello was at the opening and recalled the event years later. He felt "the vast flood of d'Annunzian rhetoric" had crushed Duse. D'Annunzio's art relied on "sensations that flourish only when fed on imagery," Pirandello said, while in Duse's art, "everything is internally very simple, bare, almost naked. Her technique is the quintessence of a pure, lived truth."

But Duse wasn't crushed. Although reviews were mixed, for the most part the theatrical spectacle, d'Annunzio's passionate verse, and Duse's acting were praised. More important, audiences liked the lavish production and the hyped-up glamour of the event. Duse and d'Annunzio had elevated Italian theatre practice on every level, producing a kind of total theatre that threatened the supremacy of opera. They continued to work on the play, making the necessary cuts and adjustments. The script is flawed, probably unproduceable by today's standards, but it also contains lines of such prescient

power they explain why Duse would submit herself to d'Annunzio's
"rhetoric." In one passage, for example, as Francesca brandishes the deadly
weapon of "Greek fire," she says:

> Life tremendous and quick! Beauty
> that is deadly! It flies through the night
> without stars; it falls in the field, seizes the man
> sonorously, it worms its way between scale and scale, hunts down
> wherever there is a vein, cracks
> his bone, searches out the marrow,
> twists him, suffocates him, blinds him;
> but before he is blinded in the eyes,
> his whole soul desperately
> screams in the brilliance that kills him.

DUSE AND HER COMPANY took *Francesca* on a tour of Italian cities.
D'Annunzio had cut about seven hundred verses, and the technical problems
of smoke and lights had been eliminated. On January 29, 1902, in Bologna,
Duse dedicated a performance to celebrate Adelaide Ristori's eighty-sixth
birthday. Earlier that month, a Paris newspaper had asked her to write a tribute honoring Ristori. Duse sent a letter warmly praising the perfection of Ristori's art. Knowing of Ristori's dislike of d'Annunzio and his work, she used
the opportunity to defend her choices. She had been reproached, she said, for
abandoning her old repertory, easy money, and sure fame to pursue a new
artistic vision. In a slap at Ristori, who had often cut plays to highlight her
own scenes, Duse wrote, "I disdain to be a virtuosa who shows off her skill. I
refuse to place my personal success above the work. Also, an evolution is
developing in our art toward 'pure art,' not mere entertainment."

Despite her claim, d'Annunzio's plays depended on her virtuosity to sell
tickets. The company moved on to the Raimund Theater in Vienna. Afterward, Duse telegraphed the response to d'Annunzio: "First act, three calls—
second, five; third, nine; fourth, four; fifth, prolonged ovation; theatre was
crowded with all the aristocracy." Critics called the production a fusion of
poetry and theatricality. One critic even quoted from *Il fuoco* to convey his
thoughts about Duse: "Her potency on the stage, when she speaks and when
she is silent, is more than human."

In Berlin, the critics hailed *Francesca* as the great event of Berlin's theatrical season, but they had a mixed response to *La Gioconda* and *La città morta*.
D'Annunzio joined Duse in Trieste and in Gorizia, where Italian patriots liv-

ing in Austria-Hungary acclaimed him as a hero. In Gorizia, d'Annunzio met Liane de Pougy, a young courtesan, who called herself an actress-dancer.

In June, Duse heard rumors of an assignation d'Annunzio planned with Liane. "Avoid, avoid, avoid, Gabri, the arrival in Florence of such a person," she wrote. Duse confided to a friend she believed in d'Annunzio's genius, but "my blindness was, that it seemed to me, that it would have been vain to make a new *form of art* without a new form of life, of thoughts, without an absolute *truth* of his being!"

Duse assumed d'Annunzio had a brief fling with Liane, but in her memoir, *The Blue Notebooks*, Liane de Pougy wrote she may have been the one woman able to resist him. She said she met d'Annunzio in Florence when she was dancing there. He sent a carriage filled with red roses for her. Young boys greeted her at the door of Capponcina and threw roses at her feet. Although she thought his conversation marvelous, his physical presence repulsed her. "There before me was a frightful gnome with red-rimmed eyes and no eyelashes, no hair, greenish teeth, bad breath, the manners of a mountebank and a reputation, nevertheless, for being a ladies' man." Liane escaped by promising to come back. Instead, she sent her maid two days later with an apologetic note.

Duse and d'Annunzio spent the summer together at the Villa Secco and later in Settignano. His infidelities dismayed her, but he always returned to her, calling her Ghisola in the caressing voice she loved. In fact, d'Annunzio felt no guilt over his fleeting affairs, believing they made him more eager for his Ghisolabella and made their lovemaking more intoxicating.

For almost a year, Duse had been negotiating with the American producer George Tyler and his partner Theodore Leibler for a tour of the United States. She proposed an exclusive Dannunzian repertoire of *La Gioconda, La città morta,* and *Francesca.* D'Annunzio wanted to accompany her and give lectures. Tyler predicted disaster. "His recent book in which the great Italian actress figured as the central character has been thoroughly discussed by the American press," he wrote Joseph Smith, Duse's representative. "He would not only be a failure himself but he would absolutely ruin her position in America." Duse doesn't need new plays, Tyler asserted. "Let her come to us and play her old repertoire—I can assure her the largest season she has ever enjoyed."

Duse insisted on d'Annunzio's plays. Tyler finally agreed but refused to budge on the lectures. "If I am forced to lose Madame Duse I shall regret it very much indeed, but I don't propose to lose a whole lot of money on d'Annunzio," he said. "Let him come if he will, but not to talk."

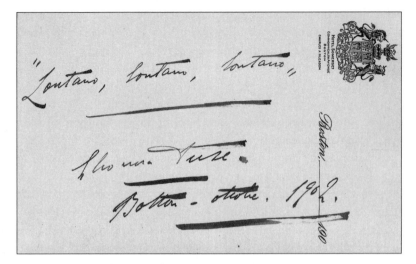

"Faraway, faraway, faraway," Duse wrote,
quoting from ex-lover Arrigo Boito's opera, *Mefistofele*

In October 1902, before leaving for America, Duse left d'Annunzio in Settignano and traveled to Paris to see Worth for new costumes. She also bought herself a full-length fur coat for 800 francs and sent d'Annunzio a plaster cast of Michelangelo's *The Prisoners*. Perhaps to compensate for the loss of his lectures, she generously agreed to give him 12 percent of the gross receipts; she received 55 percent and Leibler and Company received 45 percent.

With sixteen trunks of costumes, she arrived in New York on October 14 and was met by Joseph Smith and her old friend Helena de Kay Gilder. She marveled at the "enormous, enormous—enormous 5th Avenue!!!!" She checked in to the same room at the Holland House where she had stayed on her first tour.

Before opening in New York, Tyler and Leibler decided to try out the tour in the more receptive intellectual atmosphere of Boston. Together, d'Annunzio's notoriety and Duse's reputation as "the foremost actress in the world" generated a great deal of press and audience curiosity. American audiences rarely had an opportunity to see new European plays or any plays that might be controversial. The powerful Theatrical Syndicate monopolized American theatre at this time, controlling theatres in every major city as well as play and actor choices. The Syndicate provided what American audiences seemed to want—sentimental comedies and the pabulum of Clyde Fitch plays, with their contrived happy endings, and the excitement of melodramas like *The Count of Monte Cristo*, starring James O'Neill. Many critics supported this bland artistic diet. The critic of the *Dramatic Mirror*, for example, believed "there was enough horror, woe and misery in the world without thrusting more of it upon us in places of amusement." That Leibler and Tyler were able to sell Duse in d'Annunzio's plays to the American public was a testament to her immense drawing power.

The flaming gold and red autumn leaves between New York and Boston enchanted Duse, and she arrived in Boston in high spirits. Seats for the first three performances had been sold at auction—the top price ticket for *La città morta* sold for $26. She opened at the Tremont Theatre with *La Gioconda*. Since the immorality of d'Annunzio's plays had been denounced repeatedly in the press, the critic of the *Boston Herald* in his review assured his readers the play carried "very little moral danger to the spectators." At Duse's first appearance, he wrote, "her wonderful vitality, ease and unaffected naturalness of style took her audience captive."

The plot of *La città morta* revolted some reviewers and shocked audience members, but the play disappointed also because it was an ensemble piece, and Duse just another character in the ensemble. The audience had paid top dollar to see her at the center of the action. The medieval spectacle of *Francesca* proved more popular. To Duse, "more than to any other actress of our epoch," wrote the *Boston Herald* critic, "may be applied the expressive Italian word *immedesimare*—to bring one's self into unity with—the imagined or invented creature."

Amy Lowell, then twenty-eight, attended Duse's Boston performances, and marked her birth as a poet from the moment she saw Duse's acting. "What really happened was that it revealed me to myself," she said. Lowell met Duse and became a valuable American friend, supplying her with cases of champagne and introductions to other wealthy ladies. "I am no hero-worshipper," Lowell declared in one poem addressed to Duse, "Yet for your sake I long to babble prayers / And overdo myself in services." And in another, Lowell asked, "Where has there ever been a flesh / So rightly framing such a spirit?"

Boston's Italian Society feted Duse at a reception and presented her with a leather and gold photograph album with views of Boston. Dressed in trailing black robes sparkling with jet and accented with white, Duse moved easily among the group, chatting with them in Italian. "The sad Duse so much talked about, was not here," reported the *Boston Transcript*. "Her large dark eyes were not in the least bit sad looking, for laughter was constantly dancing there."

"If you could see how many roses I have in my rooms!!!" Duse exclaimed to d'Annunzio. She was happy he had been writing to her about his work. "What helps me the most," she said, "is to know that you are in your self."

She didn't have time to write long letters because of so many performances and recitals, but she assured him she was happy and in love with the Boston climate. "The sky is so beautiful here! So blazing!" She had won the Boston audiences, but the thought of New York was "frightening!" "Ah! What will I do?" she asked d'Annunzio. "How will I do it?"

On November 4, 1902, she opened in New York with *La Gioconda* at the Victoria Theatre on Forty-second Street and Seventh Avenue, a large musical house built by Oscar Hammerstein. The producers had prepared a handsome program book with a biography and photographs of Duse and a synopsis of the plays. English translations of the plays were also available.

The next day William Winter of the *Daily Tribune* attacked d'Annunzio's literary depravity and described Duse as "a woman of wild and lawless emotion, without intellectual purpose or control, a reveller in delirium, and a photographer of woe." However, the "enthusiasm of the house was prodigious," he concluded, "and curtain calls numerous, and tears abundant." While the *New York Times* reported Duse had "narrowed her art to one country and to one player," the critic noted "the surprise of her subtle, almost shrinking, but poignantly effective art, the joy of her strange, sad, and utterly beautiful human spirit."

After three performances of *La Gioconda*, Duse presented *La città morta* for just two performances. The *Evening Sun* reported an overheard conversation after the opening performance:

"She is fine if the play were not so rotten," a man remarked.

"Like what, for instance?" asked the woman with him scornfully.

"Well," he replied, "if it were only *Camille* or something that one could understand."

Even "the vulgarians in the audience last night," said the *Sun*, "were thrilled by the last act. As the blind wife came swiftly down to the edge of the fountain the great house was frozen into a stillness that got on your nerves." The *Sun* agreed, though, that the introduction of incest was "repulsive."

After two days off, the company opened *Francesca* on Tuesday, November 11, and ran for five performances to full houses. Except for the *New York Times*, which thought Duse played a twentieth-century Francesca, critics agreed her acting made the play bearable. The men in her company were praised as "virile, manly, and excellent." While audiences filled the theatre and reveled in the blood and gore and sheer spectacle of the piece, most critics felt d'Annunzio's play was immoral and tasteless.

"Receipts are a test of success," Duse believed, and she telegraphed d'Annunzio that *Francesca* "has won." It was a "great victory," she wrote, because audiences who understood Shakespeare understood *Francesca*. Duse's manager sent d'Annunzio an accounting of the box office, and for five performances of

Francesca, his 12 percent share amounted to $2,400, approximately 14,000 lire—an enormous amount considering the yearly rent on his villa was only 1,200 lire a year. Duse also sent him press clippings, and d'Annunzio, the most literary of playwrights, could not have been pleased with the common thread in all of them—his plays had won attention only because of the actor's art.

At the urging of Joseph Smith, Duse allowed herself to be interviewed by the *New York Herald.* The reporter met her in the lobby of the Holland House and was struck by her lack of self-consciousness. Dressed in a brimmed black hat, a long black cloak, and a black dress trimmed with white lace, Duse wore no jewelry except a single gold chain band on her little finger. Which role did she prefer? the reporter asked in French. "It is Anna in *La città morta*," she said. "Why? I can't exactly determine. One cannot always give reasons for a preference." Do you suffer as Anna suffers when you are playing the part? the reporter asked. "The great joy has been given to me," Duse said, "to enter into my roles from the moment I take them up and remain in them without effort until the end." Why did she do only d'Annunzio's plays? "In Italy every actor has his author. I have arranged to produce Signor d'Annunzio's works. No other Italian actress is at liberty to play them . . . as for playing works by other authors—Dumas, Sardou, Sudermann, Ibsen, Pinero—why, I have played them, and why should I return to old roles? One must move constantly. To stand still is fatal."

BECAUSE OF THE INTEREST in *Francesca*, Duse tried to persuade the producers to let her stay in New York instead of moving south to Baltimore. The "cretins" didn't listen to her, she said, plus the Victoria Theatre was no longer available because of another Leibler production starring Viola Allen. Duse even met with Allen in an attempt to get her to give up her engagement, but failed to convince her. The New York tour ended on November 16. Duse had time to write a long letter to d'Annunzio, primarily to lecture him. Apparently, she had heard about more of his infidelities. "Gabri! Why bring back the life of the senses?" she said. "Listen, now, now, now, still—the glorification, stupid and vain and false of the book . . . ah—Gabri—now that you've thrown this trash from you, don't reopen the door."

In Baltimore, audiences for *La Gioconda* and *La città morta* were small, but the theatre was full for *Francesca*. It had been an "atrocious week," Duse complained. As she had predicted, the box office was poor. Baltimore was "a city that could be destroyed without anything being lost in the universe," she said.

The next stop on the tour, Washington, D.C., was more successful. President and Mrs. Theodore Roosevelt entertained her at the White House, and

Anne T. Morgan, the daughter of the banker, donated $1,000 to the Albano Theatre project. Audiences and critics loved *Francesca*, but didn't understand *La città morta* or *La Gioconda*.

Duse moved on to Philadelphia. The sky there reminded her of Perugia, and she longed for Italy. "My heart hurts," Duse complained to d'Annunzio. Her "stupid imbecile" German maid (recommended by Enrichetta) had botched sending some telegrams. She worried about d'Annunzio's work, and she was also concerned about his daughter with Maria Gravina, Renata (called Cicciuzza). The girl's situation was precarious, since her mentally unstable mother had swindled a jeweler and was threatened with imprisonment. Duse urged d'Annunzio to "accept the beautiful innocent!" and to go himself to rescue the nine-year-old girl. While she was in Philadelphia, she also toured Bryn Mawr, gave a short talk in the college chapel, looked at the dormitories, and thought of sending Enrichetta to school there.

On December 15, the tour opened in Chicago. Bowing to audience preferences, the company played only *Francesca* for nine performances. Duse spent two hours the day before Christmas at the Lake Shore Drive mansion of Mrs. Harry G. Selfridge. Seated on a "throne in a bower of palms" in the library, wearing a black velvet gown trimmed in ermine, she looked suitably regal as she greeted guests. On December 29 the company gave two performances of *Francesca* in St. Louis. By January 5, they were back in New York for seven farewell performances at the Metropolitan Opera House.

A *New York Times* reporter observed a rehearsal and noted Duse wasn't melancholy at all but was extremely attentive to every detail of the production, including props and set pieces. Duse's Italian stage manager told him American stagehands were bandits, not artists. With their crossbows slung over their shoulders like pickaxes, the Irish extras hired for *Francesca* looked, the reporter said, "like a gang bound for the subway."

"Ain't oi a foinlookin' dago?" said one.

To placate the producers, Duse played Sudermann's *Magda*, and the spangles, pearls, and ermine of her showy white costumes dazzled critics and fans. Because of the size of the auditorium, Duse wore makeup, and the famous blush described by Shaw was not in evidence. Her direction of Magda's final moment, which placed Magda at the back of the stage instead of downstage center, was pointed out as a radical departure from what was expected of a star. "Time and again," said the *New York Times* critic, "she does absolutely nothing but wait for the last word or action to sink in more deeply." For her final performance, she played the *virtuosa*, a role she hated, and performed a medley of acts from *La Femme de Claude*, *Magda*, and *La città morta*.

Once again, she said good-bye to her friends Helena and Richard Gilder, whose home had been a refuge. One evening she had stayed until 2 a.m. and advised Richard to write a poem, so he wrote one to her: "Loving and lonely / Ours, and ours only." Duse responded, "She's more lonely than ever!" Before she sailed on the *La Savoie* on January 22, 1903, she telegraphed d'Annunzio: "This cruel winter is ending—and my solace is that *I have kept my word.*"

EXCEPT FOR OCCASIONAL attacks of bronchitis, Duse had been well during the long American tour. As soon as she was able to relax on the ship, she fell ill with a high fever. The crossing was the worst she had ever experienced, and when she arrived in Paris, her fever had broken, but she was exhausted. When she was well enough to travel, she joined d'Annunzio in Settignano. During her absence, he had completed *Maia*, the first volume in a poetic trilogy. He had also installed his new mistress, the dancer Loie Fuller, in an apartment in Florence. "Constancy is tiresome," he told Duse.

In March, Duse left for a northern tour. "No more pain will come from me," she telegraphed d'Annunzio on March 31. "I will tie myself to work." In a letter on the same day, she wrote, "You are free towards me as towards life itself." Her relationship with d'Annunzio in love and art would no longer be exclusive. He had licensed Luigi Rasi to present *Francesca* in Turin, and in Vienna, Duse presented *Hedda Gabler*. Art and life cannot be separated, she told him.

Their break wasn't complete, however. In April, following her Vienna tour, Duse became ill and cancelled her engagements in Russia. D'Annunzio met her in Rapallo. He proposed "an experiment in peace" for the summer months. He had a new play to write, and he needed his muse close by. He and Duse rented apartments in the huge Villa Borghese in Nettuno on the coast south of Rome. His daughter also joined them.

When d'Annunzio suggested to Duse one of his lovers join them as well, she refused and said she would leave. If he needed a "soldier," he could summon her when his play was finished. She wished him well "in life, and in art." D'Annunzio didn't get his wish of a threesome, and Duse didn't leave. Perhaps she stayed because of his daughter Cicciuzza, whom she adored, but she also stayed because she believed in his work. "I am neither *beautiful*—nor young, nor happy—nor *forgetful*," she told him. "I will never forget the sweet hours of hope—life and art and fresh pain—which I lived next to you—for your work, which still enchants me."

While Duse rested and healed her voice, d'Annunzio worked on his new play, *La figlia di Iorio (Iorio's Daughter)*. Years earlier, in the Abruzzi, he and Francesco Paolo Michetti, artist and pioneer photographer, had sat in the village of Tocco Causauria and watched as a group of drunken men chased a young woman through the town square. Michetti used the scene for a painting. D'Annunzio turned the incident into the story of Aligi, a sensitive, artistic young shepherd, who gives refuge to Mila, the girl fleeing the mob. His actions make him an outcast in the village and ruin his plans for marriage. He and Mila live chastely in a cave in the hills. When Aligi's father comes to the cave and tries to rape Mila, Aligi kills him with his sculptor's axe. As the mob attempts to execute Aligi by putting him in a sack with a vicious dog and then throwing him in the river, Mila says it's her fault—she has bewitched Aligi and murdered his father. Mila then jumps into a funeral pyre saying, "The flame is beautiful!"

When he read it to her, Duse called it a "divine work." While recognizing the dramatic merit of *La figlia di Iorio*, she realized d'Annunzio had written the part of Mila, a sacrificing virgin, for a young actress, not for her, a woman of forty-four. "As an artist, I need for *you* to be *proud* of me," she told d'Annunzio. "So that my artistic voice will not disappear." But there was no "voice" for her in the play. "It is practically impossible for me to find new roles," Duse told playwright George Middleton. "The Italian dramatists now only write for young women stars. The problem of the young alone seems interesting to the public—not the old." In fact, d'Annunzio believed his tragedy needed "virgin actors."

Alice Nielsen, a young singer, studied with Duse at the Villa Borghese that summer. "In her merry moods, Duse seemed to be joy incarnate," said Nielsen. Duse wore long Fortuny gowns that fell in a soft line from her shoulders and wrapped her head with yards of sheer chiffon. "A luminous, unearthly sort of light emanated from her face and seemed to form a halo round her turbaned head," making Duse look like an "old-time saint," Nielsen said. "Although she never mentioned it," recalled Nielsen, "I knew that the canker of the suggestion that she was growing old was eating into the very marrow of her being . . . Often she would look searchingly into my face and sigh: 'Ah, you do not know how fortunate you are to be so young and fair!' "

Nielsen rehearsed *Traviata* with Duse. "She had taught me to stand perfectly still during the delivery of the aria in the scene with the father, letting my voice and face express all the emotion. As I sang, she crept toward me quietly, stealthily, never taking her eyes from my face. When the song was finished, she was so close to me, her cheek almost touched mine. Peering searchingly into my face, she straightened herself and joyously exclaimed: 'You, you are pale, you have emotional talent; you will succeed in opera!' If she had only known it was fright at her extraordinary approach that made me lose color," said Nielsen.

When Nielsen left, d'Annunzio drove her to the station. "Why you study with Signora Duse?" he asked her in his bad English. "She can teach you nothing; she too old!"

IT'S NOT CLEAR if Duse shared her fears about being too old to play Mila with d'Annunzio. She had told him she looked too old for Francesca, and she felt he thought so too, "although he may not say it, and he is right."

D'Annunzio's actions reveal that he believed Duse was the wrong actress to play Mila. He considered *La figlia di Iorio* the most profound play he had written, and he worked feverishly to ensure the best possible production. Without telling Duse, in September 1903, d'Annunzio met with actor-director Virgilio Talli, who headed a well-respected acting company. Irma Gramatica, then in her early thirties, was the company's *prima donna*. Duse's former protégée would be ideal for the part of Mila. Excited by the prospect of producing d'Annunzio's new work, Talli was not enthusiastic about d'Annunzio's proposal that Duse join his company, act in the premieres of the work, and then cede the role to Gramatica.

At the same time that d'Annunzio was courting a new acting company, he was also romancing a twenty-seven-year-old Roman widow, the Marchesa Alessandra di Rudini Carlotti. By November 1903, they were lovers. D'Annunzio nicknamed her "Nike." Blonde, athletic, and an excellent horsewoman, Nike was eccentric and so extravagant that she bedded her horses down on Persian carpets.

Ironically, while d'Annunzio was replacing Duse both in his life and his art, her art was in full flower. During the fall of 1903, Duse was on tour, first in Switzerland and then in London. She invited the critic Arthur Symons to visit her in Zurich, and he saw her act there in *La città morta*, *Magda*, and *Hedda Gabler.* He believed her art had taken a great leap forward. "In the plays of d'Annunzio, in Ibsen, she has found the quality which she has wanted," he wrote. "Poetry, nature, sincerity, the emotion of beauty, the sensations of the soul; it is these things which she cares for supremely, it is these things which feed her insatiable hunger."

In October and November 1903 when she played London, Duse seemed ageless to the critics. "Her face is unchanged," wrote one, "the face that blends the mystery of a tragic mask with the open, wide-eyed gaze of a child. Unchanged, too, is her voice—that broken, plaintive, disquieting voice."

In London, Duse began working with voice coach Henry Russell, who treated her primarily with massage. She put him up at the Savoy, where she was staying, and they became friends. When the English censor banned *La città morta*, her rage, Russell said, was like a sudden tropical thunderstorm.

In *Hedda Gabler,* c. 1905–08

"Do you think that this idiotic Censor can be forced to change his mind?"
Duse asked. Russell shook his head, and Duse ripped the tablecloth off her
breakfast table, sending silver and dishes flying. "Her emotions were always
entirely spontaneous," Russell said, "like little bundles that she had to get rid
of, unless they impede her way."

Duse sent Russell a number of charming notes, signing herself "Nessuna"
(Nobody). Like an impulsive monarch, her moods changed abruptly, Russell
recalled, and she had no use for idle chitchat. "I never invite anyone to have
meals with me," she told him. "If it amuses you to stay, please do so; but don't
expect even the smallest courtesies of the table from me, because I shall take

no notice, and will probably not speak at all." At other times, she had to talk. "If it will bore you to listen, then you can leave me alone," she said.

Sometimes when Russell showed up for a massage session, he found Duse with her head buried in a pillow, "sobbing as if her heart would break." Duse hated getting older and onstage had begun to use a touch of makeup and sometimes covered her graying hair with wigs. Plus, the fog and rain of London depressed her. She longed for d'Annunzio and Cicciuzza.

Duse told d'Annunzio that she thought constantly of Mila and claimed that everything would be ready for her, but Duse didn't have the appropriate actors to cast the play, and after spending a fortune on *Francesca*, she also didn't have the money to produce it or help him with finances. D'Annunzio accused her of *trasgressione*—breaking their contract—but he had already broken their pact by his collaboration with Talli's company.

Around the first of January 1904, d'Annunzio finally informed Duse of his agreement with Talli. Duse wrote Adolfo Orvieto, who was acting as d'Annunzio's representative, she would "not dare to question GdA" and she "would do what you and GdA tell me to do." When Duse arrived in Marseilles for a brief tour on January 3, 1904, newspapers throughout Italy were speculating about *La figlia di Iorio*. One newspaper reported Duse and d'Annunzio had broken completely. Another said that despite the opposition of Irma Gramatica and the Talli company, Duse would play in the premiere performances. Another gossiped that d'Annunzio was bankrupt and had to sell his possessions to pay for the production. All the publicity was a press agent's dream. Much of it was probably generated by d'Annunzio himself. When asked about all the stories, Duse said, "There's only one response! They're all lies!"

On January 9, she wrote him a long letter giving up the play. It broke her heart to do it, she told him, but she was doing it all for his "beautiful destiny." The letter was forceful and dramatic, but Duse was thinking of her own "destiny" as well. She could have sought new actors or secured loans, but it was in her own self-interest not to do the play. Except for *Cavalleria rusticana*, which Verga had written for her, she had never been particularly interested in regional plays. Also, while he wanted to use her name for publicity, d'Annunzio had not written Mila for her, and she knew it.

Duse had an offstage role to play, though, and she cast herself as the victim. From Nice on January 14, she wrote d'Annunzio that since she wasn't necessary to anyone, she wanted only to disappear. While all of Duse's biographers accept Duse's role as wronged woman and blame d'Annunzio for giving the part of Mila to a younger actress, it was actually Duse who chose to withdraw from creating the role in the first performances.

Even though he believed Duse was too old for Mila, the crafty d'Annunzio had manipulated the situation in such a way to force Duse to withdraw. He needed her name to raise money for his production, which already had a deficit of 100,000 lire. Her participation also guaranteed constant publicity. On January 14, d'Annunzio wrote Michetti that contracts had been signed. Since Duse had other contractual commitments, d'Annunzio said she would play in the first performances in Milan and Florence, and then would give the part to Gramatica. D'Annunzio must have known Duse would never agree to act with a hostile company only to be replaced by a younger actress. The press had already set up a rivalry between the young *prima donna* Gramatica and La Duse. While Duse certainly would have been able to act the part convincingly, theatre is a collaborative art, and even a great actor needs the support of other actors and a sympathetic environment. For Duse to agree to such conditions was foolish, but she had made an artistic pact with d'Annunzio, and she was determined at least to *appear* to keep her side of the bargain.

At first, Duse asked d'Annunzio to delay the opening, which was scheduled for March 2 in Milan. Citing financial penalties, he refused. On January 30 in Verona, he read the play to Talli's company. Duse was in Nice. She begged him to come see her and talk things over. Busy with production details, d'Annunzio ignored her pleas. After telling him she would be free in February, on February 4, she said she had to take Enrichetta to Berlin for a week. She didn't go, but she also didn't appear at rehearsals. Then Enrichetta caught a cold and gave it to Duse. Worried about her voice, Duse sent for Henry Russell. "Whenever mother and daughter were together," observed Russell, "things went wrong with the Duse, and, although she was kind and good to the girl in every possible way, her presence always unsettled the great artist and made it almost impossible for her to work. They were, in short, not sympathetic."

Duse's cold, however, was useful—another tactic to delay her presence at rehearsals. Two days later, from the Eden Palace Hotel in Genoa, Duse wrote d'Annunzio she had fallen ill with bronchitis. She was sick, but she was mostly sick at heart and furious because d'Annunzio had not come to see her, especially since she knew he had gone back and forth to Rome to see his new lover.

When d'Annunzio refused to believe she was really ill, Duse obtained a doctor's certificate. "I have never lied," she said. Up until the opening night of *La figlia di Iorio* on March 2, Duse flooded d'Annunzio with telegrams and letters. She asserted it wasn't her fault she couldn't work and pleaded with him to write to her. Duse needed a supportive audience for her pain, and Laura Groppallo came to comfort her. Her old friend Emma Garzes sent flowers and kind words. The loyal Matilde Serao spent a week with Duse in Genoa. A few weeks later, Serao published an account of the visit in *Il Giorno*. Again acting as Duse's press agent, Serao portrayed La Duse as a great, suffering artist and corroborated her story of illness. "She was truly sick," Serao wrote. According to Serao, although her doctor had ordered her not to talk, Duse had taken up the manuscript of *La figlia di Iorio*, and sometimes reading, sometimes reciting from memory, she acted out the play. "I saw Mila," Serao reported, "in all her passionate personality."

In late February, Duse moved south to Rome. She had written to Count Primoli and hoped to see him there. On March 1, Serao contacted Primoli, who was in Paris, asking him not to tell Duse she had written. She urged Primoli to return to Rome immediately because their friend was "alone and mortally sad." Duse was also angry. Instead of comforting her in her illness, d'Annunzio had telegraphed five words: "That's the way it is."

"Ah!" Duse raged. "Blindness of words—all words!" Still, she continued her torrent of words, justifying, explaining, keeping her presence felt right up to opening night.

THE FIRST NIGHT of *La figlia di Iorio* at the Teatro Lirico in Milan was the most triumphant opening night of d'Annunzio's career. Duse was torn with conflicting emotions. Her years of belief in d'Annunzio had finally been vindicated, and she was happy in his success but devastated she was not a part of it. She also realized how she had been manipulated. *"You have killed me,"* she said, *"and with what art!!!"*

The day after the opening, she sent him a telegram: "The fable goes like this: The instrument got ill. They looked inside the instrument and saw a chord. A chord called life. When it asked for help, they found the request absurd and laughed. Because of the pain of the chord, the instrument grew even more ill. It couldn't be used anymore and was thrown away, like a dog, like a stubborn horse [. . .] But Isa doesn't die, she recovers—Foolish fable."

While she had been a loyal instrument, in the last phase of their work, "you felt nothing for me," Duse accused. He had lied to her, signed a contract that humiliated her, ignored her, and left her for another woman. He had finally achieved his victory, "but console a heart—no—no you couldn't do it," she said. When Duse went to La Capponcina to get her things, she found gold hairpins belonging to Nike in the guest room. She tried to burn down d'Annunzio's house and was stopped by his caretaker. "It's necessary!" she said. "The flame, the flame! Now!"

Duse could have called d'Annunzio's bluff and created the role of Mila in the first performances, but to do so would have meant throwing herself into the flames, sacrificing her health, jeopardizing her finances, and risking her artistic reputation. As obsessed as she was with d'Annunzio, Duse, unlike Mila, was a survivor. Duse also possessed enormous energy, and since she wasn't acting, all her intellectual, emotional, and sexual passion went into her offstage drama with d'Annunzio. The dozens of letters she wrote to him at this time seem almost alive in the sheer vitality of the writing. The letters became her surrogate self, weeping, pleading, demanding attention, and always seeking center stage.

From her room at the Hotel Bristol in Rome, Duse placed herself in the middle of d'Annunzio's new love affair. She directed her maid Nina to deliver notes to d'Annunzio, who was staying with Rudini at the Grand Hotel. "We had such hopes of work . . . Now—what has happened to divide me from you? [. . .] What is this thing that makes you sleep next to her—door to door in the same hotel?" she asked. "And me here??? . . . Now I don't want life anymore—no more, no more . . ."

Thinking that the affair would run its course, she told him that she would wait for him. She demanded words and also reminded him of their lovemaking by asking him to send her violets. She even wrote to Rudini. "Tell me," she asked, "in the name of life itself: are you ready to give everything to this love? FOREVER?"

By the middle of March, however, soothed by the presence of Giulietta and Robert von Mendelssohn, who had come from Berlin to comfort her, she calmed down. Every performance has to close, and she had exhausted all the possibilities of her offstage drama. Since she had left Genoa, she explained to d'Annunzio, she had been in a state of near madness.

"I hope soon to return to work," she wrote Adolfo de Bosis. "I should like to speak from the stage." She thanked Emma Garzes for her sympathy. "The storm has passed," she said. "I will work." To Henry Russell, she said, "I don't know what I shall do, where I shall go, how I shall live—I know nothing at this moment." To Adolfo Orvieto, she was more bitter: "He has squeezed me like a lemon and then thrown me away."

D'Annunzio finally sent her a note and violets, but it was clear he would not be returning. "I beg you to read this," she wrote him on April 15, 1904, "because it is truly the *last* letter—on the subject—and doesn't demand a response, that of *yes*, or *no*—I have taken away my body—*no longer flourishing and no longer young* [. . .] but my soul lives from another glow!"

Seven

"I WILL BEGIN AGAIN—again and again!" Duse said. Onstage and off-stage, endings followed by new beginnings had been the rhythm of her life. "I alone must hold my life in my hands," she wrote Adolfo de Bosis. She had read his translations of Shelley and asked him to translate Maurice Maeterlinck's play, *Monna Vanna*, for her.

Her letters to d'Annunzio at this time suggest she had done nothing but suffer and weep. Matilde Serao thought she was suicidal. Count Primoli found her "desperate, abandoned . . . on the brink of material and emotional bankruptcy."

In March and April 1904, though, Duse took action. For financial support and advice, she turned to the wealthy German banker Robert von Mendelssohn. She refused to touch the money she had saved for Enrichetta, which would soon amount to 300,000 francs. Mendelssohn loaned her money to pay her company, and he also took charge of her finances. "You have enriched me with your friendship," he said, "and I am always in your debt."

Her work with d'Annunzio to create an Italian national theatre had ended, and her dream of harmonizing her life and art had failed, but she refused to admit defeat. In late April, she left Italy and went to Paris to "knock on doors." Italian journalist Ugo Ojetti lamented that Italy couldn't offer Duse a permanent theatre. Although Duse certainly felt the lack of an artistic home in Italy, she had throughout her career allied herself with the future and an art that transcended national boundaries.

Like a microcosm of the multicultural world of the late–twentieth century, Paris at the beginning of the twentieth century teemed with artists and scientists of every nationality—Marie Curie, Pablo Picasso, Gertrude Stein, Maurice Maeterlinck. The most exciting, most innovative theatres that pro-

In *Monna Vanna*, c. 1905–06

duced plays from around the world were located there. Freed from the censors, André Antoine's Théâtre-Libre, an independent subscription theatre,
had challenged the conventions of the commercial theatre. Antoine inspired
other pioneering art theatres, including Otto Brahm's Freie Bühne in Berlin,
Jacob Grein's Independent Theatre in London, and Stanislavsky's Moscow
Art Theatre.

Aurélien Lugné, a young French actor-director, had worked with André
Antoine and then left to start his own company in Paris, the Théâtre de
l'Oeuvre. Enthralled with symbolism and Edgar Allan Poe, whom he believed
was a distant relative, Lugné added "Poe" to his name. Strapped for money,
Lugné-Poe used simple, highly stylized sets painted by his friends, artists like
Vuillard and Bonnard. Lugné-Poe's 1896 production of Alfred Jarry's absurdist
satire *Ubu Roi*—which opened with Père Ubu uttering something that
sounded like "Shit!"—had shocked Paris. Lugné-Poe continued to excite controversy with new productions of Maeterlinck and Ibsen plays. In 1899, financial pressures had forced him to change the status of his theatre from an
independent, art theatre to a commercial theatre. When he had founded his

theatre, he had believed "the greatest virtue of the actor will be to efface himself." Now he scrambled to entice the world's finest actor to play at his theatre.

When Duse arrived in Paris, she checked into the Grand Hotel and began contacting playwrights, producers, and theatre owners. "I had strength," Duse told Lugné-Poe later, "but I no longer knew my way." She arranged to meet with him later in Italy. She visited Worth of Paris, who designed new clothes for the women she played, including for *Monna Vanna,* a black cloak and a stunning white gown trimmed with gold.

At the Grand Hotel, she met with actress Georgette Le Blanc and Le Blanc's lover, Maurice Maeterlinck. When Georgette saw Duse, she was

With Auguste Rodin, who sculpted her
and escorted her around Paris, c. 1905–06

shocked. Dressed in gray with "lifeless eyes," Duse, then forty-five, looked pale and despairing. "The conversation began with great difficulty," Georgette recalled. When Duse left the room to order tea, Maeterlinck asked Georgette, "Why have you insisted on this irritating and useless encounter? We have nothing to say to each other. How could you find this woman beautiful?" Duse returned with the tea, and Georgette took her hand and drew her out with questions about the theatre. After an hour, "the woman that we saw on our arrival had completely disappeared," Georgette said. Maeterlinck was charmed. "I could never have imagined that a human being could perform such a transformation in such a little time," he said. "When we arrived, she was almost old, and now she's twenty-five."

Duse also saw Count Primoli and his circle. Primoli found her "revived, appeased, calmed and cured." Almost as if she were rethinking every option, Duse wrote to Arrigo Boito from Paris. Sounding confident and exuberant, she told him she planned to present *Monna Vanna* in Milan. She hoped to see him then. "What one dreams—is life," she said, "and the truth= = That which lives, lives, lives . . . !!"

Art and love are insatiable, Duse believed. As an actor, she needed audiences to love her, and she demanded love from her friends, both male and female. As a woman, particularly one who had just been rejected, she craved physical love. Taking action, doing things, had always invigorated her, but one of the reasons for her dramatic change of mood and infusion of confidence during her stay in Paris was Robert von Mendelssohn. He was portly and balding, with a full beard, and was known for his kindness. He had adored Duse for years. "I embrace you with all my tenderness, dear beloved," he telegraphed her in Paris. "My love, I am with you," he wrote, "every hour, every minute. I don't know how to say anything else today, except that I'll always love you. Robi." They met secretly. Giulietta Mendelssohn did not learn of their love affair until years later.

Duse seems not to have felt any guilt about having an affair with a close friend's husband. (According to Lugné-Poe, Duse murmured to his wife, Suzanne Desprès, as if by accident, "If, once, your lover or your husband, if I possessed him . . . once . . . just once . . . you wouldn't bear me ill will, would you? It's the golden hinge of friendship.") In Berlin, Duse often stayed with the Mendelssohns; they considered her a member of their family and even named their two daughters Angelica and Eleonora. Perhaps Duse believed her affair with "Robi" was justified because of d'Annunzio's past interest in Giulietta. There's also the possibility Duse was repaying Mendelssohn for his generosity and for his management of her financial affairs. On the other hand, love didn't need an excuse.

New work, new clothes, a new lover, and Paris in the spring all worked their healing magic. On May 12, Duse telegraphed her good wishes to d'Annunzio and Cicciuzza in Rome. Her soul still suffered profoundly, she said, but she didn't want to talk about pain anymore, she wanted to work.

Duse chose to return to work at the Teatro Lirico in Milan, where d'Annunzio's *La figlia di Iorio* had opened three months earlier. In early June, wearing her new Worth costumes, Duse alternated three different plays—*La Dame aux camélias*, *A Doll's House*, and *Monna Vanna*. Maeterlinck had written the theatrical and feminist *Monna Vanna* for Georgette Le Blanc. It had first been produced in Paris at Lugné-Poe's Théâtre de l'Oeuvre in May 1902. The character of Giovanna, played by Duse, is heroic, sexually free, and defiant. "The role is really just a cloak," wrote Hermann Bahr, "everything else the playwright left to the discretion of the actor." Milan audiences welcomed Duse back with ovations. The critics praised her beauty, found her perfor-

With her lover "Robi" Mendelssohn, c. 1904–06

mances deeper and more moving, and noted that *La Dame aux camélias* seemed like a new production.

Later that month, Duse summoned Lugné-Poe to meet with her in Turin to talk about future collaboration. Lugné-Poe had arranged with d'Annunzio to present the French premieres of *La Gioconda* and *La figlia di Iorio*, starring Lugné-Poe's wife, Suzanne Desprès. A brilliant promoter, Lugné-Poe sensed an opportunity to employ Duse's fame in his plans. "I ran there," he said. He brought his wife with him. Suzanne had idolized Duse since she had first seen Duse in Paris in 1897. Duse fell in love with their youthful ardor and enthusiasm, and they fell in love with her. "Her power of attraction was unimaginable, perhaps because it was satanic," Lugné-Poe intoned.

FOR THE FIRST TIME since 1897, Duse didn't spend part of her summer hiatus with d'Annunzio. Instead, in July 1904, she was the guest of Giulietta and Robert von Mendelssohn in the mountains of northeast Italy, the spectacular Dolomites. Duse invited one of her devoted fans, Antonietta Pisa, the wife of a prominent Milan banker, to join them at a hotel in Borca.

When Walter Wentworth, a writer from Boston on holiday in Italy, learned Duse was vacationing in Borca, he rushed there in the hope of interviewing her. He found her at the Palace Hotel. Duse, he wrote, looked slender and graceful in a brown broadcloth suit with fur trim, a white muslin blouse, and a yellow-twisted straw hat bordered with black lace. Wentworth mentioned mutual friends in America, and Duse invited him to her rooms, where, she said, she had a friend who spoke perfect English. The friend was Giulietta von Mendelssohn, whom Wentworth described as Duse's "guide, philosopher, and friend."

Wentworth suggested Duse return to America and play in English. "It would never do," Duse said. "I could learn some English, yes, but when I play, when I forget that I am Duse, when I feel my way through my part, I could never stay in the foreign language. I would dash off the track, like a runaway locomotive."

Three days later Wentworth talked with Duse again at the Miramonti Hotel in Cortina. Duse and Giulietta met him. The women were dressed precisely alike, in white woolen skirts, white silk blouses, white straw hats covered with white tulle veils, white gloves, and white shoes—confusing him in a "blur of whiteness" just as d'Annunzio had described them in *Il fuoco*. If she returned to America, Wentworth advised, "you would do well to remember that ideas about love relationships are somewhat different in our country . . . and plays which would be liked in—in some other countries would not be enjoyed in the United States."

"Oh, I could choose my list more carefully," Duse replied. There was an awkward silence.

"Duse has broken utterly with d'Annunzio," announced Giulietta.

"My greatest errors I have been led into by my emotions," Duse revealed. "The heart is not always a safe guide."

IN THE PURE AIR of the Dolomites, Duse read and rested. She enjoyed Emerson's *Essays,* and she admired the "breadth of sympathy" in William James's *The Varieties of Religious Experience.* Maeterlinck's *Monna Vanna* was adequate, but she wanted something with a stronger pulse and turned again to Ibsen. She asked de Bosis to translate *John Gabriel Borkman.* Tranquil, surrounded by friends, she was able to respond logically and calmly when a disturbing letter arrived from d'Annunzio.

Writing on July 17 from Marina di Pisa, d'Annunzio accused her again of *trasgressione.* Also, the news that she had renounced performing in his new plays humiliated and saddened him. He pledged to send her his new work when he completed it. "My imperious need of a violent life—of a carnal life, of pleasure, of physical danger, of happiness—has taken me far away," he wrote. "And you—that sometimes are moved to tears by an instinctive movement of mine the way you are moved by an animal's hunger or the struggle of a plant to climb over a sad wall—can you hold this need against me?" With eloquence and tenderness, d'Annunzio expressed his devotion and his admiration for her, but "you have always been suspicious of me," he accused. Her things at La Capponcina were being looked after, he assured her, and Cicciuzza was well and happy. "I envy your eyes that look toward the Dolomites," he concluded. "Who knows when I will see them!"

For Duse, the return address of Marina di Pisa on his letter served as a reminder of her harshest losses—her son by Martino Cafiero and the pact of art she had made with d'Annunzio. *"Don't adulterate the truth,"* she answered. "Don't write the word: *trasgressione.*" She outlined her version of their pact. Her efforts on his behalf had shipwrecked her financially. "I had an enormous weight on me—*debts, loans*—they weigh on me! I must, and I want to pay them. To do so, I need to go far away. My will is strong. I hope my health will also be so." She explained she had taken up her old repertory because she needed money. "Enough!—If I look to fix the *truth,* if I struggle to comprehend *your laws*—I advise you not to misinterpret mine—I beg you— Enough!—Let's not talk about it anymore!—Words are vain. Set aside the sword and the pen when you think of me. Don't defend yourself, my son, because I'm not accusing you: So it is—So be it.—We were united to be divided—The world is full of such miseries!—Don't speak to me of domination, of the *reason* of your *'carnal life,'* of your thirst for 'joyous life.'—I'm fed up with those words!—For years I have listened to you say them."

D'Annunzio was forty-one, but Duse, not yet forty-six, addressed him as if he were a callow boy. "Among what people who might be oblivious to human pain, will you go to live? Amid what beings of papier-mâché or of masked expressions do you intend, my son, to live with and dream of art?— What woman's love can you find that is not tied to the same laws of life?— What worthy and profound love lives *only* on pleasure?"

Since Duse's reply to d'Annunzio was not found with his papers and only exists in her draft, it's possible she never sent the letter to him. "Words are vain," she wrote. D'Annunzio's character was fixed, and nothing she could write would change it. D'Annunzio dominated through the power of his words, and Duse sought what was *beyond* words. With Duse as his muse and interpreter, a woman who possessed the empathy he lacked, d'Annunzio had reached his artistic summit. The rest of his life was one long descent. Duse continued to climb.

SHE RESUMED HER WORK in October with a tour of northern Europe. Hermann Bahr, who had first seen her in Russia in 1891, saw her perform in *Monna Vanna, Magda,* and *Hedda Gabler* in Vienna. "In all her roles," he wrote, "she is now quite different. She carries a glow as if from another freer and purer world." In *Hedda Gabler,* Duse "rips herself bloody . . . and finally, her soul excoriated, seems only to live as if on a red-hot grate." Using the language of the symbolists, he declared Duse portrayed "nameless suffering" in her acting and "the eternal desire of our poor age for transcendence of self." She embodied humanity's "eternal yearning to escape one's own boundaries." Bahr identified Duse's ability to move her art forward, anticipating and even precipitating each evolution in theatre, from *verismo* to symbolism to a kind of transcendent, poetic realism.

While she was in Vienna, Duse read an Italian newspaper story about the production of *La figlia di Iorio.* It annoyed her so much she immediately wrote to Arrigo Boito to tell him her side of the story. She explained to Boito that for almost six years she had given her undivided attention, her money, and her name to "one single endeavor" she had thought was worthy. "If my devotion, if my sincerity, if the disgrace of falling sick, was desecrated by others—I alone know what my soul had promised—what I should have stood up for—what could have endured, and what had to die." Addressing Boito as "Nome" (Name) and speaking to him as if he were a distant deity, she asked him to absolve her from any past sorrows, and she asked his pardon, *"ALSO for these words.*" She signed "Lenor" and added a postscript: "If I could speak with you! If I could see you. See you, just for a minute! Love. Love—"

At the end of October, Duse moved on to Berlin. Boito sent her a telegram there, apparently giving her his blessing. She dashed off a letter of thanks. "All my soul is *with you*, with you only!" she said. "Thank you for believing me!"

During her tour in Berlin, she stayed at the von Mendelssohns' elegant home at 51 Jaegerstrasse, in the heart of Berlin, close by the imperial palace. She had asked Boito not to write her there because the "patriarch" of the house would see the mail, and since the mail arrived at dinner "it is difficult to sneak away." Of course, Duse had other motives for not wanting Robi Mendelssohn to know she was corresponding with Boito.

Duse guarded her privacy and rarely mixed her friends. Her friends submitted to her schedule, her needs, her affectionate autocracy. She tempered her tyranny with self-mocking humor. "Unless you come here within five minutes," she wrote Henry Russell, "I shall be dead." With couples like Adolfo and Lillian de Bosis, Robert and Giulietta von Mendelssohn, and Lugné-Poe and Suzanne Desprès, she played the exciting "other woman."

When her friends attempted to control her in any way, though, she pulled away. Duse confided to Count Primoli that although she loved the Mendelssohns and was enormously grateful for their generosity and hospitality, they could be irritating hosts. Never mind that she was a difficult and demanding houseguest. Giulietta brought her children to her in the morning, Duse said, and expected her to be interested in knowing "if the little brats have gone pee-pee in the bed." Although the Mendelssohns were enormously wealthy, Giulietta was frugal. Accustomed to living in fine hotels, Duse was horrified that after dinner she was expected to fold her dinner napkin to be re-used. When Duse ordered fresh sheets every night, Giulietta protested the expense and pointed out she only changed her chemise once a week. Most of all, Duse complained the Mendelssohns wanted her to renounce the theatre. "I don't like it," Duse told Primoli. "I still have breath. I have all my teeth, and I feel the need to work. It's my reason for being. It's my life. They give to me but they do not understand me."

Duse's new friends, Lugné-Poe and Suzanne Desprès, fellow workers in the theatre, understood her and seemed to share her artistic philosophy. "Work without art disgusts me," she told them, "just as art without the beauty of craft (and therefore strength) also disgusts me." Duse missed the artistic companionship she had had with Boito and d'Annunzio, and Lugné-Poe catered to her and flattered her. Hoping his collaboration with Duse would revive the box office, Lugné-Poe asked her company to appear with his troupe in Paris in spring 1905 in rotating repertory. Duse had been courted by many established European producers, including Schürmann, her old impresario, but as an antidote to middle age, she allied herself with youth and accepted Lugné-Poe's offer.

JUST AS SHE HAD IN 1897, when Duse made her Paris debut, Sarah Bernhardt offered her seventeen-hundred-seat theatre to Duse. At this time, portions of Sarah's memoirs, in which she had written that Duse was a great actress but not a great artist, had been published. Once again, their press-fostered competition led to a flurry of publicity and gossip. With cold politeness, Duse refused Bernhardt's offer. She appreciated Sarah's past kindnesses, she told her by letter, but she had been deeply offended by Sarah's opinion of her work.

Intent on sharing in the receipts from Duse's appearance as well as the publicity value of appearing as Duse's sponsor, Bernhardt met with Duse twice to try to change her mind. Sarah's smiles and charm were lost on Duse. Still, during their meeting, she was amused by Bernhardt's overarticulated speech. Sarah was *"désolée, désolée, désolée,* leaning heavily on the *'d,'"* Duse reported to Adolfo Orvieto. Sarah disparaged Lugné-Poe and his "contaminated" theatre and warned Duse no one would be able to hear her in his theatre except in the first rows. Bernhardt offered to lend Duse all her sets and pay Lugné-Poe to get Duse out of the agreement. She even enlisted a critic to help in her campaign, but Duse had given her word to Lugné-Poe. After her two meetings with Sarah, "everything is stupid," Duse grumbled to Orvieto, "my letter, Sarah's letter, and this one. I should shut up. That's clear!!"

Her irritation stemmed from "stupid" journalists in Paris who probed into her personal life and harassed her with questions about d'Annunzio and Bernhardt. "I will *never* write my memoirs," Duse vowed. She drew a "thick veil" over her personal life, which, of course, aroused curiosity. Camille Le Senne in *La Revue Théâtrale* wrote of Duse's "pure and natural" face, the "discreet elegance" of her clothes, the "white flames" in her dark bronze hair. Duse's beauty is "an inner beauty of successive emotions which reflects her soul like the subliminal changes in the color of an April sky," Le Senne gushed in the syrupy prose journalists often lapsed into when writing about La Duse. Had Nietzsche's theory helped produce this "super-woman," Le Senne wondered?

While proclaiming her aversion to the press, Duse agreed to talk to a reporter for *Le Temps* to assert her right to privacy and freedom from prying eyes. She derided questions about her favorite perfume, her favorite food, and her favorite color, as "ridiculous and puerile." Artists, she said, "belong to the public and to the critics only in that moment in which we appear on the stage." Will you return to your palazzo on the Grand Canal? the reporter asked. "I don't have a palazzo anymore," Duse said. "I've sold everything to realize the thoughts of the poet . . . but let's not speak of past failures." Actually, Duse had never owned a Venetian palazzo, but she had reminded the readers of d'Annunzio and their affair and, most important, of her sacrifice.

Certainly as Lugné-Poe and Duse had intended, all the publicity and avoiding of publicity stimulated ticket sales. (Lugné-Poe later remarked that whether Duse performed on a particular evening depended on three things— her temperature, the city's temperature, and, most important, the box office.) On Saturday, March 25, 1905, Duse opened at the thousand-seat Nouveau Théâtre with *La Femme de Claude.* The box office couldn't handle the crowds, and there was mass confusion. The play began at 9 p.m., but people continued to pour into the theatre. "The house was magnificent," reported the *Corriere della Sera.* "The boxes were all occupied with aristocratic Parisian women in splendid *toilettes.*" Except for the noticeable absence of Sarah Bernhardt, Paris's leading actresses, Réjane, Sorel, and Bartet, were present, along with most of the artists of the Comédie-Française. As Bernhardt had predicted, at first Duse had difficulty being heard. But since most of the audience was there on opening night to be seen, no one really cared, and at the end of the play they gave Duse "a true ovation." The audience called her again and again, and she accepted their praise and bouquets with smiles of thanks.

DUSE AND LUGNÉ-POE'S collaboration was financially and artistically rewarding. "As soon as she started to act," Lugné-Poe said later, "we saw the theatre disappear." Lugné-Poe learned from her artistry, but he taught her as well. In the 1890s, he had toured Scandinavia, had met Ibsen, and performed *Rosmersholm* and *The Master Builder* in Christiania (renamed Oslo in 1925), Ibsen's hometown. Lugné-Poe inspired Duse to add *Rosmersholm* to her repertory and to explore other Ibsen plays and rethink *Hedda Gabler.* Still, Duse could be exasperating. One day when she was complaining excessively about her fragile health, Lugné-Poe exclaimed, "Shut up, already! You're stronger than all of us put together." Terrified she would turn on him for his lack of respect, Lugné-Poe recalled that instead Duse burst out laughing. "He's right," she said, "now die all of you!"

When the Paris tour ended, Duse thanked Lugné-Poe again and again for giving strength to her soul. "I love to thank you," she told him in one of her many notes, written in ungrammatical French. "Evil French devils!" she teased. "You must learn my Italian because my French, I've had it."

Duse rarely exhibited her laughing, playful side with her company. She was the first modern actor, and a director who subordinated her celebrity to

the needs of the play, but as an actor-manager, she was old-fashioned and traditional. She expected unquestioning obedience, loyalty, and devotion. In
return, she paid her company when they weren't working, advanced them
money when they needed it, counseled and advised them, and, in general,
acted like a strict and loving matriarch. She was a hands-on director, touching
her actors with a reproving tap or an affectionate caress. Duse exhorted her
company to read and study, listen and observe, and to spend less time in cafés
and in idle pursuits. Rehearsals were intense and disciplined. Her company
called her "La Signora" and when she spoke, there was respectful silence.
When an actor failed to say "Signora" after one of her directions and simply
said "Yes," she would fix him "with those imperious eyes" and say, "How dare
you show disrespect to me!" and shut herself in her dressing room.

Relentless in her pursuit of perfection, she could launch into a tirade when
an actor came to rehearsal unprepared. Once, irritated by a wooden young
actress, Duse shouted, "Perhaps you have been deceived into believing that
you are a fine actress. Nothing could be further from the truth, signorina, so
get the idea out of your head. Your acting is hopeless! Pitiful! You are nothing
better than a pretty child (and even that is questionable) who cannot act any
part she is given. Get this sad fact into your head and start studying. If I am
obliged to study, then you can study, too." When the actress began to cry,
Duse exclaimed, "Go on, cry, cry! It will do you some good. Tears wash away
a great many sorrows." When the girl began to sob in earnest, Duse said,
"That's enough now! A little weep can be interesting, but too much is irritating." She was careful, however, to mix criticism with encouraging praise.
After a performance, when she saw the girl had improved, Duse embraced
her. "Brava, well done," she said.

To play Ibsen's characters, she told her company, required an understanding of sorrow and unhappiness. If the actor were healthy and happy, he would
have to go out and look for unhappiness. "I can play them well," she said,
"because I'm filled with sorrow." She spoke often about the necessity of having a strong spirit, but she also paid attention to technique. Duse coached a
young actress whose voice was too shrill. "I urge you to practice at home," she
said, "to put every word you speak deeper inside you, down in your body, not
up in your head or in that little nose." Duse caressed the girl's face with her
"fine hand," and said, "When we know we have an enemy within us, we have
to confront it and overcome it."

RELUCTANTLY, DUSE LEFT PARIS, leaving a trail of correspondence in
her wake. "Words are meaningless and banal," she wrote Lugné-Poe, "but
they're our only way of understanding each other." In mid-May, Duse and her

company opened in London at the Waldorf Theatre. Almost immediately, she summoned Lugné-Poe and Suzanne to come to London and advise her. Henry Russell, her voice coach, had been helping her, but while he knew about managing singers, he knew nothing about the theatre. At their own expense, Lugné-Poe and Suzanne arrived in London to comfort her and help her arrange her affairs. When Duse seemed settled and happy, they tried to sneak away by writing her a letter telling her they were going home. Somehow Duse gained access to their hotel room and left a note pinned to a bed pillow. "Never have harsher words been spoken to a heart that is loyal to you," she wrote, "and of course, you have made this decision together." Overcome with guilt, Lugné-Poe and Suzanne decided to stay on for a time.

Playing in *Magda, The Second Mrs. Tanqueray, La Dame aux camélias, La locandiera,* and a few performances each of *Hedda Gabler* and *La Gioconda,* Duse enjoyed a great personal triumph in London. "The strength of Duse," said the *Daily News,* "is that she has the power of conveying thoughts and feelings to the audience as if they had some strange power of insight, and she achieves it without any apparent employment of stage tricks." But the drama critic for the *Times* also pointed out that "Duse is much too good for her company and her repertory." Critics were beginning to notice what had been plaguing her for years. "Until she appears in something worthy of her," wrote the *Times,* "we are more or less compelled to abstract her from her surroundings and dream over the perfect instrument of music and motion that she is."

Duse was sick of her old repertory as well. Yet audiences, particularly in Italy, preferred comfortable old Dumas *fils* to the controversial Ibsen. She knew her leading man, Carlo Rosaspina, was no match for her artistry. But who was? Duse had kept in touch with Virgilio Talli about possible projects with his Italian company. Perhaps working on a new play with a new company in which she would be just another member of the ensemble was the answer. Duse and Talli had worked together successfully on a production of *Fernande,* and she agreed to play Vassilisa in Talli's production of Maxim Gorky's *The Lower Depths* in late October 1905.

Another option would be to give up working entirely. "I have given my love, my strength, my youth, and my life to my art," Duse told Suzanne in August. "I've decided therefore that after this year I will move toward freedom." Duse didn't explain her idea to Suzanne, saying Lugné-Poe would tell her the details.

With the help of Lugné-Poe, Duse was ready to set a new course with a new impresario. It would be with Lugné-Poe at the helm, a man, she said, who "possesses a head and a heart." Duse longed to meet Ibsen, and Lugné-Poe began to plan a tour to Scandinavia.

Before appearing with Talli's company, Duse played a benefit performance

As Vassilisa in Lugné-Poe's 1905 production of *The Lower Depths*
with M. J. Marcy as Pepel. Duse's gestures, like a lingering kiss or
touching her fellow actor's thigh, were provocative and daring.

of *The Lower Depths* with Lugné-Poe's company in Paris. Set in a Moscow
flophouse, the play explores the lives of society's dregs, who are briefly given
hope by Luka, an illusion-spinning tramp. Duse played the small but important role of Vassilisa, the landlord's wife, and Suzanne acted Natasha, Vassilisa's younger sister. A shrewd, wicked-tempered "devil," Vassilisa cheats on
her husband, beats her sister, and urges her lover to kill her husband. Critics
liked the naturalistic play, but audiences rejected it. When Duse's appearance
was announced, though, *tout* Paris crowded the theatre to see Duse efface herself in an unattractive role. She refused any payment except a token 10 francs.

In late October, when Duse reprised the role with Talli's company in Milan, the audience greeted her first appearance with prolonged applause. The critics called her "incomparable." Instead of focusing on the play or the other actors, audiences and critics responded to Duse's star turn in a small part, which highlighted the impossibility of La Duse disappearing into an ensemble. Duse also had problems subordinating herself to another director, and her collaboration with Talli was stormy. Duse had given Lugné-Poe detailed notes and had strong ideas which she tried to impose on the Talli production. At one point, Duse apologized to Talli for the tantrums she had thrown at rehearsal. They parted cordially, however. Talli formed a new company with Emma Gramatica. Under the guidance of Lugné-Poe, Duse gathered her company and turned to Ibsen.

ON DECEMBER 11, 1905, Duse played the emancipated and tormented Rebecca West in Ibsen's *Rosmersholm* at the Teatro Lirico in Milan. After a long and careful study of the script with Lugné-Poe, Duse had "rosmerised" herself, but her company resisted the painstaking textual analysis required by the new work. Baffled by Ibsen, Italian audiences preferred the old, familiar repertory. Duse ignored the gripes of her actors and continued to portray Hedda and Nora and Rebecca, the woman she called "the most difficult, the most mysterious of all."

After engagements in Brussels and Amsterdam, Duse, accompanied by Lugné-Poe, traveled to Copenhagen, the first stop on the Scandinavian tour. Lugné-Poe arranged her travel, battled with reporters on her behalf, warded off visitors, wrote telegrams and letters, carried her bags, ran her errands, conversed endlessly about Ibsen and the philosophy of life, and rushed to her side day and night.

While Lugné-Poe tended to Duse, his wife, Suzanne, toured various eastern European cities playing *A Doll's House.* Lugné-Poe managed her tour from a distance. His decision to travel with Duse instead of his wife was much more than a business arrangement. When he had first seen Duse, he said, his heartbeat had quickened. Meeting her had eclipsed his experience of meeting Ibsen. In his memoirs, Lugné-Poe was discreet about the full nature of his relationship with Duse, but he wrote intimately and knowingly about her. He published some of her letters, but he omitted the ones that contain evidence of their love affair.

Her relationship with Lugné-Poe, like her affair with Wolkoff, was mostly based on propinquity and Duse's need for a strong, helping hand. Duse's letters to Lugné-Poe (belonging to a private collector) reveal her neediness, her passion, and what the thirty-six-year-old French director would describe later as her Machiavellian manipulation. "To understand! To understand! *It is because I do not understand*," Duse, then forty-seven, wrote in one four-page letter. "It is because this beautiful, this beautiful force has come towards me," she continued. "This force which is *so* beautiful, *so* strong, *so* good. It is because *it* alone lights up and guides my life; *it*, alone, keeps me alive. At night, I put on my ring; and as soon as dawn comes and I see the first daylight behind my window, I *hide* the ring [. . .] What a mystery! What good fortune has come towards me? I *write to you*, my beloved [. . .] I . . . a fragile woman, and I am so frightened at the thought of losing you, *the only thing* which ties me to life."

Like Duse, Lugné-Poe possessed an extraordinary imagination and a flair for self-dramatization. The Scandinavian tour "rekindled Duse's heart," wrote Lugné-Poe. "A strange fever came over her—without doubt the ultimate of her ardent life which had always aspired toward a total evolution of her art."

Actually, the Scandinavian tour was a disaster. Their engagements in Copenhagen were cancelled because of the death of King Christian IX. On the way to Christiania, they learned that Ibsen, then seventy-seven, was near death. "Soon I shall go into the great darkness," Ibsen told his son, Sigurd. Ibsen was deeply moved that Sigurd had named his third child Eleonora. When Eleonora Duse arrived in Christiania, she sent a letter and a bouquet of flowers to Ibsen's wife. When she learned Ibsen was too ill to receive visitors, Duse was devastated. Lugné-Poe found her in her hotel room wrapped in her white dressing gown, her "expression strained, hollow, as if life had left her."

"What am I to do?" she asked. As usual, she had a plan. The next morning, Duse put on heavy Norwegian boots and walked with Lugné-Poe to Ibsen's house. Tourists had often caught a glimpse of Ibsen as he sat in his corner window looking out, and she hoped to do the same. Duse stood in the snow and waited for more than an hour, but the old dying playwright did not appear.

Unable to meet the "giant," as she called him, she poured her energies into Hedda and Rebecca West and Silvia in *La Gioconda*. Christiania audiences roared out their approval. The composer Edvard Grieg, who had written music for Ibsen's *Peer Gynt*, saw her performances in Christiania and marveled as Verdi had at the musicality and variety of her voice. Years earlier, opera star Emma Calvé had followed Duse from engagement to engagement one summer to study her technique. Duse's art, Calvé wrote, "broke down the false and conventional standards of lyric expression to which I had become accustomed."

From Christiania, they moved to Stockholm, but political tensions between Norway and Sweden forced cancellation of the Ibsen plays. Discouraged, ill, and feeling sorry for herself, Duse spent most of her time in Stockholm in bed. "This period has been, perhaps, the saddest in my life," she told Lugné-Poe.

When the tour ended in late February 1906, Duse and Lugné-Poe separated. He returned to Paris and his wife, and Duse made her way slowly back to Italy. Suffering from fever and influenza, she scribbled long, sometimes incoherent letters to Lugné-Poe. As she had in writing to Boito, Wolkoff, and d'Annunzio, she used her letters as a means to release her pent-up feelings, sometimes writing two and three times a day. Since she wasn't working and was unable to escape into the world of the theatre, she had trouble sleeping.

Onstage after a performance of *Rosmersholm* in Christiania, 1906.
Her lover and manager, Lugné-Poe, sits directly behind her.

She dosed herself with valerian to combat her nervous tension and insomnia. She wallowed in self-pity.

"Here I am complaining again," she wrote Lugné-Poe from Venice on April 4. "Because the only thing I know how to do in my life is to cry, to suffer and to die. Ah! Why and how have things gone this way? I feel so lost, so out of tune with life. My work is only a trifle and my life, also, a mere nothing. The material difficulties which come up on a daily basis to 'pay' that horrible theatre company are so many; and it has been put together again to work just with you. And there you go! And I am in a quandary; and you are in Paris—and nothing has changed and nothing will ever change; ever, ever! Better to be quiet, now. You thought you could help me. And there you are!"

Lugné-Poe responded quickly to her cry for help. "I laugh and cry at the same time at your words," Duse wrote two days later. "Thank you from the bottom of my heart, because you hold me in your hands." In another letter on the same day, she said she would come to Paris "without anyone knowing it." First, she had to spend some time with Enrichetta, who was staying with her for a week, but then she would be free. She asked him to find a hotel where no one would know them. "My dear, just say yes, because I cannot stand one more pain in my life."

A few months later, on May 23, 1906, Ibsen died. In a mood of "black, black" melancholy, Duse hid herself in her Paris hotel. On May 25, she learned that Suzanne Desprès was playing *A Doll's House* that evening. Without telling Lugné-Poe or Suzanne, Duse attended the performance. She thought it a work of "power, discipline, art, and resolve." After writing Suzanne an affectionate and encouraging note, she left Paris. She had not shaken her depression.

"If Ibsen is no longer with us," Duse wrote Adolfo Orvieto, "well, then, what is the point of going on? I ask myself . . . for *whom*—and *where* can I still work?"

ADOLFO ORVIETO urged her to accept Talli's offers to work with him again in Italy, but Duse decided to continue her association with Lugné-Poe and Ibsen. "Work and life spent with you has been so rich, so rewarding, and has helped me so much to forget," she told him. "Yes, *oblivion!* It is the most beautiful, the holiest, the most human, the truest force." At the moment, though, the oblivion of work, that Dionysian abandonment of self, was out of the question. In late May 1906, depressed and troubled with a nagging cough, Duse traveled to Biarritz, a fashionable resort on the Bay of Biscay in southwest France. "The sea reminds me of another sea: mine!" she wrote Lugné-

Poe. "I am full of sorrows. Tell me one *truth*. But which one? There are so many of them—and so painful!"

Ellen Terry, then 59, had asked her to take part in Terry's fiftieth jubilee, representing her half-century in the theatre, in London's Drury Lane on June 12. "Just to feel that I am useful cheers me up a little," Duse told Orvieto. To honor Ellen, whom she adored, Duse decided to participate in the jubilee. Duse's decision to go to London and take part in the jubilee was also motivated by the fact that it would bring her closer to Lugné-Poe and to Robert von Mendelssohn. "If it was not for you, I would have no point in life," Mendelssohn telegraphed her in London.

Duse was always generous in her support of other actors. Ellen Terry's partner, the great actor Henry Irving, had died the year before, and Duse wrote a moving tribute to his art and to the gallantry of his death. Ill and failing, Irving had continued to act until he had died following a performance of *Becket*. His art was "made of infinite aspiration," Duse wrote, "lofty, dominated always by intellect, made perceptible by the power of dream purifying itself in form."

Unlike the other artists, who included Caruso, Réjane, and Coquelin, Duse didn't perform at Terry's jubilee. Instead, during the six-hour spectacle, which featured the large Terry family, Duse remained silent. To Terry and others that day, Duse was a mythic presence, symbolizing the exalting power of pure art. They had no way of knowing the bitterness and loneliness that Duse felt as she watched the English pour out their love for an actor. The next day, the event and the "radiant and exhausted face" of Ellen Terry were still on her mind. Her own country would never offer such a tribute, she realized. In London, Ellen Terry enjoyed a theatre home and a national theatre tradition that had endured for centuries. "In Italy," Duse believed, "there are no roots for such a flower!" As she aged, Ellen Terry was honored and loved. "For us," Duse said, "it would be mockery and forgetfulness."

Yet, when Italian journalists proposed honoring her with a jubilee, Duse wanted none of it. "I don't want them and their applause!" she said angrily. The wounds she had suffered from her collaboration with d'Annunzio, and the publicity generated by their love affair, were still fresh. Both in her intimate life and in her artistic life, she felt mistreated and dishonored by the Italian press, and she refused to be feted like a "clown!" Duse read the critical response to her work carefully, and she never forgave the few Italian theatre critics who had criticized her work, particularly in d'Annunzio's plays. For the most part, Italian theatre critics lavishly praised her, but the praise lacked the depth and understanding that she received from foreign critics. Her deliberate refusal of a jubilee also contributed to her mythic status, implying that such tributes were beneath one whose art was on another plane, above ordinary mortal actors.

While Ellen Terry had anchored herself in London at Henry Irving's Lyceum Theatre, Duse had chosen another route—to "go with the wind" into all the important ports of the theatre world. It was a route she shared with many of the "first moderns," who, like Duse, had giant egos and larger-than-life personalities and had left their homes to imprint their art upon the world—artists like Ibsen, Rilke, and Isadora Duncan.

IN 1899 IN LONDON, Isadora Duncan had seen Duse act in *The Second Mrs. Tanqueray.* "There was a moment," she recalled, "when the Duse stood quite still, alone on the stage. Suddenly, without any special outward movement, she seemed to grow and grow until her head appeared to touch the roof of the theatre . . . In that supreme gesture Duse was no longer the second Mrs. Tanqueray, but some wonderful goddess of all ages, and her growth before the eyes of the audience into that divine presence was one of the greatest artistic achievements I have ever witnessed . . . I said to myself, when I can come on the stage and stand as still as Eleonora Duse did tonight, and, at the same time, create that tremendous force of dynamic movement, then I shall be the greatest dancer in the world."

When Duse first saw Isadora dance in 1905, Duse thought her "a magnificent and joyous creature." Duncan, then twenty-eight, had thick, auburn hair, a creamy complexion, and a supple body, one reviewer said, that seemed to reveal her soul. Duncan had started a dancing school in Berlin in 1904, and she met Duse there at the home of Giulietta and Robert von Mendelssohn. The Mendelssohns had befriended Isadora and supported her against those who had attacked her for giving birth to Edward Gordon Craig's illegitimate daughter in September 1906.

The illegitimate son of Ellen Terry and architect Edward Godwin, Craig, then thirty-two, was a brilliant designer and theatre artist. His book, *The Art of the Theatre* (1905), had made his reputation as a theatre reformer, but most of his projects existed only on paper or in his mind. He had grandiose plans to revolutionize the theatre, but at the moment he relied on Isadora's support and contacts to get him jobs.

Isadora introduced Craig to Duse in the fall of 1906 in Berlin. Urged on by Isadora—and perhaps because Craig was tall and handsome with Ellen Terry's smile—Duse invited him to design a new production of *Rosmersholm* for her. Craig's first association with Duse had not been pleasant. In 1905, Count Harry Kessler, a diplomat, arts patron, and friend of the Mendelssohns, had arranged for Craig to design a production of *Elektra,* by Hugo von Hof-

Isadora Duncan, c. 1900

Isadora Duncan and Gordon Craig
on the day they met in 1904

mannsthal, for Duse. Duse had refused to speak or meet directly with Craig or to have anything to do with the sets or costumes until they were delivered to her in Florence. "She *never* sees anybody," Kessler assured Craig. In March 1906, Duse said she liked the sets and costumes, but she didn't pay for them until June and eventually decided not to do the play. Craig was furious and called her a "deamon—vile as I am I cannot for an instant believe such a woman really exists," he wrote Kessler, "but like phantoms they blow across our earth sometimes."

Still, Craig needed work, and he consented to work with the "deamon." Since Craig couldn't speak French or Italian, Isadora translated his conversations with Duse, or more accurately, Isadora twisted their words to make sure they agreed. When Craig asked her to tell Duse he would be responsible for the whole production or nothing, as he had done with *Elektra*, Isadora translated thus: "He would be very interested indeed."

Craig set to work on his sketches, creating not the reality of *Rosmersholm* but its spiritual environment. In November, Craig, Isadora, and their baby, Deirdre, left for Florence. Duse was there rehearsing for a short season at the Teatro la Pergola. When Craig arrived, he discovered scene canvas wasn't available in Florence. The Italians used paper backed by netting. He improvised by using lengths of sacking, which he sewed together, painted in pastels ranging from greens to blues, and then stretched onto battens. When Duse, through Duncan, asked him practical questions about doors and the enormous size of the upstage window, Craig was annoyed. "Tell her I won't have any damned woman interfering with my work!" Isadora turned to Duse: "He says he admires your opinions and will do everything to please you."

Craig threatened to leave unless Isadora kept Duse out of his way. Isadora took her for long walks. Since Duse attracted curious stares, they avoided main paths. "I will always remember those walks in the gardens," Duncan wrote, "the poplar trees, the magnificent head of Eleonora Duse, for, as soon as we found ourselves alone, she would pull off her hat and let her raven locks, just turning grey, free to the breeze. Her wonderfully intellectual forehead and her marvellous eyes—I shall never forget them."

While Craig labored singlemindedly on his sets, Duse rehearsed with her company at the Grand Hotel, dealt with problems of publicity, and conferred with the playwright Enrico Corradini on his new play, *Maria Salvestri*. Duse had replaced her leading man Carlo Rosaspina with Leo Orlandini, then forty-one, who would also act as her codirector. On November 24, Duse welcomed Guido Noccioli, then twenty-three, a new actor and crew member to her company. Noccioli had studied with Luigi Rasi, and at Rasi's suggestion, Noccioli kept a diary during the year he spent in Duse's company. Like a *pic-*

colo Boswell, Noccioli observed Duse with affection and perception. From his backstage viewpoint, Noccioli wrote down her words, described her behavior, and provided a glimpse of Duse as she moved in her natural world.

When he was introduced to Duse, Noccioli was overcome with awe. She lifted her black veil, smiled kindly at him with "perfect teeth," and offered her hand, "one of those famous hands immortalized by d'Annunzio." Two days later, when Noccioli arrived at Duse's apartment in the Grand Hotel, he found her in a "towering rage." The advertising for her Florence season had announced: "Exceptional appearance of Eleonora Duse." "Why *exceptional,* for God's sake?" Duse exclaimed. "Such billing may be all right for circus acrobats, but not for me." She ordered the handbills to be suppressed. "I demand and fully intend to have things done my way," she said. After this outburst, she gave Noccioli carefully detailed instructions about *La Gioconda* and then quickly dismissed him. Since it was so sunny and bright, she had decided to go to the countryside instead of rehearsing.

DUSE OPENED HER RUN at the Teatro la Pergola with *La Gioconda* on December 3 in front of a sold-out house. Duse was extremely nervous and acted well but not brilliantly, wrote Noccioli, but the new leading man, Leo Orlandini, was "frankly disappointing." Still, the audience applauded enthusiastically. Was the theatre-going public "one *Great Ignoramus?*" Noccioli wondered.

The following day, the *Gioconda* set was cleared to make room for Craig's *Rosmersholm* set. Isadora picked up Duse at the Grand Hotel and took her to the theatre. Since Craig was still working on the set, Isadora took Duse to a theatre box, where they sat and waited for him to finish. Finally, the curtain rose on what Isadora described as "a vision of loveliness . . . vast blue spaces, celestial harmonies, mounting lines, colossal heights." Noccioli described the set as a "strange affair, all in green and illuminated by ten spotlights." Even the furniture was green, and there were mysterious veils around the stage. "Some dream, perhaps?" Noccioli mused. The playwright Corradini reported that "the stage seemed completely transformed. The usual wings were gone. Here was a new architecture of great height, ranging in colour from green to blue. It was simple, mysterious, fascinating, and a fitting background to the complicated lives of Rosmer and Rebecca West; it portrayed a *state of mind.*" What was Duse's reaction?

For a long time she sat speechless by Isadora. Duse, of course, had seen Craig's designs and knew his work. Still, his shadowy, symbolist creation of the Rosmersholm drawing room, which was so vastly different from the

Rovescalli set Duse had been using, must have been a shock—especially since she and her company had to open the following day, with only one dress rehearsal. She quickly roused herself, and dragging Isadora behind her, rushed to the stage. She embraced Craig, congratulated him in a stream of Italian, and then called all the company together. "It is my destiny to have found this great genius, Gordon Craig," she proclaimed. "I now intend to spend the rest of my career devoting myself only to showing the world his great work." Holding Craig's hand, she continued her impassioned speech. "Only through Gordon Craig," she said, "will we poor actors find release from this monstrosity, this charnel-house, which is the theatre of today."

It was such a wonderful performance that she convinced Craig, her company, Isadora, and momentarily, even herself. Later, it dawned on Craig that Duse had been acting "the part of a great actress who is dealing with a madman and who sees it's quite useless to protest."

On December 5, the opening night of *Rosmersholm*, the Teatro la Pergola was packed. Gordon Craig had inserted an essay into the playbill to announce "the birth of the new Theatre, and its new Art." "Realism is only exposure," he wrote, "whereas Art is Revelation." When the curtain rose, "there was one gasp of admiration," Isadora reported.

Against the backdrop of Craig's drawing room of the mind, Duse appeared, not in her usual gray dress and gray veil but in a long white gown with wide sleeves. "She looked less like Rebecca West than a Delphic sibyl," observed Isadora. Actually, she looked a lot like Isadora. Unfortunately, Duse's homage to Duncan had the effect of making the other actors look like "stage hands who had walked on by mistake." Lost in Craig's unfamiliar setting, the actors, particularly Leo Orlandini, who played Rosmer, became more confused when Duse threw "her details to the wind," changing blocking and line readings. Duse improvised in Craig's setting, found shafts of light, and "moved in the scene like some prophetess announcing great tidings," Isadora said.

The Italian public didn't understand Ibsen, but Duse made them "wild with excitement." Afterward, Craig and Duncan were thrilled. "He saw his future before him," Isadora wrote, "a series of great works all devoted to Eleonora Duse."

Duse, too, was in high spirits after the performance. When the playwright Corradini congratulated her, Duse interrupted him with an ironic laugh. "So," she asked, "the audience has swallowed it?"

"I acted last night as in a dream—far away," Duse wrote to Craig after the performance, curbing her irony. "You did your work under terrible difficulties—so thank you. Last night I understood the strength of your help—so again, thank you. Let us hope that we shall work together again joyfully and unhampered." Craig interpreted this note filled with ordinary flattery as his ticket to worldwide success designing Duse productions. Duse had mentioned Ibsen's *The Lady from the Sea*, and he began working on it. He tried to learn French and imagined Duse helping him realize his theatre revolution. "I have the spirit of the greatest actress living for the most advanced idea of the Theatre," he wrote a friend, "even to the extent of getting rid of the actors themselves, which as you know, by no means implies getting rid of the great personalities."

A few months later, Duse commanded him to join her in Nice. She wanted to discuss a new play with him, and she mentioned she would be giving *Rosmersholm* on February 9. By this time, Craig had received many of Duse's telegrams, mostly about changes in plans and cancellations. When he hesitated to obey her, Isadora wrote from her sickbed in Holland. "Don't be impatient with D," she said, "but *go* to *Nice* and you will see all will turn out as you wish."

Craig arrived in Nice and went to the Casino Theatre to check on his set. Apparently Craig had not designed *Rosmersholm* to tour, and since the proscenium opening at the Casino Theatre was lower than at the Teatro la Pergola, the set didn't fit. To make it fit, Duse's technician cut a couple feet off the bottom, which threw off all the proportions. Craig was furious. "The most horrendous chaos as insults are exchanged in a bedlam of motley languages and dialects," Noccioli recorded. Since he had given up his French study, Craig couldn't make himself understood. He asked Enrichetta, who was visiting Duse, to interpret for him. Enrichetta spoke French to the administrator, who spoke Italian to the technician, who cursed everyone in Bolognese dialect. "At a certain point," Noccioli recalled, "the stage manager disappears. A heroic decision!"

Craig turned on Duse. "What have you done?" he roared. "You have ruined my work. You have destroyed my art! You from whom I expected so much."

Duse pointed to the door. "Go," she said. "I never want to see you again."

"No one has ever treated me so," Duse explained to Isadora later. When Craig asked to have his name removed from the program, she refused. But she did fire the technician who had chopped off his set. Duse replaced Craig's mutilated set for *Rosmersholm* with the previous set designed by Rovescalli. Duse's sense of visual metaphor was highly compatible with Craig's, but they never worked together again. Years later, Craig decided that what he had believed was demonic capriciousness was actually good sense. "I began to see the immensity of her colossal life performance off the stage," he recalled, "and my big scene for *Rosmersholm* appeared to me the size of a penny matchbox."

In OCTOBER 1906, Lugné-Poe had convinced Duse to sign a contract for
a tour of South America from June 1907 through October 1907. For years,
Duse had resisted returning to the place of her first foreign triumph. Her success there in 1885, when she was twenty-six, had been hard-won and grueling
and clouded by her acrimonious separation from Tebaldo Checchi. Lugné-
Poe argued that the tour would be lucrative and offer an opportunity to introduce Ibsen and Maeterlinck to South America. Duse agreed to undertake the
tour if Lugné-Poe would accompany her.

The tour began in Rio de Janeiro, where the modern world was overtaking
the old. There was "chaos everywhere," Noccioli observed. "Old houses being
demolished, new buildings going up. Roads ploughed up and new ones
traced out." Duse's South American repertory, too, was a combination of old
and new. Despite her feeling "these old plays are no longer fit to be heard!"
audiences wanted to see her in *La Dame aux camélias* and *Fédora*. "Ah! How
bored I am with this role," she sighed after rehearsing *Fédora*. When an audience gave her a frenzied ovation after a performance of *La Dame aux camélias*,
she took her bows while muttering, "Cretins . . . Imbeciles!"

Duse rushed through rehearsals of the old plays and lavished attention on
the Ibsen repertory. "La Duse's passion for Ibsen is unbelievable," said Noccioli. "Hers is a true apostolate . . . The other actors, naturally enough, end up
by loathing Ibsen. They are not accustomed to having to analyse their roles to
this extent." Noccioli believed South American audiences were too unsophis-
ticated to understand Ibsen, but he also blamed the actors. One actor, Noccioli wrote, "believes that he is acting *in the modern style* without realizing, alas,
that he isn't even capable of acting in *the traditional style*."

Lugné-Poe had prepared the press with interviews, articles, and photographs. In Rio de Janeiro, São Paulo, Buenos Aires, Rosario, and Montevideo, where Duse had received an enormous amount of press, she refused to
give interviews and make herself available to local dignitaries. In retaliation,
the newspapers attacked her. On July 6, *Fon Fon*, a local paper in Rio, castigated her for refusing to have lunch with Artur Azevedo, the prominent critic
who had championed her first appearance there.

"I am sick and tired of their nonsense," Duse said, "and I flatly refuse to
tolerate any more interviews, receptions, or any other futile activities calcu-
lated to waste my precious time. It is outrageous!"

Duse had ceded some of her directing responsibilities to Leo Orlandini,
her leading man, and Lugné-Poe handled administrative and press matters,
but Duse carried the full burden of attracting audiences to the theatre.

According to Lugné-Poe, Duse drove everyone crazy during the tour. No one suffered as much as she did, she claimed.

On the day of her gala opening in Buenos Aires, Duse asked Lugné-Poe if he knew of any surgeons. Her stomach hurt, and she feared she was terribly ill. She wasn't sure she would be able to perform. Terrified Duse was near death, Lugné-Poe found a doctor to attend to her between acts. Duse then changed her mind and said she could finish the play, and the doctor should come to her hotel instead. Lugné-Poe finally asked Duse what she thought was causing her illness. Duse told him she had accidentally swallowed a prune pit at lunch, and she was afraid she might die from it. Lugné-Poe wanted to kill her, he recalled, but instead he flattered her and told her how brave she was. When the doctor saw her, he prescribed a placebo and said it had been an honor to treat her.

As the tour progressed, and particularly when Enrichetta joined the entourage in Buenos Aires in early August, Duse's tension and irritability increased. Duse rarely saw her daughter, who was twenty-five and living in England. Earlier that year, after a visit from Enrichetta, Duse had complained to Lugné-Poe: "*Just* to see *her* was sufficient to cause a world of regret in my soul!!—A world (of regret)!—. And I can do nothing for her either." After Enrichetta arrived in South America to travel with her mother, Lugné-Poe returned to Paris and his wife, which also contributed to Duse's bad humor.

Without Lugné-Poe—lover, butler, and impresario—Duse felt neglected and lonely. Forced to deal with business matters, she lashed out at her company, who didn't seem to appreciate the "great privilege" of acting with her. When Alfredo Robert, then twenty-nine, the second male lead, who aspired to replace Orlandini as Duse's leading man, broke character and laughed during a performance, Duse was furious. "What is more," she said, "you took it upon yourself to change the entire pace of the act; you are always trying to have things your way!" Robert tried to defend himself, but Duse told him to "be quiet and think twice before contradicting Eleonora Duse." After Robert wrote a note of apology the next day, Duse forgave him.

On August 15, during a performance of *La Dame aux camélias*, Orlandini, as Armande, accidentally threw money into Duse's face. When the curtain closed, Duse ripped off her veils. As the rest of the company watched in *"terror,"* Duse released "a stream of recriminations." It was "like lava from a volcano," Noccioli wrote. "It is impossible to capture in words the bitterness, anger, and spite that consume the Signora at such moments."

Duse stopped speaking to Orlandini, and he communicated with her by letter. The atmosphere was chilly, but Alfredo Robert and the rest of the company considered Orlandini a despot and were pleased he had fallen from grace. "A cold shower every so often for those in authority is no bad thing!" Noccioli said.

In mid-September, Duse and Enrichetta traveled on the same train with the company to Rosario, a large city on the Paraná River in Argentina. They arrived in a drenching rain and were taken to the hotel through streets flooded with sewage. The critics in Rosario didn't like Ibsen, the box office was disappointing, and to no one's surprise, Duse became sick and cancelled performances. "She certainly looks very ill," Noccioli observed.

The company returned to Buenos Aires at the end of September to play four sold-out performances at popular prices. The last performance, on September 30, was "a triumphant evening . . . thunderous applause, masses of floral tributes, and, at the end, a deafening ovation." Except for Rosario, the tour in Argentina had been a success, at least financially. Ibsen, though, had failed to please.

He fared a little better in Montevideo. The critics liked *Hedda Gabler*, and d'Annunzio's *La Gioconda* was so popular it was performed twice. When they played Sardou's *Fédora*, Duse whispered in the wings before her entrance, "Good lord! What rubbish. Just listen . . . listen to that! To think that I believed there could be nothing as awful as Fernanda . . . but this is even worse!" The audience agreed with her, and the play was coldly received.

On October 6, before the second act of *La Femme de Claude*, after weeks of offstage silence, Duse finally decided to speak to Orlandini. In front of the company, she hugged and kissed him, and "with that magnificent smile on her lips" that Noccioli adored, Duse said, "Come now, let's make our peace and forget the whole affair. Everyone in this wretched profession can be mistaken at times."

Perhaps because of the release of tension, the company enjoyed "an enormous success" in Montevideo, the last city on the tour. The next day, "all the critics are hailing this sudden *revelation*," Noccioli reported. Critics and audiences in South America, accustomed to the bravura of Spanish drama and the declamation of French drama, were slow to warm to Ibsen and Duse's new art, but eventually they began to understand the work and to find a vocabulary to explain it. "La Duse does not come on to the stage casually to string together conventionalisms that are more entertaining than convincing, but rather to offer a faithful reflection of life," one Argentinian critic wrote.

Duse said good-bye to her company in Montevideo. She planned to sail immediately on an English ship, and the company would return home on an Italian steamer. Although not required to pay her actors during their layoff, she gave them half salary and passed out bonuses to the crew. "Deep down," said Noccioli, "she is really very goodhearted."

Duse with Enrichetta, c. 1908–10

On Sunday, October 14, 1907, Noccioli wrote a one-sentence entry: "The Signora embarks this evening with the sea at its roughest."

DUSE HAD EARNED 8,000 pounds (about $40,000 at that time) from the South American tour. She could have enjoyed a long rest. Instead, with young Alfredo Robert as her new leading man, she continued her tour into northern Europe and Russia. "I know the joy and the anxiety of traveling a great distance, in search of something (unknown or beautiful)," Duse wrote to Angiolo Orvieto from St. Petersburg in January 1908. She sent $20,000 to Robi Mendelssohn to invest for her. She gave the rest to Enrichetta, who planned to marry twenty-eight-year-old Edward Bullough, the Swiss-born son of a wealthy English industrialist and a German mother. A brilliant polymath who taught at Cambridge, Bullough was educated in Dresden (where he had met Enrichetta) and at Trinity College in Cambridge. Later, he authored distinguished papers on aesthetics as well as studies of Italian literature and became chair of Italian at Cambridge.

Duse was proud of her "superior, serene" daughter, but she was especially pleased Enrichetta would take her husband's name. She had succeeded in giving Enrichetta all the advantages she had lacked as a girl—wealth, education, and social status. She had kept Enrichetta from the theatre, stripped her of her Duse heritage, and made it possible for Enrichetta to marry into a world Duse could enter only as an outsider. Duse chose not to be present at Enrichetta's wedding in February 1908. "I'm happy to have her married far away," Duse told a friend, "where my name isn't profaned by legend."

Duse's name was legendary in St. Petersburg and Moscow, where people stood in line all night to get tickets. Stanislavsky and his students and the controversial director Vsevolod Meyerhold and his followers attended Duse's performances with great interest. After seeing Duse, Alisa Koonen, who had studied with Stanislavsky, declared, "If I can't act like her I must give up the theatre." Duse didn't wear makeup or wigs, Alisa observed, and her austere costumes were similar in color and line from role to role, and designed to allow her body freedom of movement. Surprisingly, this wasn't monotonous, Alisa said, but it was consistent with Duse's authority as an actor. "Measure yourself and look inside at this humanity that loans you its clothes," Duse believed. "Don't choose—there is nothing to choose here—if you dress yourself in wool or velvet or silk or false gold, it's all the same."

Duse's acting was "extraordinarily simple," Alisa said, but it wasn't the naturalism Alisa had learned at the Moscow Art Theatre. Duse had removed unnecessary details from the stage. In *La Dame aux camélias*, for example, there was no realistic eating or drinking.

Another young actress, Vera Arkadevna, understood after seeing Duse "the art of an actor is an ocean." Vera met Duse backstage and kissed her hand. "It's not right that one woman kisses the hand of another woman," Duse said. "To a woman no," Vera replied, "but to a genius, I must." Duse spoke in a whisper, Vera noted, and "total silence reigned backstage." "I can work only in the most absolute silence," Duse explained. "The slightest noise brings me back to the banalities of everyday life. When I come to the theatre it's important that I hear nothing before entering into the role."

Duse profoundly influenced a generation of Russian actors, who treasured photographs she signed for them, and who continued to venerate her all their lives. Stanislavsky and Meyerhold, who were divided on their philosophy of the theatre, agreed on Duse's art. Years later, in a speech after one of Duse's performances, Stanislavsky said he had "got his inspiration for founding the Moscow Art Theatre from witnessing a performance of Duse's," and "not a rehearsal of the company had ever gone by without referring to her or her art." Although Stanislavsky abhorred a theatre based on a great star and wanted his actors to disappear into an ensemble, Duse's acting was the ideal of what he was attempting to achieve in his actor-centered theatre. Meyerhold, who had broken with Stanislavsky to create a theatre opposed to naturalism, wanted a director-centered theatre. Like Lugné-Poe, Meyerhold aspired to an artistic "stylisation" of all elements of production. Instead of precise, naturalistic details he wanted the audience to use their imagination creatively. In Duse's acting, both men found support for their theories.

When Meyerhold saw Duse play in *La Dame aux camélias*, he was moved to tears. During the intermission, he was asked about his impressions. "This is not the place for banal criticism," he said. "Here there is only the possibility of hypnotic charisma, adoration and study." Meyerhold argued against those who believed Duse's art was spontaneous and intuitive. Noting how Duse alternated moments of "strong tension with passive and tranquil moments," he asserted she worked out her art like a maestro.

Except through example, Duse never articulated a unified "theory" of theatre or acting. Her feelings about two musical "maestros," however, illuminate her own aesthetic. "I have known Wagner in Venice," she said. "I have been in Bayreuth, and I saw in Wagner what I feel in his music, a touch of something a little conscious in his supremacy. Wagner said to himself: 'I will do what I want to do, I will force the world to accept me'; and he succeeded, but not in making us forget his intention. The music, after all, never quite abandons itself, is never quite without self-consciousness, it is a tremendous sensuality, not the unconsciousness of passion. When Beethoven writes music he forgets both himself and the world, is conscious only of joy, or sorrow, or the mood which has taken him for its voice."

Critics often used music analogies in writing about Duse. "If you want to know about Duse's art," Maurice Baring advised, "go and listen to the *Allegretto* in Beethoven's Seventh Symphony in A, in which an unobtrusive, easy melody, without effort or emphasis, naturally, so to speak, and with a gesture of complete appropriateness and divine surprise—the surprise of what is expected and yet beyond and better than all expectation—and of divine simplicity, opens the door on to the infinite."

In January and February 1908, Duse gave thirteen performances of eleven plays in St. Petersburg, closing there with *Rosmersholm*, and eight performances of seven plays in Moscow, again ending with *Rosmersholm*. Her third Russian tour was professionally and personally gratifying. She never cancelled a performance or became ill—a sure sign of happiness. The Russian public adored her and understood her. Also, she enjoyed the company of Isadora Duncan, who was dancing there. And she found a comrade in Stanislavsky. Duse attended a performance of Ibsen's *Brand* at the Moscow Art Theatre. The next day, she expressed her feelings to Stanislavsky: "Yesterday, I again found *Truth* and *Poetry*. Poetry and Truth, those two *profound sources* for your soul of art and artist. Believe me, believe me that *I* have *understood*, that I am *worthy* of understanding your effort."

After a summer hiatus in Florence, Duse returned to the road, playing cities in northern Europe in September and October. Everywhere she was acclaimed. Once, she had joked to her company that when she turned fifty, "I shall make my escape to Japan! [. . .] And you can all send me a telegram!" On October 3, 1908, her fiftieth birthday, her actors didn't need to send telegrams, because she was working with them. "Pray God that I might be able to go on working right up to the last minute," she said.

In January 1909, she played Berlin, primarily with an Ibsen repertory, including *John Gabriel Borkman* and *The Lady from the Sea*. Unlike Italian audiences, Germans revered Ibsen. After Duse had played two triumphant performances as Ellida in *The Lady from the Sea* on January 23 and 25, the *Borsen-Courier* newspaper in Berlin announced the next performance of *La Gioconda* had been cancelled because of Duse's "sudden illness."

"For the last few months, I have not been sick," Duse wrote Enrichetta on May 2, 1909, "but my body, all of my female machinery is going through a crisis that wears me out, oh so much." The crisis, of course, was menopause. "I am so often indisposed that for now any work-related responsibility is completely forbidden," she said.

Duse's crisis involved more than her physical health. For forty-six years, she had embodied dozens of characters on a theatre voyage that had taken her around the world. Audiences saw "only the person onstage," Duse said. "What do they know about me?" What did she know of herself? Shipwrecked by a natural process shared by all women, yet one no playwright had ever written about, Duse would now have time to find out.

Eight

"ELEONORA DUSE WHO MAKES NO SECRET of her years, passed her fiftieth birthday a fortnight ago," wrote Boston theatre critic H. T. P. Parker on October 18, 1909. "The actress has many and change-ful moods," Parker continued. "All last spring and summer she debated, for example, whether she would undertake another American tour, reached no decision, and left the manager, who wished to arrange it, in such uncertainty that he finally abandoned the project. Probably no one knows less than Duse herself when and how she will quit the theatre."

Duse, of course, didn't bother to inform the press she had actually turned fifty the year before, in 1908. To a few trusted critics, however, she had confided her dissatisfaction with her repertoire. The problem was she had aged, and her characters had remained young. She was deluged with new plays, but playwrights were not creating leading roles for mature women.

"Send me a beautiful Russian play," she wrote A. Yurij Beliaev, a Russian critic and dramaturg in February 1908, "a profound and beautiful work of poetry and I will perform it with all my soul." Earlier, Duse had considered adding Chekhov's *The Three Sisters* to her repertoire, but probably because of the lack of a good translation, she had dropped the idea. Chekhov had written his last play, *The Cherry Orchard*, by 1904. Again, since Chekhov's plays weren't translated into French or Italian until years later, Duse missed the opportunity to give the world her Ranevskaya, a woman who had suffered and was haunted by the death of her son.

Harassed by creditors and forced to sell his possessions and flee to France, d'Annunzio asked her to play Phaedra in his new play. She replied bitterly, "You classified me as an instrument of art which you can take up and throw away. I have already given you everything. I have nothing else left." Still, over the years, whenever d'Annunzio sent her copies of his new plays with loving inscriptions, Duse saved them.

During an engagement in Vienna in 1908, she had invited the writer and critic Hugo Wittman to her hotel room and announced she wanted to leave the stage. Duse was ill with bronchitis and inhaling steam from a kettle of boiling water. She "seemed lonely and deserted, plunged in a melancholy," Wittman said. Duse had asked Wittman to help her put together a concert recital program. She wanted to free herself from the financial and physical burden of a large troupe. She spent hours with him drawing up theoretical programs, but he finally told her she "belonged upon the stage as much as a painter before the canvas and a sculptor before the block of marble."

Duse gave up the idea of a recital program. But the time she had spent with Wittman invigorated her. "As soon as we got to work she became vivacious," Wittman recalled. "Her melancholy vanished. She smiled, then laughed, and it was quite easy to see how this woman who could not be called a beauty possessed irresistible charm when she was really interested."

SINCE SHE WASN'T WORKING, Duse didn't need to travel constantly, but still she moved restlessly from city to city, never stopping more than a few weeks in one place. The fatigue of menopause, along with weight gain, bouts with bronchitis, emphysema, and depression all plagued her and made it impossible for her to work. She called upon friends in Milan, Venice, and Paris, and rented apartments in Rome and Florence only to leave them. Sometimes she stayed alone in small hotels and let no one know where she was. Addicted to Dionysus, she was undergoing withdrawal. She longed for the ordinary, daily routine of the theatre.

"The greatest joy for an actress," she once explained, "isn't acting on a stage full of light, in front of a theatre full of people that listen in silence, eager to clap and cheer. Do you know what our greatest joy is? When towards evening we arrive all alone at the stage door and go down a long half-lit corridor and climb the stairs to find our companions that wait for us at the rehearsal. There are a few lights on the stage, long, oblique shadows from the wings, the orchestra seats are deserted, the boxes are like empty berths. There's nothing but we artists, poor actors, dressed in everyday clothes, our only companion the poet who has written the work that we must learn. We are just there ourselves, together, without strangers, without intruders and we think only of our work and not of the applause of all these unknown people that other evenings fill the theatre. In these moments, I feel I'm with my family. And sometimes I have the childish illusion that we are hidden there, in the half-light, as if for a conspiracy, a plot, something clandestine and pleasantly dangerous. All the rest is nothing more than noise, chaos, vanity, fatigue and bitterness."

As she struggled to regain her health and her equilibrium, Duse turned inward, reading and rereading her favorite books, especially the poetry of Walt Whitman and Giovanni Pascoli. She called the philosophers William James and Henri Bergson "my friends." Philosophy, she said, was "something we've invented for ourselves to keep us standing up." Duse also reached out to her women friends—old and new. She had always lived through the women she portrayed onstage. Now, in a compensating parallel, she re-created the "tender and affectionate interchange" she had shared with her fictional characters, with women, particularly younger women, who sought her out.

Just as she had taken up and studied Juliet and Nora and Hedda, Duse would befriend a woman, usually attractive and talented, sometimes for months at a time, and then she would move on to another "character" who needed her. This is not to say she discarded her women friends. With few exceptions, these "friendships from the heart," as Duse called them, were enduring. "The Duse was marvelously good to women," observed Henry Russell. "There was no moral or physical pain suffered by her own sex with which by experience she was not in sympathy, and she was always ready to extol any other woman."

For many women bound by society's conventions, Duse's life and art represented radical freedom. They idealized her as a great artist, an erotic symbol, a maternal icon, literary muse, and spiritual guide. Duse's compulsion to transcend herself was too ingrained to end when she left the stage. Women were drawn to her, and she turned her relationships with different women into little "life dramas," and with each woman Duse empathized with her "character." Her women friends also acted as an audience—someone to watch her live. In whatever setting she found herself, Duse improvised a drama from the mundane details of everyday life. Even in the moments when she was alone, quietly reading or enduring a spasm of coughing, Duse saw herself as a character in her own life. It was only on the stage that she could free herself of self-consciousness.

Helen Gansevoort Mackay left an unpublished account of her seventeen-year friendship with Duse. In her books, Mackay composed vignettes of her experiences in France and of her work as a nurse during World War I, creating a precise record of the "little things" of life.

From the time she was a girl, when she first saw Duse perform in New York, Mackay had kept Duse in a "dream place, a place of refuge." When

Mackay moved to Paris, she attended Duse's performances on the French Riviera and found the courage to ask for a meeting. Finally, Duse agreed to meet Mackay, then thirty-two, in San Remo in 1908.

The shutters of Duse's hotel room were closed, Mackay recalled, and Duse had personalized the room with "white scarves, beautiful rough peasant linen, thrown over the backs of chairs. Anemones in a thick green glass jar such as they use in the Venetia to keep oil and put up olives." Accompanied by her daughter, Enrichetta, Duse entered wearing a long dark cloak and veils, which she flung back to reveal dark hair streaked with white.

"I should never give an appointment," Duse said. Mackay couldn't speak. "Why did you want to see me?" Duse demanded. "I don't like people to ask to see me." Mackay, still too overcome at meeting her idol, remained silent. "You thought you would find an actress with plumes and glory?"

Duse opened the shutters and said, "Come, let me look at you." When she saw Mackay's expression, she began to laugh. "I have frightened you out of all your wits," she said. "Come and sit down and tell me at once everything in the world that you know." Mackay spoke quickly about parallel roads, refuge, and escaping from sadness and loneliness, but sensing that she was being absurd, she stopped talking.

"Then something passed over her face, a mask over it, as if the words made her suffer and she would not have me know," Mackay wrote. "You will go home with no illusion," Duse said. "Go away now. We will not see one another again, but we will remember." She told Enrichetta to give Mackay all the flowers in the jar. They did see each other again, though, particularly when Duse was ill and no longer working. An intelligent, undemanding companion, Mackay was sensitive to Duse's moods. "She would let me come to her nearly dark room that smelled of menthol," Mackay recalled. "I never talked of anything but the dust of the roads, the racket the grasshoppers kept up, how you could scarcely see the mountains through the heat, and how the streams were all turned to stone.

"There were days when she would not go out," Mackay wrote, "and would move about her room, arranging and rearranging odds and ends of things. Quantities of books. Like sick people feeling the weight of hours and days, she would keep asking, 'What time is it? Four o'clock, only four o'clock? Five o'clock, only five o'clock?' "

Occasionally, when Duse visited Paris, she would ask Mackay to accompany her to the theatre. Duse would arrive early so no one would recognize her, and she would leave before the rest of the audience. "She never talked about the play nor the actors," Mackay said. "I would sit silent beside her."

FOR THE FIRST TIME in her life, Duse drifted, without purpose, without a plan. She continued to read voraciously, however, searching for a playwright who could speak for her. Ermete Zacconi urged her to join his company. She declined. When the French actress Cecile Sorel played Italy, she begged Duse, even if it meant risking her health, to continue acting. Duse told Sorel her characters had abandoned her.

In Rome, where she took an apartment for a time, Duse met writer Lina Poletti. They were probably introduced by their mutual friend, thirty-four-year-old Sibilla Aleramo, author of an autobiographical novel, *A Woman* (1906). Called an Italian *Doll's House*, *A Woman* served as a beacon for early feminists. Aleramo refused to live a life of female sacrifice. A social activist who believed in free love, Aleramo had numerous affairs with prominent male writers. She also had a brief affair with Poletti, who was married (for convenience). Poletti, who had pursued Aleramo, wanted to write plays for Duse.

To this end, Poletti, then twenty-four, began a correspondence with Duse. "When do you think you should come to Rome?" Poletti asked in January 1910 of Duse in Florence. "The sun of Rome would bless you." She signed the letter "Ali," which became Duse's name for her. A few months later, the letters from Ali were frank expressions of love. "Eleon, I love you. Eleon. I have faith in you." While loving and supportive, a letter from Duse to Ali, in August 1910 urging "courage" and "patience," was not romantic. Duse complained of her "tyrant" doctor who was keeping her in bed and giving her aspirin injections.

Frustrated, Ali wrote on August 8, 1910, to Duse, who was ill in Belluno, a town north of Venice. "You speak of what must be, about what your encounter has to bring me . . . how love is far away, how this is not at all words of love. And always the separation of oblivion and distance . . . Ahi! Ahi! Eleo, in the name of God would you tell me what you have in your soul?"

Apparently, what Duse had in her soul was a need for company and someone to look after her while she was ill; plus she hoped Poletti would prove to be the playwright she was seeking. On August 22, Ali wrote she planned to join Duse in Belluno. Although there has been speculation that Duse was involved sexually with Poletti, no one who knew Duse and wrote about her suggested Duse's relationships with women were anything more than loving friendships. Poletti herself described her arrangement with Duse as a kind of barter—she took care of Duse when she was ill ("I have borne a great deal for her sake," she said) and in return, she expected Duse to produce and star in her plays.

After menopause, Duse seems to have withdrawn from the sexual arena, although she saw and corresponded with Robi Mendelssohn from time to time. (He would send telegrams reminding her of the "beautiful hours of the past and hoping that they come again.") He also continued to handle her financial affairs. Duse delighted in the company and the adulation of young women. Lina Poletti's energy and ambition as well as her devotion were an ego boost for Duse.

Poletti had two ideas for plays that appealed to Duse—one, *Arianna*, based on the Ariadne myth about an aging woman rejected by a younger lover, and the other, titled *Incest*, about a mother who abandons her young son. If Poletti had drawn on her own life, she would have had ample material for a more original play featuring characters based on herself, Duse, and Mabel Dodge, a native of Buffalo, New York. In just a few years in Italy, Dodge had transformed herself into one of the most colorful and coquettish characters in the Florentine community. In 1905, Mabel and her architect husband, Edwin Dodge, had bought and restored the Villa Curonia outside Florence. They added a loggia and a 90-foot great room, hung silk Sienese banners from the walls of the courtyard, filled terra-cotta tubs with gardenias and jasmine, and composed rooms filled with precious antiques and Mabel's vast collection of dogs in every material, period, and size. Wearing gowns of antique brocade and velvet, Mabel greeted *tout* Florence, looking as if she had just stepped from a Renaissance painting.

Mabel collected antiques, she collected celebrities, and later she collected her memories in four volumes, with a chapter titled "Duse." Through Arthur Acton, who "knew everyone in Florence," Mabel invited Duse to rest at sunny Villa Curonia. Before she accepted Mabel's invitation, Duse asked to meet her. Mabel, who had a sharp eye for interior decoration and clothes, noted Duse's Florence apartment was "austere." Duse looked like "an ascetic abbess" in a "flowing, wide-sleeved dress of ivory-colored, Capri, homespun wool," observed Mabel. "Her face was yellow-pale with darkened lids and brownish shadows. The corners of her mouth drooped dolorously, her hair was silvered all through and wound in a melancholy coil about her transparent-looking forehead."

Duse told Mabel she had her "foolish needs." Her large, wooden peasant bed had to be taken apart, packed up, and moved because she couldn't sleep in any other bed. Also, Duse was traveling with a young girl from Ravenna, a prodigy. "I am responsible to her mother for her," Duse said. Duse asked if she could bring the girl with her. It was agreed that Mabel's car would call for Duse the following afternoon, and the girl would arrive on her bicycle. Poletti and Duse arrived at the villa the next day at five. Mabel assessed the young woman, who wore a "man's straw hat with its black ribbon band, a narrow

Mabel Dodge, a temporary Italian and Duse's hostess, c. 1910

skirt which was made to hang like a pair of trousers . . . Her intelligent eyes were reddish brown . . . and they were merry and self-assured."

To Mabel's chagrin, Duse disappeared mysteriously, returned for dinner and spoke primarily to Edwin Dodge, while Poletti concentrated on wooing Mabel. On a walk with Mabel in the garden, Poletti suddenly grabbed Mabel's shoulders, pushed her down on a stone bench, gripped her hand, and said, "You are what I am seeking—*le clef majeure*—the release." Mabel pushed her away. Later, as she readied herself for bed, Mabel reported she heard a noise, turned, and found Poletti in her room. Poletti wore only a robe and a "determined look." Again, Poletti put her hands on Mabel's shoulder. "She forced me backwards from the window; little by little she had pushed me, till I had reached the side of the bed, struggling the while against her . . . I forced her out to the door and reaching it, thrust her out into the hall with a great push and turned the key in the lock. The whole incident had taken place in silence—not a word had been uttered between us."

Mabel didn't tell Duse or her husband about the incident with Poletti. The young woman was a mad, suicidal genius, Duse said. Tormented by writer's block and Mabel's rejection, Poletti couldn't write at the Villa Curonia. Mabel suggested they move to the house of a friend who lived nearby. Mabel never saw Duse or Poletti again. By 1912, after seven years in Italy, she was finished with Italy, the Florentines, and her husband, and moved back to the United States.

Since Mabel lived and dressed like a Medici, not surprisingly Poletti attempted to gain Mabel's patronage. Her clumsy efforts failed. Duse continued to encourage Poletti's playwriting, but in Venice in the summer of 1912, aided by several loyal women friends, she freed herself from any responsibility to the "prodigy." That summer, Rainer Maria Rilke recorded the drama and kept his poet's eyes firmly fixed on Duse.

RILKE, THEN THIRTY-SIX, arrived in Venice in early May 1912 and moved into an apartment with a view of the Grand Canal. Hoping to overcome his depression by writing, he ordered a new desk. Duse, who was in Venice with Poletti working on her plays, was staying in a house near Rilke's on the Zattere. Carlo Placci, a Florentine friend of Duse's, introduced her to Rilke in late June. Duse also was acquainted with Rilke's great friend and patron, Princess Marie von Thurn und Taxis, who had been born in Venice. When he met Duse, Rilke became the leading man in her daily drama and had no time to write. Although Rilke had seen Duse act, "for years and years I had longed to meet her without doing the slightest thing to bring it about." In August 1907, he had written "Portrait," a sonnet in her honor. She also appeared in his 1910 novel, *The Notebooks of Malte Laurids Brigge*, as "most tragic of women . . . so slight, so naked, so entirely without the pretext of a role."

From the beginning, the two artists were *simpatici*. Duse shared Rilke's belief in the "sanctity of the inner self, a sacred mystery, which it was the artist's duty to preserve." Rilke hated the tourist-thronged Piazza San Marco, filled with postcard vendors and beggars and lit with electric lights, and Duse introduced him to a private, shadowy Venice accessible only by gondola. In her gondola, they explored tiny canals and hidden gardens. As Duse did with all her friends, she enlisted Rilke's support, practical as well as emotional.

Rilke devoted himself to her. Her slight figure had thickened, but her smile, Rilke wrote, "is as transparent as a song and yet so full of something that is being added to it that one is tempted to stand up when it appears." Duse wanted to "remake my home—my house at Venice," and she asked Rilke to help her look at apartments. After looking at dozens, "nothing attracted me," she said. She thought of her old apartment on the third floor of Wolkoff's palazzo and wrote and asked him if she could rent it. With the "greatest regret," Wolkoff said the apartment with its separate entrance no longer existed.

Rilke accompanied Duse on other errands as well. After climbing three flights to a lawyer's office on the top floor of a palazzo, he watched as she "broke down completely" when they got to the lawyer's door. "I can't possibly see this man!" she exclaimed. Rilke even wrote letters on Duse's behalf. "I felt as though the dying Chopin were longing to play for the last time, to play his soul across, to guide it into eternity, while those around him were disputing as to whether there was a piano, whether they could bring it up to his room and—how much it would cost! I could not bring myself to believe that she would go down in sickness, misery, obscurity; she deserved, she demanded, a glorious end where she had so magnificently begun—on the stage."

Duse did not lack for opportunities, however. Max Reinhardt, the Austrian director, noted for his staging of mass spectacles as well as his work with actors, had come to Venice that summer to entice Duse to perform with his company. The young Italian actor Alexander Moissi, who had starred in Reinhardt's production of *Oedipus the King*, also urged Duse to join with him and Reinhardt in a repertory that would include Ibsen's *The Lady from the Sea*. "We talked and talked till we were breathless," Duse said. Moissi "rushed, thrust, forced himself in," reported Rilke. "At first I thought that was his natural tempo, but I am afraid it is only the tempo of the Reinhardt productions!" In late July, the *New York Times* announced Duse's return to the stage with Reinhardt and Moissi, but Duse eventually decided against the plan.

Duse introduced Rilke to Poletti and drew him into their relationship, which had become fraught with conflict. Rilke ate dinner every evening with the women and talked for hours with both of them, separately and together. Rilke found Poletti "hard, ambitious, not without a certain amount of talent but without flexibility even in her talent, . . . with more energy than vocation." Poletti had turned the early interest and encouragement that Duse had given her into an "irrevocable promise." Duse felt trapped.

"Reproaches and bitterness, sadness and helplessness come between

Rainer Maria Rilke, c. 1912

them," Rilke confided to Princess Marie, "increasingly paralysing and saddening both of them, casting a shadow." Duse grew increasingly nervous. On a garden picnic, a peacock's scream startled her just as she was passing a water glass to Rilke. The glass shattered, and Duse fled. A buzzing fly trapped in the draperies of her room disturbed her so much she left the room, and Rilke and Poletti didn't see her for the rest of the day. Another time, after an argument with Poletti, Duse disappeared for a day and a night. Rilke saw the humor in Duse's overwrought responses, but he also suspected that because of her temperament she needed to dramatize the most ordinary moments. Princess Marie warned him for the sake of his own work not to become overly involved with Duse and her problems. But Rilke, whose first play had been laughed at in Berlin, imagined her returning to the stage in his play *The White Princess.* When Duse asked for his advice about Poletti, Rilke suggested she tell Poletti to go away and finish her plays somewhere else. When Duse didn't, Rilke believed it was because she was "afraid of being left alone."

Duse had created a scenario with herself at the center pursued by competing interests, who shared one motivation—to bring her triumphantly back to the theatre. When the pressure became too intense, Duse escaped to the safe harbor of her loyal women friends, who didn't have a stake in her career. Artist Henrietta Gardner Macy, whom Duse called affectionately "Sister of Walt Whitman," had lived in Venice for years and was "the best loved American in all Venice." Macy, then fifty-eight, lived in an attic in a huge yellow house overlooking the Giudecca. Macy's chief project was creating a cast replica of the Ducal Palace. Her other project, with the help of Elizabeth Chanler Chapman, wife of the prominent American writer John Jay Chapman, and the Marchesa Etta de Viti de Marco (formerly Etta Dunham of Boston) was to look after Duse.

When Macy met Poletti that summer, she didn't like her. Macy saw a "cool young woman—shrewd, selfish, conceited, ungrateful, with the voice of a crow and the features of a bird of prey." The "shrew had the courage to tell the Duse," Macy said, "that she had been insulted on the steamboat because she had been seen in the company of an actress." "That ended it for me," Macy said. "Meanness piled on meanness, ingratitude on ingratitude! Not one word, thought or action that did not show calculating meanness."

On a Sunday evening in late July, Poletti finally read *Arianna* to Duse and a few invited guests. "And it was all a hoax," Macy reported. "If the parasite had not insulted the profession, the Art, she would not have lost her grip. That's what settled her; it was nothing personal." Still, Duse could not bring herself to confront Poletti, and Elizabeth Chapman spoke for her while Duse listened from the next room, as "point by point they had it out." Poletti left Venice immediately and moved to Rome. Rilke left as well. He had come to Venice to write and to free himself from his depression, but his efforts on Duse's behalf had drained him. Duse traveled north and joined Countess Sophie Drechsel in Tegernsee.

"Thank God she is freed from the big vampire and the little one," said Macy. "I wonder who next will utilize the sweet woman."

DUSE'S ENCOURAGEMENT of Poletti had been sincere, yet when she learned Poletti lacked talent, Duse ruthlessly turned her back. *Arianna* and *Incest* were never produced. Poletti and her "domineering mama" threatened legal action. Duse turned the matter over to her old friend, the lawyer and

Duse in retirement, c. 1910

cabinet minister Giovanni Rosadi. "Auf!—what a huge relief!" Duse sighed
when she returned Poletti's manuscript and finally freed herself from the
"nightmare."

Duse underestimated the power of her celebrity and the effect even passing praise might have on a playwright who sent her a play. On August 23,
1912, when she penciled a hasty note to Edouard Schneider, a young French
playwright, he treasured it as a talisman. Years later, Schneider met Duse,
became her friend, and wrote a kind of spiritual biography about the last
years of her life and his memories of her. His play wasn't for her, she told him.
Plus she lacked energy, courage, and health to return to the "hell" of the theatre. "I've found myself being freer faraway from the stage," she said. "Your
piece is so beautiful but to write about art is as difficult as it is to talk about
the heart."

Without the reassuring landmarks of work and art, Duse was lost in
uncharted waters. After years of looking at herself in a mirror in her dressing

room, she now refused to have mirrors around. If there was a large mirror in her hotel bedroom, she placed a screen in front of it. The lines on her hands were reminders enough of time passing. A mirror couldn't answer one central question: If she wasn't La Duse anymore, who was she?

"I'VE SPENT MY LIFE trying to perfect my art," Duse told a friend. "Now it's time I tried to perfect myself." In the winter of 1912, accompanied by her faithful old servants, Nanni, and his wife Caterina, Duse followed the sun south to a villa in Alassio on the Italian Riviera. Helen Mackay joined her there for a few days at Christmas.

When Duse picked up Mackay at the railroad station, Duse said, "There are two canaries in a cage at the railroad crossing, the guard's house. Miserable, quite black with the smoke of trains. They never sing. I have waited all this time to buy them." Mackay went with Duse to buy the canaries, and then searched all afternoon for a new cage and a bowl for them to bathe in.

The next morning Duse tapped on Mackay's door before dawn. They went to Duse's room to watch the sun rise over the sea. "Nanni had already lighted a fire of drift wood," Mackay remembered. "[Duse] sat against the cushions of her immense peasant bed . . . of unpainted wood with a sort of cupboard set into the foot of it, where the peasants would have kept their dry herbs or fruit or cheese. She had packed the place full of books. I sat on the top of it, a sort of bench it made . . . such a happy morning."

That afternoon they took a wagon up to a village in the hills above Alassio. In a shop on the piazza, Mackay bought sweets. She gave the candy to the poor children on the piazza and danced with them around the fountain. "I could not imagine why she went away and stood by the parapet, looking off to the sea," Mackay wrote. Duse was silent on the way down the mountain. The begging children, performing for a handout from a rich stranger, reminded her of her own hungry childhood when she, too, had cajoled money and sweets from strangers. "To you, their poverty is a pretty thing to play with," Duse accused.

Later, in the villa, Duse continued her coldness to Mackay and refused to have anything to do with the canaries they had saved. "You are just alike in your cages, with your grain fed to you," Duse said. "The most thieving sparrow is better." They attended midnight mass in the village, but "the signora was tired of me and the canaries," wrote Mackay. Her friends knew that when the *smara* descended on Duse, the black melancholy and depression could last for days. The day after Christmas, Mackay returned to Paris.

LIKE MOST OF Duse's friends who knew her well, Mackay accepted her abrupt changes of mood with equanimity. Duse stayed on in Alassio for a time. Not wanting to be alone, she wired her old friend Emma Garzes that she was depressed. "It would be helpful if you could come immediately." From Alassio, she moved on to Florence and Rome and Nice. Somewhere along the way in early 1913, she was joined by a new "character," photographer Helen Lohmann, then thirty-five, who was recovering from a nervous breakdown after a failed love affair. Lohmann traveled with Duse for several months.

"Though she was kindness herself to me, she would sometimes shut herself in and refuse to talk to me, or even see me, for several days," Lohmann remembered. "Then, suddenly, she would tap on my door in the middle of the night: 'I'm hungry! Come down to the kitchen with me, Elena, and eat, and have a glass of wine!'" One night, Duse talked of Ibsen's *The Master Builder*, which she called "my favorite play in all the world." The part of Hilda wasn't right for her, Duse said, but then Helen watched, "spellbound," as Duse acted Hilda Wangel, "with all the youth, the fun, the vitality, the rapacity of that troll-like creature."

Duse always carried a copy of *Macbeth* with her and liked to listen as Lohmann read the English words aloud. "Of course it is Macbeth himself one would want to play," Duse said. "What an extraordinary, complex nature! In spite of his maleness—so much woman in him!" Duse loved to read, Lohmann recalled, and often would spend the whole day reading. When she went off to be with her society friends, she would "decide to be a lady," and wear one of her Worth dresses only to return complaining of exhaustion because of too many people. Although Duse used Lohmann to run her errands and sometimes ignored her, Helen didn't mind. It was enough for her to be in the presence of a great artist, plus she believed Duse possessed a kind of "healing strength." After her months with Duse, Lohmann returned to work as a photographer and eventually, in a strange coincidence, worked at the Civic Repertory Theatre in New York with Eva Le Gallienne, whose life was also changed by Duse.

"After all, who was I," Lohmann said later, "that she should have taken the trouble to save my life."

WHEN DUSE'S old friend Yvette Guilbert toured Italy in the spring of 1913, the forty-six-year-old singer encouraged Duse to perform with her on tour. Duse toyed with the idea, even searched for material in books Guilbert sent her. Inaction had left Duse "half-dazed and self-pitying," and nothing she read—books, plays, poems—appealed to her enough to send her back to work. "But what I once was," Duse told Guilbert, "that I can no longer find. How can I begin again? What can I do?"

On August 7, 1913, Duse wrote Yvette from Viareggio, where she was ill and feverish, that she lacked the courage and the health to return to work. "People do not guess," she said, "but you and I, we know what horrible fatigue it is to cart oneself, one's thoughts, and one's trunks about between Europe and America."

Soon after she wrote this letter, Duse dismissed her pain to console Isadora Duncan. In April 1913, Duncan's two children, Deirdre, the daughter of Gordon Craig, and Patrick, her son with Paris Singer, were drowned in the Seine in a freak automobile accident. For months, Isadora traveled aimlessly. "I know you are wandering through Italy," Duse telegraphed that fall. "I pray you come to me. I will do my best to comfort you."

Duncan drove to Viareggio in a thunderstorm. "Duse was then a magnificent creature, in the full power of life and intelligence," Isadora recalled. "When she walked along the beach she took long strides, walking unlike any other woman I have ever seen." Duse "seemed to take my sorrow to her own breast," Isadora wrote, "and I realized that if I had not been able to bear the society of other people, it was because they all played the comedy of trying to cheer me with forgetfulness. Whereas Eleonora said: 'Tell me about Deirdre and Patrick,' and made me repeat to her all their little sayings and ways, and show her their photos, which she kissed and cried over."

Duse also sent notes to Isadora at her hotel, sometimes several in one day, written in pencil in her large, sprawling hand. Often, the notes would contain only a sentence or two saying, "Come to me. I love you." Then the two women would meet and walk by the sea. When Isadora received an offer to dance in South America, Duse urged her to sign the contract. "If you know how short life is and how there can be long years of ennui, ennui—nothing but ennui! Escape from sorrow and ennui—escape!"

In another note, Duse explained that a "glacial wind" made it impossible for her to go out. She also chided Isadora that if she saw any journalists, "I implore you not to tell them that I'm not feeling well—you don't know how to *hide yourself* from the public—and I, I detest that the public drives me from my nest."

One evening at dusk, Isadora danced for the first time since her children had died on April 19. Afterward, Duse embraced her and said, "You must return to your art. It is your only salvation."

Later, after seeing Isadora perform in public, Duse said, "How I wish I too could escape from reality! Without work, without risks, life is nothing—a dream empty of dreams. What joy to see you take up anew the flight toward the light!"

AT THIS TIME, two young women, Maria Osti Giambruni and Désirée von Wertheimstein, were helping Duse find her way toward the light. Two years earlier, Duse had begun exploring the idea of founding, in Rome, a refuge for actresses, a cultural center for contemplation, rest, and study—the sort of place she had never had as a young actress. On her tours to New York, she had been impressed with the beauty and the dignity of The Players Club.

In November 1911, Duse visited a villa in the Piazza Caprera neighborhood of Rome as a possible home for what she came to call her "Library for Actresses." Maria Osti Giambruni, a widow in her late twenties with two young daughters, Pierina and Luisa, lived in the villa with her mother and sister. Osti's husband had been killed in action in Tripoli a few weeks earlier, when the Italian government had declared war on the Ottoman Turks. Maria was planning to move back to Parma, where she and her husband had been born. Overcome with grief, Maria sat day after day in a dark room, too depressed to look after her daughters or even speak. On the day of Duse's visit, Maria didn't reply to the visitors who stopped in front of her, hearing only their empty words about "country" and "sacrifice." She did notice the silent presence of a woman with silver hair dressed in black velvet who stood apart from the group. Before she left the room, Duse gave Maria a "long, intense look."

"It was as if I had been awakened," Maria recalled. She moved toward Duse, who embraced her tenderly, without words. "It was like a benediction," Maria felt. Duse left, and Maria returned to her chair. "That brief light had passed." Not long after, Maria's nine-year-old daughter Pierina burst into the room with an armful of white roses. "The signora Duse gave them to me!" Profoundly moved, Maria wrote Duse to thank her. Duse soon paid another visit and advised Maria not to make any decisions about moving while she was still grieving. Maria didn't sell her home, and she and Duse became friends.

Years later, Luisa Osti Chiarelli wondered about the nature of her mother's fourteen-year relationship with Duse. "Was it friendship? Was it filial love? Was it devotion? Perhaps it was all these things together," she concluded.

Because of Maria's blonde hair, blue eyes, erect posture, and strong personality, Duse called the new "character" in her life "La Longobarda" (the Lombard). Duse suggested books for Maria to read; introduced her to Maria Montessori (who had started her first school in Rome) and advised her to enroll Pierina in the school. She also sent encouraging notes. "You will see," Duse wrote, "the little girl will grow beautiful, cheerful, strong, and sincere. Courage! Have hope! then, and we say *yes* to the fate that shapes Life."

Maria Osti, Duse's close friend
and confidante, c. 1915

"Every phrase, every word was an incitement to live, pushing me out of the tomb in which I had enclosed myself without hope," Maria said. "It was a true salvation for me." She invited Duse for visits to her house in Rome, and later to her villa in Tivoli. Sometimes Duse took her meals alone in her room when she was ill, but for the most part, Duse enjoyed being a part of the all-female household and entered into their daily life. With Duse's help and advice, Maria redecorated her villa, adding plants, oriental rugs, and sculpture. Duse's simplicity, her kindness, and her affection were a "great comfort" to Maria and her daughters.

"She didn't talk much about herself," Maria recalled, "of her glory, her triumphs, she said nothing. Mostly, and with moving tenderness, she spoke of her mother, whom she had lost when she was still very young." Duse also spoke of Enrichetta and how she had kept her daughter away from the theatre because she hadn't wanted Enrichetta to suffer as she had.

In October 1913, Duse invited Maria to Viareggio to meet Enrichetta, who had come for a visit to collect items she wanted from Duse's house in Florence. "With what joy Duse seemed to want to rid herself of everything!" Maria said. Enrichetta had left her two children, three-year-old Edward Halley and one-year-old Eleonora Illaria, in England with their father. When she saw Enrichetta with Duse, Maria was struck by "the difference in their personalities!" Enrichetta, a devout Catholic, then thirty-two, two years older than Maria, seemed typically English, straightforward and practical. Enrichetta worried about Duse's impulsive nature, which she felt could be easily exploited. She told Maria she was grateful her mother had Maria's disinterested friendship and support.

Enrichetta was not so pleased, however, about the bond that had formed between her mother and Désirée von Wertheimstein. She thought Désirée belonged in Vienna with her own family. Désirée was four years older than Enrichetta, and had been close to her and two other girls at their boarding school in Germany. All the girls had gotten married, except for Désirée. Tall, with dark chestnut hair she twisted into a roll, and a "kind face," Désirée was born in Vienna on June 28, 1877. The von Wertheimsteins were Jewish and lived in Vienna on Karntner Ring 2, opposite the Opera. Her mother was French born, and her Austrian father had an important position with the Bohemian Western railways in Austria. Désirée spoke German, Italian, and French, was unattached, and was totally devoted to Duse. Her devotion, in part, was that of a stagestruck fan. She described the moment when she first saw Duse onstage as "the most beautiful of my life."

Duse responded to Désirée's devotion. "She is like a daughter to me." Of course, Duse already had a daughter, but she had raised Enrichetta to live in a different world, and now they were separated by distance and a world of differences. Désirée had little interest in current events, art, or literature, and Duse affectionately called her a "goose." But she also praised her as Désirée, "the Good," and a "rare creature, not of intelligence, but of the heart."

Unlike Enrichetta, who wanted Duse to stay retired from the theatre, Désirée encouraged Duse to return to work. Désirée also helped Duse with time-consuming daily tasks—packing and unpacking, mailing letters, answering correspondence, doing laundry—but most important, she entered into Duse's library project with enthusiasm. In early 1914, Yvette Guilbert saw Duse in Rome and found her "quite changed! Looking in good health and beautiful!"

Duse's old friend Enrico Polese, the editor of *L'Arte Drammatica*, publicized the project and asked for support and donations in the magazine. To fund the center, Duse sold some of her jewelry and supplied the library with hundreds of her own books she had trucked from Florence. She rented a villa in the quiet Nomentana district of Rome to house the library. While actors like Tina di Lorenzo, Dina Galli, and Ciro Galvani subscribed to the plan, served on the founding committee, and helped with funding, Duse's former protégée, Emma Gramatica, who had known Duse for thirty years, refused to participate and strongly objected in an open letter to the *Giornale d'Italia*. Gramatica didn't accept Duse's new role of librarian. For decades, Duse's companies had toured the world bringing honor and prestige to Italian theatre, and her defection angered Gramatica. Successful actors didn't need the library, she reminded Duse, and the others wouldn't have the time or the desire to use it. Like a daughter lecturing an absent parent, Emma accused Duse of desertion. "For too long a time you've lived far from us, a stranger to us," she said. "You've lost the feeling and the knowledge of what was once your life. Your project is a pipe dream."

On May 27, 1914, at 5 p.m., the library was inaugurated. Since the library wouldn't open officially until the fall, books were stacked on the floor, some still in boxes. Duse's signature roses along with pots of laurel decorated the yellow and white rooms. Désirée oversaw the buffet, which had been set up on the terrace. About one hundred arts patrons, actors, and writers attended the event. "It was so wonderful, but it's a pity you weren't there," Désirée wrote Enrichetta the next day. "I was so happy when I saw that everyone was full of admiration, the young actresses were really nice. [Duse] ran up and down, and I was afraid that she would exhaust herself, but she was so satisfied with it that she forgot about her tiredness."

DUSE HAD EXHAUSTED herself, though, and spent June, July, and August recovering from a severe cold, fever, and profound depression about the state of the world. On June 28, 1914, the assassination of Archduke Francis Ferdinand at Sarajevo triggered world war. Germany declared war on Russia on August 1 and on France two days later. Soon after, Great Britain joined the Allies against the Central Powers of Germany, Austria-Hungary, and the Ottoman Empire. For the time being, Italy remained neutral.

The world was in disarray, and her small world was collapsing as well. When she returned to her house in Florence, her ground-floor apartment had been rented and the garden destroyed. She moved to a second-floor apartment. On January 10, 1915, because of the war, Duse said good-bye to a sobbing Désirée, who went home to Vienna. "I feel a great emptiness," Duse wrote Enrichetta. A few days later a massive earthquake shook an area from Naples to Rome, leaving over thirty thousand dead and destroying dozens of towns. Duse closed the library in Rome and gave the books away to schools.

On May 23, 1915, after being promised considerable territory, Italy declared war on Austria and entered the conflict on the side of the Allies. Alone in her apartment in Florence, Duse listened to the church bells ringing out the announcement. She felt useless. "I love those who can live and act because in them I forget how my day consists of so much inactivity," she told Lillian de Bosis, who had three sons in uniform. "I regret it and I am ashamed to speak to you of myself while you are living these hours." Duse signed a petition in

The only Correct Version of My Plays
Translated and Printed from My
Own Prompt Books
Under the direction of W.ᴹ F. CONNOR.
Published by FRED RULLMAN, Iɴᴄ.
At the Theatre Ticket Office, 111 Broadway, New York

Despite her infirmity, Sarah Bernhardt continued to tour—
a fact not lost on Duse, who admired Sarah's spirit, 1916.

support of Italy's war effort, and a German newspaper accused her of being ungrateful to a nation that had loved her art and given her hospitality. Duse wrote immediately to Robi and Giulietta von Mendelssohn in Berlin. She didn't hear from them for weeks. Finally, Giulietta wrote that Robi was seriously ill.

Theatre news was equally bleak. In February 1915, she heard that Sarah Bernhardt had had her leg amputated. Sarah had "seemed invincible" to Duse. Now she envisioned Bernhardt "mutilated and beautiful" like the statues of her childhood that had inspired Duse. On July 31, Flavio Andò, Duse's "dear companion in work and in pain, a magnificent comrade and a magnificent artist," died suddenly at Marina di Pisa.

"Sadness is everywhere these sad days," Duse telegraphed Isadora Duncan on October 3, 1915. It was Duse's fifty-seventh birthday, but there was little to celebrate. Death was in the air. A few months earlier, Isadora had given birth to a son conceived during a brief affair with a young Italian at Viareggio the year before. When she had first learned of the pregnancy, Duse had been critical of Isadora daring to "RECONSTRUCT her life! [. . .] to throw herself back into life, the life which bleeds—and see again—what! The smile of her dead child in another smile of another child that will be hers!" When she heard Isadora's son had lived only a few hours, though, Duse wrote and apologized for not having come to find her and for having done nothing to help her pain. "You have borne so much suffering all alone," Duse wrote. "All is anguish in the world."

AFTER SPENDING THE SUMMER between Boscolungo, in the Tuscan mountains, where she found she could "breathe without wheezing," and Viareggio, where the sea air revived her, Duse began to feel better. Using a diet regimen suggested by a friend, she also lost some weight. By this time, her menopausal symptoms had probably subsided as well. Contact with a new, younger circle in Rome that fall also stimulated her. She enjoyed musical evenings and dinner parties at the home of Olga Resnevic Signorelli (Duse's future biographer), and her husband, Dr. Angelo Signorelli. At their parties, Duse met artists, musicians, and poets, like Giovanni Papini, the brilliant philosopher and editor of *La Voce*, a literary journal.

Thinking Duse was wealthy, Papini wrote a flattering letter asking for money. In his early thirties, married, with two children, he needed calm and peace to write the important works that he felt he was destined to write, he told Duse. "Excuse this display of wretchedness," he said. "But I write it to you because you are a great spirit of woman and artist—and because you have suffered and suffer." Because of the problem in getting money out of Germany from her investments there, Duse was strapped for money herself, but she sent Papini 1,000 lire and apologized for not being able to send him more. Papini wrote to thank her, and they began a correspondence.

"Hearing you speak of art and work, I remembered, also art and work," Duse wrote. "I recognized, hearing you talk of it, the old suffering, the kind that is not healed [. . .] since the day I stopped working—I live—on nothing, I live in death, and I delude myself that I understand the suffering of others!"

Duse also met Paul Claudel and Jacques Copeau at the Signorellis. Sometimes, though, she confided to Enrichetta, these "men of the plume" are difficult. "Those people who speak to you of potatoes—they're better sometimes!" Boito also came to Rome that fall, and Duse spent several evenings with him. Everything had changed, and nothing had changed, she felt. Boito clung to Shakespeare and had little interest when Duse spoke of her interest in W. B. Yeats. She longed to talk to him about work, but decided against it. They laughed together, but there was still a great distance between them, and Boito seemed removed from life. For Duse, Boito had become an abstraction. In her mind, he was Nome and Il Santo—no longer the gentle Arrigo. Mostly his presence reminded her of all the times that work had separated them and what might have been.

When Lucien Guitry's French company performed in Rome for several months in late 1915 and early 1916, Duse attended all the plays. Duse had first met the handsome French actor in St. Petersburg when she was twenty-nine. "She was at the same time the woman of the past and the woman of the future," Guitry said. While he was in Rome, Duse wrote and asked if she could come and see him. "What a visit!" Guitry remembered.

"I bring you this book," Duse said. "Oh! It is a very simple book, and one which may be obtained anywhere, but look on this page at the cast of *King Lear*. I have written opposite Lear, Lucien Guitry." During her visit, she told Guitry she had "given up the theatre."

"Take care, take care, it is not true," Guitry said. "One believes it to be finished; it is only a passing caprice. Overcome this idea, but don't quit the theater; the theater is a family—don't abandon us." Guitry urged her to come to Paris and act with his company, proposing she play Lady Macbeth to his Macbeth. As Guitry's company prepared to return to Paris in March 1916, Duse longed to go with them. "Here, I feel that I'm losing strength," she said. "I don't know if I should leave or stay."

Duse decided to stay. She had discovered a fascinating art, a "glass that sees into souls," an art that was a logical extension of her aesthetic. The years between 1909 and 1916 have been called the golden age of Italian film. About twenty-two production companies filmed in Italy around the clock, producing costume dramas, historical epics, middle-class melodramas, and social realism. Like their American counterparts, early Italian filmmakers freed themselves from the proscenium arch and shot on location, making use of the extraordinary Italian light. From the beginning, Italian intellectuals and Italian theatre people embraced the new medium, never treating it with the kind of disdain early film aroused in other countries.

Duse discussed the new art with Giovanni Papini, who had written an article about the philosophy of the cinema in 1907, and for months, she escaped into movie houses in Rome and Florence. "Hidden in the darkness of the house, I have seen I don't know how many films and I have tried to recognize those which corresponded to my real being, those significant ones which are only a flash, like a sketch, I might say almost like a flash of lightning." She saw Mascagni's *Cavalleria rusticana* and D. W. Griffith's *Cobweb* and watched as "lightning-like living creatures appear before me . . . Like the visions which I seek."

In many of the silent films, Duse observed Woman as object—either victim or vampire—endlessly repeating images of sensuous bodies, widening eyes framed by thick, black eyeliner, and clutching hands pressed to the head or heart. Giovanni Pastrone, who had invented the dolly and used location shooting with multiple cameras, produced and directed the hit of the decade, the 1914 historical epic *Cabiria*, with subtitles by d'Annunzio. The pioneering film influenced D. W. Griffith and Cecil B. DeMille. Set in the pagan world of the third century, *Cabiria* featured erupting volcanoes, Hannibal crossing the Alps, and one hundred children fed into the great mouth of the bronze god Moloch. A huge cast, including a muscle-man hero and two beautiful leading women, the victim Cabiria, and the vampire Sophonisba, acted with grandiloquent, operatic gestures. It's likely, too, that Duse saw Sarah Bernhardt's *La Tosca* and *La Dame aux camélias*, filmed versions of the plays that made Sarah look like a hyperactive puppet. Duse admired Mary Pickford, but she criticized the work of Francesca Bertini, the first world-famous diva of Italian film, who played many of Duse's theatre roles on screen, including leading roles in *La Dame aux camélias*, *Odette*, and *Fédora*. *Odette* seemed "the exterior of a poor life, mechanically shown," Duse said, "nothing that makes the soul reflect—that, after the word, leaves the imagination free! —Nothing of what is not seen, what weaves life, none of the inevitabilities that shape it, press it in a vise."

When an offer came from D. W. Griffith inviting her to come to Los Angeles and make films, Duse believed he had asked a woman who didn't exist anymore. "Those good people out there," she confided to Papini, "sure of themselves, wrote me, offering the earth, only, those people were addressing me, remembering another person, believing—I don't know why—that they would find again, through me, E. Duse—But neither I [. . .] nor any of my friends, have any trace of her."

When Enrichetta advised her against accepting Griffith's offer—for that matter, returning to work at all—Duse snapped that she had always worked to support herself. Enrichetta never understood how much work meant to Duse. "Her work was her true life," Maria Osti believed, "and her salvation."

ENRICHETTA LATER DESTROYED most of Duse's letters to her, but during the war, she copied her mother's letters, "just as they came along," into notebooks so later in time her children would be able to read them. She then burned the originals. On her part, Duse carefully saved all her daughter's letters to her, tying them neatly into bundles. Later, when Enrichetta found the letters, she burned hers as well. Although Enrichetta explained in the notebooks she feared her mother's letters would fade, this is hardly a reason to destroy them. It is natural to treasure pages touched by a loved one's hand. It is significant that most of the letters Enrichetta chose to copy were all written during the war years when Duse was alone, without Désirée, her surrogate daughter.

The letters are a mishmash of Italian and French—at one point, Duse decided to write to Enrichetta in Italian only, but soon slipped back into French sprinkled with Italian words and phrases. The confusion of the languages reflects the confusing feelings Duse had toward her daughter. Certainly, in the portions of the letters Enrichetta chose to copy, Duse reached out on the surface to her practical daughter, telling her about her day-to-day routine, the books she was reading, the people she was seeing, and always with a subtext about her money worries. It was becoming increasingly difficult for her to receive funds from her investments in Germany. Stunningly scarce in the letters are questions or concerns about Enrichetta's life and children (of course, it's possible Enrichetta might not have copied these sections), and the letters reveal Duse to be enormously self-absorbed. In letters to her women friends, however, Duse often expressed sympathy and concern for them and their families. With Maria Osti and Helen Mackay, Duse shared her fears of poverty, and she confessed to being depressed or ill. Maria provided her with a home, sometimes for months at a time, and Mackay sent her money. Duse accepted their assistance gratefully. Enrichetta had the "family money" Duse had given her and many of Duse's jewels, and she was married to a wealthy man, but she didn't help Duse financially. With Enrichetta, Duse played the strong, self-reliant mother who didn't need help. "I don't want to be a stone in my daughter's shoe," Duse said.

Still, Duse tried to bridge the gap between them. Enrichetta recognized Duse's effort, and with indelible Chinese ink, she copied the words her mother had scrawled with an easily smudged and fast-fading pencil. "Letters seem to me such poor and cold things," Duse told Enrichetta. "How to relate the things I have seen, and the things in my soul which most of humanity never sees!"

EXPRESSING THE UNSEEN, saying the unsayable, had always been the aim of Duse's art. Ever since Griffith's offer, she had "dreamed only of films." The art of silence, she called it. She decided to create her own visions—"some of our images—old walls and churches of Italy." She read the stories of Swedish writer Selma Lagerlöf and worked on adapting one with the help of Camille Mallarmé, niece of the French poet, who wrote children's stories. She turned again and again to Ibsen's *The Lady from the Sea*, calling her "my beautiful consoler." Just as she had as a girl, she also studied sculpture and paintings, imagining the spirit that lived inside them. "Since I have been looking at them, to realize, to understand *how they are made*, it is like an enchantment for me."

In the spring of 1916, she received an offer from Arturo Ambrosio, founder of Ambrosio-Films in Turin, one of the most important and successful companies in Italy. She immediately "felt a kind of confidence" in Ambrosio. He seemed "quite nice, unaffected, 'Italian' in the best sense of the word." Perhaps the fact that Ambrosio had filmed d'Annunzio's plays influenced her, but mostly she was "determined to be disciplined and reintroduce order into my eviscerated, empty life!!! One must work—work is the bread and salt of my life—to it again!"

In early June, after weeks of tense negotiations, at times becoming ill with fear the whole project would go up in smoke, Duse signed a contract with Ambrosio-Films. She would receive 50 percent of the film's receipts and an advance of 40,000 lire (about $3,000) plus 20,000 lire for expenses. Once again, as she had so many times in the past, her faithful friend Matilde Serao publicized Duse's return to work and reminded newspaper readers of Duse's past triumphs and present beauty.

Serao interviewed Duse in Rome in early June. "Eagerly I looked on that face, that clear source of dreams," Serao wrote. "Oh, so much can be done," Duse said, "so much can be done with the cinematograph."

Finally, after seven years, "ecstatic—laughing even," Duse returned to work. "I am more in the dream than in reality!" she exclaimed.

Nine

DUSE CALLED MAKING a film a spiritual problem, part of her life-long "sweet, inexhaustible" search for harmony between life and art. Finding harmony also meant taking control ("Oh! How I love that word!"). When producers wanted to capitalize on her name and film her greatest theatre roles, she dismissed the projects as ludicrous and vulgar. Because of his admiration for her, Arturo Ambrosio at Ambrosio-Films accepted her "irritating, often brusque originality" and allowed her to choose her own material, write the script, and exercise artistic control.

For her first and only film, Duse chose the work of a woman writer—Grazia Deledda's *Cenere (Ashes)*. Set on Deledda's native island of Sardinia, the novel tells of a mother who gives up her illegitimate child for his own good. Grazia Deledda, Matilde Serao, and Sibilla Aleramo, three successful women writers, all lived in Rome and encouraged one another's work. When Aleramo was attacked for writing about her lesbian affair with Lina Poletti, Serao defended her artistic freedom. To these women writers, who struggled against a patriarchal society, Duse, an actor, represented the ideal of the new woman, "courageous, self-assured, free to love, and free to express herself through art."

"In *Cenere* you must be only yourself," Deledda wrote Duse. "Love and sorrow together, mother and child intertwined with lights and shadows, without external color." The story of *Cenere* was a familiar one to Duse. A poor and beautiful young girl (called Rosalia in the film) is seduced and becomes pregnant. To give her illegitimate son a better life, Rosalia takes him to be raised by the family of his father. While Rosalia lives as a rootless beggar and itinerant worker, her son, Anania, grows up, gets an education, and then finds the mother who has abandoned him. When his fiancée refuses to accept Rosalia, the son is torn between his mother and his fiancée. To give her son a new life, Rosalia decides to die.

Duse distilled the film of *Cenere* around the most powerful scene in the novel—the son's reunion with his mother. The "lost son" theme had always appeared in Duse's work, but *Cenere* also expressed her feelings about her separation from Enrichetta. The atmosphere of the film evoked the bleak state of war-torn Italy and the universal suffering of mothers with sons in the war—a time, wrote Grazia Deledda, when "the earth trembles under our feet, and an infinite gray extends over our horizon."

When she was invited to entertain the troops, Duse refused. While soldiers were suffering and dying in dirt and blood, the idea seemed grotesque to her. Instead, she exchanged her usual black dress for a more cheerful blue one and visited the wounded and soldiers at the front. She talked to them, listened to their troubles, and carried messages to their mothers and families. She wrote letters to soldiers and sent gift packages. She formed a close epistolary bond with Luciano Nicastro, a nineteen-year-old Sicilian officer she met in a Milan bookstore during the war. Intelligent and sensitive, with large dark eyes that reminded her of Enrichetta's, Nicastro became Duse's surrogate son. Nicastro's mother was dead, and at times he called Duse "Mama." She waited for his letters, read and reread them, worried about his safety, and sent him an Italian translation of Whitman's *Leaves of Grass*. Her letters to him, in which she addresses him intimately as *"tu"* or *"Son!,"* are eloquent and tender. "I'm not a society woman," Duse said. "I'm not a patrician—I'm of *this earth* [. . .] I see you, and I follow you, and I accompany you, and I *stay on guard,* invisible, next to you."

AFTER WEEKS OF SCRIPT work and study, Duse traveled to Viareggio in early June 1916 to film some outdoor scenes. To help Duse direct the film and also to play her son, Ambrosio hired Febo Mari, then thirty-five, an experienced actor, director, and writer. Federico Fellini recalled that as a boy he had idealized Mari and wanted to model himself after the handsome, aristocratic filmmaker.

In July, Duse moved to Turin, where the Ambrosio studios were located, to film the interior scenes. "Mystery, marvel, the machine," she said when she saw the film they had shot in Viareggio. Many of the proofs were bad, but she loved one sun-washed sequence shot in a field of flowering fava beans. Her character, Rosalia, worked in the field as a gleaner, and Duse's white hair harmonized with the silvery flowers of the fava.

For the first time, Duse was playing a character without direct audience

Grazia Deledda, author of the novel *Cenere*

communion, but her hours of film watching and her instincts served her well. "I want to be responsible for my film, the whole of it," she said. The technical side of filmmaking fascinated her. She befriended the lighting technician and the wardrobe crew, and she paid attention to every aspect of the filmmaking. "I went into the dark room to watch some clips," she said, "and something strange happened to me. I felt so detached that Rosalia seemed to speak directly to me." She served as an audience of one, evaluating and directing her own performance choices. Just as her theatre acting had defied the notion of woman as object, Duse's film portrayal of Rosalia rejected stock gestures and the stereotype of woman as victim or vampire.

Duse's insistence on her individual vision led to battles with Ambrosio and Febo Mari. When Mari wanted to shoot close-ups in full sunlight, she resisted. She begged him to "put me in the shadow." Since she was fifty-eight, feminine vanity played a part in her aversion to close-ups, but she also wanted her film to employ light and shadow, to be a universal story of life and death.

Ambrosio wanted her to make a *verismo* film, a "reproduction of life," but she sought a transposition of life, to see beyond words, into the soul.

"I have learned so much," Duse wrote Maria Osti. "Technique alone is not enough, just as *inspiration* by itself is not enough." As she worked on the movie, Duse kept in close touch with Enrichetta, Maria Osti, Helen Mackay, and Antonietta Pisa, but she was alone in Turin. Rising before dawn, working long hours, and learning something new invigorated her. She didn't mind being alone. Years earlier, when she had made her debut in Turin, she had preferred going to the theatre alone. "Return along your path," she told herself now. "Begin again!" After a day of filming, she was exhausted, but she still had "a conquering feeling in my soul!" Working made her feel young again, and like a child, to console herself in her solitude, she bought a doll, "so pretty, and all mine." When she felt depressed, she held the doll and said, *"Avanti!"*

Since she was learning by doing, Duse's perfectionism led to costly reshoots and an additional month of work. Ambrosio had given her an advance, but she wouldn't receive her share of the profits until after the film had been released. With the help of Antonietta Pisa, Duse pawned the two pearls that the Duchess of Palmella had given her, and she also asked Enrichetta to sell a pearl necklace that she had given her and send her the money. Duse explained to Enrichetta that in a moment of fatigue she had relinquished control, and in the middle of the film, "you can almost see the two different hands—almost—I would say—the two different souls."

In September 1916, Duse invited Maria Osti to come to Turin and see a rough cut of the film. Osti watched the film with Grazia Deledda, who had also come from Rome. Moved to tears, Osti thought *Cenere* was beautiful, but because of Deledda's "closed character, so different from Eleonora's," she couldn't tell if Deledda liked the film or not. Deledda complimented Duse on her acting, but she pointed out "the work is yours now, no longer mine." Unhappy with the opening sequences of mother and son that Mari had directed *"without heart,"* Duse took a cameraman and Ettore Casarotti, who played the little boy, and spent a week in a village near Viareggio redoing the scenes.

Finally, in Rome, in March 1917, *Cenere* opened. That spring, when Rome "was then bursting out on every side with wisteria, iris, and lilac," the writer Colette watched *Cenere* in a darkened movie theatre. Because of Ambrosio's budget constraints, the film is very short, just over half an hour long.

CENERE OPENS WITH a flashback of Rosalia/Duse, a young mother, saying good-bye to her seven-year-old son. During the opening scenes, Duse covered her hair with a white kerchief and is seen in medium shot with her face turned away from the camera. Her hands, with long, tapering fingers, look remarkably young and delicate. Wearing a dark, long-sleeved dress and moving with quick, firm steps, she gives the impression of a vibrant young woman. The little boy stands on a wall over a rushing stream, and Duse focuses all her attention on him, caressing his hair, embracing him. Clearly she finds it difficult to let him go. Then, like a fairy-tale ritual, she gives him an amulet filled with precious relics—pieces of paper, herbs, flowers, bits of rock and ashes—which she hangs on a strong chain and places around his neck. Mother and son leave their ancient village and take to the open road, a central image in the film. At a gristmill, Rosalia leaves the boy with his father. In a dream sequence, the boy awakens and goes to a window and imagines his mother reaching up to him. It was "her most beautiful scene," Colette recalled, "those hands were such loving, beating wings, prolonged, extended by their shadows right up to the window sill—that the emotional Italian crowd by which I was surrounded suddenly burst forth into a mist of tears and sighs, all at the same moment."

In scenes depicting Rosalia's wandering after the separation from her son, Duse allowed the audience to see her white hair and her lined face without makeup. In one scene filmed in a sunlit field, Rosalia, exhausted from her work, lies on her stomach and drinks like an animal from a stream. Refreshed, she throws her head back in the pure pleasure of the cold water. Perhaps Duse was drawing on a memory from her youth. Once, when she was a young woman, she and a friend had been walking through some woods and encountered a "savage and dangerous man." Suddenly, Duse remembered, "there was a huge watering hole for the animals and he lay down with his face in the water. When he came up his entire expression had changed, and he said to us with his Roman accent, 'The water is good.' The water calmed his inner fire, and he looked back, and he was no longer interested in us. We, all of us Italians, carry this dangerous flame inside us."

The heart of the movie is the reunion between mother and grown-up son, but the contrast of acting styles between Duse and Febo Mari undercuts what should be a moving and powerful scene. Looking dapper in a dark business suit, highly polished shoes, and white shirt and tie, Febo Mari moves his lips constantly in speech, rolls his eyes, which were outlined with thick dark eyeliner, employs stock gestures—such as holding his hands to his head—and generally acts histrionically. Duse made the decision not to move her lips in speech; she doesn't wear eyeliner or any makeup; and each gesture, each movement, as when she hesitantly touches her son on his shoulder, is motivated by the thoughts of the character. Critics had written for years about Duse's rare, dazzling smile, and she used it once in the film. Head bowed, she kneels at her son's feet while he strokes her hair. She then looks up at him, takes his hands, and breaks into a smile so spontaneous and meltingly lovely that for a moment she looks like a girl.

After an argument in which her son attempts to assert his masculine authority and Rosalia resists, he leaves to ask his fiancée if she will accept his mother. If the fiancée says no, he will send the amulet back by messenger in a colored cloth. If the answer is yes, he will use a white cloth. The scenes of Rosalia waiting are studies in stillness—she does nothing except sit with knees apart, arms folded, the tension expressed through her body line and the expressiveness of her face. Finally, there is a knock on the door of the hut. Duse waits, leaning against the wall with her back to the door. When the door opens, her hand flashes out fiercely, grabbing the wrist of the messenger. She sees the amulet wrapped in colored cloth. The caption reads, "All is ashes—life, death, man, destiny." Realizing that she is unwanted, Rosalia takes to the road. Hearing of his mother's disappearance, the son sets out to find her. Deciding to sacrifice herself again, Rosalia makes her stumbling way back to the hut, where she dies.

Duse based the last images of the film on Giotto's paintings. Inspired by Giotto's "nobility without pose" and his "resigned sadness," Duse brought together in the last sequence the two most important images of her film—the amulet and the open road. Tenderly, Mari takes the amulet from his dead mother's hand. A group of peasants lift the white-shrouded body of Rosalia to their shoulders and carry her out of the hut. Mari kisses her forehead and then holds out his hand in farewell in a simple, understated gesture—"Ashes" the caption says. In the final image, Mari stands alone in the desolate countryside with the empty road, the future, stretching in front of him.

Producers had warned Duse that a movie without a love theme and without beautiful women wouldn't be successful. Critics called Duse's performance pure and original but criticized the screenplay. With its truncated, depressing story, *Cenere* failed commercially, unable to compete with the spectacles and melodramas of the popular cinema. Duse knew that her film was "only a sketch," but she believed it was "on a different plane from others of its kind."

"The critics say that my film is too beautiful for the uncultured masses," Duse said. "Perverse hypocrites, as if I didn't know that my art film, with a white-haired woman, wasn't their kind of film."

EVEN BEFORE *Cenere* was completed in the fall of 1916, Duse had begun work on her second film for Ambrosio-Films, Ibsen's *The Lady from the Sea*. With two men from Ambrosio's company, she had scouted locations near Alassio on the Italian Riviera, finally settling on the village of Cervo. On one

A final moment from *Cenere*, Duse's only film, 1916

trip, the driver of her car made a bad turn on a steep mountain road with a sharp drop to the sea and ran head-on into another car. Duse hit the windshield and suffered superficial glass cuts on her face and neck. Shaken up, she was able to walk to a nearby village, where the local doctor treated her. She summoned Maria Osti, who traveled to Alassio to be with her while she recovered and then accompanied her to her house in Florence. Ambrosio used the excuse of the accident and the war to suspend work on *The Lady from the Sea*.

Duse talked to her friend Paul Claudel about writing a film for her, but they couldn't agree on a subject, and Claudel didn't really like the cinema. She continued to work on her own screenplays, including one about an Italian saint, Angela da Foligno, which Cines Film of Rome rejected diplomatically as too beautiful.

Giovanni Papini urged Duse to give up acting completely. "Above all, you're a writer, and a great one," he said. In a particularly "literary" letter to Papini, she wrote about her 1891 separation from Boito without mentioning her Russian lover, Wolkoff. "I know a poor devil of a woman," she said, "who on coming back from the theatre, in the rooms of the grand hotels, of the beautiful cities, which today, Bolshevism is burning and destroying, coming down a long corridor, decorated by shoes and boots and slippers, lined up on the ground, at every carefully closed door,—she (the poor devil) could do nothing but weep, and remember a distant house, an old convent hidden on the hill amid the summer's green—a Lamp burning, perhaps at the same hour, and—a dear face, unique in the world, bowed beneath the Lamp, searching, there, too, his lot and his destiny!" Her heart didn't break, she told Papini. "*If* some mysterious strength appeared (unsaid) from the depths of me, it was not, then a projection of art, but, something far stronger: *passion for life*. It was life that I sought, that I wanted: life; it illuminated me and slipped from my hands every evening, every evening, when I thought to *grasp something* of the secret of life, of the reason of our life, *this* at least; then art took possession of it (with me as medium) and stole the answer from me— and I remained, afterwards as if emerging from a hallucination, exhausted and alone, and with an irrepressible strength that the next day made me resume my war, and my defeat—! Ah! Who will give me back that grief of those days!" Suddenly, in "the tinsel of the *theatrical word*," Duse had heard d'Annunzio's voice, "sweet and sadder than love itself [. . .] and then my soul was lost—and still I haven't found it again!" Duse followed this confession with an apology to Papini. "I blush for having written you, (lately) a letter so coarse—disordered [. . .] I spoke like a *prima donna*."

The best example of Duse's taste in film and of her own screenwriting gifts was revealed in a letter she wrote to Enrichetta describing a visit she made to Boito in the fall of 1916. Boito had asked Duse to pick up a photograph and letter and deliver it to her lawyer and Boito's old friend, Giovanni Rosadi, who lived in Florence. Almost as if she were a camera recording the event, Duse presented a portrait of her former lover. She arrived at Boito's familiar house in Milan at five on a mild September afternoon. At his door, she saw his dog, a black-and-white setter, hot and miserable inside a small cage. She rang the bell and waited, sympathizing with the trapped dog. At the door, Boito, then seventy-four, didn't notice the suffering dog and barely acknowledged her presence. For half an hour, Duse sat in Boito's study while he finished the letter at his desk. Paying no attention to her, Boito argued with his servant, who refused to find a piece of string that Boito wanted. Then Boito searched for the piece of string himself, looking stoop-shouldered, confused, and old. The September light entered through the closed shutters, and Duse sat motionless, watching Boito, who seemed like a ghost. Everything in his house was closed and shuttered, with books piled everywhere. Duse noticed a portrait of her younger self on Boito's desk along with a portrait of Verdi. After small talk about when Duse planned to leave Milan, she said good-bye.

Arrigo Boito in Milan, c. 1916

HER PROBLEMS SEEMED trivial in a world ravaged by three years of war. An unusually cold winter and a shortage of coal forced her to leave her house in Florence and move into the Hotel Italie. She spent weeks in bed with bronchitis. By March 1917, she felt well enough to go to Rome for meetings only to find that the film company people "speak in another language." When Cines Film proposed that she make a biographical movie of George Sand, Duse rejected it. "Can you imagine me," she said, "with my hair in a fashionable 1840 headband, sitting between Alfred de Musset and Frédéric Chopin—those monstrous . . . louts!"

Unemployment and food rationing brought on by poor harvests had led to bread lines and riots across Italy. In August, martial law was declared in Turin, and striking munitions workers were sent to the Austrian front in "penal battalions." That month, Duse visited the Austrian front at Udine, headquarters of the Italian general staff. She traveled with other actors but refused to take part in the performances.

When she arrived at the Grand Hotel in Udine, she was greeted with cheers. Close enough to the fighting to hear cannon fire, she stood with the soldiers and watched a performance by a group of actors. She noted the soldiers' irritation and contempt. One bitter young man gave her a message to take to his mother in Milan. Duse took the train to Milan, delivered the message, and returned the next day to Udine. She found the soldier, who cross-examined her and finally became friendly when he learned that Duse had actually met his mother. Duse also had a brief reunion with the young soldier Luciano Nicastro, who had been given permission by his commanding officer to go to Udine to see her. What she saw at the front was "grotesque and magnificent," Duse wrote, "nobility and stupidity together on the loom of life."

During her stay in Udine, she learned that Robi Mendelssohn had died in Berlin. "I have lost an indescribable affection," she said. A month later she received a letter from d'Annunzio, whose patriotic odes and stirring speeches to vast crowds had made him Italy's most powerful propaganda weapon. The year before, d'Annunzio had lost the sight of his right eye during an emergency landing of his airplane. Forced to remain still during his recovery, he had written on narrow strips of paper, one sentence per strip. In just a few months, he wrote ten thousand strips and later published the work as *Notturno*. Promoted to major and awarded a silver medal for gallantry, as well as the French Croix de Guerre, d'Annunzio told Duse that he always carried three talismans: his mother's wedding ring and the two emeralds that Duse had given him. "No one has loved me like Ghisola has loved me," he wrote. In the war, d'Annunzio had found the mass audience he had always craved. He noted that "battle leaves in the sensual man a melancholy similar to that which follows great voluptuousness."

Shortly after Duse's visit to the front, Italy lost its greatest battle of the war at Caporetto, northwest of Trieste. Taking advantage of misty weather conditions, nine Austrian and six German divisions surprised the Italian forces. The Italians retreated in disarray. Venice was threatened and total military collapse was feared, but the British and French sent reinforcements. In early November the Italians held at the Piave River, near Venice. The loss at Caporetto was so crushing that today in Italy, the expression "It's a Caporetto" means a complete and utter defeat.

From Florence, "after years of silence," Duse answered d'Annunzio's letter. Fearing for his life and for the survival of Venice, she warned him to "be on guard." She wanted to travel to Padua and look for him, "but I can't," she wrote. "At *Udine*, I deluded myself that I was useful, and I seemed to come alive. But, now, after *Caporetto*, the anguish and the cold have thrown me down." She signed her letter "Gabri-Ghisola," once again linking her fate to his.

Refugees from northern Italy, particularly the Friuli area and Venice, poured into Florence. Duse sold valuable books and some of her art objects to help them. She went out every morning to be among them. "I have no peace elsewhere," Duse said, "—and all those people—I know them, I recognize them, one by one, since I possess their dialect, their speech, their silence, the turn of their thought, the hiding-place of the heart." She stayed among them, "not out of pity," she said, but because they helped her bear the emptiness of her own day. Also, in their faces, she saw that "indefinable something" and the past reappeared to her—"childhood, the cold, the hunger, a yard of a house, and my mother, poor thing, then—I can't say how—all becomes light in my soul."

Duse had found her audience again, and the necessity of making art pressed on her. "Illusion? How to bear life without illusion?" she wondered.

ON JUNE 10, 1918, Boito died. He was seventy-six. Duse had been expecting the news. Twenty-nine years earlier, Boito had sent her a glass prism that caught the sun's rays. She always kept the prism with her in remembrance of the light that Boito had brought into her life. Boito bequeathed Duse his desk lamp—both gifts a symbol of their intellectual love affair. Duse's grief for Boito, like her love for him, was primarily regret. She implored Enrichetta to love her children and not to leave them. "Love," she explained to her daughter, "is the sharing of the day and of the things of life."

The loss of Boito was a reminder of other losses. That June, on thirty-five numbered pages, a fragment of an autobiography, Duse poured out her memories in a rushing stream of consciousness written in the second person. "But the illusion of making an illusion that was yours, it's vanished, really vanished," she wrote. "Console yourself. Take heart. You will not struggle anymore for that anxiety. Now, all you have left is life, like a handle of a door, crumbling in your hand." She wrote of her childhood poverty and humiliation; she remembered the girl whose drowning she had witnessed; and she recalled the death of her mother, the birth of Enrichetta, and the years of struggle to create her ephemeral art.

She concluded abruptly, realizing that words were futile against the relentless passage of time. "Like this, in the wind, like this—you lost track of time which seemed immutable to you. The eternal in us was elsewhere—and you will not return, because if you return, at this time, you will be changed! You'll never be 29 again—you need to live, and you cannot return to the olive garden!—You have simulated on the stage, exchanging it for an altar, you simulated that which inside you dictated love, and turned around, simulating the life, and since this was not enough, also the death!" She would never be young again, but she could live and work again. "There is a life that is outside of reality," she believed, "and there is one who strives to copy it . . . good! That is for you, close to the reality!"

As long as the war endured, returning to reality, which for her was returning to the illusion of art, seemed impossible. In early 1918, Maria Osti had moved her family to the Villa del Quintiliolo, near Tivoli, a lovely hill town in the Roman countryside. She invited Duse to come and stay with her there. Maria had prepared the best guest room with a view of a waterfall, but the noise of the water disturbed Duse, and she changed to another room with a view of the mountains. After a month's stay, Duse returned briefly to her house on via della Robbia in Florence, but when she entered, "a feeling of ruin" pervaded her, and she traveled north to Bologna, searching for "a little bread for my soul."

During the fall of 1918, Duse moved between her house in Florence and Antonietta Pisa's palazzo in Milan. In early September, Duse learned that Tebaldo Checchi had died after a long illness. To her surprise, Checchi had left her and Enrichetta about $3,000 each. Finally free of the husband she had loathed, Duse was still suspicious of him. She asked her lawyer, Rosadi, to make sure that she would not be liable for Checchi's debts. The bequest was unencumbered, and the money was welcome. Still, in a letter to Enrichetta telling her of her father's death, Duse reminded her daughter that she had always been Enrichetta's sole support. Duse may have been a bad mother, but she had been, by the standards of the day, an exemplary father.

That fall, with Enrichetta as intermediary, Duse helped her son-in-law, Edward Bullough, compile an anthology of Italian literature for Cambridge University Press. Although Bullough held a lectureship in German at Cambridge, he had read Italian since he was a boy. An anthology was like a "tossed salad," Duse said, but she suggested authors, sent books from her library, and copied out poems. A few years later, Bullough resigned his German lectureship and devoted himself entirely to Italian studies. There's no evidence that Bullough was close to Duse or ever discussed acting with her, but in his most famous lecture, "Psychical Distance as a Factor in Art," he touched lightly on the actor's art. Acting illustrated, "as no other art can," Bullough wrote, "the cleavage between the concrete, normal person and the distanced personality." Almost as if she were responding to Bullough's thesis, Duse countered that when others spoke to her with haughtiness about "Art," she, "in her silent heart," replied, "Life."

Finally, after the disaster of Caporetto the year before, the Italians pushed forward on the Austrian front, culminating with a great victory at the Battle of Vittorio Veneto in October 1918. Through his rhetoric and his actions, d'Annunzio had been instrumental in lifting the spirits of the Italian forces. In August 1918, he led an air squadron of eight planes over Vienna and dropped half a million leaflets decorated with the Italian colors, red, green, and white. The message was clear—the pieces of paper might have been bombs. The daring flight made headlines around the world, and d'Annunzio, then fifty-five, was declared a great hero. Afterward, on leave in Venice, he wrote to his Ghisola that his airplane's engine had stopped briefly during the flight and then restarted. "I had the two emeralds," he told Duse. "The miracle was evident."

The armistice was signed on November 11, 1918. "This great page of history that all of you have written with your blood and your sacrifice is finished," Duse wrote her cousin Eugenio Duse. "Glory to you soldiers of Italy!"

IN POST-WAR ITALY, there was little glory. The industrial northeast had been devastated and needed to be rebuilt. The national debt was enormous, taxes were high, the lira was devalued, the cost of living soared, and the government, opposed by the radical wing of the Socialist Party, was too weak to deal effectively with the problems. Some 600,000 Italian soldiers had lost their lives in the war, and millions more had been wounded. Unemployment was at 10 percent, and if soldiers did make it home, they couldn't find work and were derided by socialists as "dupes of warmongers." Like a last, feverish convulsion of the war, the Spanish influenza pandemic raged through Europe, America, and the Orient, killing over 21 million people, double the number killed in the war. As did thousands of others in Italy, Duse caught the Spanish flu.

Since Duse had "no one of the heart close by," Maria Osti traveled to Florence several times during December and January to stay with her, until she, too, fell ill with the flu. To make matters worse, the rent on Duse's house in Florence had tripled, and she had to move out. She decided to move to Venice and began to pack her things. It had been almost five years since she had seen her daughter, and she hoped that Enrichetta and the children could join her there for a visit. An offer to make a film in Naples encouraged her momentarily, but she couldn't make a decision. "I haven't refused it or accepted it," she said, "but it's something to think about, and thinking . . . is living."

Duse looked at houses in Venice and Murano, where her friend Henrietta Macy had a school for poor children, but prices were too high, "impossible for me," she said. The bequest from Tebaldo Checchi had disappeared, most of it eaten up by lawyer's fees. She wrote to Giulietta Mendelssohn about her investments in Germany, but Giulietta was strangely silent. "*I don't know* what I will decide to do," Duse said. "I live *hour to hour* hoping that nature will free me quickly!"

Worried about conditions in Italy, Enrichetta refused to bring her children to Venice and wanted Duse to come to England in June, perhaps for a permanent stay. "Enrichetta *insists* that I come and I'm so upset!" Duse told Maria Osti. "I kiss you—I'm so sorry to leave you! So far away!—I'm sad about everything." A lawyer friend in Florence agreed to travel with her as far as Paris. Maria Osti came to Florence to see Duse off. "Perhaps it's good-bye forever!" Duse said, her voice filled with emotion.

The trip to Paris was exhausting, but when she got on the boat to cross the Channel, the fresh sea air revived her. After the initial happiness of her reunion with Enrichetta and her grandchildren, Duse endured, rather than enjoyed, her visit to the Bullough home in Cambridge. Duse felt uncomfortable in Enrichetta's regimented, proper world and longed for solitude and freedom. Although Edward Halley, nine, and Eleonora Illaria, seven, knew she was an actor, Enrichetta wouldn't allow them to tell anyone that they were Eleonora Duse's grandchildren. "Descending from a diva was nothing to be proud of," Enrichetta had taught them. They never saw Duse act onstage, but the children had seen *Cenere* and were frightened by her screen presence. Edward and Eleonora didn't speak Italian or French, were busy with their summer activities, and intimidated by their Italian *nonna*, who caught a cold and spent most of her time wrapped in a shawl by the fire. Every day, Duse would say, "I'd better go now." She occupied herself by reading and writing letters to Maria Osti, Helen Mackay, and Antonietta Pisa. Even in summer, the chill and wind of Cambridge oppressed her. "During the day I am stupid with fatigue," she wrote Mackay. "It's impossible to feel free living in my daughter's house."

"Perhaps our too orderly life wearied her," recalled her granddaughter. Also, according to Eleonora Illaria (later Sister Mary Mark), Duse strongly disapproved of Enrichetta's plan that both of her children enter religious orders. Enrichetta "took" Duse to church while she was in Cambridge, but Duse didn't believe in organized religion. She had occasionally attended meetings of the Theosophical Society in Rome with Maria Osti. The mysticism of Theosophy and the idea of a spiritual reality uniting all beliefs, a kind of all-encompassing unity, attracted Duse, but her religion had always been art and the stage her altar. Earlier that year, in February 1919, like Joan of Arc's saints, some of Duse's characters, all Ibsen's women, had appeared to her in a dream. "I saw them, calm (*they* were), around me—and they said to me: '*from us* you withdrew yourself!'"

Terribly homesick, Duse also worried about the current political controversy swirling around d'Annunzio. At the peace talks in Versailles, President Woodrow Wilson opposed the territorial agreements that the Allies had made with Italy before the United States entered the war. Wilson, along with England and the other Allies, supported Yugoslavia, who asked that the important port of Fiume (now Rijeka) on the Adriatic coast, currently occupied by Italian troops and a large Italian population, be excluded from Italy's territorial claims. Furious with the Allies for their "bad faith," d'Annunzio inflamed popular opinion in Italy and outraged the Allies with a series of stirring speeches, declaring, "The Italians should not yield as much as a fingernail." Enrichetta didn't approve of her mother's ties with a man she considered an incarnation of the devil himself. Divided by politics, country, religion, language, and personality as well as the ever present "stain" of Tebaldo Checchi, Duse and Enrichetta agreed it would be best if Duse returned to Italy to live.

Duse spent six weeks in Cambridge, but she told Maria Osti it felt like years. On her way home, she saw Helen Mackay briefly in London. Duse wore a hat and covered her face with several veils, and Helen thought she looked older, as "if sadness had molded her face." After several distraught letters from Duse, Maria Osti left her family and traveled from Rome to the French border to meet Duse's train. She waited for hours in a dark and dingy station until the train arrived sometime after midnight. Maria went with Duse to a retreat near Bergamo. They rested for a few days before traveling on to Asolo, where Duse had decided to make her home, and where she planned to be buried. "I like the stones of that corner of the world," she said.

NORTHWEST OF VENICE in the foothills of the Dolomites—"One step just from sea to land," wrote Robert Browning—the tiny stone-walled town of Asolo was a corner of the world that Duse had known as a child. Nearby, to the south, were Vicenza, her mother's birthplace, and Padua, where her grandfather Luigi had built his theatre. Majestic Mount Grappa, which turned to flame in the fall; the mild climate and fresh air; the cheaper living expenses—all drew her to Asolo. When she arrived, she stayed at the Albergo Sole in a white and blue room, which became known as the Eleonora Duse room. Soon, her friends Lucia and Pierin Casale, who had a villa in Asolo, invited her to stay with them. Their house was charming, and they made Duse feel welcome and loved. "They're good people without being geniuses," Duse said, "because people of genius are dangerous."

Meanwhile, across the Adriatic, on September 12, 1919, Gabriele d'Annunzio led about twenty-five hundred men into Fiume and raised the Italian flag. "I have risked all, I have accomplished all, I have gained all," d'Annunzio wrote to Benito Mussolini, whose fascists were challenging the government. "I am master of Fiume . . . What about your promises?" he asked Mussolini. "At least prick that belly which weighs you down, let some of the air out. Otherwise I shall make my way there when I have consolidated my power here. But I shall not deign to look you in the face." D'Annunzio commanded his city-state of Fiume like a forward-thinking Renaissance prince—a character of his own invention. He proposed a liberal charter of universal suffrage, freedom of the press, schools free of propaganda and devoted to art and music, yet at the same time he and his men indulged in cocaine and sexual orgies. Duse followed d'Annunzio's exploits in the press, but her own affairs and financial worries consumed her.

Except for a short telegram sending a greeting, she hadn't had any news or any information from Giulietta Mendelssohn about her investments in Germany. Duse wrote asking for news and begged Giulietta to send her money without delay. In late October, she received her answer in an *"atrocious letter."* Giulietta had known about Duse's affair with Robi. Their friendship "had died in her heart," and she never wanted to see Duse or speak to her again. Giulietta had only maintained their relationship for the sake of Robi, but now that he was dead, she didn't have to pretend anymore. The letter was "a

Duse with her lover Robert von Mendelssohn
and his wife Giulietta, 1909

great blow to my heart," Duse told Maria Osti. "But perhaps it's my fault! If I had remained under the dear protection of *il Santo, none* of the world's evil could have stained me! None of it! But now, far from the only light of my life, I can't read the hearts of others and I have experienced and done evil, *without wanting to.*"

Duse had idealized her romance with Robi and rationalized her actions. Giulietta's anger had exposed her relationship with Robi for what it was—a shabby affair and a deception of a dear friend. "If I am as she says I am," Duse said, "then I'm lost." Duse appealed to Giulietta's son, Francesco, who answered her with affection and promised to help with obtaining her funds. Duse apologized to him for her years of solitude and silence and for appearing "insincere, strange and venal." A year later, Duse had a joyous secret reunion with Eleonora, Giulietta and Robi's daughter. The Mendelssohn children forgave her, but Giulietta, her friend for over thirty years, never did.

To comfort herself, as she had done all her life, Duse wrote letter after letter. "Thank you for believing in me," she wrote Helen Mackay. Without explaining the reason for Giulietta's anger, Duse also informed Enrichetta that Giulietta had ended their friendship. The loss of Giulietta's friendship, and her attendant guilt and sorrow, overwhelmed Duse at times. "Not this pen, not this paper and pencil," she said, "nothing can help me shake this malaise of my soul."

She found some solace in nature. "It's a shame not to be able to stay in this peaceful house with the vineyard for wine and its vines covering the walls," she wrote of Asolo, "and the well with fresh water and a few roses here and there, along the orchard wall. Sweetness, goodness of the earth. And the trees, rendered golden by an earlier sun. To walk on leaves of gold and red, and the color of the earth. Life took away the dream and the reality of my soul. Maybe I'm already dead. But I still smell the sweetness of a flower, the scent of a tree, and feel that harmony when the sun appears at the dawn at this window."

And, as always, she escaped into books—to friends who had never failed her. She read with a pencil in hand, underlining and annotating, as if she were analyzing a script. Even the New Testament that she always carried with her bore the marks of her thoughts. She searched for new voices but turned again and again to authors who echoed her own beliefs: Dante, who urged her to find light in the eternal "Serene"; Shelley, who proclaimed that nothing exists but mutability; Whitman, who brimmed with empathy for all creation; Pascoli, who wrote lyrically of the mystery of death and the communion between all creatures; and Yeats, a kindred spirit, who believed in mystical visions and wanted to unite art with life. Duse had always rebelled against organized religion and "doctrinal intransigence," but she drew courage from Catholic philosophers such as François Fénelon, who advised, "Go forward—always forward; go forward without stopping and without glancing back." In the writings of saints, who combined faith with action and had transporting visions, she found a paradigm for her own journey and experience. *Revelations of Divine Love,* by fourteenth-century anchorite Julian of Norwich, was a particular favorite of Duse's. Julian wrote in homely images of a mother-Christ and reveled in the ecstasy of full humanity in God's love. From this book, Duse took a sentence, which she often repeated: "All will be well, and all will be well, and every kind of thing will be well."

WHEN SNOW APPEARED on Mount Grappa, Duse decided to move south to spend the winter with Maria Osti in Tivoli. She also wanted to talk to her lawyer, Rosadi, about renewing her theatre contacts in Rome in the hope of finding work. She arrived by sleeping coach in Rome in late November 1919. She brought with her the "brutal letter" from Giulietta so that she and Maria could read it together.

Soon after her arrival, Duse became gravely ill. During her visits to the front, she had contracted malaria, which was complicated by bronchial pneumonia. For five months, in addition to taking care of her own family in a villa without electricity or telephone and heated by wood-burning stoves, Maria Osti acted as Duse's nurse, even giving her injections. Duse was not a good patient. Tivoli was beautiful but isolated, and Duse worried constantly about money and longed to return to work.

Hoping to resolve Duse's problems, Maria found an apartment with a terrace and a beautiful view in Piazza Sallustio in Rome, moved Duse's belongings from Florence, and offered to pay the rent, since Maria's own family would use the apartment as well. Everything was settled, but on the morning Duse planned to move to Rome, instead of talking to Maria, she sat in her bedroom and wrote a long letter explaining that she could not accept Maria's generous offer. She was leaving for Florence and then to Asolo. She thanked Maria for her pure friendship, her patience, and her financial help, but she neglected to apologize for not having let Maria know sooner. Almost as if she were awakening from a long sleep, Duse shook herself and realized that she had to make her own way. "No one is alone in the world," she told Maria, "and *we must* be responsible not passive."

"Her letter opened my eyes to her truth," Maria said. She realized that Duse's "great destiny" was outside logic. Maria overcame any anger she felt, and the women remained close friends, but Duse no longer needed Maria in the same way. In fact, Maria had been replaced by another "friendship of the heart." After spending the war years in Vienna, forty-three-year-old Désirée von Wertheimstein was returning to Italy, where she wanted to live and "to share with me a life of work," Duse said. Unmarried and independent Désirée was free to travel and submit to Duse's schedule.

Duse and Désirée spent the summer in Asolo. At first, they stayed at the Albergo Sole. Then Countess Edith Rucellai, the daughter of Duse's old friend Katherine de Kay Bronson, invited her to move into her villa in Asolo. Called "La Mura," the house was ivy-covered and charming. Robert Browning had stayed there, and while it was run-down, it was rent-free. Still, Duse was tired of being a guest and wanted her own things around her. That fall, she rented a house—"very humble and Franciscan"—on via Canova by the beautiful arch of Saint Caterina. She furnished her bedroom with her wide peasant bed stacked with her favorite books. As usual, there were no mirrors, no photographs of herself, just her brass Libra balance and her pictures of Shelley, Beethoven, Ibsen, and Shakespeare. On clear days, from the garden balcony, she could see Venice. With a home of her own and the "dear and faithful" Désirée to attend to her, Duse, then sixty-two, felt free to navigate her life again, just waiting "for a gust of wind to fill my sails!!"

WANTING TO RETURN to work and finding the means to do so were two different things. "Why not come to America?" her old friend Yvette Guilbert suggested. "You will always find something to do with me. Come!" Duse thought about it. A theatre in Holland had invited her to guest star with their company. She tentatively said yes, then no. Producers in Paris contacted her. "These stupid people asked me to do the old plays of my youth," Duse said. They also advised her to color her hair and wear chic, modern clothes. "God forgive them their imbecility!" Perhaps it would be best, she decided, to stay in Italy.

Choice of a repertory, as always, was the biggest problem. She wrote to the playwright Marco Praga, who had recently published his memories of working with her on *La moglie ideale* (*The Ideal Wife*), and asked him to meet with her in Asolo. She liked his play *La porta chiusa* (*The Closed Door*), which had premiered six years earlier. She didn't like his advice that she revive *La Dame aux camélias*. She talked to her former acting partners Ermete Zacconi and his wife, Ines Cristina. "Maybe I'll find my destiny again if I go back to the Soul's reign that is Art's reign," she told them.

Virgilio Talli planned a season of plays in Rome with a new, young company and asked her to join them. She accepted, until she read the contract and decided that it was too demanding and declined. She met with Italian theatre managers. "They cannot make up their minds where they want me to begin," she complained. "One time, it is in Turin; another time, in Milan; and then, again, in Rome. [. . .] And in the meantime, I burn."

In Rome, Duse met Silvio D'Amico, an ambitious young critic, who wanted to create an Italian national theatre to produce the work of young Italian playwrights. It was not a propitious time to create a new theatre. Caught between socialists and fascists, the weak government presided over a country filled with strikes and violence. When Prime Minister Giolitti ordered an Italian warship to fire on d'Annunzio to dislodge him from Fiume, nationalists condemned Giolitti, and his government was thrown out of office. After his expulsion from Fiume, d'Annunzio, the only national figure who threatened Mussolini's power, had retreated to a villa in Gardone Riviera and devoted himself to interior decoration and writing. Depressed, humiliated, blinded in one eye from his war wound, he wrote Duse that the heroic life had not brought him peace. He had thought of her constantly while he was in Fiume, but now he didn't think he would be able to bear her look. "I kiss your hands," he concluded. "*In my lost eye* is your image, and no other."

When he met Duse, the critic Silvio D'Amico was fascinated by her legend, which d'Annunzio had helped create. D'Annunzio had immortalized her beautiful hands, and D'Amico longed to see them. Duse usually wore a hat and veil over her white hair and softly draped, rather nondescript black dresses, but in stylish contrast, she often covered her hands with white gloves. When D'Amico finally saw her ungloved hands, they seemed like any others, but her voice was "stupendous." His first impression of her, though, "was not entirely good." While Duse seemed "intelligent, full of intuition and the enthusiasm of a young woman; she was flooded in a tumult of confused aspirations and contradictions." Duse flattered D'Amico with personal letters and notes, gave him interviews, and thoroughly charmed him, but she had no intention of lending her name to projects controlled by others.

D'Amico championed the work of Pirandello, whose plays he gave to Duse to read. Pirandello wrote the part of a mother who keeps her dead son's memory alive in *La vita che ti diedi (The Life I Gave You)* for Duse. She considered it for a time but eventually rejected the play. Aspiring playwrights sent her scripts and Duse read them eagerly, searching for her ideal writer. When they asked for her comments, Duse explained, "I hate to write about art."

Since she disliked crowds and couldn't abide cigar or cigarette smoke, Duse rarely attended the theatre, and she kept her distance from the men who dominated the Italian theatre at this time. Most of them shared Pirandello's casual misogyny and stereotypical view of women as either instinctive or idealized creatures. Silvio D'Amico, Marco Praga, and Pirandello viewed Duse with some condescension as a capricious, demanding diva, weak and indecisive, a role she played well, but Duse had her own ambitious agenda. While she gave lip service to the idea of a stable, permanent theatre for Italy and to promoting the work of Italy's playwrights, her art and her legend depended upon moving her theatre ship from port to port. It was her great bond with Sarah Bernhardt, who had rejected the Comédie-Française for a nomadic life as an international star. Duse knew, too, that the power of her myth depended upon mystery and the right kind of publicity.

Henrietta Straus, a reporter from the *New York Times*, happened to be staying at Duse's hotel in Rome in January 1921. Duse agreed to be interviewed. As Straus waited in one of the hotel's reception rooms, "an elderly woman, dressed plainly and unobtrusively in a black suit and hat" entered the room. "Her hair was gray, her figure mature, her face etched with tiny lines of pain." Straus didn't recognize the woman as Duse until she began to speak. "Then, by some miracle of the flesh," she said, "one became aware of only the delicate charm and contour of the cheek, the wistful eagerness of the eyes, the compelling exquisiteness of the voice and hands and gesture."

Straus also met Désirée. "Madame is so unhappy," Désirée confided. "If you could only find her a manager in America!" Duse saw Straus often, invited her to tea, took her to meet Olga Signorelli, sent her flowers, and even inveigled Straus to contact American producers for her. Straus received one offer, which Duse turned down. They discussed plays and writers. Duse wanted to act again in Ibsen's *The Lady from the Sea* because it was "poetic and not too much of a strain." Besides, she told Straus, "it will be easy to costume." Marco Praga was "poetic in spite of himself," Duse said, but she believed "there has been no great Italian poet since d'Annunzio."

After a "siege of pain" one day, probably a coughing fit brought on by Duse's persistent problem with bronchitis, Duse announced, "Life is terrible."

"Because you should never have left the stage?" Straus asked.

"Ah, yes," Duse admitted, "one should always fulfill one's expression."

AFTER WEEKS of indecision, Duse decided to return to the theatre in a short season with Ermete Zacconi's company in two plays. She would perform Ellida in Ibsen's *The Lady from the Sea* and Bianca in Praga's *La porta chiusa*. Duse liked the contrast of Ibsen's "play of the mind" with Praga's "play of the heart." Marco Praga and Silvio D'Amico advised Duse against working with Zacconi. Duse ignored their advice. Zacconi offered her the freedom she craved; they had worked together before in d'Annunzio's plays; she was fond of Zacconi's wife, Ines Cristina; and they had a genuine affection for her.

When she had left the theatre twelve years earlier in 1909, Duse had closed with Ibsen's *The Lady from the Sea*, and she would return with the same play, but in a completely new production. "I wish to play only the mother, the woman without age, the eternal creature, like Ellida," Duse said. Like Duse, Ellida saw life in images and symbols. At the beginning of the play, Ellida, whose baby son has died, has lost her way and pines for the sea. After she has been tempted by the mysterious Stranger who has come from the sea to claim her, Ellida freely chooses her own fate.

Accompanied by Désirée, Duse moved to Turin to begin rehearsals with Zacconi's company. Since the cast for *The Lady from the Sea* was small, they often worked at her hotel. Using her Larousse dictionary, various translations of *The Lady from the Sea*, and her books on Norway, which she had retrieved from storage, Duse fine-tuned the script line by line. She restored a telling line of Hilde's at the end of the third act that had been omitted by the translator. As usual, she took charge over every aspect of the production, including the scenery, rejecting some early sketches because they looked more like Lake Maggiore than Norway. She ordered her costumes in varying shades of sea blues and greens with foamy touches of white from Worth and Fortuny.

Immersed in rehearsals, costume fittings, dentist appointments, and business meetings, and under the pressure of the upcoming "fixed hour" of performance, Duse had little time for Enrichetta and her two children when they came to Turin for a visit in late April. Helen Mackay also traveled from Paris for the opening, and was dismayed when Duse didn't have time to see her. Before the opening, Duse went to Genoa. She spent a day looking at the sea, breathing the sea air, and meditating. Ellida was a sea creature, and Duse filled her senses with the sea and created the character in the silence and the solitude of her own thoughts. "I'm trying to forget myself," Duse later explained to Eva Le Gallienne. "That way, perhaps I won't be so afraid."

Unlike Adelaide Ristori, who left a detailed, moment-by-moment explanation of Lady Macbeth's thoughts and her acting choices as she progressed through the play, Duse left little written evidence of her creative process. Duse's working scripts contain dashes and dots to set off her lines, slash marks for pauses, strike-throughs for cuts, a sprinkling of exclamation marks, various inventive symbols, and once in a while a word or two, but since she created the character anew at every performance, what she was creating couldn't be written down. Duse believed *The Lady from the Sea* was "a symbol of the infinite," and she had to embody that symbol onstage.

"I shall appear before the audience with my tired, lined face and my white hair," Duse told reporters. "If they want me so, I shall be happy and proud. If not, I shall return to my silence." Duse's return to the stage was an exceptional event, and on May 5, the Teatro Balbo in Turin was filled to capacity and fragrant with flowers. Ellida doesn't appear until almost ten minutes into the play. The audience whispered impatiently, wondering when La Duse would appear. They heard her before they saw her. "A voice ringing with inexpressible music, as clear as silver and as soft as velvet, called out, 'Are you there, Wangel?' " When Duse appeared, the entire audience stood and cheered. "Viva Duse! Viva Italy!"

At a time when Italy was foundering in poverty and despair, torn by strikes and violence, with the shadow of fascism growing ever larger, Duse and her art represented Italy's greatness. "They all felt in that moment that during her long silence the echo of her art had become more and more intense," wrote F. Bruno Averadi, who attended the opening, "that Italy had realized more and more what she thought to have lost with Eleonora. They saw that she was not lost, that she had come back, and they greeted her with that passion of tenderness which we would feel and express if a beloved dead one suddenly returned.

"In one scene of the first act," Averadi recalled, "she was sitting, talking to somebody about herself, but with increasing hesitation and long pauses, as if she could not or would not find the words expressing what she had in mind. While she spoke, an umbrella in one of her unforgettable hands was slowly tracing designs in the sand, and everybody in the audience followed the movements of that umbrella, as if she were tracing secret words about herself which her lips would not speak."

Ovations followed each act, and the opening was a triumph. The distinguished critic Renato Simoni wrote of Duse's remarkable communion with her audience. The twenty-year-old intellectual and liberal activist Piero Gobetti, who would be beaten to death by a fascist squad five years later, called Duse a religious spirit imbued with the Divine. Afterward, Duse cried with relief. Silvio D'Amico came backstage, kissed her hand, and said that the play was "a drama of the female soul."

"No!" Duse exclaimed. "The drama of everyone."

Luchino Visconti, then fifteen, who had been taken to the theatre by his mother, saw Duse in *The Lady from the Sea*. Watching her, "I learned how one must act," the director said later. While others commented on Duse's intellect or her voice, Visconti shrewdly maintained that her art was based on "sex, what the old actors called 'guts' and the romantics call heart."

During her engagement in Turin, Edouard Schneider, Duse's future biographer, visited her at her hotel. He asked why she had returned to the theatre. "When I left, I never thought I would return," she said. "The war changed everything, everything was ravaged, all this ruination, and so far away from the action I felt in exile."

Praga's middle-class drama *La porta chiusa*, another play about a lost son, equaled the success of *The Lady from the Sea*. Duse played Bianca, who has had a son, Giulio, by her lover. The son grows up, learns he is illegitimate, angrily confronts his mother, and at the end of the play, leaves home with his real father. Bianca, despairing over the loss of her son, remains with her husband. Duse and Memo Benassi, who played her son, transformed the sentimental story into a drama about sin and redemption.

Maria Avogadro, Duse's dresser and maid, wrote Enrichetta to say she regretted that Enrichetta hadn't stayed for performances of *La porta chiusa*. Duse looked "so much younger" in her beautiful Worth costumes, Maria said, particularly the long, ivory robe that she wore in the second act. "She shakes all our little everyday lives," Maria wrote, "and in her anguish one finds so much anguish lived by all of us."

The company moved to Milan for a short tour, and Duse gave her final performance with Zacconi's troupe. Their parting was amicable. With Zacconi and Ines Cristina's friendship and support, Duse had gained the confidence to lead her own company once again. She hired an administrator and surrounded herself with familiar faces. Memo Benassi joined her, and she hired her former company members Ciro Galvani, Alfredo and Enif Robert, and Leo Orlandini. As her codirector and lead actor, she chose Tullio Carminati. Just twenty-six, Carminati was handsome, aristocratic, and noted for his spontaneity and grace. "I don't have a captain for my little ship," Duse purred. "Will you be my captain?"

THAT FALL, Duse went to Venice for business meetings and to finalize plans for her company's upcoming engagement in Rome. John Barrymore, who was visiting Venice with his wife Blanche (also known as Michael Strange), was staying at Duse's hotel on the Grand Canal. Years later, Barrymore told Robert Edmond Jones and Margaret Carrington, Jones's wife and Barrymore's vocal coach, about the time he met Duse.

"I was drunk, as usual," Barrymore recalled, "and broke, as usual. So I went to the hotel desk to get some money. I remember I had my letter of credit on a chain that was fastened around my waist. Riveted to me, it was. As I went to the desk, I saw a little old lady sitting alone in the corridor. She was dressed all in black—shabby black, I remember, and her gloves were black, too, and worn. She wore some sort of cloak. Her hair was snowy-white. I noticed in passing, the way you do, you know, without thinking—how still she sat—how alone she seemed." The cashier gave Barrymore his money and whispered, "You may be interested to know, Sir, that that lady sitting there is one of Italy's great actresses."

"That little old lady?" Barrymore said.

John Barrymore, who was inspired by Duse
when he saw her in Venice, returned to New York
to play his legendary, modern Hamlet, 1922.

"Yes, that is Eleonora Duse."

Barrymore walked up to her. "Pardon me, Madame."

"Yes?" Duse replied.

"You speak English?"

"A little."

"I came to say . . . I mean . . . I wished to tell you . . ."

"Yes?"

"That I kiss your hands," Barrymore said. "I would kiss your feet but I cannot do that in this public place. It would be my only way of telling you how great you are and what an ineffable inspiration you have been to artists all over the world."

At this point in his story, Jones recalled, Barrymore stopped talking. Tears ran down his cheeks. "He brushed them away angrily but they still streamed down in a fountain of anguish and self-pity." Barrymore's response to Duse was not unusual. Her life and work inspired actors around the world, who dreamed of meeting her, clipped newspaper articles about her, and collected her photographs. After some moments, Barrymore controlled his tears and continued with his story. Duse had thanked him for his very great compliment. "You are an American?" she asked.

"Yes, Madame."

"Ah, America. The new world . . . You are perhaps an actor?"

"Yes, Madame."

"A very good actor, I think."

"A very bad one, I am afraid, Madame. But my grandmother was a great actress. She began her career on the stage when she was three months old."

"Ah! How remarkable," Duse said. "The American way . . . So—how do you say it?—precocious!"

ALTHOUGH DUSE had wanted to produce three new Italian plays during her first Italian tour in fifteen years, she could afford to present only one. She had known writer Tommaso Gallarati-Scotti for years, and they had seen each another at Udine. During the war, he had observed an old, poor woman praying desperately outside a church and had imagined her fate as a kind of mother's Calvary. After showing an early draft to Duse, she insisted, "the prayer is mine." Like the woman in his play, Duse, too, had once prayed for the life of her son, a *piccolo innocente* whom she had lost. "It's a prayer not a drama," Gallarati-Scotti said. *"Così sia,"* Duse replied, which became the title.

Duse had hoped to begin rehearsals in September in Rome, but she didn't arrive there until November. After traveling from Venice in "a pigsty of a coach" where the windows wouldn't close, she caught a cold and spent two weeks in bed. Maria Osti and her daughters saw her performances in Rome that winter.

To nine-year-old Luisa Osti there was nothing special about the woman who appeared onstage in *The Lady from the Sea*. From her white, disordered hair to her soft, flowing gowns and her expressive gestures, she was the same Eleonora Duse who had stayed at her family's house in Tivoli. Luisa was surprised that in the vast auditorium of the Teatro Costanzi, Duse's voice was clear and harmonious, "as if she were sitting next to me in an arm chair."

New York Times critic Carlton Miles attended the opening of *Così sia* in Rome on January 12, 1922. The Teatro Costanzi "was thronged," he wrote, "with monocled Italian dandies, officers in bright uniforms, women in evening gowns, American tourists, English tourists, artists, hangers-on of the theatre, members of the embassy." A well-fed, well-dressed crowd—not the sort of audience to appreciate a symbolist prayer or anything too provocative. The year before, Pirandello had premiered his masterpiece, *Six Characters in Search of an Author*, at Rome's Teatro Valle. From the moment the curtain was raised and the audience saw there wasn't any scenery, the muttering had begun. When the six characters entered from the back of the house, the audience chanted *"ma-ni-co-mio"* (madhouse) and *"bu-ffo-ne"* (buffoon). Afterward, as Pirandello left the theatre, people threw coins at him and derided him as "that lunatic Pirandello." The audience had continued rioting into the night.

The opening-night audience for *Così sia*, however, had come to honor Duse, and at first, they listened attentively. Set in an Italian village filled with poverty, violence, and despair, *Così sia* (translated as *Thy Will Be Done*) was also Gallarati-Scotti's and Duse's prayer for Italy. The action of the play is simple, and the characters emblematic. Duse played "Mother," and Tullio Carminati acted "Son." Characters named "the Cripple" and "the Blind One" pine for the old days when people were kind, wine flowed, and food was plentiful. The mother has a brutish, unfeeling husband and sacrifices her happiness to save her son's life. Years later, the son, an insensitive hedonist, rejects her. "There's nothing . . . ashes," Mother says, echoing Rosalia in *Cenere*. In an attempt to save her son's soul, she offers up her life as a sacrifice and dies.

At the moment when the son turned on his mother and began to berate her, "the excitement of the audience grew so intense," wrote Carlton Miles, "that it finally burst the bounds of propriety." From every part of the theatre, violent, sustained hissing and whistles broke out. The noise became so loud and disruptive that Duse and the other actors stood motionless. "Finally a few brave souls ventured applause," Miles reported. "This swelled to a point where it drowned the hisses and the play proceeded somewhat lamely to the curtain." After a long pause, Duse appeared with Gallarati-Scotti. The hisses began again. *"Sola, sola!"* shouted the crowd. When Duse reappeared alone onstage, the audience applauded wildly.

Maria Osti explained to Luisa that the applause was for Duse and the hisses for the author. Luisa was not convinced. She didn't like the play and hated the way the son treated his mother, but "after all, Duse had chosen the play, no one had forced her to act in it," she said. What amazed her most was learning that La Duse could make a mistake.

Duse, of course, didn't think she had made a mistake, and was furious with the Roman "barbarians" and with the critics, who attacked her "prayer." Determined to keep the play in her repertory, she told Gallarati-Scotti, "If it's not understood today, it will be tomorrow."

FROM FEBRUARY to May 1922, Duse played in ten cities, including Bologna (where she performed at Teatro Duse), Venice, Florence, Trieste, and Turin. Audiences loved *The Lady from the Sea* and *La porta chiusa*, but she cut the number of performances of the unpopular *Così sia*. To save money, she also had to choose between her leading men, Memo Benassi and Tullio Carminati. Probably since Carminati played the son in *Così sia*, she let him go. "My *heart is a rock*," she wrote Maria Osti.

Although critics had hailed Duse's glorious return to the theatre, her tour was not a triumph financially. Fear and uncertainty pervaded the country. Wealthy industrialists and landowners as well as conservative Catholics worried about godless communists seizing power. Black-shirted fascist squads, particularly in northern Italy, had declared open war on socialists. The squads had smashed printing presses, sacked trade union headquarters, and broken strikes. Factory workers and farm workers, allied with the socialists, feared for their livelihood and even their lives. Meanwhile, Benito Mussolini readied himself to take advantage of the government's inability to bring order.

Alice Rohe, a writer for *Theatre Magazine*, followed Duse from Trieste to Livorno. With little hope that the actress would agree, Rohe found Duse at the Palace Hotel and asked for an interview. Duse used her standard line, "You know, I have always refused to be interviewed," with the flattering subtext, *but I will be happy to talk to you.*

Wearing a dark blue silk brocade robe trimmed in white lace, Duse received Rohe in her hotel apartment, which had a spectacular ocean view. "I have never studied a more sensitive face nor have I ever seen eyes expressive of more sadness," Rohe said. "Yet her occasional laugh reveals a keen sense of humor. And when she smiles, showing her white teeth, twenty years fall from her."

"I understand that in America there are many very young actresses of real talent who dominate the stage today," Duse said. "I want to study your stage and meet these young artists who are re-creating Art. For me it will be a spiritual tour, a breath of new life."

After flattering American actors, Duse turned to American playwrights. "I understand that you are producing exceptionally exciting plays. [. . .] I am greatly interested in your young dramatists. Who knows but what one of them may write a play for me. [. . .] I am told that America today is really the land of the precocious, that every professional field has been practically taken over by astoundingly young people."

She didn't forget her devoted audience of women. "It seems to me that the American woman is the most respected and the freest in the world. I admire the freshness of viewpoint and the independence of thought and action, which characterizes these women. Of course, Italian women today are freer than before the war, but freedom as it exists in America—unconscious freedom—does not exist here."

Rohe didn't dare ask Duse about her relationship with d'Annunzio, a "tragedy," Rohe wrote, "more over-powering than any drama she has ever portrayed."

WHEN DUSE FINISHED the Italian tour in May, she went to Paris to talk to impresarios about engagements in Europe and America. She saw Helen Mackay and met with Yvette Guilbert, who was disturbed by Duse's condition. "I saw her ill . . . as though she were burning up her last embers, drugged, intoxicated by her recent triumphs!"

While she was in Paris, Duse talked with Sacha and Lucien Guitry and with Jacques Copeau about various possibilities, but nothing concrete materialized. She didn't contact her former lover and impresario Lugné-Poe, who was "surprised, hurt, perplexed, bitter" at the slight. Later, he got word to Duse that he had "suffered a bitter madness," but after long reflection he offered to place himself and his theatre at her disposal, and even guaranteed her a profit. Duse didn't respond. At a luncheon at Foyot's with Yvette Guilbert and Enrichetta, who had come from Cambridge, Yvette noted that Duse had transformed herself and "chatted gaily, and seemed to defy the possibilities of a sinister future."

"Oh, you should see Mme. Duse on the stage!" Désirée said. "You wouldn't know her, she is full of burning life!"

Duse also attended one of Guilbert's concerts. Observing Guilbert's young American students, who crowded around the singer, Duse offered her own views on arts training. "Do you imagine that you can teach your gift? Can you give them souls? No. Can they even comprehend yours? No. Well, then, keep yourself to yourself—give yourself only to your art, and not to them!"

"But it encourages them, Duse!" Guilbert replied.

"A proof that they are fools! For you are the most discouraging example in the world, Yvette! No, my dear; our talents cannot be taught, if one has not 'God under one's skin,' as the poet said, nothing to be done."

While she was in Paris, she also saw Francesco Mendelssohn, who was there studying music. Francesco reminded her of her beloved Robi, and they planned a trip together to Basel, Switzerland, but Duse became ill. Rainy, chilly weather brought on an asthma attack, and she spent a week in her Paris hotel room taking oxygen. When she recovered, she and Désirée traveled to Milan, where Maria joined them and accompanied them to Asolo.

DUSE MET WITH d'Annunzio at the Hotel Cavour in Milan in early August. She wanted to add *La città morta* to her repertory, which also would include Ibsen's *Ghosts*. Duse had made extensive revisions in d'Annunzio's script, cutting out whole pages of dialogue and speeches, and she even wrote new connecting lines. She asked d'Annunzio to okay the abridged script. He gave his approval. Duse later told Olga Signorelli that d'Annunzio exclaimed, "How much you loved me!" Duse didn't report what she told her old lover, but she confessed to Signorelli, "If I had loved him as he believes, when we parted, I would have had to die. Instead, I was able to survive."

Just over a week later, on August 13, two days before a meeting that d'Annunzio had arranged with Mussolini and Prime Minister Nitti, d'Annunzio fell from a second-floor window at the Vittoriale, his home on Lake Garda. Although he remained in a coma for three days, he recovered. Worried about his survival, Duse visited him. For years, d'Annunzio scholars have speculated about his mysterious fall—what d'Annunzio described as his archangelic flight. Some argue that Mussolini arranged the fall to rid himself of d'Annunzio and his attempt to reconcile the Italian left and right wings. Others (including d'Annunzio himself) suggested suicide or even d'Annunzio's drug use. In any case, ten weeks later, on October 27, 1922, thirty thousand armed, black-shirted fascists gathered in Rome to march on the capital and demand that power be given to Benito Mussolini. The next day, King Victor Emmanuel III asked Mussolini to head a new government. Mussolini compared d'Annunzio to a "broken tooth: he had to be eradicated or covered in gold." In return for Mussolini's gold, which supported his extravagant lifestyle and renovations at the Vittoriale, d'Annunzio remained silent (at least in public). Unlike Pirandello, he never became a member of the fascist party. In his memoirs, Prime Minister Nitti asserted, "If d'Annunzio had not fallen from the window and the meeting between him, Mussolini and me had taken place, perhaps the history of modern Italy would have followed a different course."

That fall, Duse again played Rome, and her new production of *Ghosts* was a hit. Wanting to ally himself with Italy's finest actor and d'Annunzio's former lover, Mussolini asked to meet with her. On December 4, precisely at three o'clock, he knocked on the door of her room at the Hotel Royal. "I have come as Prime Minister," he announced, as if there were some other role he could have chosen, her lover perhaps. Duse looked at his "hard face and jutting jaw," and replied with joking irony, "I am at your feet." Duse took his hand, noted that it was small, and also observed that Mussolini seemed anxious to please. He asked what could be done about the Italian theatre. They talked generally about art, and then Mussolini told Duse to submit a proposal for the Italian theatre. Duse never wrote a proposal, and later, when Mussolini offered her a pension, she refused. Duse did not overtly challenge Mussolini and his fascists, but she rejected all of his proposals and any attempts to use her art for political purposes. "An artist must work," Duse told Olga Signorelli. "I can still work and I want to work." She didn't tell Mussolini that she was working on her own project, which was contacting producers in France, England, and America in the hope of leaving Italy.

Ruth Draper, the American actress and monologuist, who was in Milan, traveled to Rome to see Duse play Mrs. Alving in *Ghosts*. Draper met Duse and performed for her privately. "Just to see her and feel her personality does something very strange to one's heart," Draper said. "You've never seen such suffering in a face, nor felt more forcefully the presence of an immortal soul."

When Duse learned that the immortal Sarah Bernhardt was performing in Turin and Genoa that fall, she asked Enif Robert to take Bernhardt two hundred roses. Duse had seen Bernhardt for the first time in Turin forty years earlier, and had been liberated by Bernhardt's pioneering example. Enif delivered the roses. When Bernhardt learned that Duse was not there, she said, "Oh, too bad! I'm truly desolate."

"If we had met," Duse told Enif later, "she would have nonchalantly said, 'I lost a leg, and you, what have you lost? And I would have said, 'a lung.' "

Bernhardt's appearance in Turin, acting in *Daniel*, a play, she said, that was "nothing but *merde, merde, merde*," was her final performance onstage. She returned to Paris. On March 26, 1923, she died in her son's arms.

Duse's Italian tour continued as a critical success and a financial disaster. Because of the political and economic instability in Italy, theatre audiences were sparse and traveling was difficult and expensive. Unable to pay her company, Duse wrote to Katherine Onslow, a fifty-year-old, unmarried, wealthy Englishwoman who had been her fan for years and often sent her flowers. "I'm nothing other than an artist who's looking for a way to save her ship," Duse said. She asked bluntly for a loan of "between 600 or 700 lire sterling," which she would return in one year. "Pardon me," she said, "but I'm not well, I'm confined to bed but I desire an immediate response. We're in rough seas—words are useless and my life is very cruel."

In less than two weeks, Duse received two checks from Onslow. "Now, the only thing that I can assure you," Duse told Onslow, "I want to *work* with all my strength." She used one check to pay her outstanding debts and her company's salaries, and the other one she kept in reserve. She also asked Onslow to use her English bank to find out what had happened to her savings in Berlin, and she directed the Mendelssohn Bank to send the money to Onslow. The bank sent Onslow a check for 300,000 marks, which because of inflation was "worth Threepence!" Duse's earnings, the $20,000 she had brought back from her 1907–8 South American tour and had given to Robi to invest, were completely wiped out. Onslow gave the check to a furious Enrichetta, who burned it. Enrichetta suspected that the German bank had actually transferred funds to Switzerland before the war and had cheated her mother out of the money she had saved for her old age.

Through the efforts of Gabrielle Enthoven, an English friend of Katherine Onslow's, London producer Sir Charles Cochran asked Duse to play six matinees at his New Oxford Theatre in June. Duse quickly recovered her health. She sent Onslow her travel plans and thanked her. "Your confidence gives me the courage and the will to work."

TRAVELING SLOWLY to allow Duse time to rest, Duse and Désirée went first to Milan and then to Paris. Charles Cochran and his wife, Evelyn, met them in Paris and accompanied them on the boat train to London. "Duse abandoned herself almost like a child to be taken care of," Evelyn recalled.

All six of her London matinees, scheduled two per week, were sold out. Her old friend Lucien Guitry and his company played the evening performances at the New Oxford Theatre. Cochran made every effort, including the installation of oxygen tanks backstage, to make his star feel comfortable. Flowers and cards filled her dressing room. Ellen Terry, elderly but still vigorous, attended the opening of *The Lady from the Sea* with her daughter Edy. Terry brought Duse flowers, which Duse used in the play, and afterward the two old friends embraced in Duse's dressing room.

Knowing that this might be their last chance to see Duse, actors snapped up many of the tickets, and a whole generation of young actors saw her for the first time during this London run. Nineteen-year-old John Gielgud stood at the back of the packed theatre during *Ghosts*. He didn't understand the play, and thought Duse in her black shawl looked more like a Spanish empress than a Norwegian mother. "What impressed me the most," he said, "was the tremendous reception the audience gave her, their breathless silence during the performance."

Eva Le Gallienne, then twenty-four, sat on the floor of the front-row aisle at a performance of *Così sia* and experienced a religious ecstasy. "She seemed to me the embodiment of Pity—Compassion—Understanding—like Christ," Le Gallienne wrote. "I felt that as Peter & John followed Him—so would I follow Her." Afterward, she sent Duse flowers and asked to see her. Duse sent a note thanking her for the flowers but regretting that "today impossible—perhaps tomorrow."

Forty-one-year-old Sybil Thorndike had a more analytical response to Duse's performances. "Because acting is the common art of mankind, because every man, woman and child is able to act, more or less, I believe it is the most difficult art to achieve perfection." She called Duse "the perfect actress—her art so controlled that her spirit could soar free; and it is in the spirit that an actress becomes great and universal as distinct from the superb technical performer." While Bernhardt "followed a tradition—followed it superbly and with perfect artistry, Duse was a revolutionary in her art," Thorndike said. "She found new ways, discovered fresh paths of invention." As Mrs. Alving in *Ghosts*, Thorndike observed, Duse had "a touch of comedy" and a "bitter irony" that heightened the tragedy. In *The Lady from the Sea*, "how different she was—how tender and wistful . . . with hair quite gray and face with no touch of makeup, she was a young woman." As the old woman in *Così sia*, she was "desolate and spiteful." Without a particularly melodious voice or great beauty, "Eleonora Duse had the universal spirit," said Thorndike. "She was humankind; that is why, to me, she is greater than all others."

The critics agreed with the actors. "What is there left to be said of her, except in poetry?" asked the critic of the *London Telegraph*. Her triumph, particularly the success of *Così sia*, which had flopped in Italy, elated and energized Duse. To live onstage again, to find grace and abandonment in art was "a great consolation," Duse said.

When Enrichetta wanted seats for *Così sia*, Duse balked at her daughter intruding into her world. "For whom?=For you? For the two of you?" she asked. "This sword of Damocles of these seats that you have asked me to buy for you disturbs me, makes me sick, and I beg you out of love not to commit an act of such blindness, for it would be an act against love—that act of overwhelming me with your presence!"

It's not known if Enrichetta bought her own tickets and went to the performance anyway, but after receiving her mother's strong protest, it is likely she did not attend.

Following the London engagement, Duse was free and could easily have spent some time with Enrichetta and her family in Cambridge. Instead, in July, she and Désirée went to Geneva to a hydrotherapy spa, where Duse rested for two weeks. She needed to build up her strength. "I've signed a contract for America," Duse wrote Maria Osti from Geneva. "I will leave in October."

DUSE'S DECISION to add *La città morta* to her repertory linked her name with d'Annunzio's, and the press rehashed their famous love affair. *Time* magazine chose her as the first woman to appear on the cover. "She set the Tiber on fire—" proclaimed the caption. From the Savoy Hotel in Switzerland, Duse wrote to d'Annunzio. "I am here because I have neither the strength nor the courage to return to Italy," she said. "To go back there, and this winter take up my wanderings again from theatre to theatre—oh no—I simply can't do it any more. I had too hard a lesson last winter. And so it's better to leave without turning back. Every morning and every night I beg my fate to allow me to accomplish what I have undertaken. I have signed a contract for ten weeks of Work in North America. I must be strong to carry this out—in any case, I must go; those who speculate with us, and do so in the name of art, use the word art as a card in the game they play with us."

Her lawyers advised her that she needed the money, and Duse reluctantly played several performances in Vienna in late September. She had asked Maria Osti to join her there, but Maria didn't have a passport. Instead she met Duse in Milan. Olga Signorelli made the trip to Vienna and reported that after completing a successful engagement, Duse drank champagne and was in high spirits.

In Cherbourg, Duse boarded the *Olympic* for the trip to America. Enrichetta and the children had spent a few days with Duse in Paris, and they said good-bye to her in Cherbourg. Among the circle of women friends who traveled with Duse were Katherine Onslow, Désirée von Wertheimstein, Maria Avogadro, and a new character, Bathsheba Askowith, a clairvoyant and mystic whom Duse called "La Russa."

Before she sailed, Duse spoke of her mission. "I should like to raise myself," she said, "through my work—and for my work—to the level of the really great subjects—sacred subjects—to the very heart of the Mystery. The theatre sprang from religion. It is my greatest wish that, somehow, through me—in some small way—they might be reunited."

The *Olympic* arrived in New York on Tuesday, October 16. The crossing was "magnificent," Duse wired Enrichetta. Duse's twelve actors and the crew, who had sailed from Italy on the *Giuseppe Verdi*, would arrive the following week. Duse's impresario, Morris Gest, then forty-two, an important producer married to David Belasco's daughter, Reina, met the boat. Gest had been born in Russia, and Duse liked his Russian soul and his taste in theatre. Gest had

Stanislavsky with producer Morris Gest, 1937

also brought Stanislavsky's Moscow Art Theatre to the United States. Stanislavsky's troupe would be appearing in New York at the same time as Duse.

Leaning on Katherine Onslow's arm and followed by Désirée, Maria, and Morris Gest, Duse, dressed in black and wearing a large, black hat with a heavy veil, made her way through the crowd. When a group of Italians at the pier cheered her, she answered, "Viva America" and "Viva Italia." With their police escort clearing the way, they traveled from Twenty-third Street to Fifth Avenue, and then to Central Park and the Hotel Majestic at Seventy-second Street. Duse marveled at how much New York had changed since her last visit twenty years earlier.

"You have made the rounds—going out and coming back, back and forth, leaving without joy and the return without respite. Going around in circles— faithful and rebellious, blessed and scattered!" Duse had written in her little memoir in 1918. Once again, she had made a complete circle. In January 1903, she had left New York after a farewell performance at the Metropolitan Opera. To celebrate her return, Gest had planned a gala event, again in the golden barn of the old Metropolitan Opera.

After much discussion, Duse and Gest had decided on *The Lady from the Sea*—Ibsen's "play of the mind"—for the Met gala. Duse preferred to open with Ibsen, and it was also an appropriate play for The Neurological Institute, the only hospital in New York exclusively for the treatment of mental illness, which sold box seats to benefit the hospital. When the box office opened to sell general-admission tickets on Monday, October 29, the day of the performance, a line stretched from the front of the Opera House on Broadway, through Thirty-ninth Street and Seventh Avenue, and almost entirely around the building. According to the Met Box Office report, 3,867 people bought tickets. Hundreds of others were turned away.

Vanderbilts, Astors, Rockefellers, Harrimans, and all their society friends filled the boxes along with most of literary New York. Ethel Barrymore, Lillian Gish (who sat in a chair in the wings), Gloria Swanson, Rudolph Valentino, and John Barrymore represented the elite of the theatre and film worlds.

"Duse came on stage," Lillian Gish recalled. "She swayed, as if she were about to faint. Then something mystical took place. There was thundering applause as the audience stood up and sent its strength to her. She absorbed it, seemed to grow taller, and went on to fill that huge theater with magic." Afterward, the audience stood and applauded for twenty minutes as Duse took call after call. She admitted no visitors to her dressing room after the performance. As she left the theatre, a crowd applauded and called her name. When they wouldn't go away, she concluded, "They're waiting for the boy." Memo Benassi, her leading man, had been starstruck when Rudolph Valentino and John Barrymore came backstage to meet him. When Duse called him outside, "the magnesium lamps dazzled me," he said.

PRAISE FROM THE New York critics rained down on Duse like "an explosion of coconut grease," wrote George Jean Nathan, the acerbic critic and champion of Eugene O'Neill. Nathan derided the other critics, who wrote about Duse's soul. Instead, he extolled her work ethic, her sensitive mind, and the fact that she "made her body the tool of that mind instead of making the mind the tool of her body." Nathan agreed that Duse was a "mystery," but mainly because she had united all the critics.

November 1923 in New York was Duse month. Her company moved to the Century Theatre, a large spectacle house on Central Park West, where they played two matinees each of *The Lady from the Sea, Ghosts, La città morta, La porta chiusa,* and *Così sia.* Everyone agreed that Duse was wonderful, but no one could agree on why and how. What makes a great actor like Duse? critics asked themselves.

To be fully appreciated, a great actor needs a great audience. After the war, America had emerged relatively unscathed from the economic devastation

Memo Benassi, Duse's last leading man,
early 1920s

that had ravaged European countries. When Duse arrived in 1923, Broadway boasted 196 productions and more theatres than either London or Paris. It was a time of intellectual ferment and rebellion in all the arts. Influenced by the Yiddish Theatre on the Lower East Side, who performed Shakespeare, Tolstoy, and Ibsen; sparked by the Provincetown Players, who introduced the plays of Eugene O'Neill; and led by the Theatre Guild, who presented Shaw, Molnar, and Strindberg on Broadway, the American theatre came of age in the early 1920s. A new generation of actors and audiences had an extraordinary opportunity to compare Duse's art to Stanislavsky's Moscow Art Theatre, whose work she had inspired. The Moscow Art Theatre was the finest ensemble company in the world, with actors able to portray characters with a surface reality as well as emotional depth. Still, the company lacked even one great charismatic actor.

Lee Strasberg saw all of Duse's performances that fall and marveled at her technique, because she didn't seem to have one. Later, in his classes at the

Actors Studio, he used Duse's example to motivate his students. "Duse achieved a fusion of the inner and the external which we have not arrived at in our theatre," he told them. "The theatre will require the next hundred years to deal with what Duse represented in this area."

Actress and teacher Stella Adler, who studied with Stanislavsky, used Duse's technique of intense and imaginative script analysis in her classes. "The text has to be filled," Adler said. "The *real* play is in the actor and behind the words." Duse would have felt right at home in scenes with Adler's students Marlon Brando and Robert De Niro. "You act with your soul," Stella Adler told her students. "That's why you all want to be actors, because your souls are not used up by life."

To describe Duse's soul was beyond the powers of John Corbin, the *New York Times* critic. He lamented that "no future generation can know what it is we admire in the art of Eleonora Duse" because "her art lives wholly within, a thing of the spirit." Duse's art, which was as revolutionary as Ibsen's plays or Picasso's paintings, could not be preserved.

A writer's work endured, but "the actor vanishes without a trace," Duse said. "Therefore she must use her ambition in the service of the art form, the only way not to be futile and ephemeral." Duse wanted her art to take root in a new generation of actors, and for this reason, she kept acting, creating her art over and over again with her body, trusting that the family of actors would carry what she had learned into the future. Drawn by her legend, audiences felt and responded to Duse's overwhelming drive to connect, to make art *with* them, and to somehow make her art endure *in* them.

Duse had refused to see Gloria Swanson, but when the young Broadway star Eva Le Gallienne left flowers and asked to see her again, Duse agreed. Le Gallienne reminded her of a young Venetian girl. They met in Duse's austere room at the Hotel Majestic, which had been stripped of mirrors, photographs, and flowers. During a series of meetings, Duse taught Le Gallienne that fear was a form of vanity and gave her a well-worn copy of *Prières de Saint-Thomas d'Aquin.* She asked Le Gallienne to read aloud one marked passage: "Most generous rewarder! Endow my body also with splendid clarity, with prompt agility, with penetrating subtlety, with strong impassibility." They discussed Ibsen's plays, but mostly Duse treated Le Gallienne as a colleague, encouraged her, and allowed her a glimpse into her private world. Le Gallienne attended all of Duse's matinees. From her front-row seat, she observed there "was no hiatus between the thoughts and feelings of the characters Duse played, and herself as their interpreter. It was *one* process." Years later, Le Gallienne wrote *The Mystic in the Theatre*, a loving tribute to Duse. Le Gallienne believed that Duse's art was a combination of "perfectly concealed technical virtuosity" coupled with creative imagination, "the power of an astute and virile mind," and a body "which had been molded into a flaw-less instrument." Her success in New York filled Duse with joy, but she was especially happy to see all "those young faces" lifted up toward her.

Robi's son, Francesco Mendelssohn, visited Duse in New York. She thanked him for bringing her "refuge, comfort, and consolation." Buoyed by her return to work, Duse felt young, and she attempted to add a new young "character" to the circle of middle-aged women around her. One day after a matinee, as Duse and Désirée walked through the Hotel Majestic, at the ele-vators, Duse saw a young woman in her early twenties with dark hair and lovely dark eyes, a woman who resembled Angelica Duse and perhaps reminded Duse also of her beloved friend Matilde Acton. The young woman was Mildred Oppenheimer (later Knopf), who had attended Duse's matinee that day with her mother. The women stared at each other as they waited for the elevator, and then Duse asked (in French) if they wanted to speak to her. "And we sat in front of the elevator and we talked like old friends for a whole hour," Mildred recalled. Duse asked Mildred to find a book in French for her. The next day Mildred brought the book and some flowers to Duse's room.

"She invited me into her bedroom where she was breathing out of an oxy-gen tank," Mildred said. "In any case, she told me a great many things that astound me now when I think of it, that she would talk to a young girl whom she had just barely met." Duse told Mildred about her love affairs, said that she disliked the theatre and had sent her daughter away to live with friends, since she didn't want Enrichetta to have the terrible life she had had. Duse rarely saw her daughter, and later, when Mildred met Enrichetta, she realized this "was the cause for great bitterness and some neurotic problems" for Enrichetta. At the end of their talk, Duse asked Mildred to go on tour with her across the United States. "I wanted very much to go," Mildred said, "but as my mother was going abroad and I couldn't let her go alone, it was impos-sible."

Playing only two matinees a week left Duse a great deal of free time. In a public tribute, Stanislavsky told Duse she "was the incarnation of all the arts, and that she belonged not only to Italy, but to the world at large." Percy Hammond, the critic for the *New York Herald Tribune,* noted that Duse looked "apathetic" during Stanislavsky's talk. Duse adored her "Russian com-rades," but public ceremonies made her uncomfortable. Stanislavsky invited Duse to their plays, but she rarely went out in the evenings, and she didn't see any theatre while she was in New York.

She talked at length with the critic and author Stark Young. "Help me," she said. "You understand my inner force as few have done." She needed new plays. She had heard of Eugene O'Neill; perhaps he could write a play for her. "When she talked with you," Young wrote, "Duse used to come straight

Mildred Oppenheimer, Duse's young
American friend, early 1920s

across the room and sit near, her fingers sometimes touching your arm. Duse
obliterated and exalted you . . . and gave you at the same moment the sense
of being taken as no mere individual but as something in yourself that was
immortal." Later, Young told her about a play he wanted to write for her.
Write the play, Duse said, but don't talk about it, since "a work of art did not
exist at all before it was expressed in its medium."

Duse gave her final performance in New York on November 30, a rain-
soaked Friday afternoon. She played *La città morta* in front of a sold-out
house and took twenty-seven curtain calls. Morris Gest leapt onto the stage
and kissed her hand and then her cheek "with a great smacking kiss."

DUSE AND HER COMPANY left for Boston the next day. To address her fear
of catching cold and to combat backstage drafts, Gest had a portable dressing

room built for her, which could be placed in the wings. In Boston, Duse played *Ghosts* and *Così sia* to sold-out houses at the huge Boston Opera House. In one matinee, she earned more than she'd received during an entire week twenty years earlier. Duse's smile at the curtain calls of *Così sia* "was more moving than any moment in the drama," wrote the critic of the *Boston Globe*. Theatre critic Elliot Norton, then a student at Harvard, was most impressed by Duse's silence. "She held you," he said. "She never did anything that was in any way theatrical, but it focused your eyes on her, and it made you think there was something extraordinary in her mind and heart." There was no sign of ill health, Norton recalled. "She didn't cough. She knew exactly what she was doing."

The company moved south to Baltimore and Washington. After playing one performance of *Ghosts* to a sold-out house in a drafty theatre in Baltimore, Duse asked Gest to cancel her Washington engagement. Actress Josephine Hutchinson recalled that when Duse left the stage in Baltimore, "you could hear her coughing in the wings." On New Year's Eve in 1924, she opened in Chicago with *Ghosts*, followed by *La città morta* and *La porta chiusa*. Although Duse's American tour was supposed to end in Chicago, Morris Gest had convinced her to extend her tour for twenty more performances and to play California. Duse wanted to see Mary Pickford and some of the other actors she had watched on film. When Gest couldn't meet Duse's terms, she signed with the Selwyns and Fortune Gallo. Duse advised Onslow, who negotiated for her, "to be on guard, because I absolutely refuse any help that is not a result of my work."

Producer Fortune Gallo traveled with Duse and called himself "a slave to the lamp," since Duse refused to do any publicity. "To ensure that she kept each engagement, it required the services of a diplomat, strategist, page, nurse, and physician." Throughout the tour, Gallo recalled, "I was the first three and sometimes the fourth." Troubled by asthma (perhaps emphysema as well), Duse kept oxygen tanks in her hotel suite and in her dressing room. "She had no business making the tour," Gallo wrote later, but during the tour he pushed her to maintain the schedule he had mapped out.

After Chicago, the company moved to New Orleans. Duse had never appeared there, and her performance was sold out. In New Orleans, Duse received a wire from Eva Le Gallienne, who was discouraged about her own work. Duse quickly telegraphed back, almost as if she were consoling herself: "You have hope. Don't ever doubt yourself. You'll find strength in new effort. All will be well."

The company had a "rough crossing" to Havana, but they were welcomed with "open arms and typical Latin enthusiasm." Spanish-speaking actors had a kind of cult devoted to Duse. The celebrated Catalan actress Margarita

Xirgu, famous throughout the Spanish-speaking world, happened to be in Cuba. She idolized Duse and was overjoyed when she found out they were in the same hotel. She sent Duse white roses. Told that Duse saw no one, Xirgu devised a plan. To get to the elevator, Duse had to pass Margarita's door, so Margarita put a chair outside the door and sat, waiting. Finally, Duse appeared. When she passed near the Spanish actress, Margarita stood up and "bowed her head." At first, Duse appeared not to notice, but at the moment the elevator opened, Duse turned her head and looked back, which was all the encouragement Xirgu needed. She ran to her, fell to her knees, and kissed one of Duse's hands. Duse stroked Margarita's head and then vanished into the elevator. Later, when Duse learned who Margarita was, she invited the actress to talk with her. "Throughout the entire interview," Margarita recalled, "Duse talked of nothing but Madrid's Prado Museum. She remembered the names of the rooms and of the paintings of the great Spanish masters." Duse gave Margarita a portrait, on which she wrote, "Best wishes in life and art." Margarita always carried it with her.

After fifteen days in Cuba, in February 1924, the company traveled to California. They played four engagements in Los Angeles and three performances in San Francisco. Duse knew California from the silent movies she had seen, and the "soft skies, the beautiful sunshine, the fragrant groves" reminded her of Italy. "I am happy here," she said. "I could be happy here always."

Duse opened with *La porta chiusa* at the Philharmonic Auditorium in Los Angeles, where D. W. Griffith's *Birth of a Nation* had had its world premiere. In every city on the tour, Duse played in large spectacle houses more suited for opera and symphony orchestras than theatre performances. That Duse was able to sell out the house and hold an audience with straight plays in these huge venues is a testament to her technique and charisma. People had traveled from Arizona, New Mexico, and Texas to see her, and the twenty-six-hundred-seat auditorium was packed with many Italians as well as members of the film community, including Alla Nazimova and Charlie Chaplin.

"A hush crept over the house as soon as the curtain rose," wrote Edwin Schallert in the *Los Angeles Daily Times*. "There was expressed an uncanny feeling that something mysterious and supernatural was about to happen." When he saw Duse, "it was as if some legendary being had suddenly assumed form and substance."

"She is art," Nazimova said at the end of the performance. "She is inspiration itself."

"Genius Enthralls Throng" with her "Super-Art" announced the headline in the *Los Angeles Daily Times* the day after the opening. To critique her "Super-Art," the *Times* invited super-artist Charlie Chaplin, then thirty-five, to write a review. Chaplin wrote from an actor's sensibility with an actor's knowledge of technique.

> Eleonora Duse is the greatest artiste I have ever seen. [Chaplin wrote.]
>
> Her technique is so marvelously finished and complete that it ceases to be technique . . .
>
> Of course, the sum of these is the perfect artist: the simple, direct child soul; the experienced craftsman in technique; the heart that has been taught the lesson of human sympathy and the incisive analytical brain of the psychologist.
>
> Bernhardt was always studied and more or less artificial. Duse is direct and terrible.
>
> The climax of *The Closed Door* is in the second act where the mother learns unexpectedly that the son knows the secret of his illegitimate birth.
>
> An actress of lesser genius would have torn this emotion absolutely to tatters. Duse sank in to a chair and curled up her body almost like a little child in pain. You did not see her face; there was no heaving of the shoulders. She lay quietly and almost without moving. Only once through her body ran a sort of shudder of pain like a paroxysm. That and the instinctive shrinking of her body from her son's outstretched hand were almost the only visible movement . . .
>
> I confess that it drew tears from me . . .
>
> When she turned at last, both hands flung out in one gesture of utter despair, resignation—surrender—it was the finest thing I have seen on the stage. Through all her grief, her self-abasement, her contrition, ran a terrible irony. It was all in that one gesture.

Chaplin praised Duse's company of strong actors, the inventive stage direction, and the lighting. Staging techniques that Duse had used for years, such as actors turning their backs on the audience and entering and exiting unobtrusively or even blocked by other actors, "overwhelmed" Chaplin. In 1924, much of American directing was still in the grip of the "Ta-Da!" school of obvious crosses and center-stage speeches. Duse also used atmospheric lighting, which sometimes left actors' faces in shadow. "If we only could direct pictures as this play was directed," Chaplin wrote.

Duse played her other performances in Los Angeles and San Francisco to cheering, packed audiences and glowing reviews. While she was in California, she paid off the loan Katherine Onslow had given her. "One does well here in the softness of the Pacific," Duse said.

Duse wanted to add four performances in San Francisco instead of going on to Detroit and other one-night stands in the Midwest, but the contracts had been signed and the tickets sold, and the producers refused. "Hope to find necessary courage to do my duty," Duse wired Morris Gest. When Gest replied that Mary Pickford was making a special trip to see her in Detroit, and when she learned that her "Russian comrades" would also be there, she said, "Now I will go happily."

"THE GREATEST STAGE DETOUR ON RECORD," one reporter called Duse's train trip east to Detroit. Since Duse feared the cold and high altitudes, her deluxe train avoided Denver and took a roundabout route through Texas. When they crossed the desert, the huge open spaces frightened her, dust penetrated the double windows of her private car, and the heat was stifling. She breathed oxygen from the tanks and cooled herself with ice wrapped in a handkerchief. They arrived in Detroit on March 23 in a heavy rain that turned to snow and high wind. Before a wheelchair whisked her away, reporters caught a glimpse of Duse wrapped in a muffler and shawl, all in black, except for white gloves.

"I am dizzy and nauseated from my long trip," Duse wrote Morris Gest in New York. The Selwyns and Gallo hadn't treated her with "sincere and cordial kindness," and she asked Gest to meet with her. Emotionally depleted and physically ill after her California triumph, Duse gave a vibrant performance of *La porta chiusa* in Detroit, perhaps inspired by the presence of Mary Pickford and Douglas Fairbanks in the audience.

Duse told her actors they were in a country where "time is money," and she forced herself to go on. Since her performances were exceptional events held in large auditoriums, she played just one performance in the smaller cities. "Am suffering from nervous breakdown owing to fatigue and I feel ill," she wired Morris Gest from Indianapolis. "Sending you all my strength," he replied.

At the beginning of *La porta chiusa*, Duse usually stood, but when the curtain rose in Indianapolis, she was seated. Eleanor Lambert, now the grande dame of fashion publicists, saw the play in Indianapolis and recalled that Duse sat in a large armchair through most of the evening. "She was beautiful, with *moonstone* face and hair," Lambert remembered. "Her voice was like a bell, very beautiful and in her white robes with her white hair, the whole impression was silvery."

The next day Duse felt better. She gathered her strength for one performance of *La porta chiusa* in Pittsburgh followed by one performance of *Ghosts* in Cleveland before she returned to New York to play two farewell performances at the Metropolitan Opera. "Counting the hours to be back in New York," she wired Morris Gest. On Tuesday, April 1, Duse and her company arrived in Pittsburgh and checked in at the Hotel Schenley. The hotel was near the Syria Mosque, where they would be performing. After the little she had seen of Pittsburgh between the train station and the hotel, Duse called it the "ugliest town in the world." An unusual cold wave had set in, and during the five days between her arrival and the Saturday performance, Duse never left her apartment at the Hotel Schenley.

On Saturday, April 5, 1924, Pittsburgh audiences had limited entertainment choices. At the Syria Mosque, they could see "DUSE World's Greatest Actress and her company of dramatic celebrities from Rome." At the Gayety, they could see Mimmie Cooper's Burlesque Revue, or they could attend a hockey game between Boston and Pittsburgh.

Duse liked to arrive at the theatre early to prepare, and two hours before the performance, around 6 p.m. on Saturday, wrapped in a heavy fur coat, she went with Désirée to the Syria Mosque. Désirée had wanted to drive to the theatre because a freezing rain was falling, but perhaps because Duse felt the need of air after being closed in the hotel for five days, she insisted on walking. A huge building, the Syria Mosque usually hosted the circus, symphony orchestras, and grand opera. When Duse and Désirée got to the auditorium, the box office wasn't open and no one was there to direct them. As they walked around the building searching for the stage door, they found nothing but locked, closed doors. Finally, shivering and wet, they found the open stage door at the back of the building.

Duse's portable dressing room had been set up on the stage. She drank some brandy, and Désirée gave her an alcohol rub. Dressed in a blue woolen robe, she warmed herself at an electric heater. Perhaps Duse considered canceling the performance, but she didn't. Almost four thousand people waited for her to appear.

When the curtain rose, Duse sat in a chair with her face partly hidden by a bowl of flowers. The audience gave her an ovation. "Her vitality is gone," observed one writer. Critic Allan Davis, who had seen her play in New York, thought she looked ill. Her breathing was labored, and she coughed several times. Backstage during the performance, Duse urged the other actors to hurry and finish. In Act II, a scenery door refused to close, but when Duse entered, Allan Davis said, "neither door nor scenery existed." The greatest moment of the play, according to Davis, was at the close of Act III, when Duse said good-bye to her son. "With an ineffable, tormented, loving-kindness she wafted [her son] a kiss; then overpowered with yearning she stepped to him, and turning her face away held him close." At the end, after her son and her lover had gone, Duse was left alone onstage. *"Sola . . . Sola!"* (Alone . . . alone!) she despaired.

After many curtain calls, Duse said, "I can't do it anymore." Shaking with fever, she returned to the Hotel Schenley. To receive proper medical attention, Duse should have been hospitalized, but she had an irrational fear of hospitals because her mother had died in one. Dr. Charles Barone, a Pittsburgh doctor, was summoned to the hotel and diagnosed influenza. The women that Duse had collected from around the world—Désirée, her "daughter" from Austria; Maria, her dresser from Italy; Bathsheba "La Russa," the mystic from Russia; and Katherine "Santa Catarina" from England— acted as a round-the-clock nursing team. Because of Duse's famous desire for privacy, reporters left them alone, and they were able to keep Duse's illness out of the papers for the next ten days.

Duse's twelve actors, including Enif Robert and Memo Benassi, were allowed to see her for brief periods. Duse worried about her actors "alone, lost in the mists of Pittsburgh." She longed for the strength to return to New York, where she could get on a boat and go to Italy. "Ah! Asolo, Asolo, how far away you are!" Duse said.

She missed her Italian doctors and didn't have faith in the treatment she was receiving. Duse's Italian doctors had often prescribed a regimen of warm sun and fresh air, but there was none to be found in Pittsburgh. The unseasonable chill wind and rain had continued all week. "Decided improvement," Katherine Onslow wired Enrichetta on Friday, April 11. The next day, Duse felt well enough to send a telegram to Eva Le Gallienne, who was opening in a new play. "I am happy to find you in full battle. All will be well. All hopes. Tenderly." It was the last telegram Duse sent.

A week later, Dr. Barone told reporters Duse was seriously ill with influenza. "It is impossible to tell which way the tide will turn," he said. That night pneumonia set in. On Saturday, Onslow wired Enrichetta: "Relapse Condition Grave."

The next day, a cold and wet Easter Sunday, Duse received cards and flowers from friends and fans around the world. Weak, with a high fever and chills, she alternated between delirium and lucidity. Désirée had never left her side. Late on Sunday, Duse told her to go and get some sleep. Then Duse slept for several hours. Shortly before 2 a.m. on Monday, April 21, Duse awoke and asked for some coffee and a little cognac. Désirée brought them to her. "Afterwards she dozed," Désirée recalled. "Suddenly she wanted to sit up on the bed. I helped her. She was shuddering. I called Maria."

"Then fixing her gaze on us," Maria remembered, "she asked us what we were doing standing there. 'Get moving! We have to leave,' Duse said. 'Act!

Alice Boughton's photograph
of Duse, 1923

Do something!' Then shivering with cold, Duse demanded, 'Cover me!'"
Maria put a shawl around Duse's shoulders. A few minutes later, Duse bowed
her head and died. She was sixty-five.

DUSE'S PERSONAL DRAMA HAD ENDED, but the public spectacle continued. The Samson Mortuary in Pittsburgh took charge of her body. Katherine Onslow supervised arrangements. Before moving on to New York,
Onslow planned a private service at the funeral home without the company
members present. Duse's actors rebelled. They insisted on remaining with
Duse as a kind of honor guard. According to the Pittsburgh *Post*, angry words
were exchanged outside the funeral home. The actors prevailed and attended
the short service along with Prince Gelasio Caetaini, the Italian ambassador,
whom Premier Mussolini sent to Pittsburgh as his representative.

The company stayed in Pittsburgh for a week while arrangements were made. D'Annunzio grieved over Duse's death, but unable to miss an opportunity to tweak Mussolini, cabled the Premier. In the message, which the newspapers published, d'Annunzio called Duse's death a tragedy for Italy. "I beg that the beloved remains be brought to Italy at the expense of the state." Mussolini's reply, also published, said he would make the necessary arrangements to bring the body back to Italy at the cost of the state. Defensively, Mussolini said he had offered Duse a pension so she wouldn't have to leave Italy. Mussolini also cabled Enrichetta, asking for burial instructions.

On Sunday, April 27, Duse's coffin, surrounded by her circle of women, her actors, and Prince Caetaini left Pittsburgh and arrived in New York at Penn Station on Sunday evening. A crowd of more than three thousand waited at the Church of St. Vincent Ferrer, on Lexington Avenue, for the hearse to arrive. Sixty altar boys in the black and white of the Dominican Order chanted the offices of the dead as the coffin was moved into the chapel of St. Joseph.

Duse's body lay in the chapel for three days. Every day from 6 a.m. until 9 p.m. a stream of people paid their respects. "No one was allowed to stop for more than a moment," the poet Amy Lowell recalled. "I cannot imagine how many there must have been in the whole three days, thousands and thousands of them." At night, Désirée, Maria, and Katherine Onslow sat vigil along with the photographer Helen Lohmann and Eva Le Gallienne.

Duse and Lohmann had spoken of Isadora Duncan while Duse had been in New York, and Lohmann wrote to Isadora, who was in Russia, about Duse's death. "You know that Eleonora was to me the light and inspiration of my art," Isadora responded. "She was my Madonna my Beatrice the most beautiful of all. I never felt myself worthy to kiss the hem of her dress—and that she should have thought of me and spoken of me makes me weep with joy."

Early on the morning of Thursday, May 1, hours before the funeral requiem mass was to begin, ten thousand people gathered near Lexington Avenue and Sixty-sixth Street, and another ten thousand congregated at the Seventy-second Street entrance to Central Park. One hundred police reserves were called in to keep order. When the doors of the church opened for the mass, "men and women of all creeds and nationalities filed reverently in," reported the *New York Times*.

A bouquet of lilies and white roses tied with purple ribbon from King Victor Emmanuel covered the top of the bronze coffin, and a bouquet from Mussolini, with the inscription "To Italy's First Daughter," leaned against the side, along with flowers from Enrichetta and a wreath of palms from Duse's com-

Matilde Serao, Duse's friend and advocate for
over forty years. Serao died in 1927.

pany. Flowers lined every part of the church. Three Dominican priests offici-
ated at the mass. "In the middle, suddenly," Amy Lowell recalled, "the sun
shot a beam of light directly down upon the coffin from the high window at
the end of the chancel. It was like a symbol taking tangible form." The
"Prince of Tenors," Giovanni Martinelli of the Metropolitan Opera, sang the
Benedictus.

Afterward, the funeral cortege made its way slowly to Fifty-eighth Street,
where the steamship *Duilio* waited at the pier. Crowds lined the route throwing white carnations and roses in the street. At the pier, two priests offered a
final blessing, and sailors raised the coffin by ropes onto the deck of the ship.

With flags at half-mast, the *Duilio* arrived in Naples on May 10. A cloud of
black smoke hung over Vesuvius, and a hot wind blew. Civic officials, pho-
tographers, and reporters met the boat. Duse's first friend in Naples, Matilde
Serao, now white-haired and ill, waited as well. After a brief ceremony, the
cortege moved by train to Rome.

On the morning of May 11 in Rome, Enrichetta and Edward Bullough,
who had come from Cambridge; Maria Osti and her daughters, carrying a

sheaf of blossoming broom from Tivoli; Olga Signorelli and Dr. Angelo Signorelli; and many of Duse's Roman friends joined the funeral procession to
the Church of Santa Maria degli Angeli, which belonged to the royal family.
Mildred Oppenheimer, who had wanted to go with Duse on her tour, was
traveling in Italy with her mother. When she heard of Duse's death, Mildred
met the train in Rome and "walked in the terribly hot dust of the Roman
streets" behind the bier. Tens of thousands of people stood in the hot sun to
pay tribute to Duse. "The whole city turned out and lined the streets," Mildred recalled.

Representatives from Milan and from Duse's birthplace, Vigevano, playwrights and critics, and actors from all over Italy, many who had worked with
Duse, attended the funeral mass in Rome. Theatres and actors around the
world sent messages of sympathy. Ermete Zacconi called Duse the logical
product "of some three centuries of art, during which with patient, quiet
work, the family of actors comes closer to the art of truth." As the only
speaker at her Roman funeral, Zacconi, in a voice choked with tears, exalted

Laurence Olivier and Vivien Leigh, who were performing *Titus Andronicus*
in Venice, visited Duse's grave in Asolo, May 1957.

"Duse, who has fallen like a soldier in battle, giving her life for an ideal of art." Over 100,000 people filed past Duse's coffin, which by the end of the day could not be seen under a mountain of flowers.

Duse had wanted to be buried in Asolo. The train carrying her coffin traveled from Rome to Florence, where a group of artists as well as members of the English community offered their flowers. The train moved on and paused in Bologna, where more people and university students added their floral tributes. The train stopped again in Padua. From Padua, the cortege made its way by automobile to Asolo.

On May 12, a sunny, clear day, another ceremony was held at Sant'Anna Church in Asolo. The mayor of Chioggia spoke last, sending Duse "a greeting from your sea." At 6 p.m., after everyone had left, Enrichetta and Désirée opened the bronze coffin and said their final good-byes. Enrichetta recalled there was a smell of pine and balsam. A filmy white-and-black silk Fortuny veil covered Duse's white hair, and she wore a white linen gown. Next to her lay the glass prism that Boito had given her. The two women spent the night with Duse in the church. The next day, she was buried in the cemetery of Sant'Anna.

Set apart by a low hedge from the plots crowded with family groups, Duse's solitary grave, marked by a white polished granite slab inscribed with just her name and dates, looks toward the mountains and beyond.

Afterword

Enrichetta stayed on for a time in Asolo to take care of her mother's affairs. Désirée moved to the Albergo Sole, where she had stayed with Duse when they first moved to Asolo. Enrichetta "resented anything or anyone connected with the theatre," Désirée said. Enrichetta felt Désirée had been a burden to Duse and careless with money. Also, Enrichetta reported to her children later that "Venerata" (her name for Duse after Duse's death) had had a "physical aversion" to Désirée, and "couldn't bear being touched by her—such things do exist & are darkly but deeply rooted." Désirée had lived with Duse for years, and no evidence exists of such an aversion. Evidence does exist, however, in Duse's letter to Boito, of the physical aversion Duse had felt for Enrichetta.

That fall Mildred Oppenheimer traveled to Asolo to visit Duse's grave. She left a message with Enrichetta, and Enrichetta wrote to her hotel in Venice and invited her for a visit. "Her daughter was much taller than she," recalled Mildred, "and a madly religious Catholic."

During Mildred's visit, Enrichetta said she had some things to do and asked Mildred to dust Duse's books, which had just come out of storage, and put them on bookshelves. Enrichetta told her she might find money, letters, "goodness knows what, as bookmarks." Enrichetta left and Mildred began her work. "As I went through the books, I found many, many letters from d'Annunzio." Mildred put the letters, with the distinctive "flashy writing," aside in a paper box. Enrichetta returned and saw the letters from d'Annunzio. "She took the whole box and tossed everything into the fire," Mildred said. "I've always thought how crazy that was. But she was embarrassed." Mildred and Enrichetta became good friends, and later Mildred visited Enrichetta in Cambridge. Enrichetta asked Mildred to let her know if she ever heard about a film being made of her mother's life. "At one time there

Duse's grandchildren, Father Sebastian Bullough
and Sister Mary Mark Bullough, c. 1938. In 1968, Sister Mary
Mark donated Duse's papers and personal effects to the
Fondazione Giorgio Cini in Venice.

was talk of Greta Garbo doing [a film] so I let her know and nothing ever
came of it," Mildred said.

In 1934, d'Annunzio, then seventy-one, wrote Enrichetta and asked her to
come to the Vittoriale. D'Annunzio claimed to have seen Duse's spirit and
had been frightened. While visiting friends in Italy that summer, Enrichetta
went to Gardone Riviera. D'Annunzio's villa looked like the house "Lucifer
might have liked to have on earth," she said. Carrying her prayer book and a
bottle of holy water, which she held tightly throughout her visit, Enrichetta
walked through the rooms crammed with furniture, books, and objects.
"When I saw the room of the phantasm," Enrichetta recalled, "it was easy
to guess, that with his one nearly blind eye . . . certain lights have formed

ghostly shapes." The house had one beautiful room, however, "bare and whitewashed," she said, where d'Annunzio worked. Enrichetta noticed two photographs there. "One was of his mother, to whom he really was devoted, and the other was of my mother." Two roses in a vase were between them. In 1938, d'Annunzio died of a brain hemorrhage while writing at his desk.

Enrichetta continued the pattern Duse had set by separating herself from her own children. Duse had objected to the plan, but both of her grandchildren entered Dominican religious orders.

The year of Duse's death, Enrichetta placed her daughter Eleonora, then twelve, in St. Dominic's convent in Stone, England. "I was disobedient," Eleonora remembered. At first, she had hated the convent. For many years, the convent adhered to a vow of silence during the week, and she was allowed to speak only on weekends. Gradually, she learned to accept the order and discipline. At seventeen, she took her vows and became Sister Mary Mark, named after the patron saint of Venice. For thirty-eight years, she headed the convent school and directed plays. Few knew of her famous grandmother or that the blue silk dress worn by the Virgin Mary in the Christmas pageants had once belonged to Eleonora Duse.

Eleonora Duse, 1896

Notes

*Please refer to the bibliography for complete publication information
on the books cited in the notes. If dates and citation are given
in the text, they will not be repeated in the notes.*

PAGE

One

3   *Duse's hair*—At the Fondazione Giorgio Cini in Venice, the principal repository of many of Duse's papers, costumes, and personal effects, I was able to hold in my hands a heavy swatch of her hair.

"I was choked"—F, 246. In this roman à clef of Duse's love affair with Gabriele d'Annunzio, Duse's voice and her memories of her childhood come through convincingly and clearly. D'Annunzio, scholars believe, was a good reporter and wrote down Duse's words verbatim. I retraced Duse's walk through Verona from the Piazza Erbe to the arena.

3   *Alessandro Duse's story of meeting Angelica*—In Enrichetta Bullough's notebooks at the FC. In *Istoria . . . di due nobili Amanti* (c. 1530), by Luigi da Porto, which may have served as one of Shakespeare's sources, the feuding families are the Montecchi and the Cappellati.

4   "the words flowed—I must have looked"—F, 246–49.

5   "ecstasy of power"—Goldman, 15.
    "Art, like love"—ED to DA, V.
    "echo of the pain"—EDA. This short memoir was written by Duse in 1918.
    "transformation of life"—S, 1938, 286.
    "No!"—Guerrieri, 1962, 79.

6   "dared not define"—"Through discipline"—EDA.
    "the outward rendered"—G. F. Young, 81.
    "And it's *art*"—ED to Polese, Oct. 15, 1882, BU.
    "Who is it"—EDA.
    "The crossing"—S, 1955, 120.
    "passionate colorist"—CS, March 9, 1905.

7   "At last"—James, 39.

8   "No more Jew"—Markus, 301.

10 "doozy"—William Safire, *New York Times*, April 11, 1999, according to the etymologist Gerald Cohen.
    "almost as handsome"—James, 39.
    "My grandfather was"—*Enciclopedia*, 1194.

11 "Asino!"—Bullo, "Eleonora Duse e suo nonno," Venezia, 1897, 15.
    Travel in Italy—John Murray's handbooks provide a wealth of information about travel in Italy during the 1850s and 1860s.

12 "Where did you"—"tightly, tightly"—EDA.
    "magic gifts"—Painter, 52.

13 "Don't be afraid"—S, 1955, 18.
    "*frutto della colpa*"—Mangini, "Note sulla famiglia Duse e sul debutto di Eleonora a Venezia," Estratto da: Archivio Veneto Serie V. Vol. CIII (1974), 124.

14 "aimlessly from one"—EDA.
    "poor meal"—EDA.
    "I know what"—F, 238.
    "disheveled, laughing"—EDA.

15 "not seeming dead"—"to look, to guess"—EDA.

16 "always swooned"—Meyer, 230.

17 "infuriated action"—Carlson, 133.

18 "light snoring sound"—D'Amico, 1929, 56.
    "I would go"—F, 245.

19 "I remember the sound"—F, 237–41.

20 "Venetian seduction"—Symons, 1969, 37.
    "communicating a great"—F, 245.
    "Only my mother"—F, 245.
    "a great knocking"—EDA.

21   "desolate and dear"—EDA.
     "broken shell"—EDA.
     "always my refuge"—S, 1955, 44.
     "What makes you"—Ridenti, 5.
22   "It was because"—Russell, 93.
23   "but consumed on"—McLeod, 33.
     "paradise inhabited by"—Hare, 1883, 84.
25   "the beautiful Miss"—G, 1993, 159.
     "I had to act"—AT, 406.
     "She was an actress"—Pontiero, 1986, 26.
     "296 performances"—G, 1993, 163.
26   "Is it Miss"—"completely modern"—Ibid., 168.
27   "I am bourgeois"—ED to Primoli, Feb. 16, 1884.
     "bristled like a"—S, 1938, 35.
28   "used her elbows"—Grisolfi, 19.
29   "burst of laughter"—Banti, 51.
     "fundamentally good"—R, 473.
     "No one could"—Banti, 337.
30   "The actors showed"—G, 1993, 170.
     "The past is dead"—Bentley, *Thérèse Raquin*, author's preface, 516.
32   "When I must"—S, 1955, 49–50.
     "must live her"—AT, 405.
     "You have to show"—S, 1955, 79.
33   "I love you"—G, 1993, 175.
     "as one signs"—Count Primoli to Dumas, quoted in *Fortnightly Review*, June 1900.
34   "Save me from"—G, 1993, 175.
     "Speak to me"—"Seven"—G, 173.
35   *Baby depositories*—According to cultural historian David Kertzer, in his study *Sacrificed for Honor*, in certain cities 40 percent of all newborns were abandoned.
36   "sweet strip of sea"—Rolland, 42.
     "If I had lost"—James, 440.
     "Your salvation was"—EDA.
37   "dark, dark"—S, 1955, 37.
     "I turn to you"—ED to Cesare Rossi, Nov. 26, 1885.

Two

39   "alone and sad"—Checchi to D'Arcais, Buenos Aires, Aug. 27, 1885.
40   "some beautiful"—Dumas to Primoli, 1881, *New York Dramatic Mirror*, July 3, 1896.
41   "Imperious, manly"—*Enciclopedia*, 534.
     "beautiful, sympathetic"—Mangini, "Nota sulla famiglia Duse," Estratto da: Archivo Veneto Serie V. Vol. CIII (1974), 125–28.
     "slim, nervous"—*Gazzetta Letteraria*, Feb. 19, 1881.
42   "is equal to"—"La Questione della Donna," ibid., June 4, 1881.
     "I no longer"—A. Duse to Enrico Duse, May 1881, FC.

42   "la signorina"—Schino, 131.
      "a memory"—Ibid., 145.
43   "Art was my"—Ristori, 246.
44   "Tebaldo is full"—ED to A. Duse, FC.
      "It is today"—ED to A. Duse, V.
      "I can't wait"—ED to A. Duse, V.
      "an unfeeling man"—S, 1959, 33.
45   "The young woman"—EDA.
46   "People spoke only"—Jules Huret interview with ED, May 24, 1897.
      "What these royals"—Gold and Fizdale, 197.
      Comparison of Bernhardt and Duse—Duse, as Simone de Beauvoir noted in *The Second
      Sex*, could forget herself and thus go beyond herself. She was one of those rare, gener-
      ous-minded artists, de Beauvoir wrote, who "make their persons the instruments of
      their art instead of seeing in art a servant of their egos."
      "She came with"—Huret, May 24, 1897.
47   "No one knows"—Salmon, 59.
      "I do not"—Ibid., 59.
48   "In America"—Ibid., 170.
      "I won't write"—Ibid., 178.
49   "An artist without"—ED to Edoardo Boutet, Oct. 25, 1890.
      "one breathes the"—Barzini, 97.
      "Then I can"—ED to Somigli, S, 51.
50   "That's Duse!"—S, 1955, 49–50.
      "I must study"—ED to D'Arcais, Sept. 13, 1882.
      La Femme de Claude—Bernhardt did play Césarine years later, but with mixed success.
      "Kill her"—Maurois, 392.
      "resounding crazy"—ED to Somigli, Dec. 8, 1882, BU.
51   "I feel that"—ED to Gennaro Minervini, AT, 379.
      "artistic personification"—Luigi Capuana, "La moglie di Claudio," *Fanfulla della
      Domenica*, Nov. 5, 1882.
53   "strange"—"unseemly"—"Acting"—ED to D'Arcais, Aug. 4, 1884.
      "wiped out every"—ED to Polese, B. Also in AT, 390–91.
      "the last word"—Oreste Cenacchi, "A Proposito di un'attrice moderna (Eleonora Duse-
      Checchi)," *Gazzetta Letteraria*.
      "betraying some emotion"—"I need"—Ridenti, 153.
54   "dearest friend"—"If I were"—Serao to Primoli, Sept. 23, 1883.
      "was good to me"—Banti, 51.
56   *Duse's measurements*—Alexander, 115.
57   "always restrained and simple"—CS, Jan. 15, 1884.
      "still too much"—Verga to Capuana, July 7, 1885.
      "a phenomenal fiasco"—ED to D'Arcais, April 3, 1884.
58   "This window"—ED to D'Arcais, April 8, 1884.
      "Dearest Gueltrini"—CS, May 9–10, 1884.
60   *"Fiamma tinta"*—S, 1955, 73.
      "she was a modern"—"La prima rappresentazione," CS, May 4–5, 1885.

"murmuring resistance"—ED to D'Arcais, May 15, 1884 (approx. date).

"every excess, every"—CS, May 5, 1884.

"becomes the impossible"—Symons, 1969, 14.

"a little mysterious"—"sympathetic communication"—CS, May 5, 1884.

61   "symbol of feminine"—CS, May 12, 1884.

"Duse is the greatest"—CS, May 10–13, 1884.

"What do you"—Nardi, 519.

"You are not"—R, 5.

63   "something that *speaks*"—R, 6–7.

"reinvigorated—young"—ED to D'Arcais, May 15, 1884 (approx. date).

"I feel reborn"—Nardi, 523.

"With all the devotion"—Schino, 147.

64   "breathe the mild"—ED to Primoli, Sept. 4, 1884.

65   "When you are"—ED to Primoli, *Ariel*, 139–40.

"*All* the Roman"—Caccia, 222.

"good man"—Serao, "La famiglia di Eleonora Duse," *Nuova Antologia*, July 1927, 174.

"she didn't give"—ED to Checchi, n.d., probably around Jan. 8, 1885, V.

66   "theatrically coarse"—ED to "Luisa," an actress friend, Mar. 20, 1885, S, 1952.

"foremost in my mind"—Dumas to Primoli, Apr. 10, 1885.

"You can well"—Primoli to Dumas, Jan. 4, 1885, published in *Fortnightly Review*, June 1900.

"How the atmosphere"—Ibid.

67   "She didn't want"—G, 1993, 293. The entire letter of Primoli is published in Guerrieri, which includes the information about the miscarriage.

68   "There's Denise"—Richardson, 126.

"heavy"—"worth the whole"—ED to Luisa, Mar. 20, 1885, S, 1952.

"has broken with"—*The Atheneum*, 1885, 1:673.

"might have tired"—Primoli to Dumas, Apr. 1885, quoted in the *New York Dramatic Mirror*.

"I seem in love"—Primoli to Giacosa, Mar. 19, 1885.

69   "unsurpassed"—*Capitan Fracassa*, Mar. 16, 1885.

"You can't imagine"—S, 1952.

70   "trilling of the tenors"—ED to Primoli, *Ariel*, 142.

"What does it"—Schino, 178.

"Do you think"—Checchi to D'Arcais, Aug. 27, 1885.

"weak and tiny"—"I wept"—ED to Serao, Aug. 28, 1885.

71   "Dumas made Denise"—Briccio de Abreu.

"You see how"—ED to Serao, Aug. 28, 1885.

72   "times of triumph"—Briccio de Abreu.

"false friends"—Checchi to D'Arcais, Aug. 27, 1885.

73   "without Duse's craziness"—Schino, 183.

"pale and disconcerted"—Ibid., 181.

"decided to commit"—"No! Not with"—Schino, 181, 174–75.

74   "I look at your"—ED to Ristori, G, 1993, 65.

"Today I'm conscious"—ED to D'Arcais, AT, 385.

Three

75 "a sadness"—"When I am"—ED to Cesare Rossi, Nov. 26, 1885.

76 "Art—and determination"—"incompatibility"—CS, Dec. 28–29, 1885.
"phenomenal"—"half-Venetian"—ED to D'Arcais, Apr. 27, 1886.
"Rossi can't understand"—Ibid.

77 "the beautiful sea"—"How can I"—ED to D'Arcais, July 6, 1886.
"A great laziness"—ED to Giacosa, July 27, 1886. FC.
"not to confuse"—CS, Dec. 8–9, 1886.

78 "artist of genius"—Renan to Duse, Dec. 8, 1886.
"The success of"—Antoine, 78.
"by the naturalists"—Ibid., 3–4.
"Ah yes!"—Ibid., 80.

79 "My art belongs"—S, 1959, 52.
"on the personality"—S, 1955, 65.
"What a child"—ED to unidentified writer, S, 1952, 29.
"greatest power"—ED to D'Arcais, S, 1955, 68.
"Every evening"—Pierre Montera, "Luigi Gualdo, Robert De Montesquiou et La Duse," *Italianistica: Rivista di Letteratura Italiana* 11, nos. 2 and 3 (1982): 283–300.
"Of all the actors"—CS, Feb. 1–2, 1887.

81 "I cannot give"—R, 8.
"He has much"—Conati, iii.
"I am made"—R, 10.
"I feel the heat"—R, 42.

82 "I did the"—R, 73.

83 "three heads"—R, 151.
"I give you all"—R, 147.

84 Duse note to Checchi—Nov. 7, 1887, V.
"Where are you"—R, 63.
"She's so important"—Caccia, 224.
"a glance, a gesture"—*Gazzetta Letteraria*, Dec. 10, 1887.

85 "it seemed to me"—R, 153.
"We will take"—R, 157.
"Now is the"—R, 160.
"I feel old"—R, 170.
"You don't need"—R, 199.

86 "Asino!"—R, 201.
"One year we have"—R, 194.
"I know well"—R, 480.
"29 years"—R, 231.
"Your work can't"—R, 238.

87 "This morning"—R, 225.
"hated everything that"—Wolkoff-Mouromtzoff, 196.

88 "indescribable moods"—Fürstin Marie von Thurn und Taxis-Hohenlohe. *Erinnerungen an Rainer Maria Rilke*. Translated by Elke Neumann. Frankfurt: Insel Verlag, 1994, 58–59.

"fine and sensitive"—Wolkoff-Mouromtzoff, 271.

Il Castello di San Giuseppe—The convent is now called the Castello San Giuseppe and is a seventeen-room hotel, featuring guest rooms named after Boito, Duse, and Giacosa.

"The place is"—R, 253.

89   "It's true, Lenor"—R, 267.

"very tired"—CS, Nov. 18, 1888.

"Help me be"—R, 284.

"Do it your"—R, 282.

"the serpent of"—R, 277.

90   "didn't have the figure"—Vazzoler, 75.

"love, hate, fury"—Vazzoler, 75.

91   "inebriation of the last"—R, 290.

"all-wise"—R, 294.

"enormous, phenomenal"—R, 817.

"If you've ever"—ED to Giacosa, Dec. 29, 1888, FC.

"What do you"—R, 303–04.

"I love you"—R, 321.

"I have a fear"—R, 328.

"The heart of my"—R, 337.

92   "If you put"—R, 380.

"I would no longer"—R, 383.

"provided that her"—Wolkoff-Mouromtzoff, 281.

"Does he have a"—R, 387.

"I'm a *chierichetto*"—R, 410.

93   "What a beast"—R, 463.

"I must work"—R, 481–82.

"impossibility at the moment"—R, 493.

"Arrigo, Arrigo"—R, 530.

"a state of high"—Wolkoff-Mouromtzoff, 281.

"taken away his"—R, 533.

"I recall her"—R, 534.

"You have me"—R, 536.

94   "I *swear* to"—R, 553.

"I couldn't do"—R, 564.

"There are those"—R, 576.

"like a lion's paw"—R, 595.

"It seems to me"—"afraid that you"—R, 590.

95   "New paper, new ink, new pen"—R, 613. Duse punned on *penna* (two *n*'s) to distinguish it from *"pena"* (pain).

"He had chosen"—R, 615.

"Duse had committed"—D'Arcais, "Rassegna Musicale e Drammatica," *L'Arte Drammatica*, Sept. 1889, 369–78.

"Work provides money"—ED to Marco Praga, Pontiero, 88.

"squatting and smoking"—R, 624.

96   "What a young"—R, 626.

"I am a man"—R, 648.

96   "I don't have"—R, 650.

"I'm *strange*"—R, 684.

"Art is not"—R, 696.

"She speaks without"—Révesz, 187–89.

97   "there is a little"—R, 692.

"It's so sweet"—R, 720.

"The public *(pigs!)*"—R, 701.

"with him the"—R, 734.

"were all hacks"—R, 736.

"What for?"—Skinner, 292.

"great neurotic"—"is like Paris"—Montera, "Luigi Gualdo," *Italianistica: Rivista di Letteratura Italiana* 11, nos. 2 and 3 (1982): 292.

98   "Lenor . . . is down"—R, 765.

"Last night I worked"—R, 772.

99   "terra-cotta red"—Skinner, 248.

"Sit there and read"—Marco Praga, "Malinconie," *La Lettura: Rivista Mensile del Corriere della Sera*, Feb. 1920, 77–84.

100   "a woman that"—CS, Nov. 13–14, 1890.

"It's the soul"—ED to Avanzini, Apr. 27, 1892.

"No declamation!"—Meyer, 569.

"an old Norwegian"—R, 706.

"Nora"—Meyer, 807.

101   "I work"—R, 784.

"Lenor knows how"—R, 788.

"Try to keep"—Wolkoff-Mouromtzoff, 299.

"not to waste"—R, 798.

"perfection"—CS, Feb. 10–11, 1891.

102   "a pale, unhealthy"—Hansson, 97–128.

103   "My God!"—*Ariel*, 88.

"*your* circle"—R, 799.

"I don't need"—R, 798.

"I promised *Wolkoff*"—R, 796.

104   "is constructed to"—Wolkoff to ED, Apr. 22, 1891.

"was like a"—Wolkoff to ED, Mar. 19, 1891.

105   "Love! Love!"—R, 798.

"I want to meet"—R, 795.

"straight for Munich"—R, 796.

Four

106   "Today I am"—Wolkoff-Mouromtzoff, 301–02.

107   "Her simplicity is"—P.

"I don't understand"—Chekhov, 185.

"Kainz clutched my"—Reinhardt, 114.

"From the Moment"—"Lucien Guitry Pays His Tribute to Eleonora Duse," reprinted from *Gaulois*, May 11, 1924.

108 "my greatest success"—Wolkoff-Mouromtzoff, 302.

"as an individual"—Ibid., 303.

"the immortal E"—P, 72–73.

"You know Lenor"—Wolkoff to ED, Apr. 1, 1891.

"But no"—Wolkoff to ED, Apr. 3, 1891.

109 "She doesn't restrict"—P, 77.

"I've never seen"—S, 1962, 73.

"physical freedom"—Stanislavsky, 463.

"but not a single"—Ibid., 79.

"If there is no"—Ibid., 286.

110 "strange costumes—"curl up"—P, 129.

"her best performance"—S, 1962, 81–82.

"Why were you"—P, 129.

112 "She did not"—Colette, 289–90.

"An actress must"—S, 1962, 82.

"by the heart"—Wolkoff-Mouromtzoff, 303–04.

"The joys of"—R, 801.

114 "Yes"—"above every"—R, 802.

"One day when"—Wolkoff-Mouromtzoff, 305.

"Take it slowly"—LP, 124–25.

"image of Nora"—Maurice Baring, "Eleonora Duse," *The Fortnightly Review*, June 2, 1924, 759.

115 "A new sun"—Hugo Wittman, "Eleonora Duse," *The Living Age*, Nov. 24, 1924.

"Duse struck chords"—G, 1993, 206.

"For her the"—Reinhardt, 122.

116 "ourselves"—"It's our era"—P, preface.

"This is how"—Leblanc, 312.

"Even when she"—Ibid., 306.

"Naturally, I have"—P, 129.

117 "whether she is"—Paul Schlenther, "Eleonora Duse," *The Looker-On*, Mar. 1896.

118 "My Magda comes"—Pontiero, 105.

"I've had enough"—P, 180.

119 "above all to"—Wolkoff-Mouromtzoff, 311.

"confusion of streetcars"—S, 1962, 105.

"was so barren"—Rosamund Gilder, "La Nostagilder—Some Letters of Eleonora Duse," *Theatre Arts*, June 1926, 370.

120 "Sir, I do not"—"Mme. Eleonora Duse Has Something to Say," *New York Dramatic Mirror*, Jan. 28, 1893.

"fear of being tainted"—Gold and Fizdale, 320.

121 "It was as though"—Gilder, 368–69.

"points"—"the first actor"—Sterling Library, Yale University, Jack Crawford Scrapbook, Apr. 24, 1893.

122 "in the arms"—*New York World*, Jan. 24, 1893.

122 "is infinitely more"—Ibid.

"new to us"—*New York World*, Feb. 5, 1893.

"There are mysteries"—NYT, Feb. 8, 1893.

"composed of two"—*New York Recorder*, "Gossip of the Stage," Feb. 22, 1893.

"does not permit"—Gilder, 382.

"Madame I need"—"You write to me"—Ibid., 379.

123 "Your crinolines wobble"—AN, 53.

"Bankrupt yourself"—Gilder, 380.

124 "by the appealing"—"Beyond doubt"—H. T. P. Parker, *Boston Transcript*.

"latent power"—*New York Herald*, Feb. 5, 1893.

Prejudice against Italians—Italian workers often were paid less than white and black workers. Two years earlier, on March 14, 1891, in New Orleans, a lynch mob killed eleven Italian immigrants who had been acquitted of murder. It was one of the worst lynchings in U.S. history.

"For giving us"—AN, 55.

"It is evening"—Gilder, 382.

125 "I bankrupt myself"—Ibid., 368.

126 "Still, in spite of"—Le Gallienne, 90.

"If I don't live"—ED to Cesare Rossi, May 12, 1893.

"rushed on the stage"—Shaw, 1965, 732.

"You have given"—Terry, 259.

128 "the most absorbingly"—*Theatrical World*, 1893, 125–87.

"I have worked"—S, 1962, 104.

"art personified"—Ibid., 109

129 "the secret voice"—EDA.

130 "And if it's the last"—"Anytime, any place"—R, 805–07.

131 "Sometimes he was"—Hermann Graf Keyserling, *Reise Durch Die Zeit*, Vaduz, Liechtenstein: Verlag, 1948, 201.

132 "Is it still"—R, 807.

"I felt the flame"—R, 817.

"Well, what about"—Archer, 143.

"You love me!"—"You have struggled"—R, 814–15.

133 "I'm telling the"—"I've said badly"—R, 817–19.

"Why does death"—"That handwriting"—R, 820–23.

"Strange thing"—R, 830.

134 "swept her audience"—Archer, 143.

"God, Arrigo"—R, 831.

"like schoolboys through"—Arnold Bennett, "Unfinished Perusals," in his *Books and Persons: Being Comments on a Past Epoch, 1908-1922*, George H. Doran Company, 1917, 235–38. Reprinted in *Twentieth-Century Literary Criticism*, Vol. 40.

136 "wishes to possess"—Woodhouse, 124.

"an endless web"—F, 3. This is the first characterization of Duse/Foscarina in the roman à clef.

"To hear oneself"—Isadora Duncan, 14.

"I see the sun"—ED to DA, undated note, V.

Five

137　"I have found"—EDA to DA, V.

　　　"When I find"—Woodhouse, 9.

138　"Gabriele d'Annunzio"—Ibid., 24.

139　"pallid face"—Antongini, 319.

140　"every trace"—R, 833.

　　　"possessed an astonishing"—Swanson, page 96. In 1904, Laurense moved to a cottage in Wittersham, England, not far from Ellen Terry's house and Henry James's home. She adopted two orphan girls, but she never married. In 1907, she lectured in the United States on *The Meaning of Happiness*. In 1915, with Paderewski she headed the Polish Victims Relief Fund. For most of her life she devoted herself to her father and her neurotic older sister. At her death, on March 12, 1940, she was so poor that she was buried in an unmarked grave in Wittersham.

　　　"everyone is taken"—"I am afraid"—Wolkoff-Mouromtzoff, 308–10.

　　　"I beseech these wretches"—ED to "Roberto," Nov. 8, 1894, BU.

141　"I blessed them"—Wolkoff-Mouromtzoff, 808.

　　　"except for kisses"—R, 837.

　　　"Don't promise"—"my malediction"—R, 843–45.

　　　"true"—"Whatever gave"—R, 847.

142　"my dear friend"—DA to EDA, Pusey Library, Harvard University Library, autograph file, undated letter on Hotel Meurice stationery. Photo included.

　　　"there is a large"—R, 847.

　　　"illustrious predecessors"—R, 851.

　　　"I've done it"—R, 850–54.

　　　"All the words"—R, 854.

143　"I hate lace"—Leblanc, 306–11.

　　　"I will shew"—Shaw, 1965, 658.

　　　"Madame Bernhardt has"—Shaw, 1922, 134–42.

145　*"Elle n'est pas"*—Gabrielle Enthoven, "An Appreciation of the Duse." Harvard Theatre collection. Unidentified clipping.

　　　"The Signora Duse"—Shaw, 1965, 658.

146　"misses fire"—Ibid., 659.

　　　"We will leave aside"—Checchi to DA, June 26, 1895, B.

　　　"Sacred to Love"—Gatti, 143.

147　"He gripped her"—F, 266.

　　　"You will help"—ED to DA, V.

　　　"Don't lie"—ED to DA, Dec. 20, 1895, V. Also in MA, 150.

148　"May light shine"—"It is only fair"—F, 27–61.

149　"the promise of Pisa"—Emilio Mariano, "Il 'Patto d'alleanza' fra Eleonora Duse e G. d'Annunzio," *Nuova Antologia*, Jan.–Apr., 1951, 1–16.

　　　"promise to my art"—N, 82.

　　　"You will smile"—ED to DA, V, MA, 152.

　　　"Your touch"—ED to DA, V.

　　　"I would like"—ED to DA, Jan. 18–19, 1896, V, and MA, 153.

149   "a book of"—Gatti, 151.
      "The nomadic woman"—F, 304.
150   "We women must"—AN, 70.
      "You are on high"—ED to DA, B.
151   "God, it's so easy"—ED to DA, Feb. 27, 1896, V.
      "Eleonora Duse"—*The Illustrated American*, Feb. 15, 1896, W.
      "I managed to"—MK, FC.
152   "work-work"—ED to DA, Mar. 3, 1896, V.
      "How is it"—ED to DA, V.
      "So be courageous"—S, 1952, 32.
153   "consign Magda"—*New York Tribune*, Apr. 30, 1896.
      "Venice seems possible"—ED to DA, July 7, 1896, B.
      "The strongest is"—R, 863.
154   "a frightful conspiracy"—Woodhouse, 148.
      "The truth is"—ED to DA, Sept. 30, 1896, V, MA, 156–57.
      "beautiful day"—Giulietta Gordigiani to DA, V.
155   "I left almost"—ED to DA, Feb. 12, 1897, B.
      "sad step"—"She had tied"—Winwar, 157, quoting from DA's notebook of Jan. 27, 1897.
156   "the dear little"—R, 881.
      "the cold knocked"—ED to DA, Feb. 12, 1897, B.
      "it's impossible to"—R, 875.
      "I want to"—R, 877.
157   *"If there's no"*—R, 893–94.
      "They change me"—R, 885.
      "dear soul"—ED to DA, Feb. 12, 1897, B.
      "The days pass"—R, 901.
      "What is it"—ED to DA, Mar. 2, 1897, B.
158   "everything that is"—ED to Adolfo de Bosis, Mar. 31, 1897.
      "lie"—"Everything cannot be"—Ibid., Mar. 28, 1897.
      "You'll see how"—ED to DA, Apr. 20, 1897, B.
159   *Axel Munthe*—Later, to commemorate her times at San Michele, Duse gave Munthe a 15th-century stained-glass window that the city of Florence had given her. He installed it over the entrance door.
      "Don't lose them"—"I know, I know"—ED to DA, Apr. 20, 1897, B.
      "To live without"—ED to DA, B.
160   "Today a new"—R, 908.
      "This is how certain"—ED to DA, Apr. 4, 1897, B.
      "It was a slow"—Woodhouse, 318.
161   "mutilation"—ED to DA, V.
      "Never, never, never"—R, 912.
      "When Ariel is"—ED to DA, B.
      "Fame, too"—ED to Liliana de Bosis, Apr. 30, 1897, S, 1952.
162   "To my mind"—Worth, 215–16.
      "It was more"—Gold and Fizdale, 271–72.
163   "As the play goes on"—Mapes, 19.

164 "the most profound"—"Oh, your Duse"—Roberto Bracco, "La Duse a Parigi," June 3, 1897.
"I feel that"—Mapes, 28.
"La Duse makes"—Ibid., 35.

165 "What fly is"—Knepler, 220.
"In La Duse we"—Mapes, 47.
"Why, signora"—S, 1959, 93.

166 "It was one of"—Mapes, 54.

167 "Go, go"—Ibid., 56.
"Now they want"—Gold and Fizdale, 274.
"I assure you"—ED to DA, July 2, 1897, B.

Six

169 "Where will I"—ED to DA, July 2, 1897, B.
"I have strong"—ED to Laura Groppallo, Setti, 1978, 199.
"withdrew quietly"—Graf Keyserling, 201.

170 "I want to possess"—Andreoli, 276.

171 "The world"—Woodhouse, 167.
"doing, taking action"—ED to DA, Aug. 6, 1897, V. Also in MA, 157–60.

172 "a stupid religion"—R, 917.
"But you can't"—R, 935.

173 "human being"—Molinari, 150.
"I love you"—ED to DA, Sept. 12, 1897, V.

174 "Oh misery!"—DA to Boutet, *Ariel*, 116.
"impossible combination"—ED to Primoli, Dec. 12, 1897.
"I have refound"—ED to DA, Nov. 7, 1897, V.
"Duse's hatred"—Anita Vivanti Chartres, "Duse and Her New Play," *The Dramatic Mirror*, Feb. 12, 1898.

176 "The boredom"—ED to DA, Feb. 13, 1898, V, and in MA, 161.
"I've earned some"—Andreoli, 312.
"There's only one"—ED to DA, Feb. 14, 1898, V.

177 "Ah . . . I see"—Sayler, 88.
"Je vois!"—Le Gallienne, 1965, 153.
"Her lips were"—Woodhouse, 178.
"precise as clockwork"—S, 1955, 181.
"Sarah contributed"—CS, 22–23, Jan., 1898.
"Ah! The sun?"—ED to DA, Jan. 15, 1898, V.

178 "I have read"—Hadley, 124.
"This is greater"—R, 944.
"with lithe undulating"—F, 186.

180 "sadness of this"—ED to DA, Mar. 31, 1898, V.
"soul of fire"—Pontiero, 170.
"I'm speaking to"—ED to DA, V.
"100 francs"—ED to Laura Groppallo, Aug. 25, 1898, Setti, 1978, 199–200.

181 "ceaseless pain"—Ibid., 201.
  "When I am"—Andreoli, 329.
  "The warm drops"—F, 215.
  "expected and poisoning"—ED to Lillian and Adolfo de Bosis, Oct. 20, 1898, S, 1952.
182 "He embraced her"—F, 123–24.
  "Speaking is one"—ED to DA, Dec. 18, 1897, V.
  "barely . . . briefly"—ED to DA, Apr. 15, 1898, V.
  "flash of energy"—Andreoli, 329.
  "like a woman"—Ibid., 281.
  "horror"—"something snapped"—"What's wrong"—Ibid., 331.
183 "smooth away"—ED to Laura Groppallo, Setti, 1978, 201.
  "The contract honored"—Zacconi, 72–73.
184 "So poor deluded"—Hadley, 168.
  "I swear to you"—Banti, 231.
  "Here I am"—S, 1959, 104.
185 "A thousand statues"—d'Annunzio, *La Gioconda*, 56–57.
  "He who stops"—Woodhouse, 186.
186 "Me?"—"I was busy"—Richardson, 241.
  "bad demon"—DA to Angelo Conti, "Lettere ad Angelo Conti," *Nuova Antologia*, Jan. 1, 1939.
187 "Among all the"—Zacconi, 75.
  "The Duse's Own"—*Boston Record*, Dec. 27, 1899.
  "Have the Duse"—Berenson, 174.
  "dear, dear"—N, 62.
  "I love your"—ED to DA, V.
189 "very gentle and"—Teresa Sormanni Rasi, *Diario*, edited by Alfredo Barbina, 129, BU.
  "Everything is"—"A letter"—ED to DA, V.
  "For you, I"—"throw it to the"—ED to DA, Aug. 13 and 24, 1899, V.
  "She's certainly not"—Rasi, *Diario*, 134.
  "crowd of snobs"—Rolland, 3.
  "What grief"—Jullian, 123.
190 "mediocre French"—Rolland, 24.
  "Curious thing"—Ibid., 31.
191 "Besides, I'm 40"—Gatti, 175.
  "All I have"—"*the horror of a lie*"—ED to DA, V.
  "What an interesting"—Rasi, *Diario*, 138.
  "your own mother"—Duchess to ED, Nov. 22, 1899, Setti, 1978, 230.
  "I was beautiful"—ED to DA, Oct. 3, 1899, V.
192 "I haven't seen"—DA to ED, Oct. 23, 1899, *Ariel*, 128.
  "There's not a"—ED to DA, Oct. 13, 1899, V.
  "I, Isa, I"—ED to DA, Oct. 15, 1899, V.
  "Detestable empty"—ED to DA, Oct. 17, 1899, V.
  "In the wings"—Rasi, *Diario*, 153.
  "If you were"—ED to DA, Nov. 21, 1899, V.
  "Who holds you"—ED to DA, Nov. 20, 1899, V.
193 "Solitude is a good"—ED to unknown correspondent, Feb. 21, 1900, BU.

"inevitable and terrible"—R, 949.

"We are nomads"—"Eleonora Duse in New York," *New York Sunday Herald*, Nov. 9, 1902.

"the event of the moment"—Hadley, 208.

"a novel of acting"—Valesio, xv.

194 "You have compressed"—ED to DA, May 21, 1900, V.

"*Il fuoco* is"—*L'Illustrazione Italiana*, Mar. 11–25, 1900, quoted in Cappello, 90–92.

"singular sensation"—Andreoli, 351.

"This is the most"—ED to DA, May 31, 1900, V.

195 "perhaps aspired to"—Ellmann, 77.

"I have less"—Cecil, 166.

"greatest rubbish"—"form without substance"—*The Saturday Review*, May 26, 1900, 648–49.

196 "an unhealthy, bad"—ED to Carlo Rosaspina, Nov. 3, 1900, S, 1952.

"Poor me"—ED to DA, letters and telegram from June 15 to June 16, 1900, V.

197 "The ideal of art"—ED to Lillian de Bosis, Oct. 1901, S, 152.

"My life belongs"—ED to DA, Oct. 1900, V.

"Can I watch"—Duchess to ED, Feb. 7, 1901, Setti, 1978, 232.

199 "slowly became alive"—"which truly seemed"—Le Gallienne, 1965, 154.

"shocked the audience"—G. Pozza, "*La città morta* di d'Annunzio," CS, March 21–22, 1901.

"Work—ah!"—ED to DA, Apr. 28, 1901, V.

200 "I wouldn't want this"—ED to DA, Aug. 20, 1901, V.

"So forgive your"—Duchess to ED, Sept. 27, 1901, Setti, 1978, 233.

"exquisite, penetrating"—"G. d'Annunzio e la "Francesca," *Il Giornale d'Italia*, Oct. 3, 1901.

201 "But why not"—Rasi, *Diario*, 219–20.

"You have spoken"—Ibid., 181.

"In three years"—"higher, more true"—Ibid., 184.

"I have to pay"—Ibid., 189.

"Go away"—Ibid., 190.

202 "The stage must"—Ibid., 193.

"All of Rome"—CS, Dec. 10–11, 1901.

"And you, dear"—Rasi, *Diario*, 198.

203 "Nobody would be surprised"—Stokes, et al., 121.

"the vast flood"—Luigi Pirandello, "Eleonora Duse: Actress Supreme," *The Century*, June 1, 1924, 244–51.

204 "Life tremendous"—Valesio, 101.

"I disdain to"—S, 1955, 222.

"First act, three"—ED to DA, Apr. 3, 1902, V.

"Her potency on"—"La *Francesca da Rimini* a Vienna," *L'Illustrazione Italiana*, Apr. 13, 1902.

205 "Avoid, avoid"—Andreoli, 279–80.

"my blindness was"—Ibid.

"There before me"—de Pougy, 72.

"His recent book"—Le Gallienne, 1965, 53–54.

206   "enormous, enormous"—ED to DA, Oct. 15, 1902, V.
207   "there was enough"—AN, 117.
      "very little moral"—AN, 105.
      "more than to any"—AN, 111.
      "What really happened"—Damon, 147–48.
      "I am no"—"Where has there"—Lowell, 551, 550.
      "The sad Duse"—*Boston Transcript*, Oct. 28, 1902.
      "If you could see"—ED to DA, Nov. 5, 1902, V.
208   "a woman of wild"—AN, 119.
      "narrowed her art"—NYT, Nov. 5, 1902.
      "She is fine"—*The Evening Sun*, Nov. 8, 1902.
      "virile, manly"—*New York Press*, Nov. 14, 1902.
      "Receipts are a test"—"Eleonora Duse in New York," *New York Sunday Herald*, Nov. 9,
      1902.
      "great victory"—ED to DA, Nov. 12, 1902, V.
209   *Box-office receipts*—Reports are at the Vittoriale. Although previous Duse biographers
      record that Duse overpaid d'Annunzio and sent him a share based on sold-out houses,
      according to the financial reports at the Vittoriale, she (or her representative) calculated
      his 12 percent based on the attendance at each performance.
      "It is Anna"—"Eleonora Duse in New York," *New York Sunday Herald*, Nov. 9, 1902.
      "Gabri! Why"—ED to DA, Nov. 17–18, 1902, V.
      "atrocious week"—ED to DA, Nov. 22, 1902, V.
210   "My heart hurts"—ED to DA, Dec. 1, 1902, V.
      "throne in a bower"—AN, 149.
      "like a gang"—"Duse at Close Range," NYT, Jan. 11, 1903.
      "Time and again"—NYT, Jan. 8, 1903.
211   "Loving and lonely"—Gilder, 218.
      "This cruel winter"—ED to DA, Jan. 18, 1903, V.
      "Constancy is tiresome"—ED to DA, Mar. 31, 1903, V.
      "No more pain"—ED to DA, Mar. 31, 1903, V.
      "You are free"—ED to DA, Mar. 31, 1903, V.
      "an experiment in"—Andreoli, 395.
      "soldier"—ED to DA, June 24, 1903, V.
      "I am neither"—ED to DA, July 15, 1903, V.
212   "As an artist"—ED to DA, June 22, 1903, V.
      "It is practically impossible"—*Theatre*, Dec. 1924, 22.
      "In her merry"—Alice Nielsen, "Duse Returns to the Stage," *Theatre*, Jan., 1921.
213   "although he may not"—Russell, 78.
      "In the plays"—Symons, 162.
      "Her face is"—"Duse Plays in London," NYT, Oct. 6, 1903.
214   "Do you think"—Russell, 79.
215   "not dare to question"—ED to Orvieto, n.d., in Nuzzi, 73.
      "There's only one"—*Il Giornale d'Italia*, Jan. 9, 1904.
      "beautiful destiny"—ED to DA, Jan. 9, 1904, V.
216   "Whenever mother and"—Russell, 87.
      "I have never"—ED to DA, Feb. 13, 1904, V.

217 "She was truly"—Matilde Serao, "Quella Che Tace," *Il Giorno*, Mar. 25, 1904.

"alone and mortally"—Serao to Primoli, Mar. 1, 1904, Spaziani, 166.

"That's the way"—ED to DA, Feb. 28, 1904, V, and Andreoli, 400.

"You have killed"—Andreoli, 400.

"The fable goes"—ED to DA, Mar. 3, 1904, V.

"you felt nothing"—ED to DA, Apr. 28, 1904, V.

"It's necessary!"—Palmerio, 206.

218 "We had such hopes"—ED to DA, Mar. 11, 1904, V.

"Tell me"—ED to DA, V, and in Piero Chiara, "Le grida e i sussurri nelle lettere inedite della Duse tradita," *Domenica*, Apr. 18, 1976.

"I hope soon"—ED to de Bosis, S, 1952, 49.

"The storm has"—ED to Garzes, FC.

"I don't know"—Russell, 88.

"He has squeezed"—ED to Orvieto, Nuzzi, 89.

"I beg you"—ED to DA, Apr. 15, 1904, V.

Seven

219 "I will begin"—AT, 407.

"I alone must"—S, 1938, 195.

"desperate, abandoned"—Richardson, 264.

"You have enriched"—S, 1938, 194.

221 "the greatest virtue"—Braun, 46.

"I had strength"—LP, 115.

222 "lifeless eyes"—Leblanc, 311.

"revived, appeased"—Richardson, 264.

"What one dreams"—R, 958.

"I embrace you"—Robert Mendelssohn to ED, FC.

"If, once, your"—LP, 83.

223 "The role is"—Hermann Bahr, *Aus Glossen*, Oct. 10, 1904, quoted in Segantini, 24.

224 "I ran there"—"Her power"—LP, 83.

"guide, philosopher"—Walter Wentworth, "Eleonora Duse in Her Holidays, an American's Impressions," NYT, Feb. 12, 1905.

"blur of whiteness"—"breadth of sympathy"—Ibid.

225 "My imperious need"—N, 66–76.

"Don't adulterate the"—N, 77–86.

226 "In all her roles"—Hermann Bahr, Mendelssohn, 24–31.

"one single endeavor"—R, 964.

227 "All my soul"—R, 965.

"it is difficult"—R, 962.

"Unless you come"—Russell, 81.

"if the little"—G, 1993, 310.

"Work without art"—LP, 129.

228 *"désolée, désolée"*—ED to Orvieto, Nuzzi, 74–75.

"everything is stupid"—"I will *never*"—Ibid.

228 "pure and natural"—Camille Le Senne, "La Duse," *La Revue Théâtrale*, 1905.

"ridiculous and puerile"—"Eleonora Duse a Parigi," CS, Mar. 9, 1905.

229 "The house was"—"La prima recita della Duse al Nouveau Théâtre di Parigi," CS, Mar. 26, 1905.

"a true ovation"—Ibid.

"As soon as"—LP, 73.

"Shut up, already!"—LP, 115–16.

230 "Yes, with those"—NO, 56.

"Perhaps you have"—NO, 53–54.

"I can play"—S, 1955, 258.

"Words are meaningless"—LP, 115–16.

231 "Never have harsher"—LP, 90–92.

"The strength of Duse"—*Daily News*, May 26, 1905, Boin, 56.

"Duse is much"—*Times*, May 29, 1905, Boin, 101.

"I have given"—G, 1993, 329.

"possesses a head"—R, 969.

233 "incomparable"—CS, Oct. 29, 1905.

"the most difficult"—Le Gallienne, 115.

234 "To understand!"—ED to LP, Apr. 8, [1906], W.

"rekindled Duse's"—LP, 132.

"Soon I shall go"—Meyer, 806.

"expression, strained"—LP, 141–42.

"broke down the false"—Calvé, 60.

235 "This period has"—ED to LP, Mar. 17, [1906], W.

236 "Here I am complaining"—ED to LP, Apr. 4, [1906], W.

"I laugh and cry"—ED to LP, W.

"If Ibsen is no"—ED to Adolfo Orvieto, May 29, 1906, S, 1955, 272.

"Work and life"—ED to LP, May 21, [1906], W.

"The sea reminds"—ED to LP, May 30, 1906, W.

237 "Just to feel"—S, 1955, 272.

"If it was not"—R. Mendelssohn to ED, June 22, 1906, FC.

"made of infinite"—S, 1955, 267.

"In Italy, there"—S, 1955, 273.

"I don't want"—ED to Laura Orvieto, Nuzzi, 88.

238 "There was a"—Daly, 38.

"a magnificent and joyous"—ED to "Lucien [Guitry]," n.d., courtesy of Lion Heart Autographs.

240 "She *never* sees"—Newman, 47. It's not clear why Duse decided against the play. Perhaps she believed that the role of Electra was too young for her, and it's possible that she found Craig's sets too complicated for a touring company. The short play was later set to music by Strauss.

He would be—Craig, 216.

"Tell her I won't"—Isadora Duncan, 213.

"I will always"—Ibid., 215.

241 "perfect teeth"—NO, 50–51.

"frankly disappointing"—NO, 55.

"a vision of"—Isadora Duncan, 217.

"strange affair, all"—NO, 56.

"the stage seemed"—Craig, 219.

242 "It is my"—Isadora Duncan, 218.

"the part of a"—Gordon Craig, "On Signora Eleonora Duse," January 1928 manuscript draft by Craig written in Genoa, Italy, B.

"the birth of the"—Craig, 219–20.

"She looked less"—Isadora Duncan, 219.

"wild with excitement"—NO, 56.

"He saw his"—Isadora Duncan, 219.

"So, the audience"—NO, 56.

"I acted last"—Craig, 220–21.

243 "Don't be impatient"—Craig, 222.

"The most horrendous"—NO, 65.

"What have you"—Isadora Duncan, 221–22.

"I began to see"—Gordon Craig, "On Signora Eleonora Duse," B.

244 "chaos everywhere"—Unless otherwise noted, all quotations about the South American tour are from the Noccioli diary.

245 *"Just* to *see* her"—ED to LP, W.

246 "La Duse does not"—Pontiero, 1986, 241.

247 "I know the joy"—S, 1955, 276.

Edward Bullough—Bullough published a number of essays on aesthetics, and his essay "Psychical Distance as a Factor in Art and an Aesthetic Principle" has become a classic. His lectures on aesthetics were the first ever offered at Cambridge. He also published several translations, and Duse helped him select the readings for an Italian anthology, *Cambridge Readings in Italian Literature* (1920).

248 "I'm happy to"—Mazzoni, 106.

"If I can't"—P.

"Measure yourself"—EDA.

"extraordinarily simple"—P.

"got his inspiration"—*Duse Art Review* 1, no. 5 (Oct. 1927): 4.

249 "This is not the"—P.

"I have known"—Symons, 1969, 4.

"If you want to"—Maurice Baring, "Eleonora Duse," *The Fortnightly Review*, New Series, June 2, 1924, 763.

"Yesterday, I again"—ED to Stanislavsky, Feb. 16, 1908, P.

250 "I shall make"—NO, 92.

"For the last few"—Molinari, 208.

"What do they know"—S, 1955, 277.

Eight

251 "Eleonora Duse"—H. T. P. Parker, "Eleonora Duse," *Boston Transcript*, Oct. 18, 1909.

"Send me a"—P.

"You classified me"—Woodhouse, 219.

252   "seemed lonely and"—Hugo Wittmann, "Eleonora Duse," *The Living Age*, Nov. 11, 1923.
       "The greatest joy"—S, 1955, 342.
253   "something we've invented"—ED to Enrichetta, Oct. 10, 1918.
       "tender and affectionate interchange"—ED to Francesco D'Arcais, Aug. 4, 1884.
       "friendships from the"—ED to MK, May 24, 1920, FC.
       "The Duse was"—Russell, 83.
       "dream place"—MK, FC. All MK quotes unless otherwise indicated are from the Mackay papers at the FC.
255   "When do you think"—BU.
       "I have borne"—Bacheler and White, 272.
256   "beautiful hours"—R. Mendelssohn to ED, Apr. 4, 1915, FC.
       "knew everyone"—Luhan, 363–82.
258   "for years"—"most tragic"—Rilke, 233.
       "sanctity of the inner"—Hattingberg, 6.
259   "is as transparent"—Wydenbruck, 48–49.
       "remake my home"—Wolkoff-Mouromtzoff, 318–19.
       "broke down completely"—Freedman, 346.
       "I felt as though"—Hattingberg, 145–46.
       "We talked and"—S, 1959, 150.
       "rushed, thrust, forced"—Wydenbruck, 49.
       "hard, ambitious"—Ibid., 53–54.
       "irrevocable promise"—Ibid.
       "Reproaches and bitterness"—Ibid., 51–52.
261   "the best loved"—Bacheler and White, xvii.
       "cool young woman"—"Thank God she is freed"—Ibid., 270–73.
       "domineering mama"—"Auf!"—ED to Giovanni Rosadi, "Il carteggio Duse nel Fondo Rosadi della Biblioteca Riccardiana," Accademie e Biblioteche d'Italia—Anno LIII, n. 3, 132.
262   "hell"—"I've found myself"—Schneider, 7–8.
263   "I've spent my"—Le Gallienne, 1965, 101.
       "There are two"—"You are just"—MK, FC.
264   "It would be"—ED to Garzes, Jan. 20, 1913, FC.
       "Though she was"—Le Gallienne, 100–03.
       "half-dazed and"—Guilbert, 297.
265   "People do not"—Ibid., 300–01.
       "I know you"—"Duse was then"—Isadora Duncan, 308.
       "Come to me"—ED to Isadora, NYPL, n.d.
       "You must return"—Isadora Duncan, 310.
       "How I wish"—ED to Isadora, NYPL, n.d.
266   "country"—"The signora Duse"—MO, 15.
       "Was it friendship"—MO, 9.
       "You will see"—MO, 17.
267   "the difference in"—MO, 34.
268   "kind face"—Author interview with Luisa Osti Chiarelli.
       "the most beautiful"—Désirée to Enrichetta, June 14, 1921, FC.

"She is like"—ED to MK, FC.

"the Good"—"rare creature"—ED to Emma Garzes, Dec. 21, 1912, FC.

"quite changed!"—Guilbert, 301.

269   "For too long"—MO, 38.

"It was so"—Désirée to Enrichetta, May 28, 1914, FC.

"I feel a"—NB, FC.

"I love those"—S, 1952, 63.

270   "seemed invincible"—Rosadi, "Il carteggio," Accademie e Biblioteche d'Italia—Anno LIII, 140.

"mutilated and beautiful"—Ibid., 141.

271   "RECONSTRUCT"—Stokes, 165.

"You have borne"—ED to Isadora, Sept. 2, 1914, NYPL.

"breathe without wheezing"—MO, 45.

"Excuse this display"—Painter, 44.

272   "men of the plume"—NB, FC.

"She was at"—"Lucien Guitry Pays His Tribute to Eleonora Duse," Harvard Theatre Collection, reprinted from the *Gaulois*, May 11, 1924.

"glass that sees"—S, 1955, 305.

273   "Hidden in the darkness"—ED to Febo Mari, "Duse and the Films," *Boston Transcript*, Feb. 14, 1931.

"the exterior of"—Painter, 56.

"Those good people"—Ibid., 54.

"Her work was"—MO, 50.

274   "I don't want"—ED to MK, FC.

"Letters seem to me"—NB, FC.

275   "dreamed only"—NB, FC.

"Since I have been"—Painter, 54.

"felt a kind"—"determined to be disciplined"—ED to Enrichetta, NB, FC.

"Eagerly I looked"—Matilde Serao, "Eleonora Duse at Work for the Films," *Boston Transcript*, Apr. 23, 1917.

"Oh, so much"—ED to Enrichetta, NB, FC.

"ecstatic—laughing"—MO, 50.

Nine

276   "sweet, inexhaustible"—ED to DA, Dec. 18, 1897, V.

"Oh! How I"—ED to Enrichetta, NB, FC.

"irritating, often brusque"—G. Piccini, "Eleonora Duse—In Retirement," *Vanity Fair*, February 1917.

"courageous, self-assured"—Amoia, 7.

"In *Cenere* you"—Martha King, *A Legendary Life*, in unpublished manuscript. Courtesy of Martha King.

277   "the earth trembles"—King.

"I'm not a"—Nicastro, 178.

"Mystery, marvel"—"I want to"—"I went into"—ED to Enrichetta, NB, FC.

278 *Victim or vampire*—Duse's lifelong effort to portray women as human beings was articulated in 1905 by German psychologist Rosa Mayreder, who wrote: "Woman as an individual exists for herself, and is as noble and as vile, as gifted or as stupid, as weak or as
strong, as good as or as wicked, as like to man or as unlike him; in short, as diversified as
is made necessary by the human species. [Therefore] . . . If they wish to achieve power
as real persons in the world they must battle against woman as fetish." Quoted in Dijkstra, 443.

279 "I have learned"—MO, 50.
"Return along your"—"you can almost see"—ED to Enrichetta, NB, FC.
Cenere—An original print of *Cenere* may be seen at the Museum of Modern Art in New
York, and it is also available on Italian videocassette. Philip Glass composed a new score
for the film, which he premiered at Messina, Italy, in 1997. The film is interesting today
for the same reason it excited interest in 1917—the exquisite photography and the acting of Duse. As a story, *Cenere* is unremarkable, but the film has become a classic
because it provides documentary evidence of Duse's creative genius.
"closed character"—MO, 51.
"the work is yours"—King.
"without heart"—MO, 52.
"was then bursting"—Colette, 289.

280 "her most beautiful"—Ibid., 289.
"savage and dangerous"—Schneider, 58–59.

281 "nobility without pose"—Cara, 46.
"only a sketch"—S, 1959, 159.
"The critics say"—Cara, 28.

282 "Above all"—Vittore Branca, "Eleonora Duse grande scrittrice," CS, Apr. 19, 1969.
"I know a"—Painter, 57–58.

284 "speak in another"—MK, FC.
"Can you imagine"—ED to Enrichetta, NB, FC.

285 "grotesque and magnificent"—MO, 58.
"I have lost"—ED to Pisa, Setti, Aug. 30, 1917.
"No one has loved"—N, 92.
"battle leaves in"—Woodhouse, 306.
"after years of"—"be on guard"—MA, 164–67.
"I have no peace"—Painter, 60.

286 "Illusion? How to"—ED to MK, Dec. 18, 1917, FC.
"Love is the sharing"—NB, FC, and Weaver, 329.
"But the illusion"—EDA.

287 "a feeling of ruin"—ED to MK, Feb. 26, 1919, FC.
"a little bread"—ED to Pisa, Aug. 24, 1918, Setti.
Tebaldo Checchi bequest—Checchi left a bequest of 40,000 lire. With an exchange rate
in 1919 of 13.075 lire to the dollar, the gift was $3,059.27 each—or $6,118.54.
"tossed salad"—NB, FC.
"as no other art"—Bullough, 127.
"Art, in her silent"—EDA.

288 "I had the two"—N, 127–28.

"This great page"—ED to Eugenio Duse, Nov. 29, 1918.

"dupes of warmongers"—Zebel, 782.

"I haven't refused"—MO, 76.

"impossible for me"—MO, 80.

"Enrichetta *insists*"—MO, 82.

289   "Descending from a diva"—"I'd better go"—Author interview with Sister Mary Mark Bullough.

"During the day"—MK, FC.

"Perhaps our too"—"took"—Author interview with Sister Mary Mark Bullough.

"I saw them"—Painter, 61.

290   "The Italians should"—Woodhouse, 318.

"if sadness had"—MK, FC.

"I like the stones"—MK, FC.

"They're good people"—ED to MK, FC.

"I have risked"—Woodhouse, 334. In an effort to draw on d'Annunzio's popularity, Mussolini published a forgery of the letter, leaving out the parts where d'Annunzio showed contempt for him and his fascists. According to d'Annunzio biographer John Woodhouse, the doctored letter was republished until 1941, and for decades d'Annunzio was falsely tied to the fascist cause.

291   *"atrocious letter"*—MO, 93.

"had died in"—MO. Duse quoted Giulietta's letter in a letter to Helen Mackay, Oct. 30, 1919.

292   "a great blow"—MO, 95.

"If I am"—ED to MK, Oct. 29, 1919, FC.

"insincere, strange"—ED to F. Mendelssohn, NYPL.

"Thank you for"—MK, FC.

"Not this pen"—MO, 101.

"It's a shame"—ED to MK, Nov. 14, 1919, FC.

293   "brutal letter"—MO, 102.

"No one is alone"—"Her letter opened"—MO, 104.

294   "to share with me"—ED to MK, FC.

"very humble"—ED to MK, FC. Duse's house in Asolo is now called "Casa Duse" and is an elegant private home. The owner allowed me to tour the house and garden. The house has been remodeled, but Duse's third-floor bedroom with whitewashed walls and worn wooden ceiling beams has not been changed.

"dear and faithful"—ED to Pisa, July 30, 1920, Setti, 1972, 197.

"for a gust"—MO, 119.

"Why not come"—Guilbert, 302.

"These stupid people"—ED to MK, FC.

"Maybe I'll find"—ED to Ermete Zacconi, October 1920. Mirella Schino, "Ritorno al teatro. Lettere di Eleonora Duse ad Ermete Zacconi e a Silvio d'Amico." Sept. 1986.

"They cannot make"—Henrietta Straus, "The Real Duse Behind the Legend," NYT, Oct. 21, 1923.

295   *D'Annunzio and Fiume*—Woodhouse, 350. "The consequences of d'Annunzio's cavalier attitude to authority, his defiant march on Fiume, and his readiness to use armed force

to sustain a nationalistic purpose," writes John Woodhouse, "were all-important examples for Mussolini and became precedents for what was to happen in Rome during the next two years."

295   "I kiss your"—N, June 3, 1921.

"stupendous"—Silvio D'Amico, "Conversazione con la Duse," *L'Idea Nazionale*, Feb. 7, 1921, Harvard Theatre Collection.

"I hate to"—Govoni, 485.

296   "an elderly woman"—Straus, NYT.

297   "I wish to play"—Schneider, 37–38.

"I'm trying to"—Le Gallienne, 111.

"a symbol of"—F. Bruno Averardi, *Theatre Arts*, Sept. 1931, 773.

"I shall appear"—S, 1959, 161.

298   "A voice ringing"—Averardi (see note above).

"a drama of"—D'Amico, 1929.

"I learned how"—Schino, 384.

"When I left"—Schneider, 14–15.

299   "so much younger"—May 26, 1921, FC.

"I don't have"—Ridenti, 106–07.

"I was drunk"—Transcript of an unpublished interview with John Barrymore. Courtesy of Barrymore biographer and scholar Michael A. Morrison, author of *John Barrymore, Shakespearean Actor*.

301   "the prayer is mine"—Gallarati Scotti, 15.

"a pigsty"—ED to Ines Cristina Zacconi, Oct. 28, 1921.

"as if she were"—Author interview with Luisa Osti Chiarelli.

302   "was thronged"—NYT, Oct. 24, 1923.

"that lunatic Pirandello"—Guidice, 116–17.

"after all, Duse"—Chiarelli, 70.

303   "If it's not"—Gallarati Scotti, 15.

"My *heart is*"—MO, 127.

"You know, I have"—Alice Rohe, "Duse Breaks Her Silence," *Theatre Magazine*, Sept. 1922, 137–38, 186.

304   "I saw her"—Guilbert, 304.

"surprised, hurt"—Warren, 1979, 56. Draper reported Lugné-Poe's feelings and his offer to Duse. Duse resented Draper's interference.

"chatted gaily"—Guilbert, 305–06.

305   "How much you"—S, 1938, 326.

"broken tooth"—Woodhouse, 371.

"If d'Annunzio had not"—Gatti, 397.

306   "I have come"—S, 1955, 369.

"Just to see her"—Warren, 1979, 54.

"Oh, too bad"—Persone, 198–99.

"nothing but *merde*"—Gold and Fizdale, 326.

"I'm nothing other"—ED to Onslow, FC.

307   "Now, the only"—ED to Onslow, Feb. 14, 1923, G, 129.

"worth Threepence!"—Letter to Katherine Onslow from Mendelssohn Bank in Berlin, May 1, 1923. Enrichetta noted on the letter: "The cheque which Katherine

Onslow has shown me was exactly worth Threepence!" and underlined "Threepence" twice, FC.

"Your confidence"—ED to Onslow, FC.

"Duse abandoned herself"—Typescript written by Cochran's wife Evelyn. Sir Charles Black Cochran Papers, B.

308   "What impressed me"—Gielgud, 40.

"She seemed to"—Sheehy, 104.

"today impossible"—Le Gallienne, 1965, 106.

"Because acting is"—NYT, Sept. 27, 1959, II, 3:1.

"What is there left"—*Literary Digest*, July 4, 1923, 29. A summary of Duse's reviews.

"a great consolation"—MO, 134.

"For whom?="—Molinari, 250–51.

"I've signed a"—MO, 134.

309   "She set the"—*Time,* July 30, 1923.

"I am here"—S, 1959, 166–67.

"I should like"—Le Gallienne, 1965, 183–84.

310   "You have made"—EDA.

311   *Box-office receipts*—Morris Gest reported that ticket sales brought in $30,000, the largest receipts ever for a regular drama. The box-office statement at the Met shows a gross of $17,510.00 for the evening, which means that either Gest added in the money received by The Neurological Institute for the benefit or perhaps he inflated the figure. "Duse came on"—Gish, 257. Writer Langston Hughes seemed to be the one person who didn't grasp Duse's magic. He had read d'Annunzio's *Il fuoco*, and he sat at the back of the Metropolitan Opera house when Duse played *The Lady from the Sea* and saw "just a tiny old woman, on an enormous stage, speaking in a foreign language before an audience that didn't understand."

"They're waiting"—Benassi, 23–24.

"an explosion of"—Nathan, 137–42.

313   "Duse achieved a"—Strasberg, 368.

"The text has"—Adler, 76–77.

"no future generation"—NYT, Nov. 4, 1923.

"the actor vanishes"—AT, 408.

"Most generous rewarder!"—Le Gallienne, 1965, 8.

"was no hiatus"—Ibid., 149.

"perfectly concealed"—"those young faces"—Ibid., 156, 112.

314   "refuge, comfort"—ED to Francesco Mendelssohn, n.d., NYPL.

"And we sat"—Taped interview with Mildred Oppenheimer Knopf, courtesy of Wendy Knopf Cooper.

"was the incarnation"—Percy Hammond, "The Theatre," *New York Herald Tribune,* Nov. 15, 1923.

"Help me"—Program Book from "Love Scenes from Four Centuries. A benefit Performance for the Eleonora Duse Fellowship Endowment." March 10, 1929, at the Ethel Barrymore Theatre, New York. Program annotated with notes by Stark Young, recalling his meetings with Duse, W.

"When she talked"—Stark Young, "Conversations with Duse: A Great Artist on Her Art," *The Century Illustrated Monthly Magazine.* May/Oct., 1925, 101–05.

315 "with a great smacking"—NYT, Dec. 1, 1923.

316 "was more moving"—AN, 198.
"She held you"—Author interview with Elliot Norton.
"you could hear"—Author interview with Josephine Hutchinson.
"to be on guard"—ED to Onslow, n.d., 1924, FC.
"You have hope"—Le Gallienne, 1934, 174.
"rough crossing"—Désirée to Enrichetta, Jan. 28, 1924, FC.
"open arms and typical"—Gallo, 175–76.

317 "bowed her head"—Rodrigo, 131–32.
"soft skies, the"—AN, 218.
"A hush crept"—AN, 218.
"She is art"—*Los Angeles Daily News*, Feb. 20, 1924.

318 "Eleonora Duse is"—Charles Spencer Chaplin, "Duse Seen as Soul of Art," *Los Angeles Daily News*, Feb. 20, 1924.
"One does well"—AN, 231.

319 "Hope to find"—AN, 232.
"Now I will"—AN, 237.
"The greatest stage"—AN, 233.
"I am dizzy"—AN, 233.
"time is money"—ED, n.d. [1924], BU.
"Am suffering"—AN, 241.
"She was beautiful"—Author interview with Eleanor Lambert.

320 "Counting the hours"—AN, 243.
"DUSE World's"—Pittsburgh *Post*, Apr. 6, 1924.
"Her vitality is"—Ibid.
"neither door nor"—Allan Davis, "Duse's Final Performance," NYT, Apr. 27, 1924, Harvard Theatre Collection clipping.

321 "I can't do it"—Persone, 228.
"alone, lost"—Schneider, 139.
"Decided improvement"—FC.
"I am happy"—Sheehy, 119.
"It is impossible"—Pittsburgh *Post*, Apr. 19, 1924.
"Relapse Condition"—FC.
"Afterwards she dozed"—Désirée to Enrichetta, Apr. 21, 1957, FC.
"Then fixing her"—Schneider, 143.

323 "I beg that"—Cables appeared in the NYT, Apr. 24, 1924.
"No one was"—Damon, 661.
"You know that"—Isadora Duncan to "Helen," Sept. 2, 1924. Mary Fanton Roberts, Isadora Duncan Collection at City Museum. Courtesy of Peter Kurth.
"men and women"—NYT, May 2, 1924.

324 "In the middle"—Damon, 661.

325 "walked in the terribly"—Taped interview with Mildred Oppenheimer Knopf.
"of some three"—Zacconi, 72–73.

326 "Duse, who has"—CS, May 13, 1924.
"a greeting from"—Ibid.
Details of the coffin opening—In a letter from Enrichetta to Adolfo Orvieto, Nuzzi, 95.

Afterword

327   "resented anything or anyone"—Le Gallienne, 1965, 89.

"Venerata"—"physical aversion"—NB, FC.

"Her daughter was"—Taped interview with Mildred Oppenheimer Knopf.

328   "Lucifer might have"—NB, FC.

329   "I was disobedient"—Author interview with Sister Mary Mark Bullough. She died April 16, 2001.

Enrichetta's response to writing about Duse—NB, FC. Over the years, as books and articles about Duse appeared, Enrichetta termed them too earnest or too imaginative and patched together with bits of gossip. Sister Mary Mark urged her mother to publish her own book about Duse. Except for the notebooks intended for her children, Enrichetta never wrote about Duse. "To be a real book about her," Enrichetta said, "it would have to tell the truth."

Selected Bibliography

Actors on Acting: The Theories, Techniques, and Practices of the World's Great Actors, Told in Their Own Words. Edited by Toby Cole and Helen Krich Chinoy. New York: Crown Publishers, Inc., 1970.

Adamson, Walter. *Avant-Garde Florence: From Modernism to Fascism*. Cambridge: Harvard University Press, 1993.

Adler, Stella. *On Ibsen, Strindberg, and Chekhov*. Edited and with a preface by Barry Paris. New York: Alfred A. Knopf, 1999.

Alexander, Alfred. *Giovanni Verga*. London: Grant & Cutler Ltd., 1972.

Alma-Tadema, Laurence. *Songs of Womanhood*. London: Grant Richards, 1903.

Amoia, Alba. *20th-Century Italian Women Writers: The Feminine Experience*. Carbondale and Edwardsville: Southern Illinois University Press, 1996.

Anfuso, Bernice Sciorra. *The Passing Star, Eleonora Duse in America*. Master's thesis, University of California, Los Angeles, 1956.

Angier, Natalie. *Woman: An Intimate Geography*. Boston and New York: Houghton Mifflin Company, 1999.

Antongini, Tom. *D'Annunzio*. Freeport, New York: Books for Libraries Press, 1938.

Antoine, André. *Memories of the Théâtre-Libre*. Translated by Marvin A. Carlson. Coral Gables, Florida: University of Miami Press, 1964.

Archer, William. *The Theatrical World of 1894*. London: Walter Scott, Ltd., 1895.

Aston, Elaine. *Sarah Bernhardt: A French Actress on the English Stage*. Oxford: Berg Publishers, 1989.

Auerbach, Nina. *Ellen Terry: Player in Her Time*. Philadelphia: University of Pennsylvania Press, 1987.

Augier, Emile. *Four Plays*. Translated and with an introduction by Barrett H. Clark. New York: Alfred A. Knopf, 1915.

Bablet, Denis. *Edward Gordon Craig*. Translated by Daphne Woodward. New York: Theatre Arts Books, 1966.

Bacheler, Clementine, and Jessie Orr White. *The Nun of the Ca' Frollo: The Life & Letters of Henrietta Gardner Macy*. New York: William Farquhar Payson, 1931.

Baedeker, K. *Baedeker's Northern Italy.* Coblenz: K. Baedeker, 1870.

Balk, Claudia. *Theatergöttinnen: Clara Ziegler—Sarah Bernhardt—Eleonora Duse.* Berlin: Gesellschaft für Theatergeschichte, 1994.

Banti, Anna. *Matilde Serao.* Turin: Unione Tipografico, 1965.

Baranski, Zygmunt G., and Shirley W. Vinall, eds. *Women and Italy: Essays On Gender Culture and History.* New York: St. Martin's Press, 1991.

Barzini, Luigi. *The Italians.* London: Penguin Books, 1964.

de Beauvoir, Simone. *The Second Sex.* New York: Vintage Books, 1989.

Becker, Jared M. *Nationalism and Culture: Gabriele D'Annunzio and Italy after the Risorgimento.* New York: Peter Lang, 1994.

Benassi, Memo. *L'ultimo viaggio di Eleonora.* Venice: G. A. Cibotto, 1967.

Benedetti, Jean. *Stanislavsky.* London: Routledge, 1988.

Bentley, Eric, ed. *From the Modern Repertoire.* Series III. Bloomington, Indiana: Indiana University Press, 1956.

Berenson, Bernard. *Sunset and Twilight: From the Diaries of 1947–1958.* New York: Harcourt, Brace & World, Inc., 1963.

Bernhardt, Sarah. *Memories of My Life: Being My Personal, Professional, and Social Recollections as Woman and Artist.* New York and London: Benjamin Blom, 1968.

Bertolone, Paola. *I copióni di Eleonora Duse.* Pisa: Giardini Editori, 2000.

———. "Corrispondenze, Paròla, visione, scena nelle lettere di Eleonora Duse. Ph.D. thesis, Universitá degli Studi di Roma, 1993–94.

———. "Parole di teatro e teatro delle parole nella corrispondenza di Eleonora Duse." *Biblioteca Teatrale.* Rome: Bulzoni Editore, 1996.

Blair, Fredrika. *Isadora: Portrait of the Artist as a Woman.* New York: McGraw-Hill Book Company, 1986.

Boglione, Giuseppe. *L'arte della Duse.* Rome: Boglione, 1960.

Boin, Ivana. "Eleonora Duse sulla scena inglese." Ph.D. thesis. Università degli Studi di Venezia, 1994–95.

Bordeux, Jeanne. *Eleonora Duse: The Story of Her Life.* London: Hutchinson & Co., 1924.

Bourget, Paul. *Cosmopolis.* New York: Current Literature Publishing Company, 1910.

Braudy, Leo. *The Frenzy of Renown: Fame and Its History.* New York: Vintage Books, 1997.

Braun, Edward. *The Director and the Stage.* New York: Holmes & Meier Publishers, 1982.

Brewster, Ben, and Lea Jacobs. *Theatre to Cinema: Stage Pictorialism and the Early Feature Film.* New York: Oxford University Press, 1997.

Briccio de Abreu, Luiz Leopoldo. *Eleonora Duse no Rio de Janeiro, 1885–1907.* Conference catalog. Companha Nacional de Teatro, Ministero da Educação e Cultura, 1958.

Brooks, Peter. *The Melodramatic Imagination.* New Haven and London: Yale University Press, 1976.

Brownstein, Rachel M. *Tragic Muse: Rachel of the Comédie-Française.* New York: Alfred A. Knopf, 1993.

Bruno, Giuliana, and Maria Nadotti, eds. *Off Screen: Women and Film in Italy.* London and New York: Routledge, 1988.

Bullough, Edward. *Aesthetics: Lectures and Essays.* Stanford, California: Stanford University Press, 1957.

Buzzi, Giancarlo. *Invito alla lettura di Matilde Serao.* Milan: Mursia, 1981.

Caccia, Ettore, ed. "Lettere di Matilde Serao a Giuseppe Giacosa." *Lettere italiane.* Florence: Leo S. Olschi Editore, 1972.

Cacciaglia, Mario. *Eleonora Duse: Ovvero vivere ardendo.* Milan: Rusconi, 1998.

Calvé, Emma. *My Life.* New York: D. Appleton and Company, 1922.

Cappello, Angelo Piero. *Come leggere "Il fuoco" di Gabriele d'Annunzio.* Milan: Mursia, 1997.

Cara, Antonio. *"Cenere" di Grazia Deledda nelle figurazioni di Eleonora Duse.* Nuoro: Istituto Superiore Regionale Etnografico, 1984.

Carlson, Marvin. *The Italian Shakespearians.* Washington: Folger Books, 1985.

———. *The Italian Stage from Goldoni to D'Annunzio.* Jefferson, N.C., and London: McFarland & Company, Inc., 1981.

Carner, Mosco. *Puccini: A Critical Biography.* New York: Alfred A. Knopf, 1959.

Cather, Willa. *The World and the Parish: Willa Cather's Articles and Reviews, 1893–1902.* Vol. 1. Selected and edited with a commentary by William M. Curtin. Lincoln, Nebraska: University of Nebraska Press, 1970.

Cecil, David. *Max.* Boston: Houghton Mifflin Company, 1965.

Cenni, Allessandra, ed. *Sibilla Aleramo: Lettere d'amore a Lina.* Rome: Savelli, 1982.

Chaigne, Louis. *Paul Claudel: The Man and the Mystic.* New York: Appleton-Century-Crofts, Inc., 1961.

Chekhov, Anton. *Anton Chekhov's Life and Thought: Selected Letters and Commentary.* Translated by Michael Henry Heim with Simon Karlinsky. Los Angeles: University of California Press, 1973.

Chiara, Piero. *Vita di Gabriele D'Annunzio.* Milan: Mondadori Editore, 1978.

Chiarelli, Luisa Osti. *Dalla Padania alle Murge: Una giovinezza.* Fasano di Brindisi: Schena Editore, 1997.

Colette. *Earthly Paradise.* New York: Farrar, Straus & Giroux, 1966.

Comacchio, Luigi. *Storia di Asolo.* Asolo, 1985.

Conati, Marcello, and Mario Medici, eds. *The Verdi-Boito Correspondence.* English-language edition prepared by William Weaver. Chicago: University of Chicago Press, 1994.

Craig, Edward. *Gordon Craig: The Story of His Life.* New York: Alfred A. Knopf, 1968.

Daly, Ann. *Done into Dance: Isadora Duncan in America.* Bloomington and Indianapolis: Indiana University Press, 1995.

D'Amico, Silvio. *Cronache del Teatro I.* Bari: Editori Laterza, 1963.

———. *Tramonto del grande attore.* Milan: Mondadori, 1929.

Damon, S. Foster. *Amy Lowell: A Chronicle.* Boston: Houghton Mifflin Company, 1935.

D'Annunzio, Gabriele. *La Gioconda.* Translated by Arthur Symons. New York: H. Fertag, 1989.

———. *Figlia di Iorio.* Translated by Charlotte Porter. New York: Greenwood Press, 1968.

———. *The Flame.* Translated by Susan Bassnett. New York: Marsilio Publishers, 1991.

———. *Francesca da Rimini.* Translated by Arthur Symons. New York: Frederick A. Stokes Company, 1902.

———. *Siamo spiriti azzurri e stelle: Diario inedito,* a cura di Pietro Gibellini. Firenze: Guinti, 1995.

———. *The Triumph of Death.* Translated by Georgina Harding. London: Dedalus, 1990.

Deledda, Grazia. *Romanzi e novelle.* Vol. 2. Milan: Mondadori Editore, 1955.

De Pougy, Liane. *My Blue Notebooks.* Translated by Diana Athill. New York: Harper & Row, 1979.

Dickens, Charles. *American Notes and Pictures from Italy.* London: Everyman, 1997.

Dijkstra, Bram. *Evil Sisters: The Threat of Female Sexuality and the Cult of Manhood.* New York: Alfred A. Knopf, 1996.

Divina Eleonora: Eleonora Duse nella vita e nell'arte (catalog). Fondazione Giorgio Cini. Venice: Marsilio Editori, Ottobre 2001.

Dumas, Alexandre. *Francillon.* Taken from the prompt-book of Signora Eleonora Duse; together with a sketch of her life, by Antonio Bracco. New York: Carl and Theodor Rosenfeld, 1893.

Duncan, Doree. Carol Pratl, and Cynthia Splatt, eds. *Life into Art: Isadora Duncan and Her World.* New York: W. W. Norton & Company, 1993.

Duncan, Irma. *Duncan Dancer.* Middletown, Connecticut: Wesleyan University Press, 1965.

Duncan, Isadora. *My Life.* London: Victor Gollancz Ltd., 1928.

Duse, Eleonora. "Frammento autobiografico." *Biblioteca Teatrale.* Rome: Bulzoni Editore, 1996.

Edel, Leon. *Henry James: A Life.* New York: Harper & Row, 1985.

Ellmann, Richard. *James Joyce.* New York: Oxford University Press, 1982.

Enciclopedia dello spettacolo. Rome: Casa Editrice Le Maaschere, 1954.

Everdell, William. *The First Moderns.* Chicago: University of Chicago Press, 1997.

Ferruggia, Gemma. *La nostra vera Duse.* Milan: Casa Editrice Sonzogno, 1924.

Fildes, Valerie. *Wet Nursing.* London: Basil Blackwell Ltd., 1988.

Finney, Gail. *Women in Modern Drama: Freud, Feminism, and European Theater at the Turn of the Century.* Ithaca, New York: Cornell University Press, 1989.

Freedman, Ralph. *Life of a Poet: Rainer Maria Rilke.* New York: Farrar, Straus and Giroux, 1996.

Fusero, Clemente. *Eleonora Duse.* Milan: dall'Oglio Editore, 1971.

Gallarati-Scotti, Tommaso. *Due drammi e la Duse.* Mondadori Editore, 1963.

Gallo, Fortune T. *Lucky Rooster: The Autobiography of an Impresario.* New York: Exposition Press, 1967.

Gatti, Guglielmo. *Vita di Gabriele D'Annunzio.* Florence: Sansoni, 1956.

Giambruni, Maria Osti. *Storia di un'amicizia.* Edited by Luisa Chiarelli Osti. Fasano di Brindisi: Schena Editore, 1993.

Gielgud, John. *Early Stages.* New York: The MacMillan Company, 1939.

Gilder, Richard Watson. *Letters of Richard Watson Gilder.* Boston and New York: Houghton Mifflin Company, 1906.

Gilder, Rosamond. *Enter the Actress: The First Women in the Theatre.* New York: Theatre Arts Books, 1931.

Giorgetti, Claudio. *Presenze fuori scena.* Viareggio: Pezzini Editore, 1997.

Gish, Lillian, with Ann Pinchot. *The Movies, Mr. Griffith and Me.* Englewood Cliffs, N.J.: Prentice-Hall, Inc., 1969.

Gold, Arthur, and Robert Fizdale. *The Divine Sarah.* New York: Alfred A. Knopf, 1991.

Goldman, Michael. *The Actor's Freedom: Toward a Theory of Drama.* New York: The Viking Press, 1975.

Gould, Jean. *Amy: The World of Amy Lowell and the Imagist Movement.* New York: Dodd, Mead & Company, 1975.

Govoni, Corrado. *Teatro*. Rome: Bulzoni Editore, 1984.

Granatella, Laura. *Arrestate l'autore! D'Annunzio in scena*. Rome: Bulzoni Editore, 1993.

Grisolfi, Anthony M. *The Essential Matilde Serao*. New York: Las Americas Publishing, 1968.

Guerrieri, Gerardo, ed. *Eleonora Duse e il suo tempo* (catalog). Treviso: Canova, 1974.

———, ed. *Eleonora Duse nel suo tempo*. Quaderni Del Piccolo Teatro 3, Milan, 1962.

———. *Eleonora Duse: Nove Saggi*. Edited by Lina Vito. Rome: Bulzoni Editore, 1993.

———, ed. *Eleonora Duse, Tra storia e legend*. Catalog. Festival di Asolo, Rome: 1985.

Guidice, Gaspare. *Pirandello: A Biography*. Translated by Alastair Hamilton. London: Oxford University Press, 1975.

Guilbert, Yvette. *The Story of My Life*. London: George G. Harrap & Co., 1929.

Hadley, Rollin van. *The Letters of Bernard Berenson and Isabella Stewart Gardner, 1887–1924*. Boston: Northeastern University Press, 1987.

Hansson, Laura M. *Six Modern Women: Psychological Sketches*. Translated by Hermione Ramsden. Boston: Roberts Brothers, 1896.

Hare, Augustus. *J. C. Hare Cities of Northern Italy and Central Italy*. London: Daldry, Isbister & Co., 1876.

———. *Cities of Southern Italy and Sicily*. London: Smith, Elder, & Co., 1883.

Hart, Jerome. *Sardou and the Sardou Plays*. Philadelphia and London: J. B. Lippincott Company, 1913.

Hattingberg, Magda Von. *Rilke and Benvenuta*. Translated by Cyrus Brooks. New York: W. W. Norton & Company, Inc., 1949.

Hofmannsthal, Hugo von. *Selected Plays and Libretti*. Edited and introduced by Michael Hamburger. New York: Pantheon Books, 1963.

Huneker, James. *Iconoclasts: A Book of Dramatists*. New York: Charles Scribner's Son's, 1917.

Irving, Laurence. *Henry Irving: The Actor and His World*. London: Columbus Books, 1989.

James, Henry. *Italian Hours*. Boston: Houghton Mifflin Company, 1909.

Jonas, Von Ilsedore B. *Rilke und die Duse*. Frankfurt am Main: Insel, 1993.

Julian of Norwich: Showings. Translated from the critical text with an introduction by Edmund Colledge, O.S.A., and James Walsh, S.J. New York: Paulist Press, 1978.

Jullian, Philippe. *D'Annunzio*. Translated by Stephen Hardman. New York: The Viking Press, 1973.

Karlinsky, Simon. *Anton Chekhov's Life and Thought*. Translated by Michael Henry Heim in collaboration with Simon Karlinsky. Berkeley, Los Angeles, London: University of California Press, 1973.

Kennard, Joseph Spencer. *Italian Romance Writers*. 1906. Reprint, Port Washington, N.Y.: Kennikat Press, Inc., 1966.

———. *The Italian Theatre: From Its Beginning to the Close of the Seventeenth Century*. New York: William Edwin Rudge, 1932.

———. *The Italian Theatre: From the Close of the Seventeenth Century*. New York: William Edwin Rudge, 1932.

Kertzer, David. *Sacrificed for Honor*. New York: Beacon Press, 1993.

Klopp, Charles. *Gabriele D'Annunzio*. Boston: Twayne Publishers, 1988.

Knepler, Henry. *The Gilded Stage*. London: Constable & Company Limited, 1968.

Kurth, Peter. *Isadora: A Sensational Life*. Boston: Little, Brown and Company, 2001.

Landy, Marcia. *Italian Film*. Cambridge: Cambridge University Press, 2000.

Leblanc, Georgette. "Mes Conversations avec Duse." *Les oeuvres libres,* Volume LXVI. Paris: Arthème Fayard, 1946.

Le Gallienne, Eva. *At 33.* New York: Longmans, Green and Co., 1934.

———. *The Mystic in the Theatre.* New York: Farrar, Straus and Giroux, 1965.

Leprohon, Pierre. *The Italian Cinema.* Translated by Roger Greaves and Oliver Stallybrass. New York: Praeger Publishers, 1972.

Lorca, Federico García. *Deep Song and Other Prose.* Edited and translated by Christopher Maurer. New York: New Directions, 1980.

Lowell, Amy. *The Complete Poetical Works of Amy Lowell.* Boston: Houghton Mifflin, 1955.

Lugné-Poe, Aurélien-François Marie. *Sous les étoiles: Souvenirs de théâtre, 1902–1912.* Paris: Artheme Fayard, 1932.

Luhan, Mabel Dodge. *European Experiences. Volume Two of Intimate Memories.* New York: Harcourt, Brace and Company, 1935.

Mackay, Helen. *Chill Hours.* Freeport, New York: Books for Libraries Press, 1920.

Mantegari, Pompeo. *Eleonora Duse Reliquie Memore.* Editrice Tespi.

Mapes, Victor. *Duse and the French.* Publications of the Dunlap Society. New Series No. 6. New York, 1898.

Margarshack, David. *Stanislavsky: A Life.* London: Faber and Faber, 1950.

Mariano, Emilio. *Sentimento del vivere ovvero Gabriele D'Annunzio.* Milan: Mondadori Editore, 1962.

Markus, Julia. *Dared and Done: The Marriage of Elizabeth Barrett and Robert Browning.* New York: Alfred A. Knopf, 1995.

Matthews, Brander. *French Dramatists of the 19th Century.* New York: C. Scribner's Sons, 1924.

Maugham, H. Neville. *The Book of Italian Travel (1580–1900).* London: Grant Richards, 1903.

Maurois, André. *The Titans: A Three-Generation Biography of the Dumas.* Translated by Gerard Hopkins. New York: Harper & Brothers Publishers, 1957.

Mazzoni, Ofelia. *Con la Duse: ricordi e aneddoti.* Milan: Alpes, 1927.

McLeod, Addison. *Plays and Players in Modern Italy.* London: Smith, Elder & Co., 1912.

Meyer, Michael. *Ibsen: A Biography.* Garden City, N.Y.: Doubleday & Company, Inc., 1971.

Modjeska, Helena. *Memories and Impressions.* New York: The Macmillan Company, 1910.

Molinari, Cesare. *L'attrice divina: Eleonora Duse nel teatro italiano fra i due secoli.* Rome: Bulzoni Editore, 1987.

Murray, John. *A Handbook for Travellers in Northern Italy.* London: John Murray, 1860.

———. *Murray's Northern Italy: A Handbook for Travellers.* London: John Murray, 1853.

Museo Teatrale alla Scala. *Eleonora Duse: Un vestire che divenne moda.* Milan: Artigrafiche G. Ferrari, 1973.

Nardi, Piero, ed. *Carteggio D'Annunzio—Duse.* Florence: Felice Le Monnier, 1975.

Nardi, Piero. *Vita di Arrigo Boito.* Milan: Casa Editrice Mondadori, 1944.

Nathan, George Jean. *The Magic Mirror.* New York: Alfred A. Knopf, 1960.

Nathanson, Richard. *Schauspieler und Theater Im Heutigen Italien.* Berlin: Verlag Hugo Steinitz, 1893.

Newman, L. M. *The Correspondence of Edward Gordon Craig and Count Harry Kessler 1903–1937.* Published by W. S. Maney & Son Ltd. for the Modern Humanities Research Association and the Institute of Germanic Studies. University of London, 1995.

Nicastro, Luciano. *Confessioni di Eleonora Duse.* Milan: Gentile Editore, 1945–46.

Nuzzi, Cristina. *Eleonora Duse e Firenze.* Catalog of the exhibition, Fiesole, Oct. 8–Nov. 27, 1994. Florence: Firenze Viva, 1994.

O'Leary, Liam. *The Silent Cinema.* London: Studio Vista Limited, 1965.

Painter, Borden W., Jr., ed. *Perspectives on Italy: Essays in Honor of Michael R. Campo.* Special issue of *The Cesare Barbieri Courier.* Hartford, Conn.: Trinity College, 1992.

Palmerio, Benigno. *Con D'Annunzio alla Capponcina (1898–1910).* Florence: Vallecchi Editore, 1938.

Pandolfi, Vito. *Antologia del grande attore.* Bari: Editori Laterza, 1954.

Penzel, Frederick. *Theatre Lighting Before Electricity.* Middletown, Connecticut: Wesleyan University Press, 1978.

Perria, Piera. *Tra applausi e fischi: La Gioconda di Gabriele D'Annunzio.* Firenze: Firenze Atheneum, 1992.

Persone, Luigi M. *Fedelissima della Duse: Scritti di Enif Angiolini Robert.* Prato: Società Pratese Di Storia Patria, 1988.

Peters, Margo. *Mrs. Pat: The Life of Mrs. Patrick Campbell.* New York: Alfred A. Knopf, 1984.

Phillips-Matz, Mary Jane. *Verdi: A Biography.* Oxford and New York: Oxford University Press, 1993.

Pierazzi, Rina Maria, and Carlo Vittorio Duse. *Eleonora Duse e la guerra: Lettere inedite ricordi—episodi.* Turin: Istituto Editoriale, 1927.

Pierce, John A., and Brander Matthews. *The Masterpieces of Modern Drama.* Garden City, New York: Doubleday, Page & Company, 1915.

Plazzotta, Anastasia. *Les tournées in Russia di Eleonora Duse.* Ph.D. thesis, Università degli Studi di Venezia, 1994–95.

Pontiero, Giovanni. *Duse on Tour: Guido Noccioli's Diaries, 1906–07.* Amherst: University of Massachusetts Press, 1982.

———. *Eleonora Duse: In Life and Art.* Frankfurt am Main: Verlag Peter Lang, 1986.

Puppa, Paolo. *La parola alta sul teatro di Pirandello e D'Annunzio.* Bari: Laterza, 1993.

Primoli, Joseph-Napoléon. *Pages inédites.* Rome: Edizione di Storia e Letteratura, 1959.

Pullini, Giorgio. *Marco Praga: Documenti di teatro.* Bologna: Capelli editore, 1960.

———. *Teatro italiano del novecento.* Bologna: Cappelli, 1971.

Radice, Raul, ed. *Lettere D'Amore.* Milan: il Saggiatore, 1979.

Rampersad, Arnold. *The Life of Langston Hughes, Volume 1: 1902–1941.* New York: Oxford University Press, 1986.

Rasi, Luigi. *La Duse.* Rome: Bulzoni Editore, 1986.

Rava, Gino. *Eleonora Duse: Note di un suo medico.* Venice: Zanetti Editrice, n.d.

Révesz, Andrés. *La vida patética de Eleonora Duse.* Barcelona: Editorial Iberia, 1947.

Rheinhardt, E. A. *The Life of Eleonora Duse.* New York/London: Benjamin Blom, 1969.

Riccio, Luigi Del. *The True Story of Eleonora Duse's Love Affair with D'Annunzio.* Kansas: Haldeman-Julius Company, 1924.

Richardson, Joanna. *Portrait of a Bonaparte: The Life and Times of Joseph-Napoléon Primoli, 1851–1927.* London and New York: Quartet Books, 1987.

Ridenti, Lucio. *La Duse minore.* Rome: Gerardo Casini Editore, 1966.

Riedt, Heinz. *Carlo Goldoni.* New York: Frederick Ungar Publishing Co., 1974.

Rilke, Rainer Maria. *The Notebooks of Malte Laurids Brigge.* Translated by Stephen Mitchell. New York: Random House, 1982.

Ristori, Adelaide. *Memoirs and Artistic Studies.* Translated by G. Mantellini. New York: Benjamin Blom, 1969.

Rodrigo, Antonina. *Margarita Xirgu y su teatro.* Barcelona: Editorial Planeta, 1974.

Rolland, Romain. *Gabriele d'Annunzio e la Duse.* Paris: Les Oeuvres Libres, 1947.

Russell, Henry. *The Passing Show.* Boston: Little, Brown, and Company, 1926.

Sacchetti, Lina. *Grazia Deledda.* Bergamo: Minerva Italica, 1971.

Saligeri, Dada, ed. *Eleonora Duse: Un vestire che divenne moda.* Catalog. Introduzione di Carlo Fontana. 3 marzo–1 aprile 1973.

Salmon, Eric, ed. *Bernhardt and the Theatre of Her Time.* Westport, Connecticut: Greenwood Press, 1984.

Sayler, Oliver M. *The Eleonora Duse Series of Plays.* New York: Brentano's, 1923.

Schino, Mirella. *Il teatro di Eleonora Duse.* Bologna: Società Editrice il Mulino, 1992.

Schneider, Edouard. *Eleonora Duse: Souvenirs, notes et documents.* Paris: Bernard Grasset, Editeur, 1925.

Schneider, Ilya Ilyich. *Isadora Duncan: The Russian Years.* Translated by David Margarshack. New York: Da Capo, 1968.

Schorske, Carl E. *Fin-de-Siècle Vienna: Politics and Culture.* New York: Alfred A. Knopf, 1980.

Schürmann, J. J. *Derrière le rideau.* Paris: Maurice Bauche, n.d.

Segantini, Bianca, and Francesco von Mendelssohn. *Eleonora Duse.* Berlin: Rudolf Kaemmerer Verlag, 1926.

Serao, Matilde. *The Conquest of Rome.* Translated by Dora Knowlton Ranous. The National Alumni, 1906.

———. *Vita, opere, testimonianze.* Edited by Gianni Infusino. Casoria: Polisud, 1977.

Setti, Dora. *Eleonora Duse ad Antonietta Pisa Carteggio inedito.* Milan: Casa Editrice Ceschina, 1972.

———. *La Duse comèra.* Milan: Pan Editrice, 1978.

Shaw, George Bernard. *Collected Letters: 1874–1897.* Edited by Dan H. Lawrence. New York: Dodd, Mead & Company, 1965.

———. *Dramatic Opinions and Essays.* Vol. 1. New York: Brentano's, 1922.

Sheehy, Helen. *Eva Le Gallienne.* New York: Alfred A. Knopf, 1996.

Signorelli, Olga. *Briefe.* C. Bertelsmann Verlag, 1952.

———. *Eleonora Duse.* London: Thames & Hudson, 1959.

———. *Eleonora Duse.* Rome: Gherardo Casini Editore, 1955.

———. *La Duse.* Rome: Angelo Signorelli Editore, 1938.

———. *Vita di Eleonora Duse.* Bologna: Capelli, 1962.

Simone. *Sous de nouveaux soleils.* Paris: Gallimard, 1957.

Simoni, Renato. *Trent'anni di cronaca drammatica.* Turin: Società Editrice Torinese, 1951.

———. *Teatro di Ieri, ritratti e ricordi.* Milan: Fratelli Treves Editori, 1938.

Skinner, Cornelia Otis. *Madame Sarah.* Boston: Houghton Mifflin Company, 1967.

Smith, Winifred. *Italian Actors of the Renaissance.* New York/London: Benjamin Blom, 1968.

Sorel, Cecile. *Cecile Sorel: An Autobiography.* Translated by Philip John Stead. New York: Roy Publishers, 1953.

Spaziani, Marcello. *Con Gégé Primoli nella Roma bizantina.* Rome: Edizioni Di Storia E Letteratura, 1962.

Stanislavski, Constantin. *My Life in Art.* New York: Routledge/Theatre Arts Books, 1924.

Stokes, John, Michael R. Booth, and Susan Bassnett. *Bernhardt, Terry, Duse: The Actress in Her Time*. Cambridge: Cambridge University Press, 1988.

Strasberg, Lee. *Strasberg at The Actors Studio: Tape-Recorded Sessions*. Edited by Robert H. Hethmon. New York: Viking Press, 1965.

Stubbs, Jean. *Eleanora* [sic] *Duse*. New York: Stein and Day, 1970.

Swanson, Vern G. *The Biography and Catalogue Raisonné of the Paintings of Sir Lawrence Alma-Tadema*. London: Garton & Company, 1990.

Symons, Arthur. *Cities of Italy*. New Rochelle, N.Y.: Knickerbocker Press, 1907.

———. *Eleonora Duse*. New York/London: Benjamin Blom, 1969.

Talli, Virgilio. *La mia vita di teatro*. Milan: Fratelli Treves Editori, 1927.

Taranow, Gerda. *Sarah Bernhardt: The Art within the Legend*. Princeton, New Jersey: Princeton University Press, 1972.

Teasdale, Sara. *Sonnets to Duse*. Boston: The Poet Lore Company, 1907.

Terry, Ellen. *The Story of My Life*. London: Hutchinson & Company, 1908.

Troyat, Henri. *Chekhov*. New York: Fawcett Columbine, 1988.

Tyler, George C., in collaboration with J. C. Furnas. *Whatever Goes Up—The Hazardous Fortunes of a Natural Born Gambler*. Indianapolis: The Bobbs-Merrill Company, 1934.

Ulivi, Ferruccio. *D'Annunzio*. Milan: Rusconi Libri, 1988.

Valentini, Valentina. *Tragedia moderna e Mediterranea sul Teatro di Gabriele d'Annunzio*. Milan: Francoangeli, 1992.

Valesio, Paolo. *Gabriele D'Annunzio: The Dark Flame*. New Haven and London: Yale University Press, 1992.

Vazzoler, Laura, ed. *Due copioni da Shakespeare per Eleonora Duse*. Rome: Bulzoni Editore, 1984.

Vecchioni, Mario. *Saggi ricerche e schede: Eleonora Duse*. Pescara: Tontodonati, 1975.

Verga, Giovanni. *Opere di Giovanni Verga*. Edited by Gino Tellini. Milan: Mursia, 1988.

———. *Teatro*. Milan: Mondadori Editore, 1952.

Walkely, A. B. *Drama and Life*. New York: Brentano's, 1908.

Warren, Dorothy. *The World of Ruth Draper*. Carbondale: Southern Illinois University Press, 1999.

Warren, Neilla, ed. *The Letters of Ruth Draper*. New York: Charles Scribner's Sons, 1979.

Weaver, William. *Duse: A Biography*. New York: Harcourt Brace Jovanovich, 1984.

Wharton, Edith. *A Backward Glance*. New York: Viking Press, 1990.

Whitfield, Eileen. *Pickford: The Woman Who Made Hollywood*. Lexington: University Press of Kentucky, 1997.

Wilde, Oscar. *The Letters of Oscar Wilde*. Edited by Rupert Hart-Davis. New York: Harcourt, Brace & World, Inc., 1962.

Winwar, Frances. *Wingless Victory: A Biography of Gabriele D'Annunzio and Eleonora Duse*. New York: Harper & Brothers, 1956.

Wolkoff-Mouromtzoff, Alexander. *Memoirs*. Translated by Mrs. Huth Jackson. London: John Murray, 1928.

Woodhouse, John. *Gabriele D'Annunzio: Defiant Archangel*. Oxford: Clarendon Press, 1998.

Worth, Jean-Philippe. *A Century of Fashion*. Boston: Little, Brown, and Company, 1928.

Wydenbruck, Nora, trans. *The Letters of Rainer Maria Rilke and Princess Marie von Thurn und Taxis*. Norfolk, Conn.: New Directions, 1958.

Young, G. F. *The Medici.* New York: Modern Library, 1930.

Young, Stark. *The Flower in Drama.* New York: Charles Scribner's Sons, 1923.

————. *Glamour: Essays on the Art of the Theatre.* New York: Charles Scribner's Sons, 1925.

Zacconi, Ermete. *Ricordi battaglie.* Milan: Garzanti, 1946.

Zangwill, Israel. *Italian Fantasies.* New York: The Macmillan Company, 1910.

Zebel, Sydney H. *A History of Europe Since 1870.* New York: J. B. Lippincott Company, 1948.

Index

Berlin, 105, 118, 158, 161, 220, 222; Duse's
performances in, 128, 129, 155–6, 191–2,
194, 204–5, 227, 250
Bernhardt, Sarah, 17, 38, 46–7, *47*, 48–9, 59,
62, 66, 97, 142, *270*; acting style, 17, 46–8,
61, 62, 99, 107, 117, 162, 308; in *La città
morta*, 176–8, 197, 198; in *La Dame aux
camélias*, 61, *62*, 164, 177; Gabriele
d'Annunzio and, 154–5, 159, 176–7, 193;
death, 306; Duse's rivalry/friendship with,
48–53, 78, 91, 92, 98–9, 109, 117, 119–20,
124, 128, 134, 143–5, 151, 155, 158–66, 228–9,
296, 306; film work, 273; first meeting
with Duse, 162–3; illegitimate son, 37, 163;
late tours, 270, *270*; leg amputation, 270;
in *Magda*, 117, 144–5, 151, 164; physical
appearance, 143–4, 163; George Bernard
Shaw on, 143–5
Bertini, Francesca, 273
Biarritz, 236
Boito, Arrigo, 61, *64*, 81, *82*, 128, *284*; death,
286; Duse and, 61–4, 79–81, 83–105, 108,
113–14, 129–34, 139–42, 153, 156–60, 172–3,
178, 192, 206, 226–7, 272, 282–3, 286, 326;
Mefistofele, 61, 63, 81; *Nerone*, 85; personal-
ity, 81, 85; as Verdi's librettist, 79–82, 88,
92, 93, 94, 96, 134
Bologna, 50, 51, 53, 58, 180, 199, 204, 287,
303, 326
Booth, Edwin, 42, 119, 153
Borghesi di Pontarcy, 23
Borsen-Courier, 250
Boscolungo, 271
Boston, 124, 187; Duse's performances in,
124, 152, 206–8, 315–16
Boston Globe, 316
Boston Herald, 207
Boston Opera House, 316
Boston Transcript, 124, 207
Boughton, Alice, photograph of Duse
by, *322*
Bourget, Paul, 28, 54
Boutet, Edoardo, 26, 30, 32, 170
Bracco, Roberto, 163, 164
Brahm, Otto, 158, 220
Brando, Marlon, 313
Brazil, 70–2, 244
Bréal, Clothilde, 189
Bronson, Katherine de Kay, 87, 120, 294
Browning, Elizabeth Barrett, 8
Browning, Robert, 87, 290, 294
Brunetti-Pezzana troupe, 21–2

Brussels, 142–3, 233
Bucharest, 192
Buenos Aires, 75, 244, 245, 246
Buffi, Alberto, 101
Bullough, Edward, 247–8, 287, 324
Bullough, Enrichetta Checchi, 14, 44, *45*,
113, *247*; birth, 44–5; childhood and
education, 45–6, 54, 63–4, 77, 83–6, 92,
112–13, 131, 133, 156, 171–3, 191, 210, 216;
children of, 267, 286, *328*, 329; Duse's
death and, 323–9; Duse's letters destroyed
by, 274, 327–8; finances, 180–1, 219, 247,
274, 287, 307; illnesses, 172, 181; marriage,
247–8; relationship with her mother,
44–6, 54, 72, 85, 94, 112–13, 133, 152, 156,
172–3, 191, 216, 236, 245–6, *247*, 248,
267–8, 273–4, 279, 288–90, 308, 314,
327–9
Bullough, Father Sebastian, 267, 289–90,
328, 329
Bullough, Sister Mary Mark, 267, 289–90,
328, 329
Burghtheater, Vienna, 194
Byron, Lord, 7

Cabiria (film), 273
Caetaini, Prince Gelasio, 322, 323
Cafiero, Martino, 24, 29–30, 33–8, 39, 81,
225; death, 65, 66
Calvé, Emma, 234
Cambridge, 287, 289–90
Cambridge University Press, 287
Campbell, Stella (Mrs. Patrick Campbell),
128
Capitan Fracassa, 54, 69, 75
Caporetto, 285, 287
Capponcina, La, 178–9, *179*, 200, 205,
217, 225
Capri, 159
Capuana, Luigi, 51–2; *Giacinta*, 78–9
Carlotti, Marchesa Alessandra di Rudini,
213, 217
Carminati, Tullio, 299, 303
Carrington, Margaret, 299
Casale, Lucia, 290
Casale, Pierin, 290
Casarotti, Ettore, 279
Casino Theatre, Nice, 243
Cavalleria rusticana, 56–7, 59, 78, 100, 121,
126, 150, 215
Cavour, Count Camillo, 8
Cenacchi, Oreste, 53

Davis, Allan, 320
de Bosis, Adolfo, 158, 180, 181, 218, 219, 225
de Bosis, Lillian, 269
Deledda, Grazia, 276, *278*, 279; *Cenere,* 276–83
de Marco, Marchesa Etta de Viti, 261
DeMille, Cecil B., 273
Demi-Monde, Le, 26–7, 181
De Niro, Robert, 313
Denise, 36–7, 66–7, *67,* 68–70, 97; Rome performances, 68–70
Depanis, Giuseppe, 84
de Pougy, Liane, 205
Desclée, Aimée, 38, 50
Després, Suzanne, 166, 222, 224, 227, 231, 233, 236
Detroit, 319
di Lorenzo, Tina, 163, 170, 174, 268
Diotti, Arturo, 71, 73, 75
divorce laws, 27, 41–2
Divorçons, 41–2, 61, 126
Doche, Eugénie, 163
Dodge, Edwin, 256, 257
Dodge, Mabel, 256–7, *257,* 258
Doll's House, A, 100–102, *102,* 103, 117, 126, 161, 236; Milan performances, 101–3, 223; Moscow performances, 114
Donatello, 6
"doozy" (term), inspired by Duse, 10
Dostoevsky, Fyodor Mikhailovich, 103
Draper, Ruth, 306
Drechsel, Countess Sophie, 87, 93, 101, 112, 172, 173, 261
Drury Lane Theatre, London, 143–5, 237
Dumas *fils,* Alexandre, 23, 26–7, 54, 56, 64–5, *98,* 231; *La Dame aux camélias,* 26–7, 36, 43, 46, 50, 61–2, 108–10; death, 164–5; *Le Demi-Monde,* 26–7; *Denise,* 36–7, 66–70, 97; *La Femme de Claude,* 50–3; meeting with Duse, 97; *The Princess of Baghdad,* 40–2
Dumas *père,* Alexandre, 26–7
Duncan, Isadora, 136, 238, *239;* children of, 238, 240, 265, 271; Duse and, 238–43, 249, 265, 271, 323
Duse, Alessandro, 3–4, 6, 10–11, *11,* 12–15, 18, 21, 25, 34, *35,* 37, 38, 44, 75, 76, 92; death, 114
Duse, Angelica, 4, 11, 12–13, *13,* 14–15, 27, 112, 173, 267, 314; illness and death, 18–21, 22
Duse, Eleonora, *13, 19, 43, 45, 51, 52, 59, 62, 67, 80, 90, 102, 111, 120, 125, 135, 138, 166,*

186, 188, 198, 203, 214, 220, 221, 223, 232, 235, 247, 263, 282, 291, 322, 330; acting style, 5–6, 18–23, 27, 32–3, 40, *43,* 48, 51–3, 57, 60, 68, 78, 90–1, 109, 115–17, 124, 135–6, 162, 165, 199, 203, 230, 234, 248–9, 278, 280, 297, 308, 313, 318; aging of, 173, 182, 200, 212–13, 263, 278, 286; Albano theatre project, 170, 210; Ambrosio-Films and, 275–83; artistic views, 5–7, 15, 48, 53, 60, 78–9, 96, 119, 129, 158, 176, 193, 222, 249, 252, 287, 303–4, 309, 313; Sarah Bernhardt's rivalry/friendship with, 48–53, 78, 91, 92, 98–9, 109, 117, 119–20, 124, 128, 134, 143–5, 151, 155, 158–66, 228–9, 296, 306; birth, 12; birth of her daughter, 44–6; Arrigo Boito and, 61–4, 79–81, 83–105, 108, 113–14, 129–34, 139–42, 153, 156–60, 172–3, 178, 191, 206, 226–7, 272, 282–3, 286, 326; break with d'Annunzio, 217–19, 225–6; Martino Cafiero and, 29–30, 33–8, 39, 65, 66; in Cambridge, 289–90; childhood, 6–7, 12–21, 112, 263, 286; in Ciotti-Belli-Blanes troupe, 22–6; collaboration with d'Annunzio, 136, 137, 148, 158, 165, 170, 174, 182, 187, 193, 201, 203; Compagnia della Città di Roma and, 81, 83–105, 129–31; Craig's set designs for, 238–43; critics on, 20–3, 26, 30–3, 41, 42, 48–53, 57, 60–1, 68, 70–1, 78–9, 84, 90–1, 96, 101, 106–8, 115, 122–4, 128, 143–6, 151, 164–6, 173, 174, 195, 203, 207–10, 216, 223, 228–9, 231, 237, 249, 281, 297, 302, 308, 311–18; Gabriele d'Annunzio and, 134–7, 142, 146–9, 151–67, 168–206, 211–19, 222, 237, 251–2, 285, 295, 304–6, 309, 323, 327–9; death, 322–6; Isadora Duncan and, 238–43, 249, 265, 271, 323; in Duse-Lagunaz troupe, 3–5, 9–21, 44; "La Duse" persona, 33, 116–17, 158, 174–5, 190; early acting experience, 12–37; education, 7, 15–16, 18, 20; in Egypt, 94–6, 131–2, 181; facial neuralgia, 145; fame, 5–6, 45, 137, 151, 170, 180, 224, 262; film work, 272–3, 275–82, *282,* 283, 284; finances, 7, 42, 72, 76, 101, 119, 131, 133, 174, 176, 177, 180, 190, 197, 201, 219, 225, 246–7, 252, 256, 271, 274, 287, 288, 291–2, 303, 306–7; first meeting with Bernhardt, 162–3; first pregnancy, and death of her son, 33–8; *Il fuoco* controversy and, 193–7; German tours, 115–17, 128, 129, 140, 143, 154–6, 191–2, 194, 226–7, 250; grandchildren, 267,

A NOTE ABOUT THE TYPE

THIS BOOK was set in Adobe Garamond. Designed for the Adobe Corporation by Robert Slimbach, the fonts are based on types first cut by Claude Garamond (c. 1480–1561). Garamond was a pupil of Geoffroy Tory and is believed to have followed the Venetian models, although he introduced a number of important differences, and it is to him that we owe the letter we now know as "old style." He gave to his letters a certain elegance and feeling of movement that won their creator an immediate reputation and the patronage of Francis I of France.

Composed by North Market Street Graphics,
Lancaster, Pennsylvania
Printed and bound by Berryville Graphics,
Berryville, Virginia